Felix Bovet

Egypt, Palestine and Phoenicia

A Visit to Sacred Lands

Felix Bovet

Egypt, Palestine and Phoenicia
A Visit to Sacred Lands

ISBN/EAN: 9783337231873

Printed in Europe, USA, Canada, Australia, Japan

Cover: Foto ©Andreas Hilbeck / pixelio.de

More available books at **www.hansebooks.com**

EGYPT, PALESTINE, AND PHŒNICIA.

BY

FELIX BOVET.

TRANSLATED BY

W. H. LYTTELTON, M.A.,

RECTOR OF HAGLEY AND CANON OF GLOUCESTER.

*WITH A BIOGRAPHICAL SKETCH OF THE AUTHOR,
BY PROFESSOR F. GODET, D.D.*

New York:

E. P. DUTTON AND COMPANY,

39, WEST TWENTY THIRD STREET.

1883.

PREFACE.

THE book of which the eighth French edition * is here translated for English readers was originally recommended to me by my friend Professor Godet, some of whose theological works I have published in English, and whose opinion of the value of a book would always weigh much with me. And if it may be truly said, as I think it may, that the chief characteristics that make a book interesting and profitable reading are, first, a good subject, secondly, a good method and style of treatment, and last, but not least, a tone of thought and feeling in the author which makes it a pleasure and an advantage to be brought into contact with his spirit, few books, it seems to me, have more to recommend them than this of M. Bovet's.

With regard to the translation, I may be allowed to say that I began it when disabled by illness from other and harder work, and that, though the completion of it has cost me far more of time and labour than I expected,

---

* M. Bovet has allowed me to see the proofs of the eighth edition which is now passing through the press.

the narrative and conversational style in French being to me much more difficult to render into easy and idiomatic English than the argumentative and disquisitional style of essays, which alone I had before attempted, I shall not at all regret the time and labour spent upon it, if the book give its readers anything like the pleasure and, I may truly say, edification which it has given me.

In correcting the proofs, I had very valuable help and criticism from a near and dear relation of my own, which has added much to the terseness and ease of the style—merits not easily given to a translation from French narrative or conversation into English.

M. Bovet has, at my request, added several footnotes to this translation, which   not occur in the original, but which will, I hope, add to the usefulness and interest of the book for English readers.

In the subjoined letter, written to me at my request by Professor Godet, the principal facts of M. Bovet's life are stated, which may serve to introduce him to English readers. But, as Professor Godet has well said, his own words in his delightful book will best picture and recommend the man himself.

W. H. LYTTELTON.

HAGLEY RECTORY,
   November, 1882.

My DEAR FRIEND,

What need can there be, it might perhaps be said by one who had read this book before reading its preface, to give an account to the English public of its author, when his own book pictures him so perfectly? The remark is just; but as the translator presses for a few lines of introduction, and it will always be a pleasure to me to associate my name with that of my friend, M. Félix Bovet, I cannot refuse the request.

M. Bovet was born in 1824, in this little corner of the earth, which an American author—giving way, no doubt, to too favourable a bias—was pleased to call "the choicest spot in this loveliest of lands," in my native town of Neuchâtel. In 1843, he went to Berlin, to study law. I was living there at that time. We became intimately acquainted, and formed a friendship which has now lasted, without a single break, for forty years. We entered also upon an active fellowship in work, of which I have increasingly felt the value, and reaped the fruits.

M. Bovet, as all his readers will feel, was not made for the law. Accordingly, he soon quitted that occupation for theology. Hebrew in particular attracted him. He studied it less at the university than in the company of some learned Rabbis, with whom he met in Berlin. After completing his studies, he determined not to receive holy orders; but to dedicate his life to the profound study of Scripture, and to labours, quietly carried on, in the cause of Christ.

He held for some years the offices of Librarian and Professor of French Literature at Neuchâtel, which he afterwards exchanged for the Chair of Hebrew in our Faculty of Theology. During this time he published the "Life of Zinzendorf:" it was a thank-offering made by him on behalf of his whole family, which in successive generations had received many blessings through its relations with the Moravian Church. At a later time he published the "History of the Psalter," a work of great erudition, and full of interesting information.

The present volume was written in the year 1858. The reader who can enter into the account here given by M. Bovet of his travels, will soon feel that this journey also was offered in repayment of a debt of gratitude, and that the impulse which led him to Palestine was, above all, the desire to kiss the ground trodden by those blessed feet which have left upon that soil so ineffaceable an impress.

This work, in its French form, has reached its eighth edition; it has been translated into German, Swedish, Dutch, and Italian. I hope that it will not be less well received in England, notwithstanding the great number of books of this kind which appear there, one might almost say every year. M. Bovet's book has a character all its own. It is a flower gathered in Palestine, and brought away in all its freshness and fragrance. Every reader will say to himself, I cannot doubt, " Here is the friend I should choose to accompany on such a journey." For my own part, I thank God that He has granted me such a travelling companion for life's journey.

F. GODET.

CONTENTS.

INTRODUCTION.

FROM my earliest years the vision of a journey in Palestine and in Greece had been to me, as to so many other men, a dream of delight. Many a time had I pictured myself tossed on the waves of the Archipelago, in the midst of the "shining Cyclades," * following in the track of the ships of Æneas, or of Themistocles ; many a time, tracing the footsteps of Jesus, had I scaled in imagination the mountains of Galilee, and run with Elijah before the chariot of Ahab across the plain of Jezreel. Whether our education be pagan or Christian, or whether its character be æsthetic, philosophic, or evangelical, it always carries us back to the East ; and that common fatherland of all the religions, of all art and speculation, becomes in consequence—even more than our own native land can be—the true home of our spirit. Generally speaking, indeed, we only begin to understand nature through the mediation of art ; consequently we need not be surprised if we find ourselves touched with admiration by the scenery of Sicily and of Greece, when reading Virgil or Theocritus, before we become in the least conscious even of that peculiar kind of beauty that is characteristic of our own country. For my own part, I learnt to enjoy the beauty of nature from reading poetry, and specially classical poetry, long before

* " Nitentes Cyclades," say Virgil and Horace.

I

I recognised it in the scenery of Switzerland. Our
great mountains, shrouded in autumnal mornings with
transparent mists, our great cedars, the freshness of our
meadow-lands, all these had fewer charms for my eyes
than the little hillocks, burnt by the sun's rays, which
surround my native town; I loved to look at them when
an oppressive summer sun brought out their aridity, and
assimilated them more closely to the idea which I had
formed to myself of the islands of Greece or of the
mountains of Judæa. I loved to gaze upon our lake
when the "bise," sweeping before it the vapours which
with us so often veil the brilliancy of our sunny skies
was shadowing the water with a deeper azure: I fancied
myself at such times standing by that "black-waved
sea," of which Homer speaks ; and the greatest happiness I could picture to myself was that of some day
wandering in search of adventure over that archipelago
so rich in memories of victories, in marvellous legends,
and famous shipwrecks.

*With new times, new cares.** I have been describing the feelings, the impressions of childhood ; but
never have they been quite effaced from my mind ;
and, besides, the thoughts that have succeeded them
have still brought me back to the East, to which the
study of the Bible added in my mind a new kind of
interest ; it seemed to me that the actual sight of the
scenes in which the events of sacred history took place
must set those events in their true light, stripping them
at once of that halo of legendary glory with which fanatics
have invested them, and of that, as it were, *abstract* character, which they owe to their treatment by theologians,
—giving them, in short, a higher degree of life, of simplicity, of reality. If I wished to see Jerusalem, it was

* Racine.

not with any idea of seeking to experience there vague
religious emotions, which one might often fail in reaching ; it was in the hope of thereby throwing a more
distinct light upon the facts, the words, even upon the
very spirit, of the sacred writings.

And, besides, acquaintance with the various nations
of the western world does not satisfy the desire which
we feel to contemplate humanity in more than one
aspect. The nations of Europe are but slight variations
of one and the same type. The distinct features which
characterise the Frenchman, the German, the Englishman, the Spaniard, or the Dutchman, are as nothing in
comparison with the points of mutual contact and
resemblance, by virtue of which each of these remains,
above all, a European. Our peoples remain, after
all, but buildings constructed out of the *débris* of the
ancient Empire of the West ; they are but Roman
provinces, more or less Germanised, more or less
indocile, of one and the same Latin Church. From
Naples to Edinburgh, from Koenigsberg to Salamanca,
the Latin syntax, the institutes, and the pandects,
constitute the common groundwork of education. It
was the same French Revolution which more or less
shook and renovated all these nations ; the industry of
our time comprehends them in one and the same network of railroads, and tends to obliterate every day,
more and more, the differences already so slight which
still serve to distinguish them the one from the other.

The wish, then, to see other lands was not the least
among the motives which attracted me towards the
East. It was in my mind more than a wish, it was a
real need of my intelligence. It appeared to me that I
could not in any way succeed in apprehending the spirit
of our changeful West till I had provided myself with a

standard of comparison in the unchanging East which preserves, in its traditions, and in its manners and customs, the changeless image of the primitive ages ; just as it also preserves the embalmed bodies of its kings and of its gods, in the necropolises of Memphis. I wished to look for once upon a world that should be neither Latin nor German, neither Catholic nor Protestant ; I wished to come into contact, in the Semitic race, with the other pole of historic mankind.   I had seen the progressive races, I wished to see the stationary ; I wished to sit for once under the tents of those veterans of humanity from whom we have received our traditions and our beliefs, and the first elements of our sciences and arts ; to whom, in short, we owe everything, but who owe us absolutely nothing.

My travels were nevertheless not the result of a plan long premeditated, and elaborated at leisure. My dream had remained a dream.   For a long time many things had held me back,—" my family, my studies, a thousand cares, and, above all, that vague feeling of restlessness which makes a man sometimes shrink in timidity from realising wishes."*   But one day, when I was thinking of anything rather than of the East, an article in a newspaper drew my attention.   The *Univers* brought me the news that there existed at Paris—rue de Fürstenberg, 6—a society whose object it was to facilitate travels in the sacred lands, by putting within reach of pilgrims the benefit of the principle of association.   For a sum of 1,250 francs this society, called " *L'Œuvre des Pèlerinages,*"

* . . . . " La famille, l'étude,
Mille soins et surtout la vague inquiétude
Qui fait que l'homme craint son désir accompli."
        Feuilles d'Automne, de V. Hugo.

conveys you to Jerusalem, lodges you in the Latin convent during the feast of the passover, conducts you afterwards through Samaria and Galilee, and, two months later, brings you back, free of expense, to Marseilles. You start on March 7, on board the packet *Des Messageries Impériales;* you arrive at Jaffa on St. Joseph's day, and *before Trinity Sunday is past** you are at home again.

Never had the idea of a pilgrimage to the East presented itself to me in so concrete a form. The dread of a decision that must be come to, and of a plan that must be fixed upon for the journey, would, I have no doubt, have kept me back all my life. But now the *rue de Fürstenberg* opened its arms to me. I had but to pack my portmanteau, and to draw a cheque upon Paris, payable to the treasurer of *l'Œuvre*, or to his order.

I wrote at once to the secretary to tell him of my wishes. M. Bettencourt answered me in a very good-natured letter, to which he appended the prospectus. But I found it stated that for admission into the "caravan" one must be furnished with a recommendation from the president of the *Conférence de Saint-Vincent de Paul.* And, besides, it was added, that as the scheme bore a special religious character, one should "apply to this intention a recitation of the *Ave Maria* and of *l'Angelus.*" These words shewed me that I had been misled ; *l'Œuvre*, as I ought to have foreseen, was intended only for Catholics, and I at once gave up my whole project.

Nevertheless, I tried in vain to put it out of my thoughts ; such a plan once admitted into the mind is not so easily put aside. The East had once more laid hold of my imagination ; Jerusalem presented itself to

* An allusion to a popular song.

me anew "more charming and more fair;"* the snowy tops of Hermon and of the Taygetus, the plane-trees of Ilyssus, the palms of the valley of the Jordan, rose in vision before me; I fancied I could hear the booming of the bees of Hymettus, and the voice of the *Muezzin* descending upon me with its shrill notes from the tops of the minarets.

And besides, there was nothing in the way of the accomplishment of my design. Just then I had no duty, no engagement, no work begun, to detain me at home; and though I had not the necessary qualifications for associating myself with the so-called "children of the crusade," still I had the opportunity of embarking with them. The *Messageries Maritimes* are for the service of all the world; I made up my mind therefore to undertake the pilgrimage with them, but alone and on my own account; and I started immediately for Marseilles, that I might avail myself of the packet of the 7th of March.

In mentioning all these particulars to those who are good enough to read my book, my object is to guard them against misunderstanding as to the nature of this journey of mine, and so risking a disappointment. Though the curiosity which took me to the East was less that of the eyes than of the mind, and the object I had in view was rather to gain knowledge than to amusement, yet my expedition had no claim to be called one in the interests of science. I had not the kinds of knowledge needed for such an undertaking. I travelled, not in the hope of carrying science a few steps forward, but for my own instruction. I was, above all, a pilgrim. I wished to visit places that were dear to me, and to plant in my actual memory things which had hitherto existed for me only in imagination. "*J'ai voulu voir, j'ai vu,*"† ("I wished to see, and I saw.")

* Racine, in *Athalie.*   † *Ibid.*

Yes, I saw; God gave His blessing to my pilgrimage, and enabled me to draw from it as much profit as I had hoped for, and more.

Every one who has had the happiness of seeing the East has brought away from it a ray of light in his soul, which none of our mists can ever dim, and of which the pale suns of our climate can never efface the impression. Such has now been my experience. Nothing that I have seen has been able to compare for interest in my imagination with Greece and Syria. Last winter, at the foot of the picturesque mountains of Guipuscoa, "*at the bottom of the gulf where sleeps Fontarabia,*"* I was walking upon the shore, still wet with the waves, from whence the tide was noisily receding; I was looking with admiration at the rocks pierced into open-work, fretted into a thousand fantastic forms, and torn by the fury of the ocean; but my imagination would still recur with delight to that purple sea,† without ebb or flow, that bathes the coasts of Ionia. The Atlantic, that Mediterranean of our modern world, pictures for us wonderfully by its ceaseless stir the active and restless spirit of the nations of our day; whilst the Mediterranean, the "*Great Sea*" of the ancients, seems to reflect in its waters, so calm and pure, the serene genius of antiquity, to which nothing seemed great that was not marked with repose. And still, now, by the banks of that sea which I love, and on that shore of Provence from which I embarked for my journey in the East, my eyes rest with delight on the silvery foliage of the olive trees; and I love to recall the image of those which I saw flourishing in those gardens of Academe, in which the Eternal Wisdom spoke through the lips of Plato, and of that other Garden of Olives in which Jesus suffered for us!

Toulon, December 7, 1859.

* V. Hugo.   † *Mare purpureum,* says Virgil, after Homer.

I.

THE PASSAGE.

"Our religion, our laws, and almost everything which raises us above savages, comes to us from the Mediterranean."—JOHNSON, in Boswell.

I.

FROM MARSEILLES TO MALTA.

THE few days which passed away between my decision and my leaving home had been so completely taken up with the preparations for my journey that I had had no time for reflection. I started without having sketched for myself any sort of itinerary, without even having had leisure to look forward joyfully to the sights I was about to look upon, or back sorrowfully upon the friends to whom I was bidding adieu. I had left snow in Switzerland, and found rain at Lyons; at Marseilles I found sunshine and the "mistral." With the exception of the mistral at Marseilles, I found myself already well into spring, and I cannot express how delicious was the feeling that came over me when I caught sight at Château-Colomb of the Italian pine, the laurel and the aloes—advanced guards of the vegetation of the south. I had already visited some northern countries, but never before had my steps been turned towards the lands of sunshine and light. So, like a child who is taken for the first time to a show at a air, and who, seized already with admiration as he sits before the curtain, stamps his feet with impatience in his eagerness to see what is behind it, so did my heart beat with joy at the thought that these specimens of the beauties of the fair lands of the south at which I was now·looking, were but like the little performances of playwrights at a fair outside their theatres, by which they tempt spectators to enter.

I consider my readers my friends, and shall accordingly not scruple to transcribe, from time to time, without alteration, portions of my letters, or pages from my journal ; not from any indolent unwillingness to work up my materials afresh, but from the belief that others may feel pleasure, as I do, myself, in recognizing in their simplicity the impressions of the moments in which they were written.

The following is what I wrote from Marseilles :—

Thursday, March 4th.—I have just secured my place on board a ship which bears the melodious name of the *Céphise*, and I shall set sail to-morrow morning. The lot, then, is already cast, or rather, let me say *Dieu le veut!*—as the Crusaders used to exclaim on starting, like me, for Jerusalem. . . . I was travelling all day yesterday, in dark and rainy weather, which prevented my enjoying the beauty of the country. I reached Marseilles very late. To-day the sky has been bright, and I have already felt the effect of the beneficent heat of this southern sun. This harbour of Marseilles, with its forests of masts hung with their network of cordage, its quays crowded with Greeks, Turks, Armenians, and in which one overhears on all sides the melodious languages of the south,—all this has been charming to me, an agreeable prelude to the new world now about to open before me.

I was interested in noticing, on the seashore, shops

with Greek inscriptions over their doors. . . . I do not know whether I shall land at Beyrout or at Jaffa; I have only taken my place as far as Alexandria. For the moment I am more taken up with the thought of what I am leaving behind me than of what lies before me; for the imagination follows the lead of the heart, and Greece is much more vividly before my mind's eye than Alexandria and the Pyramids.

This letter of mine will have to wait long for its answer; it will find me, please God, on Mount Sion. Do you remember those beautiful *Pilgrim Psalms* which I translated for you some time back? They have always been dear to my heart, and at this moment they recur to my memory as if they had been written expressly for me. Look at the first of them, written for those starting on their journey; and at the second, describing the arrival at Jerusalem. In the first (Psalm cxxi.) are the words, "*He will not suffer thy foot to be moved; He that keepeth thee will not sleep. The sun shall not burn thee by day,*" etc.

I continue my journal.

Monday, March 8th, 9 a.m., on board the Céphise, anchored in front of the Magdalene (Sardinia).—The sea is rough; it struck our ship with such violence that it broke one of the engines; we have been compelled to take refuge in this bay, in which we enjoy at the same time the pleasure of rest after our troubles of yesterday, and an outlook upon a picturesque country, lighted with the brightest of suns. The wind is very high, but it is no longer so cold; we feel that we have changed our skies. It is the first moment I have been able to write.

We left Marseilles yesterday morning. The "mistral," which is blowing in all its vehemence, makes

our ship roll with extraordinary violence. Breakfast is
served, but only three of the passengers take their
places ; the rest are in bed in their cabins, suffering
already from sea-sickness or from the fear of it. I stand
my ground, notwithstanding the rolling of the ship; I
hold on to the deck with both hands; plates, glasses,
bottles, dance about the table, in spite of the net which is
intended to keep them in their places.* At last a pitch
of the ship, smarter than usual, tosses everything on
to the floor ; it is amusing to see oranges and olives
rolling about in all directions, and bounding from one
side of the saloon to the other. Chairs are broken, the
captain is stretched at full length on the floor. At last
I give up the case as hopeless, and think it best to
take to my bed. There I fall asleep, and after half an
hour, waking in good force, I go on deck. We can
still discern, in the distance, the coast of France, the
islands of Hyères. With a feeling of pleasure I take
out a letter that had been put into my hands on
starting, and my heart expands, and then again sinks
a little, at the memory of the warm hearts from whom
I am being parted, further and further, as the hours
pass away.

Here then am I actually on that Mediterranean Sea,
the home of my imagination, the common theatre of
the whole history of antiquity—the sea which the
Hebrews called the Great Sea, which they contem-
plated, not without a sort of terror, from the tops of

* This net—ill-omened piece of furniture—is well known to those
who have made a sea-voyage ; it is a frame with strings stretched
across it, between which one puts the things which are in danger of
being upset by the violent motion of the ship. It is called "the
fiddles," on account of its shape, and it is only used, say the sailors,
when the ship *begins her dance.*

their heaven-blessed mountains, and which represented
to their imaginations the sterile agitation of the godless
nations of the earth—that sea, beloved of the Greeks,
and made illustrious by the great deeds of their heroes
and the travels and misfortunes of Ulysses. The north-
west wind, which is driving us before it with so much
violence, is the same which cast Æneas upon the
shores of Carthage, and shattered his ships. I also
might dread the fury of Æolus, but I know that, like
Æneas, I am under the protection of a mightier God
than he—of a God who can, when He pleases, pronounce the *Quos ego.* . . . I abandon myself therefore,
without fear, to these tumultuous waves, and allow
myself to be rocked in the arms of Amphitrite, while
trusting to the God of Israel.

At five o'clock in the evening I am taken ill; I
can no longer remain on deck ; it is too cold. Night
soon overtakes us. It is well known that the farther
one travels from the poles, the shorter grows the
twilight, and even where we now were, we began to
become conscious of that fact,—*Ruit oceano nox.* How
long a first night at sea seems! You must imagine
yourself with twelve hours of darkness before you, im-
prisoned in a narrow bed, hearing no sound but the
roaring of the waves close to your ear, and the dismal
creakings of the ship's timbers, which might seem every
moment about to give way. Some words of Virgil
had just recurred to my mind ; then I began to understand how it was that Horace could have said without
hyperbole :—

> " Illi robur et æs triplex
> Circa pectus erat," etc.

I was, however, fortunate in having, alone among the
passengers, escaped sea-sickness; and I will mention,

by the way, that a precaution recommended to me at starting had contributed not a little, I believe, to this result. It consisted in always wearing a tight-fitting strap round my waist.

And besides, I fell asleep pretty soon, and when I awoke, the day was at hand. When the light began to break, I thought I caught sight of a mountain ; I could scarcely believe my eyes, for I had imagined that our course lay in a direct line north and south, and I did not expect to see land again so soon. I came on deck. . . . Even after a single day at sea it is a pleasure to see land again,—and land it really was.

We are in the straits of Bonifacio. On our left is a small island of bare rock, and far away in the distance are the snowy mountains of Corsica. In front of us the little town of La Madeleine shines in the sun, white and coquettish. On the right rise the lofty mountains of Sardinia. Its coasts are nothing but bare rocks, torn and battered, covered here and there with dark bushes.

The same date, at sea.—All day the sea is calm, and our voyage a pleasure party. The passengers, frightened yesterday by the storm, begin to shew themselves on deck; they venture out one by one, enter into conversation, and investigate with curiosity the floating hotel in which they find themselves. The *Céphise*, Captain Guérin, is a screw-steamer, with an engine of 250 horse-power, belonging to the Syrian line of packets. She is a fine vessel, constructed somewhat luxuriously, and still new, this being only her fourth voyage. The captain is a man of experience, well-informed and agreeable,—the officer second in command, a good-looking young man, twenty-nine years old, who has already been seventeen years at sea, and has twice circumnavigated the globe. A physician, and a commissary bearing Government dispatches, are also attached to our ship.

Among the passengers I may first mention a fellow-countryman of my own, M. B——, an amiable and kindly man, with quite an English cast of countenance; having been long settled in London, he is on his way to Beyrout, to undertake the superintendence of a great commercial establishment there. I have only just had a sight of Madame B——; she is an invalid, and scarcely leaves her cabin. Their family consists of two young daughters, of ten and twelve years of age, and of two taking little boys, under the care of a German governess. Next come the pilgrims of the rue de Fürstenberg. Among them are some ecclesiastics, a gentleman from La Gironde, a lawyer from La Haute Garonne, who talks much and well; two natives of Marseilles, nineteen years old, of a very marked type, expanding with delight at the prospect of a long journey; some Parisians, some Normans and Picards, carrying with them guns and camera obscuras, having quite made up their minds, if ever they reach the East, to kill or to photograph everything they come across; some Spaniards, some Irishmen; finally, my companion in my cabin, a man of gentle and religious turn of mind,—a retired ribbon manufacturer from St. Etienne.

Among the other passengers are a native of Languedoc, a magnetiser; a Jerusalem shoemaker, Arab by birth, but in religion a member of the Latin Church; a Russian Jew and his family, etc.

To-day we go to bed later, and stay on deck enjoying the beauty of the starry night. I admire for the first time the phosphorescence of the sea; the track of the ship is of luminous whiteness; and all around us little star-like points of light from time to time gleam out at us from the waves. Towards nine o'clock the sea begins to work again, and the ship to roll.

Tuesday, March 9th.—To-day I am up early; I go on deck, impatient to see what new coasts will discover themselves. This time it is Sicily.

"Tum procul e fluctu Trinacria cernitur."

She is still in the distance; but we have before us, close by, as the advanced guard of this fair land, two of the Ægades islands. We are shewn, built upon the top of sharp-pointed mountains, some fortresses, used as state prisons. But I must not stop to dwell upon the sad thoughts that this word awakens; I fancy myself in another age of the world. Virgil and Theocritus, Ulysses and Polyphemus,—all these are present, and living before me. *Sicelides Musæ!* . . . We draw near to Sicily, and sail pretty near its coasts; next to the coast is a plain; behind it rises a first step of the mountain staircase, then high mountain-tops, which lose themselves in the clouds. This coast is that of the Cyclops. Here are Trepani, where Anchises was buried, the rocks of Lilibée, Sélinonte and its palm-trees. Away to the right is Carthage. We cannot see the shore; but from this point, no doubt, Æneas could discern the smoke of Dido's funeral pile ascending to heaven.

Meantime there is great disturbance on deck. Some of the crew are still busy cleaning it, whilst others, in the forepart of the ship, are already at breakfast; the Sicilian sun inspires them, and, for want of Homer's verses, which are perhaps unknown to them, though the modern Phocæans thought they had a

right to erect a statue to his honour, one of them
chants *l'Andalouse :*—

> "J'ai fait bien des chansons pour elle,
> Je me suis battu bien souvent."

In the midst of all this, the curly-haired Jew, in his
grey gown and Russian cap, seated on a coil of rope
by the side of his wife and his two little children,
devoutly chants his morning prayer, not disturbed by
the looks of astonishment and the shouts of laughter
of some sailors who stand round him looking on, as
at a play. This man, the object of scorn and derision
to them all, interests me most of all the passengers.
As soon as he has finished his prayer, I go up to
him and address him in German. Upon this his
rough face lights up with pleasure, his countenance
kindles, he rises eagerly. It is the first time any one
has spoken to him since he left Marseilles. He is
going to settle at Jerusalem, and die there. His little
daughter looks pale, and will not eat, because she is
suffering from thirst ; they have taken with them the
bread they will want during their passage, but they
have no water, and have not yet been able to procure
any from the sailors, who do not trouble themselves
to make out their signs. I run to fetch a glass, and
bring it them. What a blessing from God to have an
opportunity of giving a glass of water in His name
to one of His people, despised and forsaken by Gentiles,
as He Himself was by Israel ! I sit down by the
side of the Jew ; he is a Rabbi and of sacerdotal
race, as is indicated by his name, "Saul Benjamin
Haccohen." He enquires of me in his patois, full of
Hebrew words, what is the sea on which we are
sailing ? and when he learns that it is the *Yam Hag-*

gadol of Scripture, he hastens to pronounce the solemn benediction which every Israelite should utter at the sight of it : "Blessed art Thou, O Lord our God, King of the world, Thou who hast created the Great Sea !"

I say a few words to him in Hebrew, and show him my Hebrew Bible. He is glad to find some one who can understand him ; he asks me whether I have read this whole book, and whether I believe what is written in it. I ask him in return whether he expects the Messiah, and he answers in the affirmative, with a bright smile of joy and hope.

Two hours after midday.—The sea becomes steadily calmer ; the African sun begins to burn so fiercely that we are obliged to seek shelter. I spend some delightful moments in the hinder part of the ship, where my Rabbi comes and sits beside me ; and I have a long conversation also with the young Arab from Jerusalem. He gives me some useful information upon travelling in Palestine. "You usually," he says, "engage a dragoman, to whom you pay thirty or thirty-five francs a day ; for that sum he undertakes to keep you in provisions, and to find you lodging, either in a tent, or in convents and hotels ; he provides you with horses, with *moukres*, even with a cook and a valet ; nothing but escorts, when any are wanted, are paid for by the travellers." My Arab's name is Hhannah (John) ; he tells me that if I want him at Jerusalem, I shall find him at the *Casa Nuova* of the Franciscans.

In the evening a light in the distance—the Gozzo lighthouse (island of Calypso)—announces to us that Malta is not far off. At midnight we enter the Quarantine harbour.

2

II.

FROM MALTA TO ALEXANDRIA.

How eagerly we land as soon as day dawns! It is but six o'clock in the morning, but the rays of the sun are already hot. Rocks, shores, villages, stand out clear in the dazzling light, as if bleached by the sun. No vegetation is visible but some enormous cactuses and a few scattered palm trees.

In Malta we are already in the east, so far, at least, as nature is concerned ; for in the architecture of her palaces and the manners of her inhabitants, Malta re-minds one most of her neighbour Sicily. She wears, too, the livery of her mistress, England ; and the clean streets and well-kept roads—in a word, the fault-less good order that prevails—shew that the country has been for a long time under the influence of the most civilized nations ; I say the country—not the people—for from the Carthaginians to the Romans, from the Saracens to the English, none of the rulers of Malta appear to have bestowed much thought upon the Maltese. Under Nero, after a century of Roman rule, they were still reckoned among barbarians. So St. Luke calls them,* who nevertheless praises them for their " *no little kindness* " (such is the expression he uses), and for their benevolent hospitality. Modern travellers pique themselves less upon their gratitude, and they have given the Maltese an odious character. If we are to believe them, the distinctive feature of their character is still " Punic faith."†

There was something sad to me in the sight of this

---

* Acts xxviii. 2.

† The Carthaginians were, in fact, the first owners of the island, then the Greek towns of Sicily, and after them the Romans. The

island population, which has never had any independent existence as a people, and whose only history is that of its transitions from one state of servitude to another. But afterwards I became convinced that, like all other members of the human race, the Maltese have had their part to play—and that an important one—in the world's history. Placed between the Western and Eastern worlds, they serve as intermediaries between the two. Speaking with ease the three idioms most in use in the Levant—Arabic, of which their native tongue is a dialect, Italian, which is the official language of their country, and English, which is that of their masters—they-feel themselves at home everywhere, all the more naturally as they have no real fatherland of their own. There is no country in the East in which some Maltese are not to be found as dragomans, couriers, or brokers, and thanks to them I have often, to my surprise, found in Syrian hotels the *cuisine* of Europe and the comfort of England.

La Valette * is a city of palaces, in the brilliant style of the Renaissance. There are few of the houses —one might even say there is not one—of which the

Saracens conquered Malta from the Eastern Empire, and were expelled from it in the eleventh century by the Normans. From that date the island remained under the rule of the kings of Sicily. In 1530, Charles-Quint gave it over to the Knights of St. John, who had just lost Rhodes. Buonaparte took it in 1798 ; it now belongs, we all know, to the English.

* The capital of the island is called the city of Valette, or *La Valette* simply, after John de Valette, Grand Master of the Order, who built it in 1566. It was erected with amazing rapidity ; eight thousand workmen were employed upon it without pause ; Pope Pius V. had given them license to work without interruption, not stopping on holy days. Though built in such haste, La Valette is nevertheless the best built city in the world.

façade would not offer a good subject of study to architects and sculptors. The streets are straight, but as they are for the most part very steep, there is something more than commonly picturesque about them, notwithstanding their regularity. The *trottoirs* by their sides are often in steps, and in the narrowest streets, where there is no thoroughfare for horses, these steps extend across the whole breadth of the street.

I go first into the church of St. Augustine. A preacher, seated and motionless, is delivering a sermon. It takes me some time to realise that the language he speaks is not Swiss-German ; so much does Maltese resemble that dialect in its sounds and intonation. Maltese is an Arabic patois, mixed with Punic, and enriched with many Italian words. Italian is the language in which one addresses strangers, and it is even, as I have said, the official language of the country, that of the courts of law, for instance.

I have a letter from C—— to her friend Miss G——. I take it to where she is staying, a beautiful palace in the *Strada Teatro*. On my arrival I am shewn into vast *salons* worthy of Versailles, and furnished in a style suited to the requirements of British *bon ton*. Picture to yourself everything in the way of knick-knacks and of *bric-à-brac* that could be procured to furnish, to decorate, and to encumber these vast Oriental apartments in accordance with the bad taste of modern Europe !

The first thing that strikes one on landing at La Valette is the costume of the women, who are all dressed uniformly in black petticoats, and their heads covered with black veils (*manfilles*), which reach below the waist, and in the folds of which they wrap themselves up scrupulously, leaving nothing visible but the face. The carriages are also among the curiosities of the country.

Some are little shut-up rooms resting upon two-wheeled trucks, others, still simpler, consist only of two enormous wheels, an axletree, and a pair of shafts ; the two shafts are connected at the end nearest the wheels with a small wooden frame, on which rests a cushion; upon this the traveller sits, his legs hanging down behind. The driver takes his place by his side, his legs in front. We go at a great rate, and the horse's action is at least as perceptible as if one were riding him. I have never seen in Malta any but handsome, well-bred horses, even of those employed in the most ordinary and laborious kinds of work.

After breakfast I hire a carriage of the kind last described, to go as far as Città Vecchia, the ancient capital of the island, seven miles from La Valette. The look of the country surprises me much. The soil is of brilliant white rock, covered in places with a little verdure. The houses of the country people are built of blocks of hewn stone, laid one upon another without mortar or cement. They are of the shape of dice, and have generally only one door, and one window, a foot square. The town is built on the top of the hill, commanding a magnificent view over the island and the sea.

I am taken to see the cave called St. Paul's, and then the catacombs. All Città Vecchia might be taken for a part of the latter, particularly the city itself, when you have left the suburb and come within the circuit of the walls. The streets are narrow, formed out of the native rock. The houses are deserted palaces, which may be hired, it is said, for from 150 to 200 francs a year. Their style of architecture is noble and severe, more like that of the palaces in Rhodes, which I visited later, than the more florid style of those of La Valette. The streets are deserted; in the gateway only did I come upon a swarm

of beggars.   Some women, their heads all behooded
with black, and carrying their children in their arms,
attack me with a flood of words in Maltese, in the
midst of which I recognize these two European words,
"*carità!*" "*something!*"

The convent of the Augustinians, which my guide
wishes me to see on account of a garden (*una verdura*)
which is in it, is not open.   To make up for that, I
visit that of the Dominicans, which is large and handsome, but has nothing remarkable about it.   What they
most like to shew is again a *verdura;* that is to say, an
inner court planted with orange trees.   These *verduras*
are the thing in the world which the Maltese most
admire and prize;   one can understand that;—the
country round is so bare and naked.   I see why it is
that the Eastern nations have always taken a garden, a
paradise, as the fittest image of terrestrial or celestial
bliss.   We are told, however, that some beautiful cultivated ground is to be found in other parts of the island;
but it is affirmed that all the cultivable soil in Malta
has been imported from Sicily.

Thursday, March 11, *at sea.*—We were to have left
Malta yesterday evening, but had to wait till this
morning for the arrival of the packet from Italy; it
was detained by bad weather.   It brings us some new
passengers; amongst them several pilgrims, come to
join the French caravan, including its president, l'Abbé
B———, an amiable man of pleasing address, and another
ecclesiastic, l'Abbé Pascal, a missionary, lately arrived
from La Réunion, where he has spent twelve years.
And now, for the first time, the deck, hitherto essentially
French, begins to have a decidedly foreign look.   Four
Mahometans have seated themselves close together, in
the middle of the ship, and do not stir from that position

during the remainder of the voyage. They are veritable
Orientals of *the Orientales,** who exceed all that I had
dreamed of in markedness of local colouring and costume.
All four come from Tunis, and are making a pilgrimage
to Mecca. One is a Turk, a Morefti, in pink embroidered
robe, with long grey beard; the other three are Arabs.
There is something refined and gentle about their countenances. One of them seems a real gentleman ; his
manners are *distingué;* in his pocket he carries the order
of Nicham; his dress has an air of elegance about it.
His turban is red and white ; he has a fine moustache,
and wears a large blue " caftan," with green pistache
border, etc. His companions are savages, and dirty.
With them one of the plagues of Egypt begins to invade
our ship.

We have also taken on board at Malta a "*cafedji;* "
that is to say, a dealer in coffee. These marine coffee
dealers are Levantines, who set up their stalls in the
forepart of the ship, and sell coffee *à la Turque* to the
Arabs on board and to other fourth-class passengers.
They act as interpreters between the ship's company
and the Arab and Greek passengers, and are commissioned by the captain as police over these gentry;
very frequently an Arab smuggles himself on board
without having paid his fare, and does not shew himself
till it is too late to land him. The *cafedji* receives a
fee for every case of illicit embarkation which he discovers in time, or for which he succeeds in obtaining
payment.

Friday, March 12*th, at sea.*—Life on board ship is
very like the life of the waters themselves. Even when
one is not ill, one always has a feeling of being at
sea, which incapacitates one for reading, studying, or

* The title of a volume of poetry by Victor Hugo.

thinking. So people walk to and fro, or inquire after each other's health, and ask questions ten times a day of the captain as to how many knots an hour we are making.

After some days, the curiosity which one felt at first about the sea and the ship begins to lose its edge, and each passenger is taken up only with reorganizing around him the little habits of his ordinary life. As evening falls, we leave Cyrene and Libya displaying their desert coasts along the horizon, and whilst the stars silently shine out over the vast sky, we retire early into the saloon, and gather round the lamps and the piano. Some of the pilgrims have succeeded in organizing a complete whist party, others have assembled round the piano, where Miss S——— executes some brilliant variations, with *obbligato* accompaniments of exclamations and complimentary murmurs. Then l'Abbé Pascal attempts a hymn, and two other pilgrims chant the duo of " *La Reine de Chypre* "* :—

> " Vous qui de la chevalerie
> Suivez si dignement les lois. . . . ."

While all this is going on I make an attempt at writing, in spite of the increased rolling of the ship ; and M. B———, tired with doing nothing all day, falls asleep in a corner of the saloon, as happens to those who, accustomed to a very active life, find themselves suddenly condemned to idleness.

The sky becomes overcast, the wind changes, the ship pitches violently. We shall have a bad night. . . . .

* An opera by Halévy.

II.

EGYPT.

Insuetum miratur limen.

I.

ARRIVAL AT ALEXANDRIA.

Alexandria, March 16, 1858.

To M—— A——

. . . . Another word or two on my passage. The sea is not so manageable as I had imagined, and, most of the time, it is impossible to write or even to read ; take it altogether, a passage by sea is a very fatiguing business ; it is true we have had contrary winds which have retarded us, and knocked us about. The engine has been twice disabled, and, consequently, we have had some anxiety and disturbance of mind.

Thanks to the French caravan, and the Mussulmans who were on their way to Mecca, our ship was in the main occupied by pilgrims. At the first dawn of day I went aft, to go through my morning devotions ; I found there the French, Irish, and Spanish ecclesiastics, busy with their breviaries ; a little farther off, in the middle of the ship, the Arabs, prostrate upon the ground, were saying their prayers, and in front my Jew was reading the law and repeating his *Krishma*. It gave me a feeling of inexpressible sweetness to see all these prayers offered together by this little floating world, isolated in the middle of the sea, each in its own language, to that God who is " Father of all, and above all."

I was deeply moved also in the evening at seeing by the light of the stars Madame B—— sitting on deck, with her two little girls leaning their heads on her shoulders, and her little boys resting theirs on her lap, and singing together in a sweet voice a whole repertory of well-known German songs: *Wenn die Schwalben* . . . . and others of the same sort. You cannot imagine what good that did me! In the midst of this world of travellers, this isolation from everything which recalls family and fatherland, amidst the brilliant and glaring colours with which everything is arrayed in the East, these sweet sounds had, by contrast, and in virtue of the association of ideas which they awakened in me, a charm that I cannot describe.

. . . . To-day I am in a world, new, strange, even unexpected, often as my imagination had pictured it to me; for all the ideas I had formed of it fall short of the reality. In short, the East is even much more eastern than I had pictured to myself. It is an immense pleasure, as you may imagine, to have such a feast for eyes, imagination, and reflection spread before one, but it is also extremely fatiguing; the mind finds no familiar object on which to rest; and it is not easy to collect one's thoughts. . . . I slightly modified the plan I had made for my journey, and instead of spending only one day here, I determined to make it a week or two. The native country of Joseph, of Moses, and of the Pharaohs, seemed a necessary introduction to the Holy Land. I therefore let the French steamer sail without me for Jaffa, and waited for the Austrian packet. That will give me time to see Cairo and the Pyramids.

Yesterday, on waking, after a night often disturbed by alarms, I went up on deck, to see if land was visible. A narrow strip of yellow sand, bordering the sea, close to us, told us we were off the coast of Egypt. This first sight of it was melancholy; no trees, no verdure, no mountains. There were a few windmills scattered along the shore. We were on the point of entering the port of Alexandria. After a few minutes, our ship stopped, and was instantly surrounded by some hundreds of boats, full of human creatures, of all colours and all costumes, who sprang on board to take possession of our things and of ourselves;—all this farrago of living things shouting, storming, quarrelling, in languages unknown to us. . . . Yes, the impression upon me was sad; I felt that this was Egypt, " *the house of bondage.*" Before landing I thought I would read the *text* for the day:* I took out my Bible, and read, "*Joseph was in prison, but the Lord was with Joseph.*" These words seemed written especially for me; the sort of dread with which I had been filled at the sight of this great crowd of strange creatures, and at this first step which I was about to take in solitude into this, to me, unknown world, gave way: I landed with a light heart and a feeling of thankfulness. I will not attempt to tell you what I saw yesterday and to-day; I should not have time, and besides, nothing is more difficult than to describe things which present not a single point of likeness to anything known to one. Awaiting the time when " *the wilderness* " itself will " *blossom as the rose,*" I enclose you a little flower which I gathered for you on entering an oasis; for I have to-day paid a visit to the desert, which begins almost at the very gates of Alexandria, or, to speak more accurately, at a short

* *i.e.,* The text for the day of the Moravian brothers.

league's distance from it. I mounted a donkey (it is
the animal one rides in this country; the donkeys are
stationed in great numbers in the open places, like
cabs on a stand), and I rode him all day. I went to
Ramleh, a village a league and a half from here.
Ramleh is an oasis; the desert here is of fine sand,
with single palm trees growing at long distances from
each other. To-night, as I return, the sun is just
setting; the far horizon is tinted with purple; under
a palm tree a camel is lying down, with his load of
sacks upon his back; by his side an Arab, in a
white turban, arrayed in long, ample blue robe, adorned
with a red scarf, is saying his prayer, smiting the
ground with his forehead. It is a vignette one has
often seen in books, a very familiar picture; but the
first time one sees it in real life it seems to one something quite new. I might give you a number of sketches
of this sort, but I will abstain; if once I begin such
talk, I shall never stop.

To A. M. L. B—— A——

Alexandria, the same date.—Here I am staying in
the land of the Ptolemies till the day after to-morrow,
when, please God, I shall be in that of the Pharaohs.
I am glad of this moment of repose, the first I have
had for writing. I tell you nothing of our passage, nor
of Malta; all that has been fading out of my memory—
effacing itself from my imagination—since I have seen
Alexandria! What will it be then when I see Cairo?
You know that in travelling one is often disappointed,
because the reality does not come up to what one had
pictured to oneself in one's dreams. That, however,
has not been the case with me—quite the contrary;
never could I have believed that there existed any place

in the world in which the local colouring was so marked.
With the exception of one small quarter of the town,
which has just a little of a European look about it, and
where one meets carriages, though few in number, and
sees a few dresses *à la française*, everything here is
pure Oriental ; these barefooted men, dressed in red and
blue, these veiled women, these donkeys and camels, look
like figures cut out of old pictures in the *Histoire Sainte*,
The excursion I have made to-day in Alexandria reminds me of those in the *Thousand and One Nights*. I
wish I could fix in my imagination all I see ; for everything—yes, absolutely everything—on which my eye
falls is new to me.

Scarcely had I reached the hotel when W—— made
his appearance. Passing the Consulate, he had seen
my name advertised in the list of passengers on board
the *Céphise*, and had been on the look-out for me. It
was a great pleasure to me to see him again ; we have
spent the day together, and he has just left me. He
is well, but finds life here wearisome. Charmed though
I am with the *colouring*, so to say, of Egypt, I can
quite understand his feelings. Not to mention the
isolation in which a European finds himself here, this
country is extremely melancholy. In that respect
Egypt is different from what I had imagined ; I thought
that there was something in the open sunshine of Africa
to expand the soul ; but it is not so. I could not
express, still less could I describe accurately, the impression of a sort of moral as well as physical dryness
made upon me by all I see here; everything is surprising,
everything strikes my imagination, but I have as yet
seen nothing on which the eye rests with pleasure. The
grandest and most beautiful objects have had the same
effect upon me as those pieces of brilliantly coloured

Turkish tapestry which we admire, but which have no definite meaning, and of which we have nothing to say, except that they are *original;* that, however, it is true, is much, in this age of fusion.   I give you my first impressions, which no doubt will modify themselves.

I do not undertake to give you descriptions ; where everything is new, one does not know what to bring into relief, it would be necessary to photograph.   I will only say that I have already had occasion to realise what this climate of Egypt is : yesterday it was very hot,— thirty-six degrees in the shade, I was told ; to-day my thermometer stands only at twenty-three,—it is therefore a mild summer temperature ; the wind has even something sharp in it, as in our mountain valleys ; I had to button my coat in facing the wind, and yet the sun's rays were so piercing that it made head and eyes ache, in spite of every precaution.   In the expedition which I made to-day to Cleopatra's needle, I had, in a single quarter of an hour, caught a sunstroke on my face.

Thank God, I have not yet had to make use, for myself, of the little medicine-chest which you gave me, and yet it has been very useful ; I started as a doctor on my own account on board the *Céphise ;* by the help of effervescing powders I cured the digestion of one gentleman, which had been greatly disturbed; with two little glasses of *absinthe* I set right an Arab who was suffering horrors from sea-sickness ;   and lastly, with the *pâte d'orgeat* which Elise gave me, I made some milk of almonds, wherewith to suckle, for want of anything better, a poor little Jewish child, whom they were at a loss how to feed.

Write to me soon, and believe me ever, etc.

The founder of Alexandria—that young conqueror who, like that other son of Jupiter, Bacchus, led his victorious troops beyond the Indus, and of whom, in his short career, we catch sight in the midst of the conquered populations of Asia and of Africa, as the genius of liberty and civilization, rather than of conquest —Alexander—could not have chosen for his empire a capital more worthy of it. It might seem as if there must have been in his plans something greater even than the divination of genius; we might think we discerned in them the direct intervention of Providence touching the springs of the world's history. Alexandria, it is true, was never the capital of an empire ; the death of the Macedonian conqueror left her orphaned, even before she was full grown; but none the less was she the centre of the world. Rome inherited from Alexander nothing but his sword : it was to Alexandria that the pupil of Aristotle left the legacy of his thought and of his mission. It was there that by the philosophy of paganism was sketched, and then by the theology of Christendom was realized, the union of the East and the West. All the nations came there to deposit their religions, their cosmogonies, their creeds—as they deposited their sacred books in the library of the Ptolemies. Thither it was that the East came to unveil to Greece its symbols and its mysteries, and that the disciples of Plato re-baptized the doctrine of their master in those ancient springs from which it had originally derived its inspiration ; and it was there, finally, that the Gospel itself, under the hands of Clement, of Origen, of Athanasius, became Greek for the Greeks, and conquered the intellect of mankind, as it had already conquered their hearts and consciences.

But it was not in the domain of mind only that Alexandria was to assert her sovereignty. Her founder had wished to raise up a rival to Tyre ; and she was in reality, during the whole of antiquity, and till she was taken by the Saracens, the great mart of all the nations, the focus of the commerce of three continents. Upon the waves of the Mediterranean and of the Red Sea, across the sands of Libya and the deserts of Sinai, Alexandria beheld approaching her the ships and the caravans of Persia, of India, of Africa, of Rome, of Constantinople, eager to pour into her bazaars the products of the whole world. The sword of Omer dealt a fatal blow at the commerce of Alexandria, which nevertheless rose again in the fourteenth century, to fall once more at the end of the fifteenth, after Vasco di Gama had opened a new road to the Indies, and Christopher Columbus had shifted the centre of the world. In our own age, thanks to the steam which has dethroned the Cape of Good Hope, Alexandria has regained some part of her ancient importance; she is now the principal site of the commerce of the Levant, and who knows whether in the future the Suez Canal will not once more gather around itself, as to its centre of gravity, the commerce of all lands?

Alexander had desired that his remains should repose in this city, which was the creation of his genius, and of which he had with his own hand traced the outline. After his death, his body was transported thither. It was laid in a sepulchre worthy of it, in the midst of a temple dedicated to his memory ; but, alas! O vanity of vanities! O Bossuet! O Yorick! the dust of the conqueror was carried off to mingle with the ashes of Pompey, amidst the sands of the desert, and his sarcophagus, before which in former days the priests of Egypt used to burn incense, is in our day being dusted by the servants in the British Museum (*Egyptian Hall*, No. 10). There remains nothing of the ancient Alexandria but a vast space covered with bricks and fragments of pottery, and two remarkable monuments—the column called Pompey's and Cleopatra's needles. These needles are two obelisks of red granite, which form the entrance to the palace of Cæsar. One of them is still standing, the other lies prostrate in the sand. It has been pro-posed to transport this latter into England for the adornment of one of the squares in London.* The cost of its transport has been estimated at £15,000 sterling. The column, 117 feet in height, still towers over the walls of the town ; its capital and pedestal are each made of a single block of granite. It is con-sidered the finest column in the world.

II.

CAIRO.

The railroad from Alexandria to Cairo has been open for two years; it is being continued to Suez. It will. therefore connect the Mediterranean with the Red Sea, and Europe with the East Indies, awaiting that famous cutting through of the isthmus of which we have heard so much.

One might have thought that so modern a product of civilization would have seemed an offensive patch of new cloth upon the old garment of this the most ancient country of the world. A railroad in competition with the navigation of the Nile ! a viaduct over the Lake Mareotis ! a station on the shores of the Red Sea !

* It was erected on the Thames Embankment a few years since.—*Tr.*

But it does not strike one so ; it is but one additional oddity in the land of oddities. Indeed, one must not expect here the punctuality of European railways. The Arabs have not yet learnt from the English that time is money; or, rather, perhaps they think that if it is pleasant to gain time and money, it is doubly so to spend them. There is only one train a day. You start at, or near, nine o'clock in the morning, and count upon arriving at Cairo at three o'clock, but you do not in fact reach it till six in the evening,—or morning, if you ever arrive at all. It is not that the train does not travel fast, but one amuses oneself at the stations, the times for stopping not being fixed, and the servants and the labourers are Arabs or Levantines, whom it would be impossible to bring under proper discipline. And then the railroad has but one line of rails. Accordingly, when the pacha is at a village, and puts off his departure—which happens continually—he retards, not only the train in which he himself is a passenger, but the one also which travels in the opposite direction.

The first and second-class carriages are very comfortable; the third-class are occupied almost exclusively by Arabs. One carriage is reserved for women— frightful women; faces veiled, throats bare; veils, noses, ears, chests, covered with gold ornaments. They smoke their cigarettes. It is needless to say that there are neither rooms nor carriages reserved for smokers. In the East, where both sexes practise it, smoking is under no restriction.

The first station is Kefr-Nawar, a miserable village rather like the suburbs of Alexandria, and composed of little huts, very low, with mud walls, and roofs made of rushes. Here, for the first time, Egypt, which at

Alexandria is only a sandy shore, begins to shew itself in its beauty, as a rich, fertile country; it is indeed "*green Egypt*," as Virgil calls it. Cornfields and meadows stretch right and left over a plain, as far as the eye can reach. One might fancy oneself in France or Germany. From time to time a red turban gleams out like a poppy from amongst the wheat or fresh verdure, and reminds you that you are in the East. Here you see shepherds stripped to the waist, or quite naked, in charge of buffaloes, oxen, or sheep; elsewhere camels with their conductors, or splendid horses, their riders armed and brilliantly caparisoned; poor fellahs in long blue tunics, with sad, hard-looking faces, their skins burnt, and almost blackened, by the sun.

At another station,—Lamorha, we find a number of soldiers in green uniforms (green is the sacred colour to Mahometans); they are the viceroy's guard of honour. I sit down by the side of the road to breakfast; they bring me some hard eggs and disk-shaped rolls (whence the Hebrew כִּכָּר לֶחֶם, properly speaking, *a circle of bread*); these rolls are coarse, soft, and badly baked, made of a sort of paste not unlike that of the *salées* we make in the country. Some little girls come and offer me water, which they carry on their heads or shoulders, in earthenware jugs of antique forms, and made after the most artistic models. Men carrying bottles made of undressed leather mingle among the crowd, chanting odd cries. They press their bottles with both hands, and squeeze out of them into large goblets a refreshing drink,—a sort of Egyptian cocoa.

We reach the banks of an arm of the Nile; the water in it is muddy, of a blackish yellow colour, which explains clearly the name of Shikhor,* which was given

* From שָׁחַר, *niger fuit.*

to it by the Hebrews.   There is a steamer to cross
it. Soon after, we see before us, on our right, illumined
by the setting sun, the tops of the Pyramids ; the forty
centuries invoked by Buonaparte look down upon us in
all their majesty.

It is night when we arrive in Cairo.   The landing-
place is lighted only by torches.   There is an immense
crowd upon it ; it is plain enough that we are in the
neighbourhood of a great town.   But it is a crowd to
frighten one ; nothing in a European town could give
any idea of it : they shout, they howl, they hustle one
another, they fight—it is not a crowd, it is an insurrection !

I forgot to mention that among the passengers who
embarked at Malta on board the *Céphise* was a Russian,
M. de Lukieff.   We had become acquainted with each
other the night before we arrived at Alexandria, and it
was with him that I travelled to Cairo.

The *Esbékieh*, in which is the Hôtel d'Orient, is a great
square at the entrance into the town, and the plantations of trees and shrubs in the middle of it, green and
well grown, are a pleasant rest to the eyes.   This
square is frequented principally by foreigners, for the
Arabs scarcely ever take walks ; it is full of little cafés,
half Arab, half European ; they are simply plank-built
huts, in front of which are chairs and tables.   Refreshments are to be had there, and one can smoke narguilehs. These refreshments consist of coffee and lemonade,
and various bonbons and confectionery of a kind totally
different from European sweetmeats.   The bonbon
most in fashion is a sort of paste, soft, transparent,
gelatinous, stuffed with almonds and powdered with
flour ; it is perfumed with attar of roses, for the object

is not so much to please the sense of taste as of smell ;
savoury morsels are not so much in request as perfumes.

We begin our expedition at nine o'clock in the morning, mounted on donkeys, our dragomans going before
us. There is nothing here to remind one of a European
town ; the streets, not one of which is paved, are narrow
and crooked ; the houses are two or three stories high
(a thing not to be seen in the other cities of the East),
but miserable in appearance. There is nothing in the
town monumental in character, nothing artistic. The
higher stories do not correspond with the lower, they
project beyond them,—the great object to be attained
being shelter from the sun ; and as this device is insufficient for the purpose, whole streets are sometimes
spanned with beams, or with wicker-work, or even very
thick carpeting. The linen blinds which suffice in the
south of Europe would be quite useless here.

The doors of the houses are the most noticeable
objects ; they are often striped with brilliant colours, and
have inscribed upon them some verse out of the Koran.
There are no windows, in our sense of the word ; the
openings in the walls which take their place are barred
with open wood-work, and project into the street ; this
open work is much varied, and very artistic in design,
and it often costs, we are told, a fabulous sum. By the
help of these trellises and window blinds (these are the
best comparisons we can use to describe them) the
inhabitants of the houses see what passes in the street
without being seen themselves. This feature of the architecture we can see must have prevailed in the East even
in the most ancient times. The Song of Deborah,* for
instance, represents the mother of Sisera, expecting the
return of her son in triumph, trying to see *through the*

* Judges v. 28.

trellis-work whether his chariot is coming. And Solomon also says in the Book of Proverbs,* " At the window of my house I looked *through my casement* (trellis-work), and beheld a young man passing through the street," etc.

Neither are the warehouses nor workshops at all like any of those to which we are accustomed, unless it be the booths at fairs. They are shallow and narrow sheds, quite open in front, and raised two feet above the ground. The shopkeepers sit cross-legged in them, smoking their chibouques. Indeed, it is rare to see an Arab, whatever be his occupation, without his pipe, or unarmed. I remember to this day the surprise I felt the first time I saw a tailor busy at his needle, with his pistols in his girdle; and a carpenter handling his axe with one hand, and with the other holding up a chibouque, more than three feet long, which he was diligently smoking.

If you have a purchase to make, you sit down on the edge of the shop floor, cross-legged if you are an Arab, your legs hanging down into the street if you are a European, and prepare to wait patiently till the shopkeeper is pleased to serve you. He never hurries himself; and before dreaming of looking for what you want, he first takes his pipe from his mouth, and puts it into yours. If you refuse it, he sends one of his servants to the nearest café to fetch you a narguileh. If you still refuse, he rolls you up a cigarette. You get impatient, and repeat your demand—a trouble you might have spared yourself. He compels you to undergo his hospitalities to the end, and you do not get off till you have accepted cups of coffee or glasses of lemonade *ad libitum*. It is not till you have resigned yourself to your fate, and at last forgotten the object

* Prov. vii. 6, etc.

for which you came, that the shopkeeper appears to remember it. Then he unrolls his stuffs, displays his jewels, and calls upon you to make your choice.

But everything here seems contrived to wear out the patience of a European. The subdivision of the *specialités* is pushed so far, that to possess yourself of the commonest object—a pipe, for instance, and four thousand are sold per day in the various bazaars of Cairo—you often have to visit two or three shops. On arriving in Alexandria, I thought the first thing I had to do—I may say my first duty—was to arm myself with a chibouque. After having bought a pipe-bowl at one shop, I had to go to another to buy an amber mouth-piece, and to another to look out a pipe-stick. Sticks of rosewood, citron, cherrywood, or jessamine, were to be found in profusion. I fixed upon a jessamine stick, but my troubles were not yet over. I found the stick was not yet bored ; this operation is not performed till the purchase is completed, and is paid for separately. I therefore waited patiently till the stick was ready, and went away charmed with my purchase. I wished to make use of it at once; I fastened the mouthpiece into one of the ends of the pipe, I fitted into the other end the bowl, made of red earth of Stamboul ; I lighted it, I drew in my breath—but in vain ! The wretches had only bored the tube as far as the middle of its length. They had observed that instead of following their proceedings with my eye, I was amusing myself looking at the people passing by, and they had been too lazy to go on with their work a moment longer than I watched them.

And this, after all, is but the smallest part of the troubles a purchaser has to go through. They can only be said to begin when the question of the price to be paid has to be settled. Then Rabelais' quarter of an hour is often stretched to a full hour. The shopkeeper begins almost always by overcharging you enormously. Not content with asking twice the real value, he will demand, without shewing the slightest shame, ten or a hundred times the right amount. You protest, and he then asks you what price you are willing to give ; you offer twenty piastres for what he had offered to sell you for two hundred, and he closes with you eagerly, for he is still a gainer of seventy-five per cent. on the bargain.

You think you have reached the end of your troubles, and set yourself to pay the account. But after fighting your battle over your purchase, you have next to fight it out over the worth of the money itself. If it is observed that you have *sovereigns*, they will reckon the price for you in piastres and in *medjidiehs ;* if you have *medjidiehs* and piastres, they will reckon it in *guineas.* They refuse to allow more than sixteen piastres for a piece of money which you know to be worth twenty-two ; and even after that they will best you down yet another half-piastre, because the coin you offer is worn, and its stamp effaced. Suspicion will be cast upon the genuineness of the stamp, and upon the sufficiency of the weight; the shopkeeper rings it on the floor to make sure it is not bad money; he tests it with his tongue to see if it is really gold ; and, for greater security, he will almost always end by sending for scales to weigh it.

But one may, of course, provide oneself with the kind of money which is believed to have the widest currency, by applying to a money-changer. It is true that he also will try to overreach you, since you are a foreigner. And that he will easily do, since in the East the value of the currency varies strangely with times and countries. That I discovered later in my journey, in passing from Judæa into Galilee, and from there to Constantinople. A napoleon at Jerusalem was worth ninety-six piastres, at Nazareth a hundred and four, and at Constantinople a hundred and twenty-seven. The services of money-changers are none the less necessary, on account of the great variety of coins ; calculations are made sometimes with one sort, sometimes with another. Besides the piastre (twenty centimes), and the parah (half a centime), which are indigenous, one reckons principally in dollars, shillings, and guineas ; or else with francs and napoleons. But you continually meet with Indian rupees, Turkish medjidiehs, Russian roubles, and crown-pieces stamped with the head of Maria Theresa, which are here called *talari della Regina.*

Some of the money-changers are itinerant ; they circulate through the streets and bazaars, rattling a pile of piastres in their hands. Others are stationed in the public places, seated on the ground, and setting out their little tables in the open air. These are the little tables which it had gradually become customary to set up in the temple at Jerusalem, and which Jesus overturned.*

It is difficult to ascertain, even approximately, what is the population of Cairo. It is calculated, at the lowest reckoning, at two hundred thousand, and at the highest, at six or seven hundred thousand souls. The same uncertainty prevails as to all the towns of the East, even those which ought, it might seem, to be the best known ; I have before me two books, each printed within the last ten years, and one of which gives to Alexandria a hundred thousand inhabitants, and the other only twelve thousand five hundred. This latter

* Matt. xxi. 12 ; Mark xi. 15 ; John ii. 15.

number is, it is true, evidently too low, and rests probably
upon an estimate made at the beginning of this century;
for the population of Alexandria has increased considerably of late years.

The most populous streets of Cairo are more populous and more crowded than any street in Paris, but
their life is of a different kind.   There is no regularity
in it ; in one place the street is blocked up by a group
of musicians, around whom a group of idlers gather ;
in another a pedlar attracts the crowd, shewing the
stuffs which he carries on his shoulders ; another man,
his fingers covered with rings for sale, displays them
in the eyes of customers.   Often we are stopped on
our way by flocks of sheep and goats, or camels laden
with great stones or beams of timber, that we en-
counter as we pass.   The greater part of the passengers in the streets are mounted on donkeys.   How
often in the streets of Cairo I have seen the well-known
picture of the Flight into Egypt reproduced ! Mounted
upon a donkey is a veiled woman, with a child in her
arms ; by her side a man with white beard, wearing a
long robe, holding in one hand a long stick, and resting
the other upon the neck of the beast, to guide and
urge him.   But there is one point in which the *tableau
vivant* of which I am speaking differs from that of the
pictures ; that is, that in the East the women do not
sit on the animals they ride, as ours do, but bestride
them like men.   When they go on foot, they generally·
carry their children astride upon their left shoulders,
the little creature leaning with both hands upon the
head of its mother.   It is a picture less familiar to us
than the other, but not less attractive.

Besides the first-class donkeys, there are, we are
assured, in Cairo, forty thousand common ones, stationed

at the corners of the streets, and consequently forty thousand donkey drivers. These donkey drivers never leave their beasts, but run after them, hitting them mercilessly and incessantly. The consequence is that most of the donkeys have an open sore on their haunches; a cruelty altogether unprovoked, as they are lively and tractable, and to make them trot the rider has but to swing his legs backwards and forwards.

A sound of music, shrill and sharp, announces the approach of a nuptial procession; it soon comes into sight. In front march the players on fifes and tambourines. The national music of the Arabs is summed up in these two instruments. We know from the Bible that they were those most in use among the Hebrews in the most ancient times. It was on fifes and tambourines (or "timbrels") that the Israelitish women celebrated the passage over the Red Sea.* It was with a fife and timbrel that the daughter of Jephthah came to meet her father.† Later on, in the time of David, we see that the Hebrews in similar circumstances made use also of cymbals,‡ cornets, psalteries, and harps.§

Behind the musicians come, in two lines, a long train of women and girls. In the middle is the bride, walking between two older women. Four men hold up over her head a dais of pink gauze, a woman waves in front of her a large fan made of feathers. The bride is entirely covered with a veil. She has on her head a red cloth surmounted with many coronets of gold, which wraps her down to the feet in its ample folds. The whole party utter cries of joy. A second group of musicians closes the procession.

This scene is often to be witnessed, for the wedding

* Exod. xv. 20.   ‡ 1 Sam. xviii. 6.
† Judg. xi. 34.   § 2 Sam. vi. 5.

ceremonial lasts many days, and each day this procession takes place, with but slight modifications. The first
day I spent in Cairo I met no fewer than four of them.
This is, indeed, one of the characteristic features of
oriental towns; and one can understand how it was that
the first image that presented itself to the minds of the
prophets to describe the desolation of Jerusalem was the
absence of these joyous and noisy processions. "*I will
cause to cease from the cities of Judah, and from the streets
of Jerusalem, the voice of mirth and the voice of gladness,
the voice of the bridegroom and the voice of the bride; for the
land shall be desolate.*" And in another passage, "*The
mirth of tabrets ceaseth, the noise of them that rejoice
endeth.*"*

At the head of these nuptial processions one sometimes sees a child on horseback; a boy of thirteen, who
is to be circumcised. As this ceremony gives occasion,
like that of a marriage, for long and expensive festivities,
people of small fortunes manage to combine the two
festivities into one, when a marriage and a circumcision
are about to take place in the family.

The large number of blind persons to be seen feeling
their way along the streets in Cairo and Alexandria
has been already noticed by Volney. " Walking in the
streets of Cairo," he says, " out of a hundred persons
whom I met, there were often twenty blind, eighteen
one-eyed, and twenty others with eyes red, purulent,
or spotted. Almost every one wears bandages, indi-
cating that they either have or are recovering from
ophthalmia." Ophthalmia is in fact one of the scourges
of Egypt, as all physicians know. Its prevalence must
be attributed in a great degree to the sand which the
wind blows into the eyes ; but one can understand

* Jer. vii. 34 ; Isa. xxiv. 8.

how in Oriental countries in general the excessive heat of the sun must make blindness much commoner than it is among us. In compensation we have toothache, catarrhs, and chest complaints, all of which are unknown in Egypt and in Syria.

It is not therefore surprising to any one who knows the East, to find the blind so often mentioned in the Gospel history, and to meet in Scripture with so many allusions to this infirmity. Of the twelve maledictions of the Levites, there is one against him " *who maketh the blind to go out of his way.*"* " *The Spirit of God hath anointed me,*" said Jesus, quoting from Isaiah, " *to preach the gospel to the poor, and recovery of sight to the blind.*" † " *The Lord,*" says David, " *setteth at liberty them that are bound; the Lord giveth sight to the blind.*" ‡ " *I was eyes to the blind,*" § says Job, in calling to mind past days. The Bible makes mention also of eye-salves ; || it is an image which would hardly have occurred to a European, for we do not generally make more use of eye-salves than Arabs do of " eau de Bottot." In the East, on the other hand, where even the soundest eyes are constantly irritated· by the sun and the dust, eye-salves must be in daily use for hygienic and toilet purposes. As I have said above, I had occasion for it myself, even in the first half-hour of my stay in Egypt.

We leave the town on the side opposite to that which faces the Nile, and find ourselves in the desert. Before us is an immense tract of country filled with tombs, behind which rise deserted mosques and palaces in ruins. Mahomedans never destroy tombs ; they

---

* Deut. xxvii. 18. § Job xxix. 15.
† Luke iv. 19. || Rev. iii. 18.
‡ Psalm cxlvi. 8.

know nothing of *terminable grants* in such matters ;
with them they belong to the domain of piety; besides,
here, in this wide desert, the dead have no occasion
to quarrel for ground ; each may claim for himself his
own place beneath the sun. These ruined palaces date
from the time of the Soudans ; one of these mosques
serves them for a tomb. In another we are shewn two
blocks of marble, on each of which can be distinguished
quite clearly the print of the feet of the Prophet, one
naked, the other with a slipper on.

A· poor woman squatting on the sand is pouring out
of a great jug some camel's dung ; she kneads it into
a little cake which she dries in the sun. We have
already met in the high roads graceful little girls
carrying on their heads round baskets, resting on a
crown woven of grass, and collecting in these the
dung of camels and asses. These cakes constitute the
commonest and most useful sort of fuel in countries
where wood is so scarce. We find from the Bible
(Ezek. iv.) that the Israelites also were acquainted with
this substitute for wood to burn, but that they had
recourse to it unwillingly, and only when driven to it
by distress. Voltaire made sport of this passage in
Ezekiel, which he thought *bizarre;* Père Guénée made
a good reply to his flippant jests. Now that we are
acquainted with Egypt, we see nothing that is not quite
natural, in the words of the prophet.

We return into the town, and climb the hill to the
citadel, which overhangs Cairo and commands a splendid view ; beneath our feet stretches the great city, all
bristling with minarets, under the shadow of which
are grouped the cupolas of more than four hundred
mosques. In the distance is seen the rich wide plain
watered by the Nile, and farthest of all stand the pyra-

mids. Within the circuit of the citadel is the palace of
Mehemet Ali, now uninhabited. Such deserted houses
are common in Egypt; every pacha builds himself a
palace, and forsakes that of his predecessor; that of
Mehemet Ali seems to me not so handsome as that of
Ras-et-Tin, at Alexandria, built by the present viceroy,
Saïd-Pasha. At its entrance is a small garden redolent
with the perfume of citrons. At a few steps' distance
took place the massacre of the Mamelouks.

The history of the Mamelouks is well known. A
set of slaves, mostly of Circassian origin, they formed,
under the successors of Saladin, the body-guard of the
sovereign; trained from childhood to the profession
of arms, they became the *élite* of the army, and the
principal force in Egypt. In the middle of the thir-
teenth century, in the time of the crusade of St. Louis,
a Mamelouk took possession of the throne, and founded
in Egypt a new dynasty. Egypt was governed by
Mamelouk Sultans till it was conquered by the Turks
in 1517. The Ottoman Sultan, Selim I., who took
from them the sovereign power, and hanged their chief,
did not succeed in overturning their power. The
Mamelouks still formed a military aristocracy, nominally, rather than really, subject to a pacha sent from
Constantinople; they were rather vassals than subjects
of the Porte.

The pacha, Mehemet Ali, who in our century made
an attempt to form an independent Egyptian monarchy,
and to unite under his sceptre all the Arab tribes, had
two obstacles to overcome, two enemies to defeat, before
he could attain his object—one above, the other below
him. He had to shake off at once the yoke of the
Sultan and that of the Mamelouks. His audacity and
genius almost succeeded in making him independent of

the Porte, and he would have succeeded completely had it not been for the intervention of the European powers, who forced him to give up the greater part of his conquests. It might have seemed more difficult still to overturn the power of the Mamelouks, to reduce to obedience those who had raised him to power, to crush this ancient, rich, and valiant aristocracy which the Sultans had failed in subduing, and which the victories of Kleber and of Buonaparte had shaken, without succeeding in overturning it. But nothing is impossible to the man who does not stop at crime. Mehemet got rid of the Mamelouks in the same way in which Peter the Great rid himself of the Strelitzes; and Mahmoud, some years later, of the janizaries. He did not even wait, as they did, for his enemies to give him an excuse for passing sentence upon them. Pretending that he wanted their assistance for some military expedition, he assembled them all in the citadel ; he received them with a pretence of friendship, and prepared them a banquet in his gardens. At a signal given, assassins sprung upon them: the Mamelouks, taken off their guard, could not make any attempt at resistance. The larger part fell under the daggers of their assassins. Others jumped from the top of the terrace at a terrible height, and were dashed to pieces in their fall, with the exception, it is said, of one of them, who, having hazarded this leap on horseback, reached the ground safe and sound, and survived this frightful massacre.

A stream of blood flowing from under the gates of the citadel into the steep street which leads into the town, announced to the people of Cairo the success of this *coup d'état.* From that day—it was March 1st, 1811—the authority of Mehemet Ali was firmly established within his dominions, and recognized outside of them. The Porte began to fear him, and the Christian powers no longer ignored him, or accounted him a barbarian. But, from that time also, attacks of a gloomy melancholy came over him from time to time, troubling him in the midst of his grandeur and his victories. He would no longer occupy the citadel of Cairo, which had hitherto been his favourite residence ; and, tormented by remorse, he determined to expiate the massacre of the Mamelouks by erecting a magnificent mosque upon the very place where that scene of horror was enacted.

This mosque, built after the model of that of Saint Sophia at Constantinople, is in exquisite taste and of great magnificence. It is entirely built of white marble. In its centre is a vast paved court, in which graceful fountains pour forth their fresh pure waters for the ablutions of the faithful. But the Lady Macbeth bloodstain seems to be continually reappearing upon the marble pavement, and this splendid mosque, intended to expiate a crime, serves but to immortalize its memory.

Whilst they were building this edifice, a dervish foretold that the Viceroy would die as soon as the work was finished. Mehemet Ali, seized with superstitious fears, wished to counteract the effect of this prophecy by never finishing his mosque ; and during all the remainder of his long reign he never ceased enlarging, beautifying, and adorning it.

I mention in this place, only because I happen just now to remember it, a well dug in the rock to a depth of two hundred and seventy feet, and which is shewn to travellers as the principal curiosity of the citadel. It is known under the name of *Joseph's Well;* and this Joseph cannot be, as has been sometimes suggested, the Sultan Saladin, for the well appears to be of the highest antiquity, and if it was really the work of a Joseph, it must have been, rather, the son of Jacob.

Descending again into the town, we visit the mosque of Sultan Hassan, built upon the slope of the hill which leads down to the citadel ; it is ancient and imposing in aspect. Its architecture is that of many other mosques. It has the form of a cross, for it is from the Greeks that the Arabs borrowed the elements of their arts. The square in its centre is an uncovered court-yard, with a fountain in the middle of it ; on each of its sides is a building, also square, surmounted with a cupola, but entirely open on the side towards the court. There is something grand and simple in this archi-tecture, which has a truly religious character about it. It is shut out from the world round it, but it is open to the sky. The birds sing there, and build their nests. Seeing the swallows in the mosque of Hassan, these words of one of our Psalms (the 84th) recur to one's memory : "*Yea, the sparrow hath found her an house, and the swallow a nest where she may lay her young. . . . My soul hath a desire and longing to enter into the courts of the Lord.*" If ever Protestantism has an architecture suited to its temples, it seems to me that it must be something like this. I know no churches but the ancient Byzantine ones, of the purest and most ancient style, such as that of St. Ambrose at Milan, which can compete with the mosques in solem-nity, simplicity, and religious beauty.

We visit, when we once more quit the walls of the city, the tombs of the Mamelouk sultans, now neg-lected, and beginning to fall into ruins. At the highest point of the cupola of a mosque there, they show us a great bowl, filled with water and grain for the birds—a touching piece of humanity, and one which since that time I have also noticed elsewhere in the East. It is not that the Arab is sentimental by nature, or disposed to much tenderness to animals ; I have often even remarked with indignation the cruel treatment to which he subjects them. But there is in all religious feeling a power of unlimited expansion, which has the tendency to embrace in the comprehensiveness of its love all the creatures of God. " Blessed be Thou, O Lord," said St. Francis d'Assisi, in his celebrated canticle, " blessed be Thou, who hast formed our brother, the sun ; our sister, the moon ; and our mother, the earth."

Now for the first time I begin a little to understand the costume of the Egyptians. I will say nothing of that of the men; there is no one who does not know it from having met specimens in the streets of some great European town. That of the women is more interesting, but much less ornamental. The women of rank never go out unless wrapped in an ample black silk mantle ; the women of the people dress themselves by preference in dark blue, the Copts and the negresses in white. They all wear on their heads a black mantilla, falling over the back and upon the shoulders, and in front coming down to the eyebrows, entirely hiding the forehead. The face is covered with a veil of black cloth, which falls from immediately under the eyes, and descends, narrowing, to the waist. It is suspended not only by two fastenings at the corners, between the eyes and ears, but also by a third cord in the middle · this last passes through a large ring, or, to speak more accurately, a tube of gold or copper, like a pistol barrel, and completely covers the space between the eyes. All therefore that is visible of the face is the eyes only.

On the veil beneath this ring are hung, one over the

other, little pieces of gold money, sometimes as many as a dozen.

These fashions, which seem to us strange, are not mere fashions. Orientals are slaves of habit, almost as much as we are of change. The particulars of the dress of the women of Cairo may be studied even as far back as in ancient Scripture history. Genesis makes mention of *a ring for the forehead,** weighing half a shekel, presented to Rebecca by the servant of Abraham ;† and Ezekiel also speaks of this ornament.‡ Isaiah, proclaiming the condemnation which will fall upon the daughters of Jerusalem on account of their vanity and coquetries, enumerates in a curious passage the whole apparatus of the dress of the women of his times, and does not forget, among other things, the *nose jewels.*

This ring between the eyes, such as I have described, has thrown a new light, in my mind, upon an image made use of by Moses in Deuteronomy :‖ " Hear, O Israel," he says. . . . " These words, which I command thee this day, shall be in thine heart : and thou shalt teach them diligently unto thy children. . . . . And *they shall be as frontlets between thine eyes."* He says the same thing in Exodus,¶ when speaking of the institution of the passover: " It shall be for a sign unto thee upon thine hand, and for a memorial between thine eyes." A striking image, and perfectly applied ; for the person who wears between his eyes one of these *rings for the forehead* cannot help seeing it. The habit of wearing this frontlet between the eyes has even had the effect of making most of the Cairo women squint.

---

* See margin in English Bible.—*Tr.*   § Isa. iii. 21.
† Gen. xxiv. 22—47.   ‖ Deut. vi. 4—8.
‡ Ezek. xvi. 12.   ¶ Exod. xiii. 9, 16.

Instead of this heavy ring, people of rank prefer for a frontlet a plain band of embroidered cloth. Those who live in the country do not wear a veil, but they are not the less careful to conceal their faces, which they do by drawing forward the corner of their mantilla in such a way as to leave nothing visible but one eye.

Women of all ranks, and most of the men too, stain their nails from the middle to the tip with leaves of henna, which give them a rich orange-rose colour.

The poor women tattoo their chins with little blue points, which look like a beard. The hands are also tattooed with marks symbolising some talisman or some verse of the Koran. Compare with this custom the passage in Exodus, which I have just quoted: " This shall be for a sign to thee upon thine hand."

Friday.—This morning an old Russian, who accompanied us yesterday, and who is set upon seeing, and making us see, as many things as possible, is at our door early with dragoman, donkeys, and donkey drivers. He summons us to get up to *see Egypt;* I obey, grumbling to myself at this violence done to my free will. I give myself up to be led, whither I know not. We are to go to Hieropolis. We cross the town, and come first upon a little corner of the desert entirely filled with tombs, amidst which sits an old beggar, smoking with dignity his long chibouque, and holding out to passengers a lacerated hand. We pass on our left a little miserable-looking village, and soon find ourselves in a beautiful part of the country—a real garden: and fields of barley, of clover, and beautiful orchards, reminding one of those of the canton of Berne. If the trees are different from those in our climates, the grasses seem to me to be much the same. By the side of the

road the stiff and prickly thistle lifts its purple head ;
our donkeys, as they trot by, cast a greedy look at them ;
the *belle-de-jour** droops its fragile, transparent bells,
now freshened with the morning breeze, but soon to be
burnt up by the sun's rays. On the road we meet
donkeys and camels laden with heavy loads of clover,
for it is the haymaking season. The sky is flecked with
clouds, which give the scene still more of a European
look.

   All the land is carefully cultivated and perfectly
irrigated. Wells are dug to a depth corresponding with
the level of the Nile; water is drawn from them by a
wheel working horizontally. This wheel is turned by a
buffalo or by a slave, who pushes it before him as he
walks round and round. This is what is called in the
Bible "*watering with the foot.*" Moses has brought out
in a striking manner, in Deut. xi. 10—12, the contrast
between Egypt, of which the fertility depends altogether
upon human labour, and Palestine, which God Himself promises to water with rain. "*The land whither
thou goest in to possess it,*" he says, "*is not as the
land of Egypt, from whence ye came out, where thou
sowedst thy seed, and wateredst it with thy foot, as a
garden of herbs : but the land, whither ye go to possess
it, is a land of hills and valleys, and drinketh water of
the rain of heaven : a land which the Lord thy God
careth for : the eyes of the Lord thy God are always
upon it, from the beginning of the year even unto the
end of the year.*"

   After an hour and three-quarters of donkey-riding
(so are distances measured in Egypt), we arrive at the
site of Heliopolis,—so the Greeks named the ancient
city of On, so called in Genesis, where was a temple

      * *Convolvulus sepium.*

dedicated to the sun. The patriarch Joseph married the daughter of the priest of that temple ; and it was thither that Herodotus went to be instructed in the wisdom of the Egyptians. The only remains now to be seen there are an obelisk, still standing in the garden of an Armenian; and a little further on in the country are two great stones covered with hieroglyphics, lately discovered in a search instituted there. The other obelisks which formerly thronged the approaches to this temple were carried off to Rome in the time of the emperors, and now preside in their majestic changelessness over the palaces of that *eternal city,* which came into existence so many centuries later than they, and of which they have so many times witnessed the fall and resurrection.

After having paid our respects to this obelisk, the most ancient of them all—for according to the Egyptologists it is the only one which dates from before the invasion of the Hyksos, and according to that it would have witnessed the marriage of Joseph—we visit in that neighbourhood another monument, a witness, though no doubt less well authenticated, of the sojourn in Egypt, later in time, of another Joseph and another Saviour of Israel. It is an old and venerable sycamore of huge size, and overshadowing a great extent of ground, under which, if we may believe tradition, Joseph and Mary and the Holy Child rested on their flight into Egypt. Abbas Pacha planted around it a large kitchen garden, fenced in with rose bushes, breathing a delicious perfume.

After breakfast we visit an ancient mosque at some distance from the town, near old Cairo. To-day is Friday, and we intend to be present at the religious service of the *Howling Dervishes.* We find in the court

a score of persons come to attend the opening of the
ceremony. We are soon introduced. The mosque is
extremely simple, but decorated with flags and old
armour. We are placed near the entrance, along
the wall; those who are to take active part in the
devotion of the Dervishes are placed at the other end
of the building. The following is what we witnessed;
I recorded it on the spot, as it took place, pencil and
watch in hand, like a conscientious tourist.

Some forty men of all ages and conditions, as one
sees by their dresses, are squatted in a circle upon goat
or sheep skins. I remark among them many blacks,
wearing the uniform of the pacha's soldiers. They all
set to work chanting for a long time, over and over
again, the words, *Lâ Allah illâ Allah* (there is no God
but God). Then one of them stands up, without leaving his place in the circle, and chants by himself a
few words. Then all together repeat for a long time,
Allah! Allah! Allah! Then follow sighs or groans
in cadence, and more and more accelerated. They all
prostrate themselves; then the mats are taken away,
and all remain standing. A man takes his place in
the centre of the circle, and sings a chant, in which the
others join. Shortly after, two flageolets are heard
playing a sweet melody. They bow, they stand up,
they bow again, uttering all the time a guttural sound,
a sort of snore, deeper and deeper in sound, and coming
at last from the pit of their stomachs. While this is
going on, two Dervishes, wearing pointed felt hats, come
into the centre of the circle, and begin spinning round,
one arm stretched out horizontally, the other raised a
little higher. Another man who has just entered the
circle beats time to mark the rhythm of the snores and
the bows which never stop for a moment. Some other

Dervishes, who form part of the circle, and who are distinguished by their long hair, have taken off their tarbouches, and bow so low that their hair beats the ground.

A few strokes on a great drum begin to accompany all this ; from time to time one hears a frightful cry, drawn, no doubt, from some of these wretches by fatigue, for they have never stopped sighing and bowing themselves to the ground, faster and faster.

All this is frightful, and yet I confess I never have seen a ceremonial more intelligible, or which seemed to me a more frank and natural expression of the religious sentiment. One understands so well the impulse to throw oneself into delirium, to rise out of oneself, to annihilate oneself, in order to express to God that adoration which is past expression, and to arrive at contemplating Him, while realizing, so to say, one's own nothingness. And besides, I recognise in these men the same race as those priests of Baal who shouted the name of their god from morning till noon, who leaped upon the altar, and cut themselves with knives and lancets till the blood gushed out.* These priests of Baal were certainly not impostors. What Elijah rebuked in them was this very frenzy ; for the worship of Jehovah is the worship of life, of light, of freedom. It does not allow the soul to absorb itself in this sort of contemplation, so as to lose its consciousness ; but would have man arrive at such self-mastery as will enable him to *give* himself,—and at giving himself, so as to reach true self-mastery.

But what also strikes me is the sentiment of admiration and of pure happiness which irradiates the faces of these blacks, when absorbed in these exercises. One

* 1 Kings xviii. 26—28.

can see that they feel themselves transported into a sphere of being higher than that altogether material one in which their race habitually vegetates. For them this is in itself a step in advance; it is an initiation, it is the dawn of a religion, a search after God, the rudimentary stage of a form of worship.

The movements and the sighs at last cease, the sound of the flageolet alone still continues; but the respite is short; soon they begin again with renewed energy, and once more reach, after a few moments, a state of true delirium, in which they utter frightful cries.

This *ronde du sabbat* calms itself for a second, and begins a third time, proceeding always from *piano* to *forte.* At last the circle breaks; one man alone continues bending himself double, his hands clasped behind his back, and uttering from time to time horrible cries. Now he dashes himself against the wall, which he strikes violently with his head; now he sweeps the ground with his hair. The rest meantime, at intervals, offer a prayer. The miserable man finishes by entering upon a nervous *crise*, and continues his irregular movements till he falls at last upon the pavement, stiff and unconscious.

Since that time I have many times witnessed this form of worship, of which the essence is always the same, though the form is modified in different countries; and it is often accompanied by a whole set of superstitions. I shall take opportunities of time and place to recur to this subject.

On coming away from this scene, my travelling companions go with their dragoman to visit old Cairo, where is to be seen an enormous mosque, a Coptic church, and a grotto in which it is said that the Holy Family rested. I do not accompany them, being already weary of seeing so many sights, and I have not yet fulfilled the intention I have entertained since my arrival of taking a leisurely walk through Cairo. What always most interests me in any town is not its *curiosities*, but the town itself. If one is to know a place really, it is not enough to visit it ; one must live in it, or, at least, lounge about it at one's ease ; for what you come upon in that way, unexpectedly, is always worth more than what you look for, deliberately. I therefore allow my Russian officers to ride off, full trot, in a cloud of dust, and I retrace my way to Cairo, riding at a foot's pace, and accompanied only by my donkey driver, Ibrahim, with whom I try to enter into conversation. This turns out easier than might have been expected : these Egyptian donkey drivers have all of them picked up some shreds of the foreign languages they have heard spoken by travellers ; English particularly is familiar to them, on account of the great number of English who pass through Cairo on their way to India ; and if they speak it inaccurately, they make up for that by remarkable purity of pronunciation. It is a mistake to suppose that Italian is the only European language spoken in the East ; that is only the case at Alexandria and some other seaports ; but here, in the hotel in which I am now lodging, French and Italian would not help me much ; my host is a German, the waiter is a Hindoo, who knows no European language but English, and the porter a negro, who speaks only Arabic.

" What is your name, and how old are you ? " I ask my donkey driver.

" My name is Ibrahim, and I am fourteen years old."

" Have you never left Cairo ? "

"No; I should very much like to go to England with you. But I cannot leave my wife."

"Ah, you are married! And what do you want to see in England?"

"I should like to see Paris. That must be the place for fine mosques! They say there is so much money in Paris, that no one goes on foot, and every one has his donkey. Is it true that every one there wears boots?"

"Yes—pretty nearly."

"And that the women do not wear veils when they walk in the streets?"

"Yes, that also is true."

"How then do they dress?"

"They wear a gown made of iron, covered with cloth or silk."

"That is curious! And are there many Europeans in Paris?"

"The people are all Europeans."

"What! Surely the donkey drivers are Arabs! You don't mean that they employ Europeans as *sâis* and water carriers?"

I spare my readers the rest of our conversation, and stop only to explain what is a *sâis*. The thing, like the word, is wholly Egyptian. The mass of the population of Cairo ride on donkeys, but people of rank prefer horses, and are preceded by a slave, armed with a *courbache*, hitting out before him right and left recklessly, to announce the coming of his master, and to clear a road for him through the narrow and almost always crowded streets. This *avant-courrier* is called a *sâis*. Great personages employ a number of them. We read in the first Book of Kings that Adonijah, aspiring to the throne, set up chariots, horsemen, and *fifty men who* *ran before him.** The same thing is told us of Absalom. Whatever be the length of the journey, whatever the pace of his master's horse, the *sâis* has to keep in front, and must not, on any pretext, stop for a moment to rest his naked feet, bleeding from the stones in the road. The life of these men is one of the most miserable that can be imagined ; one finds it hard to understand how the human body can stand such an amount of fatigue. The condition of these poor people is often aggravated by the cruelty of their masters. I was told, for example, that a sâis of Abbas Pacha, overcome with fatigue, and no longer able to move his feet, which were swollen with running. . . . . But I spare myself the details of this story, and will not again horror-strike my imagination with them. The records of human tyranny are full enough already, without adding new facts. A sâis is also employed to run before carriages ; for there are a few carriages in Cairo. They all belong to rich people, and are almost exclusively for the use of women. I have met to-day a score of them in a row, with the blinds down, carrying a whole harem.

On re-entering Cairo, I send back Ibrahim, and bury myself, alone and on foot, in the labyrinth of dark and crooked streets. There are many so narrow that one could not ride through them on a donkey. The upper stories, which project from the house, almost touch those on the opposite side of the street, and allow only a narrow streak of light to fall on the pavement. There is probably no other town where it is so easy to lose one's way. In fact, one comes across neither public places nor monuments, to serve as way-marks,˙ and the streets are generally so tortuous that you never know towards what point of the compass you

* 1 Kings i. 5.

are walking.   Besides, most of them are *impasses*. You may sometimes travel along one street for a quarter of an hour, and then be obliged to retrace your steps, from there being no way out.   Or, sometimes, the only way out is through a dark court, into which a suspicious-looking man opens the door, demanding *baksheesh*. If the tumult of the bazaars and of the commercial streets is stunning, the silence, as of death, of these narrow streets is terrifying.   At last I completely lost my way, and could find no one to enquire from.   I met only a group of women, veiled and wrapped in their mantles, who at the sound of my footsteps ran away, shuffling their great slippers, like frightened bats. At last I found a *gamin* who brought me by a roundabout way to a more frequented street; I followed it faithfully, and came to one of the gates of the town, where, wearied out, I stretched myself under a palm tree.

III.

THE PYRAMIDS.

To MADAME —— A——

Cairo, Sunday, March 21st.

I spent fourteen hours yesterday on my donkey, and ascended the great pyramid ; so I have a right to be a little tired to-day.   Happily it is the day of rest, and I avail myself of it.   Except a short walk in the garden of Shubra, I and my donkey do nothing all day. It is three weeks since I left you ; they seem to me three centuries !   It is true I am in a country where days are as centuries, and centuries as days, and where one treads in the footsteps of Moses and Abraham.   I shall have much to tell you, but one's experiences multiply too quickly for me to dream of recording them all ; I must be content with telling of my yesterday's journey, of which the memory is still fresh in me.

Yesterday, then, Saturday, before sunrise, I left Cairo, to visit the ruins of Memphis and the pyramids of Ghizeh. I had for my companions in this excursion two Russians and a dragoman, all mounted on donkeys. Each of these donkeys is followed by its driver, a little *gamin*, in a white turban and a blue frock, with bare legs and feet ; he runs after his beast, hitting it and shouting, and, like it, he will travel his fifteen leagues a day in the blazing sun without complaining.

We reach the banks of the Nile. We get into a boat to cross the river. The Nile, always covered with boats, as broad as a lake, and sometimes even having its tempests, has really something majestic about it. The Rhine, with its little castles on the hillsides, the Rhone and the Danube, can only be called *pretty*, compared with this great river, flowing slowly, amidst islands filled with palaces, between richly cultivated plains and tall forests of palm trees. Our boat passes in front of the island of Rhodah : it was at the head of this island, now crowned with a pacha's palace, that Moses was taken up by the king's daughter. How is this known ? To me that is unimportant ; let it have been here or elsewhere, it could not have been very far off, since we are close to the capital of the Pharaohs. At any rate, I see before me the scene in which this event took place.*

The view is most beautiful. On one side the sun is rising behind the citadel of Cairo, of which we see the

---

* It may, however, be inferred from the last records of the Exodus, that in the time of Moses, or, at least, at the moment of the departure out of Egypt, the king did not reside at Memphis but probably at Belbais, or at On.

colossal cupola and the many minarets, standing out
against the sky ; on the other, its rays are already illu-
minating the summits of the two great pyramids, of
which we catch sight in the distance.   These pyramids
impress us here much as the Eiger and Jungfrau do in
Switzerland ; they are visible everywhere, so to say ;
and, touched as with silver by the rising sun, they have
the same soft tint that one admires on the Alps in
summer mornings.

We land at Ghizeh, a little village on the left bank
of the Nile.   We find there a great commotion on the
banks of the river : it is the haymaking season; camels
laden with lucernes in flower come down to the river ;
one might take them for walking hills of verdure.   They
come and lie down in the boats in which they are to
cross the water.   We stop a moment at Ghizeh, in front
of one of the *cafés* which are everywhere to be found
here—quite unlike those in Europe.   Then we continue our journey, ascending the banks of the Nile.   I
can give you no idea of the richness of the scenery.
On the opposite bank we can still see Cairo at the foot
of its citadel; on our side of the river are immense
fields, full of all manner of crops, and meadows carefully watered.   This wide and noble river, this wide-
spreading valley, this splendid sunshine, all give the
scenery a look of vastness and grandeur harmonising
admirably with the thought of the enormous and
sumptuous palaces which imagination delights in
picturing to itself here.   Flights of doves or crows
with pearl-grey necks and wings ; ibises, something
like our storks, but smaller and better propor-
tioned, with black heads, and wings of brilliant white,
like the plumage of swans, alight on the side of the
road.   We then pass through a forest f palm trees, in

which are several villages ; the houses in them are huts built of unbaked bricks, and barely rise above the ground ; we see some poor people busy fashioning, and drying in the sun, bricks of this kind, such as the Israelites used to make in this very place, under the rod of Pharaoh's officers. Near the house, dogs are barking,—yellow, like jackals. Dogs abound in Egypt, almost always wild,—not belonging to any one. Then there are turkeys, chickens, pigeons, donkeys, horses, buffaloes, long-haired sheep, camels, goats with long dependent ears, *spotted and striped* like Jacob's flocks. The variety and number of domestic animals is as great in Egypt as that of plants and human beings. Some countrywomen, drawing with one hand their mantillas across their faces, and with the other holding up gracefully shaped jugs, which they carry on their heads, are returning leisurely from the banks of the Nile ; children run to meet us, smiling, and crying out, *Baksheesh ! baksheesh !* This word signifies a *pre-sent ;* sometimes—when used by a donkey driver, for instance—it answers to our *pourboire ;* when by a beggar, it means an alms ; but oftenest it is neither one nor the other, but means simply a present ; and the man founds his claim neither upon his needing it, nor upon any right he can plead for it. The men let us pass without looking at us ; they squat on the ground and smoke their long pipes ; nothing awakes them out of their torpor. But in this country you never salute any one in passing, for it would not be enough merely to nod, or touch your hat, like a European ; such in-complete salutations would be taken as impertinences in Egypt. To salute an acquaintance, you stop, touch his hand, and then press it to your lips. I say you *touch* his hand, for it is not usual to press it, as

5

with us, or to shake it, as in England. But Oriental salutations are complicated with a multitude of other ceremonies, which I have noticed without fully understanding them, and which have explained to me the meaning of the saying of Jesus to the disciples whom He sends out on a mission : "*Salute no man by the way.*" * That was as much as to say, " Do not lose time on your way." Elisha, in the same way, urging his servant to go quickly, said to him, " Gird up thy loins, and take my staff in thine hand, and go thy way : *if thou meet any man, salute him not; and if any man salute thee, answer him not again.*"†

As I am upon the subject of salutations, I must tell you something also of insults. I have hitherto only been insulted once: it was at Alexandria, as I was going to the Catacombs. In the village near them, a child, who saw me pass, cast a look of anger at my European dress, crying, "Cursed be thy mother !" This curse, so Oriental in character, is the exact counterpart of that ancient form of benediction which we find mentioned in the Gospel : " Blessed be the womb that bare Thee, and the paps which Thou hast sucked."‡ Remember, too, that passage in Genesis, in which the earth out of which Adam was taken is " cursed for his sake."§

To return to my narrative : All these villages are in the middle of the palm trees, and the palm trees are in the middle of the villages ; they grow even in the houses themselves, and their shoots force their way between the reed-mats which are used as roofs for the houses ; sometimes the hut has no roof but the shadow of the palm tree.

Luke x. 4.   ‡ Luke xi. 27.
† 2 Kings iv. 29.   § Gen. iii. 17.

After five or six hours' march we reach Memphis. What vague ideas of magnificence and grandeur is this grand name privileged to awaken within us ! As I have said, the scene before us fits perfectly with these ideas ; by the side of this enormous river, these vast plains, these tall palms, in view of these pyramids, still surviving witnesses of the enormous power of the men of that far distant age, one feels driven to attempt to reconstruct in thought a city worthy of it all. Till now we have been walking on a perfectly level plain, but here the heaps of the *débris* of Memphis encumber the ground ; sandhills, in which one finds, mingled with the dust of past generations of men, innumerable fragments of pottery. Explorations have lately been carried on here ; two colossal caryatids, and stones covered with hieroglyphics, are to be seen, still lying at the depth of a few feet beneath the soil, in the trenches in which they were discovered. We sit down in the shade, and take our provisions out of our bags ; our dragoman consents to breakfast with us, when we have assured him that our beef is not pork, and our ale not wine. Out of a neighbouring hut come stark-naked children and women tattooed on their chins, arms, and hands. They bring us a little muddy water, and offer us some small antiquities which they have found among the ex- cavations. All the Egyptian women whom I have seen unveiled have been ugly, notwithstanding fine eyes, magnificent teeth, and an agreeable expression.

We make our way towards the desert. The cul- tivated part of Egypt consisting only of the valley formed by the Nile, the level of the desert is higher than that of the cultivated ground, but only by some forty feet. When one comes up to it, one finds only a slope of limestone rock covered with sand, something like the dunes at Ostend. The border-line therefore between the desert and the cultivated land is clearly marked, but not sufficiently so to prevent there being, at the base of these dunes, a little neutral or ambiguous strip, which may be compared to the part of the sea-shore left dry by the retreat of the tide. Upon this narrow strip of ground these two variations upon the order of nature wage war ; the sands of the desert pour themselves upon it, and cover it up, but cannot succeed in altogether stifling all its life ; tufts of grass force their way through, here and there. But the dune itself, and all that lies beyond it, is literally a sea of sand. Looking on at the ceaseless war here carried on between the desert, as the agent of destruction, for ever threatening death, and the Nile, as the source of all life, one can understand how the ancient inhabitants of the country came to look upon their river as a god ; —many a human being has been deified with less reason. It is easy even to understand how, having always so near at hand the spectacle of the sterility of the desert, they came to consider as gods all things that had life,— animals and vegetables, even leeks and onions, oxen and crocodiles.

On the border of the desert, or rather buried in it, are found the ruins of Zaccareh, which we are now about to visit. Zaccareh has perhaps never been any-thing more than a subterranean town, serving as a necropolis to Memphis. On the slope of the dune is the entrance to a cavern ; we go in, armed with torches, and accompanied by some of the Bedouins who prowl about the neighbourhood, and act as cicerones. The insides of the walls are covered with bas-reliefs and hieroglyphic inscriptions. Their text, with a trans-lation, is to be seen in Champollion or Lepsius.

We climb the dune to the top, and continue our walk. Our progress is laborious, the sand giving way under our feet. The heat of the sun is intolerable; notwithstanding a blue veil which Madame B. gave me at Alexandria, and the cotton skull-cap which every one here wears under his hat or turboosh, my forehead breaks out into great red pimples, of which I have not yet got rid, known as 'Nile pimples.' Very soon, from the dryness of the air, you find yourself taken with a burning thirst. We come upon the entrance into another cavern, much larger than the former one. We go into it; it is enormous. To the right and left of an endless passage are side-galleries, and at the entrance of each is a six-foot black marble cube, covered with hieroglyphics. These blocks are hollowed into basins at the top, and were used, it is said, as tombs for the Apis bulls.

After a long subterranean walk, we are glad '*riveder le stelle,*' like Dante coming out of the infernal regions. But in our case, *le stelle* are unhappily still this burning sun of the desert. I once more mount my donkey; the stirrup burns me through my boot. For a long time we are still on the sand; then we descend again upon the border strip I mentioned above. I catch sight of a pond, or little pool of water—no doubt what the Hebrews called an *âgâm.** I go up to it; a bevy of wild ducks take flight at sight of me. I wish to quench my thirst, but the water is not fit to drink. The pyramids are ahead of us, and seem close by, but they are still at two hours' distance. They are in the desert itself, on its furthest limit, on the edge of the dune. There are, as we all know, three of them. That of Cephren, the second in height, is the only one

* For instance, Exod. vii. 19, viii. 1.

on which, near the top, there is still left a part of that coating of polished stone which formerly covered them all three from top to bottom. At a distance it seems equal in height to that of Cheops, for the level upon which it is built is a little higher; but that of Mycerinus is perceptibly smaller.

Seen from near, the pyramids no longer produced upon me the impression of enormous size that I expected. When you see them from a distance, as, for example, from the walks in the neighbourhood of Cairo, or rising suddenly from behind the houses and trees, commanding with their overpowering majesty the whole country at their feet, you are seized with astonishment and almost with stupor, and feel moved to bow in reverence before "these majestic monuments," which, as Bossuet* said, "seem to wish to offer to heaven a magnificent assertion of our nothingness." But the *major e longinquo reverentia* is true even of the pyramids. As, in approaching them, they are always in sight, they grow larger only by insensible degrees; and on reaching them you are surprised not to find yourself more surprised by them.

By degrees, however, the feeling of wonder begins to revive, you take to pieces mentally these huge masses, and compare their dimensions with those with which you are more familiar, and astonishment returns with reflection.

The solid contents of the pyramid of Cheops alone amount to eighty-five million cubic feet. During his leisure at St. Helena, Napoleon calculated that the stones which go to the construction of this one pyramid would suffice to build a wall five (French) feet high, and proportionately thick, round the whole of Spain.

* In the *Oraison funèbre du Prince de Condé.*

And yet the height of this monument, the highest ever erected by the hand of man, does not exceed by more than a few feet that of the spire of Strasburg Cathedral. But be it remembered that the pyramids, far from being spires, are solid masses of stonework, much wider than they are high, and having bases exceeding their height by more than two-fifths. And then, deducting the chambers (very small, relatively to the whole building) found in them, they are absolutely solid masses. Lastly, bearing in mind the depth, the extent, the solidity of the foundations upon which these colossal structures must rest, it will not be difficult to believe the assertions of Herodotus, who tells us that a hundred thousand workmen were employed, without stopping, for twenty years, in constructing a single one of these monuments.

For what purpose were the pyramids intended ? or rather, what was their essential and original destination ?—for it is clear that such structures might have been utilised in many ways. It is well known how many different answers have been suggested to this question. I remember reading with great interest, some years ago, a dissertation upon this subject by M. de Persigny. According to him, the pyramids were a sort of dykes, or masses of masonry, built at the entrance, into the desert, to break the incursions of the sands and so to shelter Egypt from the invasions of its primæval enemy. I have been since told that this ingenious hypothesis has been completely refuted. But it is impossible not to be reminded of it when one looks at the pyramids and their situation.

I have, however, no doubt that these monuments had primarily a religious purpose. It is well known what an important place the pyramid occupies in the

symbolism of all antiquity. This form, which combines
in itself the triangle and the square, the number 3, the
symbol of God, and 4, the symbol of the world, was
the simplest and purest expression of the religious idea,
the most perfect and the holiest form which the mind
of man could conceive. You will find all this very
well set forth in the works of those who have treated
of the symbolism of the ancients, and particularly in
Bähr's fine book on the Mosaic worship. There is
no lack of parallel instances and analogies.

Our habits of abstraction have made symbolism so
foreign to our thoughts, that we are always in danger
of forgetting that it was during many ages the only
language of religion and philosophy. Moses was the
first who systematically opposed to the contemplative
mysticism of the ancient religions the authority of a
moral law, and substituted for vague and obscure
symbols a book, written, and intelligible to all. And
yet, notwithstanding, we have but to read the Pentateuch, and to study the construction of the Tabernacle,
and the ritual of the Mosaic sacrifices, to perceive how
much use he makes in them of symbols. He has not
suppressed, but only dethroned them. But in the depths
of Jehovah's sanctuary, under the fourfold curtains of the
Tabernacle, between the wings of the mysterious Cheru-
bim, and in the very Ark of the Covenant, is placed,
not any symbolic image of Nature and of the Deity,
but the Table of the Law, the Ten Commandments,
the Word of the Living God!

It must not be objected to this way of explaining
the pyramids, that it is improbable that such gigantic
labours should have been undertaken and executed for
no practical object, but only in obedience to a religious
idea. On the contrary, it would be more true to con-

clude, from the vastness of this work, that it could only have been inspired by a religious idea. The history of pagan and Oriental, like that of our Christian and Germanic antiquity, would afford facts enough in support of this assumption. The greatest of the monuments which the primitive civilisations have left us are religious ones. Recollect the cathedrals of Cologne and Strasburg, the temples of Ellora and Baalbek!

Without travelling so far afield for examples, what is this colossal Sphinx which keeps watch at the foot of the pyramids, but a sacred symbol, and " a great misapplication of labour and capital," as is judiciously said by an English guide-book which I have just come across ?

This sphinx is a monolith, cut out of the very rock upon which the pyramids are built; it is very probable that, with other similar sphinxes, it adorned the avenue which led up to the entrance into the Cephren pyramid. One may conclude that the base of the pyramids, now buried in the sand, is at the same level with the base of the sphinx, and, consequently, is at a considerable depth below the present level of the soil ; the mass of the pyramids is therefore far greater still than it appears to be in our day. The pedestal of this monster has been lately discovered ; its body is almost destroyed, and its face much mutilated. Pliny has already given us its dimensions ; it is the largest of the sphinxes. It is 117 (French) feet long, and fifty-one high from the head to the feet, and without taking in the pedestal. The circumference of the head is eighty-one feet. This colossus was almost wholly buried in the sand. Belzoni had the approach to it cleared, and discovered two temples in the body of the creature, one between its legs, the other in one of its paws.

As we approach the pyramids we find ourselves

surrounded by Bedouins who offer us antiquities—
sepulchral lamps, urns, scarabees—and, without leaving
us a moment to rest in the shade, press us to begin
at once the ascent of the great pyramid.   An Englishman, a few years back, broke his neck in the attempt
to ascend it alone, since which time the pyramids have
their guides, like Mont Blanc.   Two tribes of Bedouins,
thirty-five men under two scheiks, have constituted
themselves *cicerones* of these monuments.   They are
dressed only in a short white linen shirt, with long
sleeves, and wide open at the chest.   They are true
Bedouins of the frontier, not having the nobleness and
dignity which I liked to think were characteristic of
all children of the desert ; but they are none the less
picturesque.   They are covetous and mercenary, like
most Orientals—and Occidentals ; but their cupidity has
nothing of that *finesse* and astuteness which we pro-
verbially attribute to the Jews and Greeks ; their eagerness for gain shows itself in a *naïve* impudence, which
perfectly justifies the quite special sense which our
language attaches to the epithet, " Arab."

The ascent of the pyramids is laborious enough ;
you have to climb them like a rock, looking out for foot-
holds on the projections formed by the layers of stone,
and these layers are sometimes four (French) feet in
height.   One of my Russian companions decides that
he had rather stay where he is and await our return.
The other, M. de Lukieff, determines to make the
attempt ; but when he has climbed three-quarters of the
way up, he loses courage and returns.   For my part,
though already faint with fatigue, I ascend ; or rather,
I allow myself to be pulled up.   Two Bedouins drag
me up by my hands, three others push me from behind ;
a little fellow runs after us, carrying a jug of water

to refresh me when I reach the top. They drag
me up with fabulous speed, not leaving me time to
breathe, nor liberty to protest, and relentlessly compel
me to move on, cracking my joints, and flaying me
against the burning stone. In vain I protest: the
Bedouins "*have severities not to be paralleled elsewhere;*" *
they disregard my cries, and excite each other to climb,
chanting in chorus, in the Turkish of the *Bourgeois
gentilhomme :*—

> " Allah ! Allah ! Monsir buono,
> Allah ! Allah ! baksheesh buono ! '

Monsir is " Monsieur ; " *baksheesh* I have already explained ; it is the first Arabic word one learns on one's
travels ; but this one word costs one as much as the
whole of Freytag's Dictionary.

I fancied myself carried off by demons or *djinns*,
when surrounded by these half-naked phantom forms,
these muscular skeletons blackened by the sun, these
strange, wild faces, and listening to their discordant
cries resounding in my ears. I was, besides, fainting
with fatigue and exhaustion. At last I reached the
top, out of breath and no longer able to hold up.
The refreshing breeze, which wanders for ever round
isolated peaks, visited my lungs with its life-giving
breath. My outlook extends over an immense horizon.
On my right is the desert ; in front of me, to the
south, I see rising out of the sand more pyramids,
those of Dashour and Sakkârah ; to my left stretches
Egypt, the Nile, Cairo, and the chain of the Mokattem
Mountains. On the border, almost at my feet, between
the desert and the Nile, is the famous battle-field which
takes its name from the pyramids. I could have wished

* Malherbe.

to have studied all this at my ease, and realised for a moment my position on the summit of this monument, unique in the world, and which, from its grandeur, as well as antiquity, strikes one as a sort of link between the works of the Creator and those of man.

" Mais les *Bedouins* n'ont pu me laisser respirer."*

These wretches spoilt Cheops for me. Scarcely have I set foot on the summit when they fall at my feet to beg for a *baksheesh*, in addition to the fee for this expedition which I had paid them in advance ; then they take possession of me, and carry me down again as fast as they had carried me up. At half-way down, or thereabouts, I stop to rest myself upon a terrace formed by a breach in one of the angles of the pyramid. The Bedouins take the opportunity to offer me a *fantasia*. *Fantasia* is another of the stock words of the East, applicable almost to anything. This time it is a dance of a very irregular sort, which is executed by one of my guides, while in measured cadence the others clap their hands. Then they beg for another *baksheesh*.

This word *baksheesh* still pursues us long after we have reached the plain again. The more we give, the more they ask, as is natural. We mount our donkeys again. Some Bedouins, and among them one of the two scheiks, run after us for half an hour, expecting another fee. We return home by moonlight. As we cross the Nile, I lie down at the bottom of the boat, and fall asleep ; but nevertheless, as we pass the island of Rhodah, I catch the sweet scent of the orange trees borne on the wings of the breeze.

Before nine o'clock we have reached home again, having very pleasantly accomplished an expedition which every one told us it was impossible to complete

* An allusion to a verse of Berchoux's.

in one day, but which nevertheless turned out practicable, though "by the grace of God, and not by our own strength," as our dragoman Mohammed piously remarked.

IV.

THE TANTAH FAIR

I ought to have mentioned that, on arriving in Cairo, we got out at the Hôtel d'Orient. We were as yet but little trained to the peculiarities of the hotels of the Levant, where such places chance to exist, and we had made the mistake of expecting from this one something quite different from what, in fact, we found. I had pictured to myself a hostelry such as one reads of in the *Thousand and One Nights*, filled with the perfume of jessamine and attar of roses ; M. de Lukieff, on the other hand, reckoned upon a hotel like those of Europe. And he thought himself all the more justified in this expectation by the fact that the household was almost entirely French, and that the language ordinarily spoken was that of *la Canebière.* I say the language *spoken*— I ought to have said that which *should* have been spoken, for the innkeeper was at that time away on a journey, and the house was left in the hands of half a dozen waiters, who, careless of their "travellers," enlivened the dulness of their exile by playing at *bouchon* or *cheval fondu*, under the sycamores of Esbékieh. I should have been glad to have joined them ; youth must pass away, and the waters of the Nile have not, like the lotus, the power of making one forget one's native land and the sweet memories of school. But my travelling companion found it less easy to resign himself to his fate ; it wearied him to hear, night and morning, the long passages of the hotel re-echoing to the sounds of his voice calling in vain for hot water to shave with ; and so, two days after we arrived, he told me he had made up his mind to go elsewhere. I was glad to accompany him, as I found our hotel not Oriental enough for my tastes ; I wished to enjoy more completely the characteristic life of Egypt. We therefore went in search of something different, and ended in settling in a small inn near the entrance of the *Mouski*, called the *Hôtel des Pyramides*. But neither was this just the thing I had dreamed of; the innkeeper was an Esthonian, and though he had been settled in Cairo for thirty years, his broad ruddy face still retained under his tarbouche that look of jovial *bonhommie* which belongs to German innkeepers. Having to see every day on our dinner-table *saurkraut* and a pot of beer, I grumbled at so many infractions of proper local colouring ; but M. de Lukieff comforted me with the assurance that at least the waiters were Nubians from the third cataract ; that he had found a scorpion in his bed ; and that, to crown all, we should find, when we took our departure, the bill would give superabundant proof that our host himself was as complete an *Arab* as could be desired.

The time for us to leave the place was, however, drawing on; Egypt was not the goal of our journey, and I was in a hurry to reach Jerusalem. I should have preferred to have gone there by the way of the desert of Sinai, but the year was too far gone to allow us to think of it. The khâmsin was just about to begin, and we might not risk staying in the desert at that time of year, and facing the danger of being buried in the sands, or burnt up by the fever. The simoûn, which is called the khâmsin, because it lasts fifty days (that is the meaning of the word in Arabic), is a terrible wind which blows periodically during spring in Eastern lands. From that time I learnt to recognize it in Syria ; you feel under it much as you might in the neighbourhood of a stove. When it reaches Europe, under the name of the *sirocco*, it has already changed its character; it retains part of its original heat, but it has got rid, on its passage over the sea, of that *desiccating* power which it has in the East. I had no choice but to take the way to Jerusalem by sea, embarking at Jaffa; and I was bent upon not missing the first Lloyd steamer, so as to reach the Holy City, if possible, before the passover festivities.

But I had a chance, without delaying my departure, of seeing one sight in Egypt, which I thought worth attention. I had heard mention in Alexandria of the fair of Tantah, which was to take place in a few days' time. Tantah is a little town, about equi-distant from Rosetta, Damietta, and Cairo, and which has the honour of being the burial place of a saint famous in Mussulman legends, Ahmed-el-Bedaoui. His sepulchre works miraculous cures; and twice a year, at the vernal equinox, and in the summer solstice, more than a hundred and fifty thousand pilgrims, Egyptian or Abyssinian, inhabitants of Palestine or of the States of Barbary, come to offer there the tribute of their prayers. This pilgrimage is as much commercial as religious; all the nations bordering upon Egypt give each other *rendezvous* under the walls of this little town to exchange their wares ; it is the Beaucaire, the Nidjni-Novgorod, the Leipzig of the East. During the fair, Egypt is no longer to be found at Cairo or at Alexandria, it has all adjourned to the great plain of Tantah.

One day, therefore, coming back to dinner at the Hôtel des Pyramides, I proposed to M. Lukieff to accompany me to Tantah.

"It is not out of our way," I said to him, "as Tantah is on the railroad; we can reach it by the middle of the day, sleep there, and the next morning take the train that goes from Cairo to Alexandria."

Lukieff approved of my proposal; but a gentleman and lady, dressed *à la française,* and sitting at table opposite to us, asked us where we meant to lodge, if we went to Tantah.

"It does not matter;—in the first inn we come across. We are not hard to please, and if there is no room elsewhere, we can sleep on the billiard table."

"I see you do not understand Egypt yet," said the Frenchman, smiling, "and I am afraid you may get into great difficulties. You seem not to be aware that in this country one must carry one's tent with one, like a snail. But no matter, I shall be at Tantah, and you may command me."

I did not care to avail myself of this obliging offer, for I was in a hurry to get out of sight of Europeans and their ways; but I thanked him, and asked him his name and address.

"When you get to Tantah, you need but mention *Shinnik,* and they will bring you to me."

"I am speaking then to M. Shinnik . . . ?"

"No," said he to us, as he went out of the room; "my name is Ruggieri; but '*Shinnik*' means a firework, and so they call me here."

The connection between these two words was easy to see. I knew that Ruggieri was a classical name in the pyrotechnic world, and connected for more than a century with all the fireworks in Paris, though, it is true, I did not expect to come across it in Egypt.

After spending a few more days, visiting the burial places, the mosques, the palaces, and gardens in the neighbourhood of Cairo, we settled to start on our journey. We took leave, not without regret, of the city of the caliphs, and went to the railway station. The hour for starting is announced as twelve o'clock ; but we are told that to-day it will not be till two. At two they ask us to wait another hour ; when three o'clock strikes, we are told to get into the train, and that we are sure to start at five. But I have spoken already of these little unpunctualities on the Egyptian railways, and shall have other occasions to refer to them. So it was not till eight o'clock that we reached Tantah. The train stops, drops us by the wayside, and goes on, and we try in vain to make out where we are to go. We have our travelling bags and trunks, and don't know which way to turn. A negro overtakes us ; we make signs to him to carry our things, and walk before us. But where are we to go ?

" A lodging, if you please," said M. Lukieff.

The negro did not seem to understand French, but he made out that we were asking him a question, and answered us provisionally.

" *Ma fiche.*" ("There is none.")

This word is, like *baksheesh*, one of the stock expressions of the language. With it the Arabs answer everything, and the phlegmatic way in which they utter it, the sort of delight they seem to feel in lengthening out its last syllable, make it all the more irritating— " *Ma fiiiche !*" It is the "*not to be*" of the English poet, the *nicht seyn* of German philosophers. It is simple *negation*, in its most absolute and terrifying form.

" Show us, at least, some place where we may deposit our things, a *locanda*, a *locale*, a *luogo dove si può andare,*" said Lukieff, hoping, by running through a series of

6

variations of expression, to reach the point at which
Italian ceases, and Arabic begins.

The negro slowly turned his white eyes towards
a starless sky, saying, " *Allah kerim!*" (" God is
bountiful.")

The night was dark and cold; for in Egypt, however
hot may have been the day, sunset always brings with
it at this season of the year an icy wind.   We could
not stay all night by the railway, and I proposed to
Lukieff to go at once to M. Ruggieri.

" Ruggieri," I said to the negro.

" *Ma fiche.*"

" Ah, true ! I was forgetting that he is only known
by his Arabic name.   Well, *Boutchnik.*"

The negro made no answer.

" You are mistaking," said Lukieff.   " *Boutchnik* is a
Russian word.   We were told another."

" Do you remember it ?"

" No."

We were just in the position of Ali Baba, when he
had forgotten the *sesame,* which was to open to him
the doors of the cave of the Forty Thieves.   This time
there was no deficiency of local colouring.

It was in vain that, to supply the place of the word
which had escaped our memory, we tried to picture by
signs the splendours of a display of fireworks.   Our
gestures represented, one after another, in a way that
seemed to us effective, the rockets, the stars, the Roman
candles.   The Ethiopian looked on with admiration, but
without seeming at all to understand.

" Don't you know any other Arabic word besides
locanda ? " said I to Lukieff; " now would be the time
to make use of it."

" Oh, yes, half a dozen; but none that fits the

occasion. Let us see: *Djebel-et-Tarich, Biléduldjerid, Clot-Bey* . . . Ah! now I have it!—*Said Pacha !*"

" Said Pacha!" echoed the negro respectfully ; and, bowing at the name of the viceroy—" Said Pacha," he set off.

We followed him, glad to have hit upon the magic word to bring us out of our difficulties. We knew that Said Pacha was not yet at Tantah, and we placed ourselves with the more confidence under the ægis of this redoubtable name. The negro's heels had become winged, and we urged him from time to time in his progress by crying, " *Baksheesh ! baksheesh ! Said Pacha !*"

A little way on, we come within sight of innumerable fires scattered over a vast plain. Then after ten minutes' walking, we reach the camp : all is silence, it being the hour of prayer. We pass under a scaffolding hung with lamps; this is a sort of triumphal arch, serving as an entrance into a great square. To the right, to the left, and in front of us, are the tents of the pilgrims ; in the centre is that of the governor. We see our guide is taking us to head-quarters. The crowd round this enclosure stands still and silent ; some are finishing their evening prayers, others are sitting as in solemn expectation of some great event.

Having reached the tent of the governor, we enquire of an official, who seems not to understand us, but who, in order that we may explain ourselves, brings us to the only European at Tantah. He turns out to be M. Ruggieri himself.

" I will be with you directly," says he; " but prayers are just over, and my fireworks are now to begin."

And in fact in a moment one rocket shoots up, then another; then follow Bengal fires, bombs bursting into stars, etc., etc. We compliment M. Ruggieri, who apologises for the imperfections of all this. He reserves, he tells us, his finest show for evenings when Said Pacha will be present. He is expected to-morrow.

Madame Ruggieri is there too. They welcome us with perfect friendliness, and like old acquaintances; take us into their tent, and hospitably compel us to accept a place in it. They offer us supper—some remains of grilled mutton and a glass of Greek wine; then we go out to enjoy the sight of what is going on in the camp. To the religious silence which prevailed during the fireworks have now succeeded the noises of a crowd, but not of a European one. In the East, one's ears are not made less conscious of being in a foreign land than one's eyes, for in every country voices have their peculiar character; and besides, this confused hubbub of different sounds which goes to make up the noise of a crowd is here made up of quite different elements from those which make it in Europe. We pass in front of many open tents, in which the Dervishes are carrying on religious services similar to those I saw in Cairo; some stand in circles, and dance in time; others utter that hideous abdominal cry of *Allah!* which might be mistaken for the bellowing of a wild beast. *Cafés* also are numerous;—in long tents, furnished with benches on both sides and in the middle, but *lengthwise*, like omnibuses in Europe. In the East, there are benches in most of the *cafés*, though Orientals do not sit; the benches are commonly ledges projecting from the walls at a height of more than three feet from the ground, on which people sit cross-legged.

The *cafés* we see here are *cafés chantants et dansants*. We go into a good-sized one, holding from one hundred and fifty to two hundred persons, but lighted with only

three or four little lamps of the kind used in illuminations, fastened into the posts of the tent. In the
two narrow passages kept open between the benches,
two dancing women continually pass up and down ;
they sing that monotonous and melancholy air to which
all Arab songs are set, and accompany it with the
clanging of copper cymbals, which they strike one
against the other, holding them both in one hand, as
Basques do with their castanets. At the same time they
dance, but their dancing is not like ours ; the feet are
not employed in it ; the dance consists only in a move-
ment and contraction of the body, which moves and
twists itself like a serpent ; the knack of it consists just
in the fact that the arms and legs are not moved, while
the rest of the body is in continual motion. These
kinds of dances and dancers belonging to the *cafés* have
been known in the East in all ages ; Virgil, in one of
his minor poems, pictures a Syrian woman, *copa Syrisca*,
at once an innkeeper and dancing woman, skilled,—so
he says,—in twisting her body to the sound of the
castanets :—

"Sub crotalo crispum docta movere latus."

These dancing women are ugly; the next morning I
saw many more of them, not one pretty. Their complexions are very much sunburnt, and they are loaded
with necklaces, bracelets, ear-rings, and diadems made
of pieces of money, and falling in strips on each side
of the face ; from their right nostril hangs a large ring,
to which also are fastened gold coins, reaching down
to the chin. This ring is not peculiar to persons of
this kind, it is part of the costume of certain provinces,
and I saw at the fair a great number of women
adorned with it. It was perhaps known even to the
ancient Hebrews ; and it is quite possible that in trans-

lating that passage of Isaiah * which I cited above, one ought not to say *the nose rings,* but *the rings which hang from the nostrils.* At least it might seem that this was the closest rendering, though it is true the Hebrew says only " *the nose rings."* The various decorations of the Tantah dancers are also enumerated in these words of Ezekiel, " *I decked thee also with ornaments, and I put bracelets upon thy hands, and a chain on thy neck. And I put a jewel on thy forehead* " [or on thy nostrils], " *and earrings in thine ears, and a beautiful crown upon thine head."* †

Though they do not wear veils, their dress is decent, at least according to the ideas of that country ; they wear long gowns, open at the chest.

As the tent is barely lighted, one would scarcely see them, were they not preceded by a *gamin* carrying little candles fitted into the ends of sticks. You see the spectacle therefore only at the moment at which it passes before you. The women stop for an instant as they come across any official ; and as they sing, dance, and with one hand sound their cymbals, they hold out the other to beg for a few *parahs.*

We return to sleep in the hospitable tent of M. Ruggieri. The cold prevents my sleeping. All night through I hear the braying of the donkeys, the cries of the camels, and the voices of the sentinels. Early in the morning we—Lukieff and I—go out, eager to see the *ensemble* of the encampment, the fair, and the town. The walled town crowns with its grey brick houses a low hill ; the encampment spreads around it in the form of a crescent. There are tents of all sorts. Many people, too, sleep in the open air ; others take shelter under a sort of house of cards, made of

---

* Isa. iii. 21.　　　　† Ezek. xvi. 11, 12.

three or four mats. Most of the tents are made of canvas ; those belonging to personages of importance strike me by their great likeness to the *tabernacle of Jehovah* in the wilderness, as it is described in the Pentateuch. The form and proportions are just the same. The pavilion, properly so called, is divided into two parts, and surrounded by a court open to the sky, formed of canvas curtains stretched over posts.

The cattle fair is held in the encampment itself ; we pass in succession through the donkey fair, the camel fair, and the horse fair. The rest of the fair is in the immediate neighbourhood of the walls, and in the town itself. The articles of dress are generally the most remarkable objects, and specially the stuffs embroidered with gold and silver ; these, and armour, constitute the principal luxuries of the East ; the brocades are always very effective, and often of incredible richness ; they are sold in the bazaars of the town. The cheaper articles are to be found outside the walls ; there are to be seen heaps of tinsel rings, terra cotta bracelets, copper ornaments of all sorts. This fair, round the walls of the town, is frightfully noisy ; the dealers make but little use of arts of display, and trust only to noise for drawing attention. They try to attract customers by cries that would be enough to frighten them away, were their ears not Egyptian. The whole picture has a strange look of savagery, laying a hold on the imagination, which one cannot efface from it. In one place ballet dancers are figuring in the open air ; further off are to be seen women squatted on the ground with tattooing implements ; girls come and lie down before them, ready to be operated upon in that disagreeable process which is to give the finishing touch to their ugliness ; in another place are wandering

musicians sounding the tambourine, or the sharp notes
of the flageolet ; and to complete the picturesque effect
of the whole scene, in the air hideous vultures are
wheeling over the crowd at only a few feet above our
heads ; now and then they light on the ground to seek
for food among the heaps of filth, as sure of not being
disturbed in their feasting, and of being treated by the
people with respect, as in the days when Memphis
numbered them among the gods.

Said Pacha never fails to come and spend some days
at the fair ; it is one of his recreations ; he has announced himself for to-day, but it is very possible that
he will not come yet.

" He is a real specimen of a fairy-tale prince," said
Madame Ruggieri to me, " and never comes to Tantah
without an immense suite, many hundreds of horses
and dromedaries, and some thousand soldiers.   He is
not in favour of Europeans, nor of progress, and likes
nothing of our civilization except the fireworks."

In his absence, another pacha holds a court of
justice in the central tent, into the neighbourhood of
which we arrived last night.   The tent is open in
front ; at its entrance are little columns holding up
the canvas, which is lined with strips of cotton print of
different colours and patterns, of which the ends are sewn
together.   The ground is covered with mats and carpets.
The pacha sits cross-legged on a divan in the middle of
the tent.   At his left, at the other end of the divan, sits
an *ulemah* with long white beard.   An *ulemah* is something like a doctor in divinity ; he is an authority on
matters relating to religion.   Some other assessors occupy
places to the right and left, seated on lower seats.   The
pacha, the *ulemah*, and the other members of the court
have their chibouques in their hands.   Two secretaries

are seated on the ground, at the feet of the pacha ; they have neither desk nor portfolio, and write with uplifted right hand, holding in their left their paper, which is not rested on anything. Arabs always write in this way in the air, and I have, since that time, often had occasion to admire their cleverness in so doing. Behind the pacha are seen a *cawass* and two young slaves. Other servants stand by the doors. The advocates wait outside, standing before the tent.*

We had been but a few minutes there, stopped, like them, on the threshold, and contemplating the spectacle before us attentively, when, at a sign from Moustapha— that, if I remember right, is the name of our pacha—a *cawass* came up to us. At first I thought that our curiosity had been judged indiscreet, (for I saw that we two were the only spectators), and that idlers kept at a respectful distance from the prætorium. I was

---

* This tent—in the centre of the camp—in which the pacha holds his court of justice, answers exactly to the *tent* or tabernacle of assignation (אהל מועד), round which the Israelites encamped. It was at the *entrance* into this Tabernacle that Jehovah used to assemble His people to receive His commands (Exod. xxix. 42) ; it was thither also that we find He summoned Moses, Aaron, and Miriam, in order to decide their disputes (Numb. xii. 4). The priests, or literally the officers, the *ministers* of Jehovah כהנים (see, in the Hebrew text, 2 Sam. viii. 18, compared with 1 Chron. xviii. 17), alone had the right to cross its threshold. Rosenmüller was therefore in error when he referred to the *portable temples* of the Kalmucks for an illustration and explanation of the Israelitish Tabernacle, for which he might easily have found analogies among the Semitic races. It is also a mistake when the expression אהל מועד is translated " Tabernacle of the congregation." The French expression, " Tabernacle d'assignation," used in our ancient French versions (and of which the word *prætorium* would be an equivalent), is the only translation which is well founded grammatically. The Latin words, *tabernaculum fœderis*, used in the Vulgate, are by no means as accurate.

about therefore to withdraw before being summoned to
do so ; but I did not do justice to the courtesy of
the pacha.   The *cawass*, defiant as he looked, was
but the bearer of a message of peace ; he signed to
us to come in and take our places within the court.
We came forward with slow steps, our hands crossed
over our breasts, like true *Mamamouchis*,* and endeavoured to give our faces that look of diplomatic gravity
which is so becoming in Europe, and is *de rigueur* in the
East.   Soon, on another sign from the pacha, a black
slave went out, and then returned immediately bringing
us two little cups of boiling coffee carried on a silver
waiter and covered with a scarlet cloth embroidered
with gold, the object of which is to guard the heat and
aroma of the precious liquor.

I might, if I wished to impose upon my readers,
represent these courtesies of the pacha as a special
honour done to us; but they were nothing of the kind;
as I learnt afterwards, when I came to understand the
manners of the East, when one intends really to do
honour to a guest, one offers him the chibouque.   The
cup of coffee is but an act of courtesy without special
significance.   A pacha will not fail to offer it to a vice-
consul in giving him an audience; but etiquette requires
that he should reserve the chibouque for a consul, if
not, indeed, for a consul-general.   I do not say this at
all in disparagement of my gratitude to Moustapha,
whom I sincerely thank for his *demi-tasse.*

All this time the court was carrying on its work ;
two causes had been settled, and a third had just come
on for decision.   A great merchant and a poor wretch
were at the bar, both holding forth with great vivacity;
it was easy to see by their gesticulations that one was

* An allusion to a comedy of Molière's.

accusing the other of theft, or of an attempt at theft. There was not a moment's delay in passing sentence. The pacha dropped, at his leisure, between two puffs at his pipe, a sentence which the secretaries forthwith entered in the registers, and which two or three officials standing by the door proceeded immediately to execute. The culprit was stretched upon the ground just at the entrance into the tent; two men laid, and held down upon his hams, a heavy piece of wood, to prevent his moving, and a third administered the number of blows upon his back decreed by the sentence of the court.

This immediate execution of the sentence is not in accordance with our customs, but we must allow it is a mitigation of the severity of the punishment. By refusing the criminal any delay, he is spared the agonies of expectation, and of that time of looking forward to the punishment, which is a hundred times worse than the punishment itself. Whatever the punishment may be that is to be inflicted, it is but an affair of a few minutes. The wretch whom I have just seen flogged got up again immediately, and came back rubbing his back, as free as he had been a quarter of an hour before, but with one care the less, and with the look of deep-seated satisfaction of a man who has had a tooth drawn.

But, not to exaggerate Arab philanthropy, I must explain what is meant by a courbache. A courbache is a whip made of hippopotamus-hide. We all know that the skin, or, so to say, the bark, of this animal is of a thickness, consistency, and elasticity which make it bullet-proof. Thongs, or rather rods, are cut from it, which make the best of whips. One need but touch with the end of these the laziest of donkeys, or the most stubborn of horses, to make him jump as if he had received an electric shock, and set off galloping.

It is interesting to see by the Law of Moses, that, even from the most ancient times, Orientals administered justice in the same way as modern Egyptians ; among the Hebrews, as here, the execution of the sentence followed immediately upon the setence. "*If there be a controversy between men, and they come unto judgment, that the judges may judge them, then they shall justify the righteous, and condemn the wicked. And it shall be, if the wicked man be worthy to be beaten, that the judge shall cause him to lie down and to be beaten before his face, according to his fault, by a certain number.*"*

To this statement, which probably does but record a custom already obtaining, Moses adds an injunction which does not occur, as far as I know, in the Egyptian code : "*Forty stripes he may give him, and not exceed; lest if he should exceed, and beat him above these with many stripes, then thy brother should seem vile unto thee.*"† The ground upon which this law is rested seems to me even more remarkable than the law itself. It is not to a simple motive of compassion that the legislator here makes his appeal ; it is to respect for the dignity of human nature, which retains its rights, even in criminals. To inflict upon a man a punishment of an excessive and degrading nature is to offend those who witness it ; it is to outrage humanity itself. This character of the legislation of the Pentateuch has perhaps

* Deut. xxv. 1, 2.

† Perhaps it will be objected that the punishment of flogging is in itself degrading, with whatever precautions it is inflicted. But we must remember that the ancients had ideas different from ours upon that subject. "Among the Romans," says *le Repertoire de jurisprudence*, "the punishment of flogging was not infamous, even when inflicted upon free and ingenuous persons." (Article on Flogging.)

not been sufficiently noticed ; strict as it is, it provides for respect to the dignity of man ; it punishes the criminal, it never degrades him.

After having breakfasted in the tent of M. and Madame Ruggieri, and taken leave of these kind friends, we betook ourselves to the railroad. We were told that the train would arrive *at about sunset*, and we waited patiently, paying occasional visits to the outskirts of the fair, without venturing upon going to too great a distance. We saw the sun slowly set over the Libyan plains, and night wrap Egypt in darkness, but no train arrived. We seemed in danger of having to wait over yet another display of fireworks. At last, after seven o'clock, the whistle of the train was heard, and the train made its appearance. Two trucks laden with bales of cotton had caught fire *en route*, and had caused the delay. We took our places in the train, which started at great speed on the way to Alexandria. Three hours ought to have been enough to take us there ; but at nine o'clock at night, on reaching the banks of the Nile, we learnt that we could not at once continue our journey; that a train was about to start from Alexandria, and that we must wait till it had passed. It was not till midnight that we were able to resume our journey. Scarcely had we been ten minutes on the move, when suddenly we heard a cracking sound ; we felt a slight shake, and the train stopped. I understood that the engine had undergone some accident. So it was ; but no one seemed to care. The travellers slept, the railway officials sate down on the grass and smoked their chibouques, repeating, *Allah kerim!* and saying to themselves, no doubt, that as an unknown cause had stopped their engine, there was nothing to prevent an equally unknown one setting us in motion again.

Fatalism is contagious ;, I soon resigned myself to this mishap, though there was a danger of its delaying by a week my departure from Alexandria. I determined to pass the night like my companions, smoking and sleeping. One froze, it is true, in the open air, but one was stifled in the carriages ; I preferred freezing. I went and sate down at a few steps' distance, on the banks of the divine river, which I saluted for the last time, and for a long time I watched its grey waters flow past my feet, giving back their reflections under the starlight.

At last, with the first gleams of the dawn, the engineer having been taken with some happy inspiration, the train began to move slowly, and we arrived safe and sound at the neighbouring station.

At nine o'clock in the morning we arrived at Alexandria.

Allah kérim !

III.

JUDÆA.

Parvusque videri
Sentirique ingens.

I.

FROM JAFFA TO JERUSALEM.

W E all know how dependent our impressions are
upon our surroundings at the time,—upon the
wind that blows, upon the state of the air, the colour of
the sky,—upon a thousand trifling circumstances, and
above all, upon our humour at the moment. Travellers
who have shed tears at the sight of Jerusalem, or have
felt their heart beat on landing at the Piræus, ought not
to charge others with insensibility who have remained
unmoved at the same sights; and these last, on the
other hand, have no right to set down as over-excitable
beings those who have been happy enough to undergo
emotions of this kind. One and the same person can,
I can say from my own experience, receive at one
moment the most vivid impression from sights which
at another leave him quite unmoved.

When the Austrian steamer *L'Imperatore*, on which
I had embarked at Alexandria, arrived, after a passage
of twenty-four hours, in sight of the coasts of Palestine,
I was under a feeling of sadness and depression from
which I had not suffered for a long time, and the sight

of the land of promise which for so long had been the object of my desire and the dream of my imagination, did not deliver me from the fit of melancholy in which I was plunged. And yet yonder mountains filling the horizon were the hills of Judah ! But the very multitude of the recollections which this sight called up in me prevented my laying hold of any one, and one saying of the Psalmist, which fitted my feeling at the moment, alone occupied my memory : " *I will lift up mine eyes unto the hills from whence cometh my help.*" *

At half-past eleven we cast anchor, in sight of Jaffa, and at some distance from the shore ; for Jaffa has no roadstead, but a little harbour fit only to receive small craft. It happens continually that the packets which ply round the harbours of the Levant are prevented by the state of the sea from stopping off Jaffa, and that travellers who had intended to go straight to Jerusalem find themselves unable to land before they reach Beyrout. It has often been remarked in what a state of isolation the geographical situation of Palestine placed the Israelites,—an isolation conformable to the purposes of God respecting them, since He had called them out from among the rest of the nations to save them from the corruptions of the pagan world. The sea, which to other nations was a help to intercourse, to them was a barrier of isolation ; for Syria, which has good harbours on the coast of Phœnicia, has none on that of Palestine; St. John d'Acre was not conquered by the Hebrews,† and Jaffa, their only maritime town, is less a harbour than a place of danger for ships—*statio malefida carinis.* A few days after my arrival, a steamer arriving from Marseilles was lost, with all its cargo and passengers,

---

* Psalm cxxxi. 1.   † Judges i. 31.

off this part of the coast. I should have been among these passengers, if the delay of the Tantah train had led, as I had feared it would, to my missing my passage by the *Imperatore.*

Some small craft put off from the coast, and gathered round our ship. The greater part of the passengers land here ; for they are almost all pilgrims. With some others I get into one of these boats, and after being knocked about by the waves for nearly half an hour we reach the shore. But here an unexpected difficulty meets us : the harbour of Jaffa has no steps by which to land, and the only means of ascending the shore is to climb a steep coast, some ten feet in height. So one has either to clamber up, getting bruised against the rock, or to let oneself be pushed up by a boatman, who with an energetic shove of his shoulder lands one in the arms of the coast-porters. A stout Englishman by my side absolutely refuses to go through this gymnastic feat ; he demands to be taken back to the steamer, and landed at Beyrout. For my part, I climb upon the back of a boatman, and stretching up my right hand, it is grasped by a muscular *facchino*, who holds me for a moment suspended between earth and heaven, and at last deposits me upon the desired soil, *optatæ telluris gremio.*

It is by this act of faith that I get my footing at last in the Holy Land.

" *I will not describe to you,*" as is said in the *Henriade,* " *the tumult and the cries,*" and the really indescribable confusion which strike upon the eyes and ears of a traveller on arriving at Jaffa. It is enough to frighten one, even when newly arrived from Egypt. Indeed, it struck me later on, as I left Palestine, as strongly as

7

it had when I first arrived there; but in the midst of
the general decadence of the Ottoman Empire, Palestine
has fallen even lower than the rest ; it is decadence in
decadence.   If I were not afraid of exaggerating, I
should be tempted to say, in describing the impression
it made upon me, which corresponded, I believe, with
the truth, that there is as wide a difference, in point of
civilisation, between Palestine and Egypt, or the Syro-
Phœnician coast, as there is between these countries
and the civilized states of Europe.   I shall have occasion at a future time to point out some of the causes
which, latterly again, have helped to plunge this country into a state of anarchy, well-nigh unparalleled.
At first, one only of these causes occurred to me—
the judgment pronounced upon it by the Lord.   I
recognized it as indeed the Holy Land, by the very
fact that it is now the land under the curse.

   "O God," exclaimed Asaph, "the heathen are come
into Thine inheritance."*   That is still to this day
the first thought, the first sigh, that breaks from one
on landing in the Holy Land, on seeing and hearing
around one this barbarian and brutal crowd.   But I am
wrong to call them barbarian : the Turks have custom-
houses as well as we ; nowhere indeed do they more
ostentatiously claim the right of search than they do
at Jaffa.   The officers spread out my trunks in the
street, in the middle of the crowd, and open them all
together.   When I am about to continue my journey,
I find that one of them is missing ; I send the rest
on before me ; I run after that which has disappeared,
and come upon it at the corner of a street, on the
back of an Arab, who gives it up to me without resistance.   As I once more pass "*la marine*" (so are the

* Psalm lxxix. 1.

quays, or, in a general way, the part of a town which borders on the sea, called in the East), I find myself stopped, a second time, by the custom-house officers, who, notwithstanding my protests, begin again rummaging my things, and give me to understand that I shall not this time be allowed to pass ; at first I try to give them good reasons in Italian, in Turkish, in Arabic ; for why should not indignation which inspires poetry also turn one polyglott ? But as I get nothing by this, I fall back upon my native tongue, and declare with energy in French . . . . that I *will* pass. I soon see that assertion is the most effective of arguments, and that, as says Charles Quint, "*it makes very little difference, when the voice speaks loud, what language it speaks.*"* It is not till I have attended to all these sublunary cares that I am set free to give myself up to the feeling of happiness and of gratitude which fills my heart, as I say to myself that my feet are treading the soil of Israel.

Jaffa, called Jafo by the Jews, and Joppa by the Greeks, is not less celebrated among the profane writers of the ancient world than it is in the Sacred History. If we are to believe Pliny and many other authors, the foundation of this town dates from before the Deluge ; it was upon one of the rocks that guard its approaches that Andromeda was exposed to the marine monster from whom Perseus delivered her. In the Bible its whole importance rests upon the fact that it is the only seaport town of the Israelites, and is, therefore, the point of contact between them and the nations who inhabit "*the isles*"—that is to say, the regions on the other side of the Mediterranean. It is to Jafo that Jonah goes, when he wishes to escape

* V. Hugo, *Hernani.*

from the presence of Jehovah; it is there that he
embarks on board a ship (Phœnician no doubt) sailing
for Tarshish.*   In the time of Solomon, as in that of
Esdras, the cedars cut down upon Mount Lebanon by
the Tyrians and Sidonians arrived at Jafo on rafts,
and were from thence conveyed to Jerusalem to build
the Temple.

The fact of much the greatest importance, connected
with the name of this town, is that of which we read
in the Acts of the Apostles :†   I mean the revelation
by which St. Peter received the command to preach
the Gospel to the Gentiles.   Through this event,
entirely in harmony with the part constantly played
by Jafo in the history of Israel, this city became the
cradle of all the Gentile churches.   Not long after the
death of the Saviour, and the foundation of the Christian community, Peter, visiting the churches of Judæa,
Galilee, and Samaria, arrives at the little town of
Lydda, lying at the foot of the mountains, and is
summoned to Joppa by the Christians living there.
It is, no doubt, the first time, at least since the death
of his Master, that the fisherman of the Lake of Gennesareth finds himself on the shore of *the Great Sea.*
His life has hitherto been spent among his native hills.
Who can tell what new thoughts arose in his mind
when, on going up to the top of his host's house, which
was by the seaside, to pray,‡ his eyes swept that vast
extent of water furrowed by so many ships, and saw
the arrival in Jaffa of the navies of Rome and of
Greece?   Would he not ask himself what was to be,
in the future, under the new covenant of grace, the
position of those heathen nations whom travel, commerce, conquests, were daily bringing more and more

* Jonah i. 3.   † Acts x. 1.   ‡ Acts x. 6, 32.

into contact with Israel ? Perhaps the revelation which God granted him was an answer to a question or perplexity which was troubling his conscience. Jesus had commissioned him to teach and to baptize all nations ; but how was this command to be reconciled with the principles of the Law which established a marked distinction between what was clean and what was unclean? He did not as yet understand that this difficulty had been solved by a fact, and that upon this question, too, Jesus, far from having destroyed the Law, had fulfilled it. If the Jewish sacrifices, offered for the Israelites only, purified them alone, the Blood of Christ, shed for all men, was a universal sacrifice, and cleansed in the sight of God the whole race of man. This was the truth which the voice from Heaven revealed to him in the vision, by its threefold repetition of the words, " *What God hath cleansed, that call not thou common.*"

The road from Jaffa to Jerusalem is not considered a safe one ; and accordingly travellers scarcely ever travel by it except in caravans. Immediately on landing, the passengers of the *Imperatore* disperse in groups to secure the horses and men they want for the journey; the Russians betake themselves to the Greek convent; the English and Americans to their consuls ; the Catholics to the *Hospice des Franciscains*, where everything is ready for their departure. The French pilgrims, with whom I travelled as far as Alexandria, have already reached Jerusalem ; those now with us are Austrians. Horses ready saddled are waiting for them at the door of the convent, and, after a meal, they set off,—one of the Fathers, well armed, conducting them as their guide and protector.

I had let these caravans go, one after another, as I

did not wish to leave Jaffa without having inspected it. But meantime the sun was beginning to sink, and I went to look for horses. Those that I had at first engaged had failed me ; the Arab who had promised them had afterwards given them up to an American. I succeeded, not without difficulty, in finding others, and hired, at 150 piastres (thirty francs), two horses attended by their *moukre.* One of the horses was for me to ride, the other to carry my things ; the *moukre* is the driver, or rather the groom, who is to follow his horses on foot, and, the journey ended, to take them back to his master. My *moukre* is not an Arab but a Turk, as one easily sees by his smooth and somewhat soft features ; his dress is miserable ; he wears on his head an old handkerchief tied in a *bizarre* way round his head, giving him a kind of spurious likeness to Marat.

Jaffa is built on an amphitheatre on the sea-shore ; it is a little town, with five thousand inhàbitants at most. After passing through some nearly deserted streets, we come to the gate, where is assembled a considerable crowd of people ; it is here and at *la marina* that the life of the place seems to collect. The Hebrew name of Jafo signifies beauty ; and Jaffa certainly deserves the name, if one looks at its environs. Like Beyrout, Nablous, and Sidon, it is surrounded by gardens of admirable fertility ; its oranges, among other things, are famous throughout the Levant for their extraordinary size, and constitute its principal source of wealth. It is well to remark, by the way, that the gardens of the East are not like ours ; they are neither kitchen-gardens nor flower-gardens, but parks, planted with fruit trees,—citrons, almond trees, pomegranates,—or with sweet-smelling shrubs, such as rose trees and jessamines. The gardens of Jaffa are enclosed with great hedges, made of that cactus, with broad and prickly leaves (*cactus opuntia*), which is with good reason called among us the *Jewish fig tree*, for it is one of the commonest plants in Judæa and one of those which is most characteristic of that country ; even within the walls of Jerusalem it is to be found disputing possession with the heaps of rubbish. I walked a little way down a sandy road, overshadowed by these thick walls of cactus, and after passing over the region occupied by gardens, I came in sight of all that fine vale of Sharon which I am now crossing. In the background stretches the range of the hills of Judæa. Scattered here and there through the plain are to be seen pieces of cultivated ground ; the rest is pasture land, lighted up with a multitude of bright-coloured flowers,—violets, lilies, narcissuses, white and red anemones,—amongst which I like to recognize an old acquaintance—the little daisy of our regions of the earth.*

This plain of Sharon is still seen by the traveller just as it was in the days of David and Solomon ; even in those days these pastures were famous, and it would seem, from a passage in Chronicles, that it was a royal estate.† The Song of Solomon compares the Shulamite to a rose of Sharon,‡ and we see from Isaiah that the splendour of this plain enamelled with flowers

* I gathered on my way three of the flowers which seemed to me most characteristic of this plain : one was a white *cistus;* the other two, which I showed to M. Boissier, are, he tells me, the *iris sisyrinchium* and the *linum sibthropianum* (Reut. and Marg.) They are also found as frequently in Greece.

† 1 Chron. xxvii. 29 ; Isa. lxv. 10.

‡ So, at least, many interpreters translate the Hebrew word חבצלת (Cant. ii. 1 ; Isa. xxxv. 1). It might well mean one of these white cistuses so like a rose in appearance. The Septuagint and the Vulgate call it simply the *flower of the field* (*flos campi*).

was proverbial, like the beauty of Carmel and the
majesty of Lebanon.*

We have before us the little town of *Lod* or *Loud*
(in Greek, *Lydda*), which retains to this day its ancient
name ; it was from thence that the Gospel, preached
by St. Peter, spread abroad through the many villages
of Sharon.† I leave it on my left, and take the road
to Ramleh, at a league's distance, and which is believed,
rightly or wrongly, to be the *Arimathæa* of the New
Testament. Ramleh is about four hours' walk from
Jaffa, and eight from Jerusalem. It is here that pilgrims generally halt, to sleep in the convent. This
convent, built by the crusaders, is a kind of fortress, like
all the convents in the Holy Land. It is night when
I reach it. The Austrian caravan has also just arrived ;
there is a great hubbub round the gate ; monks, pilgrims, *moukres*, horses ; loud disputes in Arabic, in
German, in Italian : a real Babel. I dismount, and
succeed, not without difficulty, in reaching the postern,
at which is stationed one of the monks, who only allows
one traveller at a time to go in. I am asked if I
belong to the caravan, and on my answering that I do
not, am told that the convent is already more than full,
and that it is impossible to find room for me. I was
much disconcerted, but they hastened to reassure me
by directing me to go and ask hospitality from the
English consul. An English consul ! that was enough
abundantly to make up for my failure in getting shelter
from the Franciscans, and as I went under the guidance
of my *moukre*, and by a round-about way, to the favoured abode of *l'Inglese*, I pictured to myself vividly

According to other authorities, the Hebrew word rather signifies
the autumnal colchicum or the narcissus.

> * Isaiah xxxv. 2.   † Acts ix. 35.

the British comfort which was to refresh me after all
my fatigues, the singing of the kettle, the slices of
bread and butter, the tea-table, surrounded by the fair-
haired heads of the children, and the young ladies'
faces flanked with long curls, and then the consul himself,—his feet on the fender, his head buried in the
columns of the *Times.* I was not yet aware that the
consuls of the European powers, and particularly the
ordinary consular agents, are oftenest Arabs. I knock
at the door. A little fellow of twelve years old, with
intelligent face, opens the door, and says to me with
empressement—

" *Speak English ?*"

" *Yes.*"

" *Buono.*"

Alas! so ended the conversation, and to every question I asked, I could get no other answer than "*Yes,
yes, buono !*"

I was not the only guest of the British—or rather
the American—consul,—for such the coat-of-arms at
the door shewed him to be. Four Americans, passengers like me, on board *l'Imperatore*, were already in
the courtyard, seated on their trunks, and confidently
expecting the supper which their representative was
preparing for them. I took my place by their side,
and after a time we were shewn into an upper room,
round which is a divan ; where they brought us hard
eggs, bread, and milk.

It was not without some emotion that I found myself, for the first time, in one of these upper chambers,
so often spoken of in the Bible, and forming, to this
day, one of the characteristic features of Syrian houses.
The tops of the houses forming terraces, it is common
to erect upon them a supplementary room, opening

upon the platform: it is like a small house erected upon
the large one. This room is not intended for any
special purpose ; it serves as an extra, to be used in
emergencies. It is principally a room for visitors. The
private life of Orientals is so walled in from the outer
world, that they do not like to admit a guest into the
part of the house occupied by the owner and his family.
Naturally these upper chambers, being appendages
which can be dispensed with, are only to be found in
towns, or in the houses of the rich. The rich Shunam-
mite, who wished to have the opportunity of shewing
hospitality to Elisha, had a little upper chamber built
for the prophet to occupy when he passed that way.*
Thither, too, one retires, when one wishes to be alone ;
and there, as we see by the story of Dorcas, the bodies
of the dead are laid out before burial. Jesus, wishing
to celebrate the Passover in privacy with the Twelve
sheltered from the world's notice, chose for this purpose
an upper chamber ; whilst we generally see Him take
His meals, as is still the custom in Palestine, in the
open courtyard of the house, accessible to all comers.
As strangers, homeless in Jerusalem, it was also in an
upper chamber, lent or let to them, that the Apostles
lodged, after the death of their Master ; it was there,
out of reach of the noise of the world, and out of sight
of their enemies, that the disciples of Jesus, His mother,
and His brethren, " *continued with one accord in prayer
and supplication.*" †

    I lay down upon my divan, but I did not sleep ; the
pleasure of finding myself in the Holy Land was not
the only cause that kept me awake ; certain cruel and
voracious guests, whom one had rather not describe
more particularly, but whom I shall too often have

* 2 Kings iv. 8, *et seq.*　　　　† Acts i. 13, 14.

occasion to mention, prevented me from closing my eyes. All night long I heard the barking of the dogs and the bleating of the sheep. My *moukre*, who, as is usual, slept in the open air by the side of the horses, for fear they should be stolen, woke early. We start with the first gleam of daylight, but nevertheless we are the last to set off; the Austrian caravan has left the convent a long time past, and our Americans followed it closely.

I shall transcribe a few pages from my journal, written the very evening I arrived at Jerusalem. A traveller is, above all men, a witness whose report carries the more weight, the sooner he writes after the events he records.

Saturday, March 27th.—We set off with the dawn. The sky is perfectly clear. The sun rises behind the mountains of Ephraim. We pass over the upper part of the plain of Sharon ; it ascends imperceptibly, and is less beautiful and less rich than the region we crossed yesterday ; there are no more roses, nor violet irises, but still great red adonises and other flowers. There are a few cultivated fields, but chiefly pastures ; the cattle are under the care of shepherds armed with guns, and often mounted on donkeys or horses. Passengers salute us at times with a sort of *bonhommie*, saying to us, *Marhaba !* which in Arabic, as in Hebrew, signifies *enlargement;* that is to say, " May thy heart be enlarged !" This salutation may be addressed to any one, but among Mussulmans they say also *Salamalek.* In the New Testament the word χαίρειν * corresponds, no doubt, with the first of the above expressions, as ἐιρήνη ὑμῖν (" peace be unto you")† with the second. My *moukre*, who always calls me *hadji* (pilgrim), is

* St. James i. 1.   † St. Luke xxiv. 36, and *passim.*

to-day in good humour, and sings the Arab melody, which is less like a song than a plaintive declamation, or the voice of a child crying. One of my Ramleh Americans, whom I have just fallen in with again, tells me that the North American Indians sing just the same air.

We approach the mountain country. The scene before us is very bare, and like that of our high plateaux. In 'front of us is a range of mountains, which, as seen from here, seems of small elevation, its shape, as well as height, very much like that of the summits of the Jura, seen, for instance, from Pontarlier. It is a treeless region, the ground slightly broken ; in it are little hillocks, oblong and rounded ;—the underlying rock breaks through, and the grass is scarcely able to grow. In the valleys wheat-fields alternate with pastures ; there is no longer that crumbling soil, that earth as fine as sand, which we saw yesterday ; stones in considerable numbers cover both fields and road.

All this country which we are crossing is the ancient territory of the Danites. We know, by the Book of Joshua, that Dan only came in for the last apportion-ment in the distribution of the land of Canaan among the tribes of Israel.*   This territory, one of the least roomy originally, and still further encroached upon by the Amorites,† became insufficient for the tribe which inhabited it ; and they went and conquered another at the northern extremity of Palestine.‡   It was the most exposed part of the country, not only on the side towards the sea—where Jaffa might easily be made a landing-place for conquerors coming from a distance— but principally on the side towards Philistia ; for the plain of Sharon is but an elongation of the Philistines'

---

* Joshua xix.   † Judges i. 34.   ‡ Judges xviii.

country, and there is no barrier of any kind between it and Sephéla. Accordingly, it needed *"a young lion"* to defend this exposed side of the land of Israel. But the tribe did defend it valiantly. Altogether taken up with so doing, it sometimes neglected associating itself with its brethren in repelling enemies coming from another quarter. It is clear from Deborah's song, that when the country was invaded by the Hazor Canaanites, Dan took no part in the battle (which was fought at a distance from it in the plain of Jezreel), but *"abode in its ships."** The only enemy Dan recognized was the Philistine, and when he, with a power greater than his, succeeded in invading his land, *"Dan was a serpent by the way, an adder in the path, that bit the horseheels,"*† etc. This is seen in the history of Samson, one of the sons of that tribe, who in this very place set fire to the crops of the Philistines, and who *"judged his people "*—that is, reigned over them—*" as one of the tribes of Israel."*‡

The costume of the people here is slightly different from those I have seen in Egypt; one sees fewer turbans and tarbouches ; mostly they cover their heads, like the Bedouins, with a striped handkerchief, which falls down on all sides, and which is fastened round the head by two turns of a stout string, usually of two colours. I notice the way they make the white mantles with large brown stripes which are generally worn here; they are simply two square blankets laid one upon the other, and sewed together on three sides ; in short, a sack with a hole for the head, and two holes for the arms. That through which the head passes is decorated with a wide border. It is to this opening—to this *mouth*, as it is called in Hebrew—that Holy Scripture refers in speaking of the dress of Aaron.§ The sides are not

* Judges v. 17. † Gen. xlix. 17. ‡ Gen. xlix. 16. § Ps. cxxxiii. 2.

sewn together to the bottom, as the legs must have free room to move, so that this garment has at its lower part four corners. The *arba canphoth* (literally, the *quadrangle*), which the modern Jews hide under their other clothes, is but a smaller specimen of the mantle worn by their fathers, to the skirts of which the Law commanded them to append fringes.*   I may mention in passing that the burnous which I wear myself has fringes just like those which the Jews wear in our time.

Dresses such as these, made of only two pieces of equal size, and not cut, can easily be divided ; one can understand therefore why it is that St. John expressly says that it was not so with the tunic worn by Jesus, but that it was without seam.†   If the dresses of Orientals were like ours, the remark of St. John would have been idle; for, though our dresses are sewn, it would be difficult to part them in the middle, and one would not quite know what to do with half a paletot ! In this country, on the other hand, many people possess only half a robe ; that is to say, a single square of cloth, which they throw over their shoulders.   If, again, we did not understand the costume of the East, we should be puzzled on reading of their habit of *rending their garments*, in token of mourning or of vexation.   The word *garment* in our versions, almost always means the mantle ; in Hebrew, שמלר, בגד; in Greek, ἱμάτιον, στολή.

We come to a village, which we leave on our left ; it looks miserable ; it is made up partly of little huts, like the poorest villages in Egypt ; but I notice that here the huts are round, with dome-shaped roofs like our beehives, whereas in Egypt they are cubical. A number of women and children, some of them diseased,

---

* Num. xv. 38.   † St. John xix. 23.

press around us, asking a *baksheesh.* So they used to follow in the footsteps of Jesus, as He went from place to place doing good. Here is a poor woman leaning on a crutch, who really excites my compassion. I wish I had faith enough to say to her, like St. Peter, " In the name of Jesus of Nazareth, rise up and walk !"* But I, alas! have nothing but *"gold and silver;"* that which I have, however, I, too, very willingly give her.

After passing the village, the arid look of the country begins to be more striking, and at last we fairly enter the mountain district. There are deep and narrow ravines between round-topped hills ; no trees, but only shrubs ; the rock everywhere crops out. In the only place in which a few olive trees give shade, we sit down for breakfast. The Americans are, above all, practical men ; if in the Western world they travel without luggage, because all one wants is to be had everywhere, in the East, on the other hand, they never move without a complete apparatus of provisions, vessels, and all things needful. After resting a good quarter of an hour, we continue our journey. With the exception of these moments of repose under the olive trees, we have not enjoyed a moment's shelter from the sun all day; the temperature of the air is mild, but the heat of the sun intolerable ; there is no protecting oneself. I have to put my hat in my pocket—it is quite useless —and to twist my neckcloth round my head, as well as my handkerchief, and a cloth *dolben,* many an ell in length, which I bought at Cairo ; over it all I put the hood of my burnous ; it is a terribly hot head-dress, but easier to bear than the sharp arrows of Apollo.

We go up and down many successive hills, very like one another. In general, there is no trace of culti-

* Acts iii. 6.

vation or of human dwellings on the hill-sides. It is on the summits ordinarily that one comes upon olive gardens, hedged in with thick walls formed of heaped-up stones, such as we make in our own mountains. Near *Kuryet-el-Enab* were to be seen, amongst the olives, several vines and fig trees. These vines are large, and planted at intervals, like the trees in our orchards ; and some donkeys are grazing round them. I am reminded of the prophecy about Judah, "*Binding his foal to the vine, and his ass's colt unto the choice vine.*"*

By a curious coincidence it is just on this spot that the territory of the tribe of Judah begins. For this *Kuryet-el-Enab* ("the city of the grape"), which a tradition identifies with *Anathoth,* the native town of Jeremiah, is thought with much more probability to be the ancient *Kirjath-Jearim* where the Ark of the covenant was kept from the time of Samuel till the taking of Jerusalem by David.

Excepting these few traces of cultivation, all this district wears a look of desolation ; it is not, however, entirely without water ; there are a few streamlets at the bottom of the valleys. One sees that it is a land that has been "cursed for man's sake ;" it is easy to imagine that it might be made beautiful and fertile—perhaps all that would be wanted would be trees ; it had some formerly, as is shewn by the name *Kirjath-Jearim.*†

The further one travels into it, the more forbidding is the aspect of the country ; but from the top of the first hill we catch sight of the plain of Sharon and the sea, and on reaching the top of the last, we come upon a very extensive view over hills and valleys ; it would

* Gen. xlix. 11.   † "The forest town."

be as beautiful as the scenery of Switzerland, if it had not about it the sadness and monotony of death.

Arrived at this hill-top, I find myself completely overpowered by the heat of the sun and by fatigue from the rough action of my horse in passing over the stony road ; I know that I am coming near Jerusalem, and I am vexed to find myself unfit to feel the delight I have so often promised myself at that sight. All on a sudden, however, at about four o'clock —I was alone with my *moukre*—after passing over a little dip in the ground, I catch sight, at not more than ten minutes' distance at most, of the embattled walls and cupolas of Jerusalem ; my emotion conquers my fatigue. The impression made upon me surpasses all that I had imagined. My eyes fill with tears. . . . My first feeling was a kind of softening of the heart, that indescribable mixture of admiration and of pathos which is inspired by the sight of that which one loves. Here, then, lies before me that poor little town which has felt itself greater than all the greatest things of the earth, and has recognized itself as the principal city of the world ! That city which was so much loved by David, which Jesus so much loved, and in which Jesus suffered for the sins of the whole world, and for my sins !—Such are the thoughts which pass rapidly through my mind on coming suddenly within sight of Jerusalem. At a few steps in front of me I see a group of men and horses ; they are the Austrian pilgrims, who, at sight of the Holy City, have dismounted to pray. I also dismount and kneel down with indescribable emotion, "*For my brethren and companions' sakes, I will wish thee prosperity, O Jerusalem.*" *

The part of the town on which my eyes are resting

* Psalm cxxii. 8.

8

is Sion, the City of David ; it is close to us ; but though
the pilgrims generally enter by the nearest gate—therefore called the Pilgrims' Gate, or else the Jaffa Gate—
we descend the hill to the left, at no great distance
from the walls, in order to enter by the Damascus
Gate. As we advance, the City seems to expand, and
grow ; but the first impression made upon me by
Jerusalem, of its smallness and lowliness, will not be
effaced from my memory. I still look with admiration
at this little town, which has been the light of human
kind, and towards which the desires of all nations have
been drawn ; I think of all the tears that have been
shed over her, by Jeremiah, by the psalmists, by the
prophets, by the Saviour, and I feel that I love her for
all the love which she has inspired.

The situation of Jerusalem is very fine ; seen from
where I stand, the distant background is occupied by
the range of the blue mountains of Moab, extending
in a straight horizontal line ; on each side are the
Israelitish mountains, somewhat widely spread out. It
is but an hour or two since we had at our feet that sea
which is the boundary of the Holy Land on the west,
and here we find ourselves facing Moab. We realize by
actual sight the smallness of the country—another
instance of how God "has chosen the weak things of
the world to confound the strong." *

As I come near the town, I see in the midst of this
uncultivated soil a vine with a wall round it. But the
wall is falling into ruins ; a great breach has been
made in it, and the beasts of the field have laid waste
the vineyard. Here is a literal realization of the fine
parables of Asaph and Isaiah.† This ruined vine,
meeting one at the entrance into Jerusalem, is at once

* 1 Cor. 1. 27.　　　　† Psalm lxxx. 9—15 ; Isaiah v. 1—7.

an instance and a symbol of the desolation of the Holy City, and of the miseries foretold her by the prophets. "*O God*," says the Psalmist, "*Thou hast brought a vine out of Egypt : Thou hast cast out the heathen, and planted it. Thou madest room for it, and when it had taken root, it filled the land. The hills were covered with the shadow of it, and the boughs thereof were like the goodly cedar-trees. She stretched out her branches unto the sea, and her boughs unto the river. Why hast Thou then broken down her hedge, that all they that go by pluck off her grapes ? The wild boar out of the wood doth root it up, and the wild beasts of the field devour it. Turn Thee again, thou God of hosts : look down from heaven, behold, and visit this vine.*"

. . . On our way into the town, at a few feet from the gate, we come upon the skeleton of a horse, to which still hang a few shreds of putrid flesh, over which gather swarms of flies. Hundreds of men have passed this way since this hideous, fetid, unwholesome object has encumbered the public road, but no one has taken the trouble to remove it. In the very streets I tread upon the dead bodies of dogs and cats. This may give you an idea of the state of degradation and filth into which the town has fallen.

Jerusalem, on entering it, strikes one much as other Oriental towns do. The streets are very crowded. It is not so, I am told, always ; but the pilgrims are very numerous just now. The convents overflow with them. It is not easy to find lodging. Happily for us, there are now two inns in Jerusalem. I go to the *Malta —Melita Hotel*—kept by a Maltese called Antonio Zammit.

Scarcely have I entered when I hasten out again, to

explore the streets once more. That in which I first
find myself is a steepish hill, at the top of which is
a gloomy-looking vault, and at the bottom a group
of shabby houses. I ask what is its name, and am told
it is the *Via Dolorosa*, the street leading from the
Prætorium to Calvary, through which Jesus passed,
bearing His cross.

The feeling that seizes one on hearing this announced, quite naturally, by the first comer—a
dragoman it may be, or a cicerone—is indescribable.
"But," it will be said, "Jerusalem is so changed in these
eighteen centuries! It is mere superstition to think
of re-discovering in the streets of the modern, those
of the ancient town." Yes, I know it, but I cannot
think of that. When one hears Jesus mentioned in
the very place in which He died, one is thrilled with
a sense of the reality of all this. Looking at this *Via
Dolorosa*, this street—gloomy, dirty, narrow—filled
with a noisy crowd, I see here for the first time a
fitting frame for the passion of the Saviour. I see
Him, bowed down under the weight of His cross, in
the midst of all this opprobrium and obscurity, surrounded with this savage crowd. . . . Never did I
so realize this scene. I feel as if it had happened
yesterday.

I come upon M. Lukieff, my former travelling companion, who takes me to the Greek convent in which
he is lodging. It is a great building, attached to the
Church of the Holy Sepulchre ; the courts are crowded
with Oriental pilgrims. We climb up to the platforms
which form the roofs of the houses here ; thence we
enter one of the windows of the church, from which we
can look down into the interior as from a pulpit. Just
now the Armenians are celebrating a service there.

Indeed, many different religious bodies may be carrying on their worship simultaneously. Partitions, something like those one sees in English taverns, divide the Christians of one communion from those of another. At the height at which we stand, we can look over the tops of these barriers. We hear the chants, we see the priests swinging their great censers.

The first sight of these holy places might have impressed me painfully, as I saw here pictured before my eyes the many divisions which exist among Christians, and witnessed their style of worship, so little in conformity with spirit and truth. But for my part it only set me musing, in wonder and adoration. All these people may be far enough, perhaps, from being imbued with the spirit of the Gospel; but what a striking testimony to the power and the divinity of Christ are these men coming from every corner of the world to do homage, each in his own way, to the Man who was crucified in this place as a malefactor; and contending, as for a supreme honour, for the right to visit His sepulchre! No evidence of Christianity seems to me so eloquent. Here are men of every language and every land—men who have not been able to come to an agreement upon any one Christian doctrine, who have to a great degree lost the spirit of the Gospel,— divided among themselves, excommunicating each other, hating each other in the name of this very religion, and yet agreeing upon the one point which is the most wonderful, the most miraculous, the most incredible in Christianity, the resurrection of Jesus Christ! Christ is risen! That is the truth to which they rival each other in bearing testimony! That is the truth which every one of these Churches, and every sect, develops, comments upon, expounds, applies in its own way, but which for each of them remains the foundation of its faith and hope, the inexhaustible spring of its joy!

Palm Sunday, March 28*th.*—I woke late, and still tired with yesterday's exertions ; but my first thought is that I am in Jerusalem. I retain all day the impression made upon me yesterday by the sight of the *Via Dolorosa ;* the thought of the sufferings of Jesus Christ, made so real by the sight of the places in which they took place, absorbs and eclipses all the other memories awakened in one's mind by the sight of Jerusalem. One cannot put faith in all that is shewn one, but how unique is the feeling of being in a town where every sight is connected with Jesus, and which is full of His memory !

The first person I met yesterday, on my arrival, was Hhannah Ahouâd, the young Arab whose acquaintance I made on board the *Céphise.* He seems very much to wish to be my guide to Nazareth. Meantime he accompanies me to-day in my walks.

We enter the Church of the Holy Sepulchre ; a great crowd is pressing into it ; again, like yesterday, a procession of the Armenians and Copts ; it marches round the Chapel in which is the Holy Sepulchre. No one is bare-headed ; Orientals never uncover their heads. Some priests throw palms and olive-branches among the people ; the crowd fight, wrestle, throw themselves on the ground to get possession of them ; they laugh, they shout, and here a man who has got hold of a branch flourishes it with a saucy look in the face of another less fortunate. As at this moment there do not happen to be any rival processions, there is no risk of seeing this scramble degenerate into a fight. And besides, authority is represented in the Church by a double line of Turkish soldiers, their guns on their shoulders, who seem to be greatly amused at the sight of this exhibition of popular excitement.

The scandal is greater on Holy Saturday, when the sacred fire issues from the Sepulchre, and every one rushes to light his candle at it. Generally on that occasion blood is spilt. In these holy places, therefore, on Calvary itself, Jesus is crucified afresh continually—these places, which witnessed the infinite love of the Saviour, witness also the quarrels and fury of Christians. It is sad, but it is just ; it is in accordance with the truth of things ! God permits it in order to bring home to our very senses that which is in truth going on throughout Christendom ; so long as Jesus Christ is being crucified in the whole world by the superstition and the divisions which prevail among those who call themselves by His name, there is a fitness in its being so on this spot of the earth.

The Church called that of the Holy Sepulchre is of considerable size ; it is a combination of many churches built over the sites of the death and burial of Jesus. I am shewn the prison in which He was detained for some moments before He was crucified ; then I am made to ascend Calvary ; here is the place where He was nailed to the cross, here that on which the cross was set up, the hole in which it rested. . . .

I might have expected that so much superstition, so gross a credulity, would have stirred my critical faculty to rebellion. . . . But, listening to these announcements, I found myself incapable of investigating or criticising ; I could only shed tears and pray.

The streets of Jerusalem are partly paved, but they are not levelled ; down the middle of many of them you see an open drain running down their whole length. There are not many through which it would

be possible for a carriage to pass; accordingly (as
is the case also in the rest of Palestine) one never
meets a carriage of any kind, neither are there to be
seen any horses or donkeys, as in Cairo; everything
wears a look of wretchedness, such as I did not remark
in Egypt. One cannot just now make any safe guess
as to the amount of the population of Jerusalem; it is
at this moment more than doubled by the crowd of
pilgrims. The Anglican Bishop, M. Gobat, to whom I
paid a visit last night, tells me that never since he first
arrived here had there been so great a number; he
fears that this year there may be some terrible scenes
at Easter. It is affirmed that there are now here fifteen
thousand Greek, and ten thousand Armenian pilgrims.
One meets very few Europeans, but Orientals of every
nation and costume. O how fair will be the sight
when true life—that is, truth and charity—shall have
been restored to these feasts, and when the nations
shall come and worship in Jerusalem in spirit and in
truth !

On coming out from the Church, we walk down the
whole length of the *Via Dolorosa.* Hhannah draws my
attention to the various *stations;* first, the gate of judgment (*porte judiciaire*), by which the Lord went out of
the city; then the house of St. Veronica, who gave
Him the handkerchief to wipe His face; the place
where Simon of Cyrene relieved Him of His cross,
and that in which for the first time Jesus staggered
under its weight. It has pleased the imagination of
the people and of the monks to connect with a certain
spot each of the steps, each of the words of Jesus; on
our right, for instance, is the house of Dives, on our
left that of Lazarus. My guide even wishes me to
turn back a few steps, because he had forgotten to

shew me, in passing, *the stone which cried out.* . . . Alas!
what is the good? . . . Do not all the stones of this sad
city cry out with loud voice that the Son of David came
in the Name of the Lord, and that Israel rejected his
King?*

We pass under the *Ecce Homo* arch; then under
another connected with Pilate's palace (now the residence of the pacha), and we issue from the town by St.
Stephen's gate. In front of us is the Mount of Olives;
at its foot, enclosed in a white-washed wall, is the
Garden of Gethsemane: we are separated from it by
the Valley of Jehoshaphat, at the bottom of which is the
dry bed of the brook Kedron.

In a few minutes we reach the summit of the mountain. The panorama before us is very fine. Facing
us is the city; on our left, overhanging the road to
Bethlehem, is the Hill of Evil Council, green and cultivated, like a hill-side in Switzerland. Behind us are
hills and valleys; in the distance, the conical Hill of
the *Mont des Francs;* nearer, the district of Bethany,
then the Dead Sea—brilliantly blue—the Jordan, and,
beyond it, the long range of the mountains of Reuben
and Moab, straight, and drawn to line, like a wall; and
indeed it was a wall by which the people of God, shut
into the Holy Land, as into a fortress, was locked in

---

* We find it stated also in the narratives of the ancient pilgrims,
that their curiosity was gratified by having pointed out to them
"*the stone which the builders rejected*" (Ps. cxviii. 22). The cicerones
of our day have given up shewing it, but it is not difficult to find it
again. It was, no doubt, a great stone seven feet and a half in
thickness which forms the south-east corner of the walls of the
town, and which appears to be a fragment still preserved of the
ancient walls; it had, in fact, become *the head-stone of the corner.*
This is an instance of the way men used to attempt to find a literal
and material application of every passage of Holy Scripture.

on the east, as it was on the west, by the sea, on the south by the desert, towards the north by the snowy mountains of Lebanon.

On the summit of the Mount of Olives is the mosque of the Ascension. We climb the minaret, to command a still more extensive view. In a building near us, attached to the mosque, but in which the Latins are allowed to say mass once a year, they shew us for a *baksheesh*, upon the rock, the print left by the foot of Jesus, when He ascended into heaven. Some Mussulmans come in with me, and offer their prayers.

We re-descend the mountain. I shall not attempt to put into words the impression made upon me by these places. It is different from that of the town itself, where everything is open to examination, and where, besides, everything has been changed by the hand of time and of man. But nature is always the same: this view at which I am looking is that on which the eyes of the Saviour rested from the top of this Mount of Olives, whither, we are told, " He went as He was wont." * These stones, these olive trees, these little flowers that grow at my feet, looked the same even to the eyes of David and of Jesus. It was here that Jesus, looking upon Jerusalem, as I look at it now, wept over it, and cried, " *If thou hadst known, even thou, at least in this thy day, the things which belong unto thy peace! but now they are hid from thine eyes. For the days shall come upon thee, that thine enemies shall cast a trench about thee, and compass thee round, and keep thee in on every side; and shall lay thee even with the ground, and thy children within thee; and they shall not leave in thee one stone upon another.*"† The scene I now see before me is that which Jeremiah

* St. Luke xxii. 39, xxi. 37.   † St. Luke xix. 42—44.

beheld when he mourned over the ruins of his well-
beloved city; it is that of which the image floated
before the mind of the excited Psalmist, when he cried,
" *If I forget thee, O Jerusalem, let my right hand forget
her cunning.*"*

II.

JERUSALEM.

We all know that noble passage in Pascal,† in which
the great Christian philosopher distinguishes between
the *three orders;* a passage radiant with light, of
which the sacred simplicity, unparalleled, perhaps, in
the works of other modern authors, recalls the style of
the inspired writers.   In it Pascal sets forth what is
called, in the technical language of theology, St. Paul's
trichotomy; that is to say, the distinction drawn by him
between the three elements which make up human
nature—body, soul, and spirit.‡   These are three essentially distinct spheres,—that of material force, that of
thought, and that of the will ; the physical domain,
the intellectual, and the moral.   These three orders
of being are incommensurable.   The slightest move-
ment of thought is in itself a greater thing than the
whole visible universe ; but the sum of all conceivable
thoughts is unworthy to be compared with the slightest
emotion of faith or of charity.   From a great man of
the world to a man of genius,—from a man of genius
to a hero or a saint,—the distance is incommensurable.

* Psalm cxxxvii. 5.
† It is in the chapter of the *Pensées* which begins with the words,
" La distance infinie des corps aux esprits . . . ."
‡ It is true that Pascal's categories do not absolutely correspond
with those of St. Paul.   But this is not the place in which to point
out wherein they differ.

This distinction, already to be found in Plato and in Aristotle, but which Pascal was the first to set forth in all its definiteness, throws as much light upon the history of humanity as upon psychology and morality. In some treatises, rich in profound views, and in ingenious observations, M. Molitor, and after him M. de Rougemont, * have made an attempt to shew that each of the three great human families represents, or at least was destined to represent, one of these "orders" in particular. Who knows whether the progress of ethnography, or the future development of humanity, may not ultimately establish the truth of this interesting hypothesis ? Meantime, if we confine our attention to the three great historic nations of antiquity, we cannot fail to recognize in them the representatives of Pascal's three orders. Rome, Athens, and Jerusalem have remained to this day the leading symbols of material power, of intellectual greatness, and of moral force. Each of them understood the part it was commissioned by Providence to play ; or, at least, their prophets and poets understood it for them. If at times the kings of Jerusalem attempted to draw their nation away from its proper function, if they aimed at making of Israel an earthly power by giving it the *éclat* and the support of riches, of arms, of arts, or of diplomacy, the prophets, faithful organs of the purpose of God respecting this people, were never led astray upon that point. They did not cease reminding their nation that its glory consisted wholly in the Law which it had received from the Lord, and that its only strength lay in its faith. There would be no difficulty in finding in the Greek authors passages quite analogous ; they continually institute comparisons

* Molitor, *Philosophie der Geschichte.* Rougemont, *Géographie de l'Homme.*

between their own compatriots and the barbarians, and shew that the greatness of the former is to be seen exclusively in the development of thought. As Jerusalem is the Holy City, so is Athens, the city of Minerva, the home of the intellectual life. As to Rome, at the very time when she seemed to be rivalling Greece in the noble efforts of mind, her greatest poet tells her in a declaration, which has become a standard one, that she must leave to others the glory of surpassing her in the fine arts, in eloquence, in the sciences, and remember that her function is to rule. We all know by heart, these famous verses :—

> " Excudent alii spirantia mollius æra . . . .
> Tu regere imperio populos, Romane, memento ;
> Hæ tibi erunt artes." *

To this let us add that, even in the domain of thought, the most original and the most imperishable of the products of the genius of Rome still bears the stamp of this special characteristic. Rome did not create a philosophy, nor a morality ; but she was the first to study, to regulate, to reduce to fixed principles, the science of the most external relations which bind mankind together—the science of Law.

We must not attempt to discover among modern nations the representatives of the three tendencies which we have just indicated among the three great nations of antiquity. It would be a waste of time to do so. Since Jesus Christ, there is no longer—as St. Paul used to say—either Jew, Greek, or Roman ; there is, in fact, but one people, one civilization, one only History. Each of the nations of antiquity played its part, fulfilled its appointed task, accomplished its

* Æneid, vi. 848.

mission. The whole world has been brought into
subjection by the arms of Rome, and into order by
its laws ; the philosophy, the arts, the poetry of Athens
have become the common inheritance of the mind of
man, and all the nations of the Earth bend the knee to
the God of Israel. Jerusalem, destroyed by the Baby-
lonians, taken by Titus—in a word, conquered in turn
by all the nations—has ended in conquering them all,
and still reigns over them from the midst of her ruins,
for the possession of which Europe and Asia fought
for two centuries. She is in our day an object of
homage and of desire to the nations of the Earth ; the
Christians venerate in her the place of the sufferings
and of the glorification of their Saviour ; the Jews come
hither to seek the memory of their Temple, and to weep
over its ruins ; the Mussulmans, who claim her in the
name of their father Abraham, have forgotten the name
she used to bear among men, and no longer call her
anything but " the Holy."

No city has been so often taken, destroyed, and
rebuilt, as Jerusalem. Melchisedek, who reigned over her
in the time of Abraham, perhaps still belonged to one of
the Semitic tribes which seem to have inhabited Palestine
before the Canaanites, and to which, no doubt, Jerusalem
owes her origin. Later on, at the time when Joshua
conquered the country, we see her subject to the Jebusites, a tribe of Amorites of which she had adopted the
name, and of which she had become the capital. The
men of Judah ravaged,* but did not succeed in taking
complete possession of her ; the fortress, situate on
Mount Sion, remained in the hands of the enemy ;
and accordingly the Jebusites continued to inhabit the
city,† with the sons of Judah and Benjamin. One may

* Judges i. 8.   † Judges i. 21.

suppose that each of the two peoples, perhaps even
each of the two Israelitish tribes, occupied a different
quarter of the city. So it is that in our day, within
the same walls, the Jews, the Mussulmans, the Armenian
and other Christians, Greek or Catholic, dwell side by
side, but in distinct quarters of the town. Later, even
after David had taken the fortress, and had made it
his residence,* it does not seem that Jerusalem ever
became the property of this or that tribe ; Judah
and Benjamin continued no doubt to inhabit it in
common, and the Jebusite lived in it as a relic of the
past, by the side of its new masters.†

The fate of Jerusalem under the kings of the house
of David, under the successors of Alexander, under the
Asmoneans, under the Herods, under the Roman go-
vernors, her heroic resistance to the armies of Titus,
and her deplorable fall,—all these facts have been sufficiently popularized by the Bible and by Josephus, to
make it needless for me to dwell upon them. Every one
also knows that the Emperor Hadrian, provoked with
the Jews, and wishing to rob Jerusalem of the prestige
both of its name and its ruins, caused it to be rebuilt
under the pagan name of Ælia Capitolina, and dedicated it to Jupiter. He positively forbade the Jews
to enter it, and, in order to insult them, placed his own
statue on Mount Moriah, on the very spot that had been
occupied by the Holy of Holies. As to the Christians,
the policy of Hadrian with regard to them appears to
have been this :—perceiving that he should not succeed
in extirpating this sect, already so powerful, he flattered
himself he could annex them to his own system. He
had stopped the persecutions to which they had been
subjected, and he made an attempt to incorporate

* 1 Chron. xi. 5, 7.   † 1 Chron. xxi. 18.

Christianity into that great amalgam of varied doctrines and rites which constituted at that time the Roman religion. For this purpose he wished to do honour, in his own way, to the places sacred to the memory of Jesus ; he thought he could combine the worship of Christ with another religion of Syrian origin,—that of Adonis, dead, risen again, and deified,—which he caused to be celebrated at Bethlehem, in the grotto marked out by tradition as the birth-place of the Saviour. He erected upon the Holy Sepulchre an image of Jupiter, and upon Calvary, where had been consummated the supreme mystery of Divine love, he caused to be erected the pagan symbol of natural love, the statue of Venus.

Constantine and his mother, St. Helena, swept out of Jerusalem these monuments of paganism. The pious Empress filled the city with churches and chapels. Ælia—for so Jerusalem was still, for a long time, called—had never ceased to be the object of pilgrimages for Christians ; it became so more than ever. Involved in the general decadence of the Eastern Empire, taken by the Persians in the year 614, re-taken by the Greeks in 628, it was, shortly after, besieged by the Mussulman Arabs under the command of the caliph Omar, and was compelled to capitulate (637).

The Turkish hordes who, under Togrul-Beg, destroyed the Caliphate of Bagdad, also took possession of Jerusalem (1077). This ill-fated city had to undergo at the hands of these hordes of savages unheard-of exactions and outrages. The Christian population which it still contained, and the pilgrims who continued to flock thither, were the special objects of the persecutions of the Turks. These new excesses were the determining causes of the Crusades. I shall not tell their history ;

it will be enough to record a few dates. In 1099, Jerusalem was taken by Godefroi de Bouillon, and became the capital of a Frankish kingdom. In 1187, Saladin took it from the Christians. The Emperor Frederick II. appeared under the walls in 1299, and the Sultan of Egypt agreed to sell it to him. The Emir David took it back in 1239; it was restored to the Franks in 1243; but in the following year it fell back finally into the power of the Mussulmans.

The Sultan, Sélim I., the same who in Egypt de-throned the Mamelukes, also conquered Jerusalem, and incorporated it, with the rest of Syria, into the Ottoman empire. Under the Ottoman Sultans, the ancient capital of Judæa has till lately been brought down to the position of a sub-prefecture (if I may be allowed the expression) of the pachalik of Damascus; it is not yet twenty years since it became the head-quarters and residence of a pacha. During three centuries, the Ottomans have reigned as undisputed masters of Jeru-salem. In 1824, a conspiracy of its inhabitants did but momentarily succeed in withdrawing it from under the authority of the pacha, who compelled it, the follow-ing year, to capitulate.

A new future seemed to open before Palestine, and before all the neighbouring races, when the Viceroy of Egypt, Mehemet Ali, and his son, Ibrahim Pacha, attempted to reconstruct an Arab empire upon the ruins of a part of the Turkish empire. They proposed to themselves to re-unite all the Arab races into a single state, independent of the Porte. In 1831, already masters of the Hedjaz, they rapidly conquered Jerusalem and the whole of Syria. The victory of Konieh, in 1832, seemed to put into their hands the fate of the empire of the Sultans; but the intervention of the

9

European powers snatched this prey from their grasp, and set a limit to their conquests. In 1840, a coalition of England, Austria, Prussia, and Russia succeeded in rescuing even Syria out of their hands. We recollect the bombardment of St. John d'Acre by Admiral Stopford ; Mehemet from that moment saw himself reduced to the hereditary viceroyalty of Egypt, under the *suzerainety* of the Sultan ; and Palestine, with the rest of Syria, was restored to the Porte.

Let us take this opportunity of describing the present state of Palestine. At a distance, one might be tempted to picture it to oneself as an oppressed country, incapable of any resistance, and groaning under the iron yoke of a pacha, whose slightest wishes are instantly obeyed. This very European definition of what despotism means is, to a certain extent, true of Egypt, half civilized by Mehemet Ali, but it by no means fits the Ottoman empire. This empire is ancient; the above doctrine is ancient too, and it is so true that, notwithstanding all that may be done at times to explain it away, it recurs continually to take its place among received political aphorisms and historical commonplaces. The Turkish Government—and it is of the Government I am speaking—cannot abuse a power which it does not possess. No doubt, in the provinces nearest to the centre, one discovers still some remains of its ancient power ; but, as says Mithridates—*

> ". . . . Ce n'est point au bout de l'univers
> Que Rome fait sentir tout le poids di ses fers."

("It is not at the extremities of the universe that Rome makes the whole weight of its fetters felt.")

If this could be said of Rome, it is a hundred times

* In Racine's tragedy which bears that name.

more true of Constantinople. When the life withdraws from a body, the heart is the organ which longest retains any heat, but a long time before it ceases beating, the extremities grow cold ; Syria, and more especially Palestine, is one of these extremities of the Ottoman empire. The sovereignty of the Porte is, in these countries, no longer anything but a distant suzerainety, not often sufficient to keep in order the emirs and the scheikhs of the various tribes, who make war upon each other when they please, and would be greatly surprised if the pacha meddled with their affairs. I said just now, that the English and the Austrians, who became rulers of Palestine by the taking of St. John d'Acre, had placed it once more under the dominion of the Porte. That statement is not quite accurate, or at least it needs explanation. They took Syria from Ibrahim, but the Sultan never succeeded in re-establishing his power there. To kill is easier than to restore to life. It was easy for the arms and the political power of Europe to destroy the power of Mehemet ; but it would not have been possible for them to re-establish that of Abdul-Medjid. Accordingly, Palestine, snatched from the Egyptian tyrant, found itself, from that time, without a master, so to say ; it is in our day delivered over to anarchy—or, to use the orthography of M. Proudhon,* an *an-archy ;*—with or

---

* According to this well-known Socialist (whose ideas were, at one time, the subject of much discussion) human Society, after having tried all the different forms of government,—monarchy, oligarchy, etc.,—is at last to arrive at dispensing with all government. This ideal state, which we are to reach in the future, is called by Proudhon *an-archy*. He writes the word in this way in order to draw attention to its etymological sense, and to guard his readers against supposing that it conveys the idea of disorder, which in our ordinary way of speaking is inseparable from the word *anarchy*.

without the hyphen, this word exactly describes the present *régime* of that country.

But let me explain. The Turkish Government is not absolutely without power in Palestine, but it is without *authority*. Its power extends as far as the range of a pistol-shot or the reach of a bayonet. It has not that sort of ascendency which, everywhere else, and even in other Ottoman provinces, adds to the real power of a government, and makes it respected or feared even in the absence of its agents. The pacha is obeyed when he is present ; they send to him from Damascus, to stay with him during the Easter festivities, a reinforcement of 800 soldiers, to enable him to protect the pilgrims, and to save him from the recriminations of the French and Russian consuls. While he keeps his troops, order reigns in Jerusalem, and even, *to a certain extent*, in the immediate neighbourhood of the city ; but when the 800 soldiers have returned to Damascus,. the pacha can no longer answer for anything.

In a word, though the Turks are, it is true, one of the powers that rule in Palestine, there are many others by the side of it. Each tribe preserves a sort of independence, and carries on its affairs on its own account ; there are whole villages which pay taxes, not to the pacha, but to some Bedouin émir, and there is many a district of Palestine in which the representative of the Porte could not adventure himself without as much certainty of being robbed as any chance comer. During my stay in Palestine, notwithstanding the presence at that time of the Turkish soldiers, the Arab tribes were fighting with each other at Hebron, and some caravans of pilgrims returning to Jaffa were robbed at a few hours' distance from Jerusalem. On this same Jaffa road, not far from the ruins of a fortress traditionally called the

Castle of the good Thief, another thief, called *Abou-Gosch,* celebrated in the tales of travellers, managed to create for himself, some forty or fifty years back, a little independent principality. He had six brothers and eighty-five sons, and made himself feared in the whole country round. No pilgrim could reach Jerusalem without paying tribute to this redoubtable family. In 1832, Ibrahim Pacha sent to the hulks one of these little *Abou-Gosches.* The pacha of Jerusalem having succeeded, fifteen years back, in seizing another of them, banished him from Palestine. But their dynasty is not yet extinct; and although its power is now much diminished, none the less does it reign; the village of Kuryet-el-Enab, which it makes its head-quarters, is generally known only as that of Abou-Gosch. It is scarcely three leagues from Jerusalem.

We, with our customs, can scarcely imagine such a state of things. It seems to us as if a society could not exist in a condition of complete anarchy, and that the inhabitants of Palestine would, in a short time, have either destroyed each other, or else submitted themselves to some one tyrant more powerful than the rest. This conclusion would be logical, if we were speaking of a country as thickly inhabited as the European states, and in which the necessities of existence were of a nature less simple than they are in the East. But this condition of things, which, besides, differs but slightly from that which has prevailed over almost the whole of Europe during some part of the middle ages, is not new in Palestine. This country finds itself once more in very much the same condition as in the time of Abraham. We do not see there, in that distant age, any state of much extent, but only towns absolutely in-

dependent of each other, each with its king or scheikh,
entering into alliances or carrying on war with each
other, according to the circumstances of the moment.
Then, as now, between the towns belonging to the
different tribes, other nomad tribes pitched their tents
on the plains and on the sides of the hills, wandering
from north to south, with their huge flocks, and no other
possessions under the sun, but a few wells dug by their
fathers and some caves in which to bury their chiefs ;—
possessions often attacked, occasions of contention, of
mutual accommodation, and of wars.   The campaign of
Chedorlaomer and the three kings, his allies, against
the five kings of the plain of Sodom ; * the expedition
of Abraham in pursuit of them ;† the fights of Abraham
and Isaac with Abimelech,‡ the sojourn of David and
his followers in the land of the Philistines, the incursions or *razzias* which he made from thence upon
the Geshurites and Amalekites,§—all these are characteristic traits of Arab life, and are continually repro-
ducing themselves in Palestine.   The East never grows
old ;   institutions and empires come into existence
and fall into ruins, but manners and customs are un-
changeable.   The race of Abraham is of a vigorous
fibre ; Israel, it is well known, never bent its *stiff
neck* ; ‖ the iron sceptre of Rome broke, without subduing, it ; dispersed among the nations, like a ball
driven far by the wind, it mingled among them without
ever losing its distinctness.   As to Ishmael, I doubt
whether those who have observed his race could define
better than is already done in Genesis the indocile and
defiant character which it has retained even to our own

* Genesis xiv. 1—12.   § 1 Samuel xxvii. 5—11.
† Genesis xiv. 14—16.   ‖ Exodus xxxii. 9.
‡ Genesis xxi. 25, xxvi. 15.

day, and to which indeed it owes the persistence of its nationality. "*Ishmael will be a wild man, his hand will be against every man, and every man's hand against him.*" *

I return to Jerusalem.

The watershed which separates, in the mountains of Judah and Ephraim, the basin of the Mediterranean from that of the Jordan and the Dead Sea, passes by Jerusalem or, to speak more accurately, by its side.† Jerusalem is situated at a height of 2,450 feet above the level of the Mediterranean, and consequently of 3,750 above that of the Dead Sea. The whole of this region therefore is in considerable relief relatively to the surrounding country, for it rises with a rapid ascent. From the plain of Sharon, which is but little above the level of the sea, one can get to Jerusalem in an easy day's journey; and to descend from Jerusalem to the Jordan is the work of a few hours. The environs of Jerusalem have, in a high degree, the aspect peculiar to a mountain district; it has often surprised me not to have seen this more definitely noticed by travellers. For my part, having been familiar from my childhood with the high plateaux of the Jura, I never came out from the

* Genesis xvi. 12.

† That is, no doubt, the reason why Josephus says that Jerusalem is *in the midst of* Judæa. The Rabbis, indeed, founding themselves upon Ezek. v. 5, make of it the centre of the whole earth. And that is not with them, as might be supposed, a geographical *naïveté;* it is the expression of a profound historical and religious truth. M. Boissier assures me that, looked at from the botanical point of view, Jerusalem is also a central point of singular interest. It is at the summit of the Mount of Olives that the Mediterranean region terminates, and the Oriental begins. There is, he assures me, less difference between the flora of Rome and that of Jerusalem, than between the latter and that of Bethany, a village on the eastern slope of the mountain.

walls of Jerusalem without being struck with wonder on recognising, in the midst of scenery in so many respects new to me, such close analogies with the mountains of my native land.   Many indefinable circumstances contribute, no doubt, to give a sort of family likeness to these two countries so distant from each other.   The aridity and want of cultivation of the plateau, which forms the background to Jerusalem, adds still more to the likeness.   One fancies oneself in that colder region which is to be found in our mountains above the pine forests.   A slight carpeting of thin and fine turf covers the uneven soil, under which one can detect the bony skeleton of the mountain, and through which in many places crops out the polished rock of Jurassic limestone. There are no great trees, only here and there a few shrubs ; low walls, made up only of heaps of stones gathered in the country round.   It was pleasant to breathe the air, which is always, even in the hottest season, fresh and life-giving.   A slight but unceasing breeze was blowing over the hill-tops, and brought to my ear a silver-tinkling sound—that of the little bells, worn on their necks, by the pilgrims' horses grazing round the walls of the town, under the care of their *moukres.*

But it is not only in virtue of its elevation that Jerusalem may be said to be on a mountain.   Though some of the heights in its neighbourhood are higher, none the less is its site very distinctly a mountain-top ; it is only connected with the plateau by a tongue of land, and it overhangs the narrow valleys which surround it, and towards which it descends in a steepish decline. The plateau with which Jerusalem is connected lies to the north of the town ; it is the only side on which the city is without natural ramparts ; accordingly, it is from

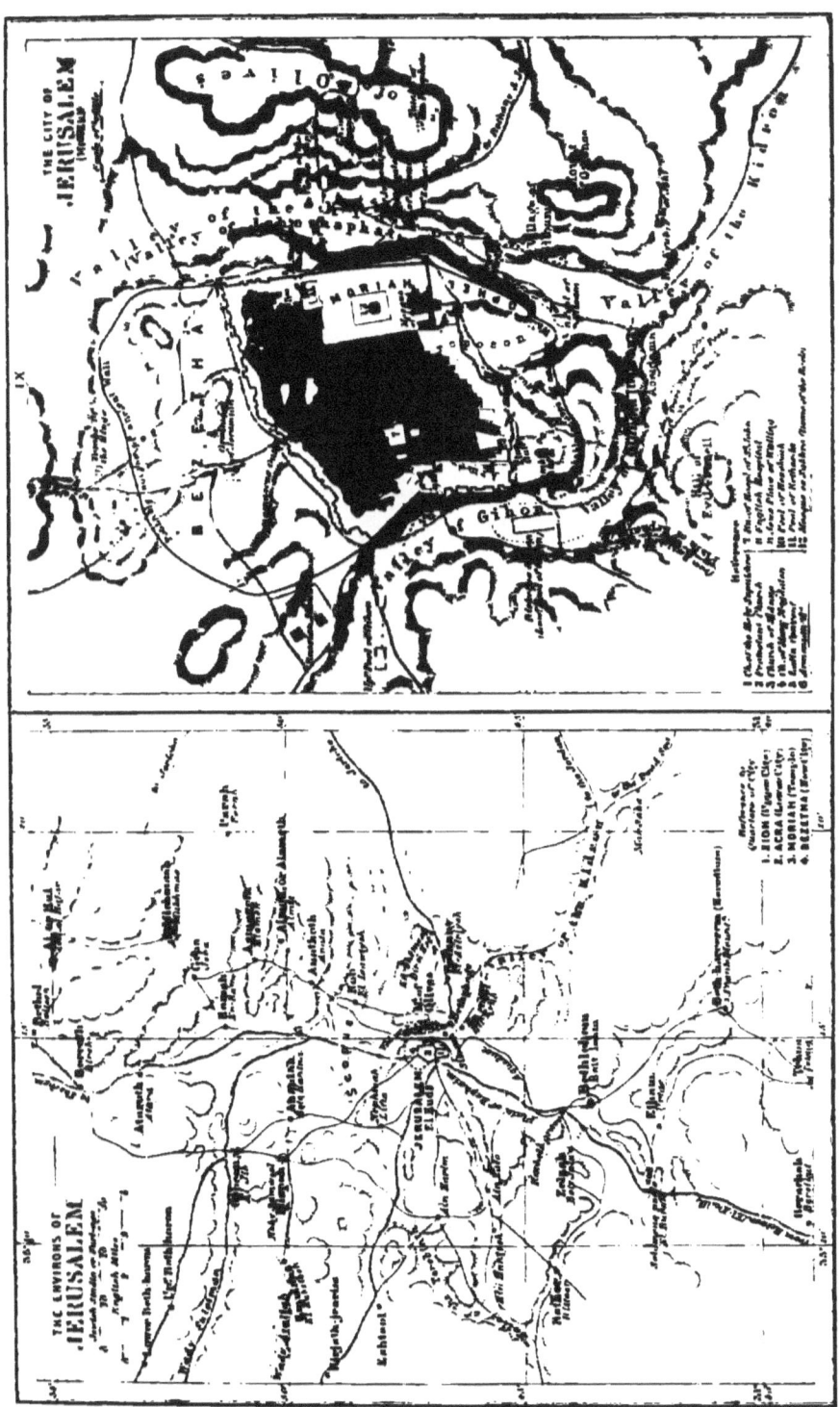

that quarter that it has oftenest been attacked, and that the Crusaders took it by assault.

On the three other sides Jerusalem is protected by deep ravines. To the East is the valley of Kedron, or of Jehoshaphat, running from the north to the south of the city ; to the west and south, that of Hinnom,* which for part of its length runs nearly parallel to the first, but then trends towards, and at last runs into it, at the south-east corner of the city.

On the other side of these valleys rise mountains† which slightly out-top that on which the Holy City stands. To the south, beyond Hinnom, a mountain, on one slope of which is the *field of blood* (Aceldama), terminates in a round top, called by the Arabs *Djebel Deir-Abou-Tor*. European travellers designate this summit the Hill of Evil Counsel, because, according to the legend, it was there, in a house belonging to Caiaphas, that that high priest persuaded the Jews to put Jesus to death.

To the east, the other side Kedron, rises a mountain with three tops, visible from a considerable distance as one approaches Jerusalem. It is the Mount of Olives. These hill-tops, at a slight distance from

---

* According to some archæologists, the valley which bounds Jerusalem to the west and south is that which the Bible calls " *the valley of Rephaim;*" that which is called the valley of Hinnom, or Gehenna, would then be the same as the *Tyropœon* of Josephus, of which we shall have presently to investigate the situation. This hypothesis has been advocated chiefly by Rabbi Schwarz and by M. Horace Bonar. What makes it very plausible is that this Tyropœon is never mentioned in the Bible, and that Josephus, on the other hand, never mentions the valley of Hinnom. But I shall nevertheless adopt the received usage, and continue calling the valley to the west of Jerusalem that of Hinnom ; for the other topographic questions which I shall have to investigate are quite independent of this one.

† Psalm cxxv. 2.

each other, are arched in a long curve, and present to
the eye a long soft outline, with nothing harsh or abrupt about it.   The Mount of Olives faces Jerusalem,
and is distant from it, one may say, but a few steps.
Two minutes suffice for descending from the walls of
the city to the bottom of the vale of Kedron, and
the valley itself is but of the breadth of a streamlet.

The southernmost summit of the Mount of Olives is
known by the name of *the Mount of the Prophets*, on
account of a vast sepulchral grotto which is to be found
in it, called *the Prophet's Tomb.*   The northernmost
summit is called by the Franks the *Viri Galilæi ;*
there, it is said, the men in white raiment appeared
to the Apostles after the Ascension of their Master,
and said to them, " *Ye men of Galilee, why stand ye
gazing up into Heaven ?"* * According to the same tradition, the Apostles would have been at that moment
on the intermediate peak, which is therefore called *the
Mountain of the Ascension.*   We shall see further on
that, according to all appearances, it cannot have been
there that the scene occurred.

To the south of these three peaks there is a fourth,
forming part of the same chain, but which we must
nevertheless distinguish from the Mount of Olives, properly so called.   It is called the *Mount of Offence* (Mons
Offensionis).   This is, according to tradition, that " hill
that is before Jerusalem," on which Solomon built an
altar for Chemosh, the abomination of the Moabites.†

Unless they were themselves fortified, these hills,
standing so close to the city, and commanding it, would
in our day be a source of danger.   But, before the

* Acts i. 11.

† 1 Kings xi. 7.   The *Mount of Offence* is, in fact, the only
one which stands directly before, *i.e.,* to the east of Jerusalem.

invention of artillery, they were with reason considered a sort of natural rampart, and the Israelites saw in them a visible image of the invisible protection of Jehovah over His chosen city. " *The hills stand about Jerusalem,*" says the Psalmist in Psalm cxxv., " *even so standeth the Lord round about His people, from this time forth for evermore.*"

The summit of the hill on which Jerusalem is built does not consist of a plateau, but of two crests running parallel to each other, from north to south. The western crest rises towards its extremity, and commands from a considerable height the valley of Hinnom ; this summit is Mount Sion, the most ancient part of the city, the fortress of the Jebusites, the city of David.

The eastern crest, on the contrary, which faces the Mount of Olives, is at one end of it broken ground, and then sinks very perceptibly as it approaches the southern end. This lower part is Mount Moriah. It is probable that its summit, before it had been levelled and worked into terraces, in preparation for the building of the Temple, was rather higher than it is at present.

The two crests of which I have now spoken are divided from each other by one of those depressions so often seen in the Jura, and to which geologists give the name of "combes," commonly applied to them by the mountaineers. The one of which I am now speaking, which is shallow at its origin, becomes more and more marked, and finally meets the valleys of Hinnom and of Jehoshaphat at their point of junction.

This "combe," now called simply *el Ouâd* (the valley), was known to antiquity under the name of the Tyropœon, or *Valley of the Cheesemakers*, an interesting name, altogether patriarchal, preserved to us by Josephus, which, even in the days of Herod and of Titus, still kept alive in the Holy City the memory of the primæval pastoral age.

Some travellers, led astray by an excessive love of system, or deceived by the ruins and fragments of buildings which here cumber the ground and often make the topography of Jerusalem obscure, have been unable to make out the upper part of this valley; they have thought that the Tyropœon descended first from west to east, and then turned at a right angle towards the south. Such is the opinion of Robinson among others. But, as I have just said, the inhabitants of Jerusalem recognise only one valley in their town, that which runs almost directly north and south. I myself for a long time searched for Robinson's "*upper Tyropœon*," but could never find it ; what he so names is the foot of a slope, but cannot be called a valley. On the other hand, I had recognised through the whole length of the city, and even before I had begun looking for it, the *combe* called *el Ouâd.* There is but one point where it might seem interrupted. Opposite to the Haram-esch-Chérif (the ancient boundary of the Temple) it is cut across by a roadway, which may be thought to have been destined in former times to connect the Temple with Mount Sion, and which I rather consider to be a part of the ancient ramparts. And in fact this roadway is in the lower *Ouâd*, which it has never been disputed formed part of the Tyropœon.

This question respecting the Tyropœon, upon which the whole topography of Jerusalem turns, is still a subject of controversy in Europe. The authority of Robinson gives weight to his hypothesis. But in Jerusalem I did not find a single person in favour of it, though I often had occasion to discuss it with Europeans well versed in the topography of that city. I have, however, just come upon it once more in a book published this very year, by an old inhabitant of Jerusalem.* It is true that the author, who revives this hypothesis, gives it its death-stroke in the act of defending it. This is what he says of his Tyropœon : *" Let us at once warn our readers that this valley has completely disappeared, having been filled up since the days of David and Solomon."* So naïve a confession may surprise us, but leaves nothing to be desired. Robinson had been less candid, and had allowed this vanished Tyropœon to figure on his plan of Jerusalem. One might, however, ask M. Saintine how the Tyropœon could have still existed in the time of Titus, or even, as he had said before, in *" Nehemiah and the Maccabees,"* if it had been filled up *" since the days of David and Solomon."* But I will not quarrel with his arguments ; I will be satisfied with taking note of the fact which he has acknowledged.

The various plans of Jerusalem, which were to be had till latterly, had all been founded upon insufficient data ; there was not one to be depended upon. It is only since the year 1858, and unhappily for me subsequently to my return from Palestine, that there has existed a good map of that country and a trustworthy plan of Jerusalem. These two fine works are due to M. Van de Velde : they have taken as their bases, —in addition to his own measurements,—those which were taken, in 1841, by the engineers of the English navy, after the bombardment of St. John d'Acre. In drawing up the plan of Jerusalem, he availed himself

* *Trois ans en Judée.* Par P. Gérardy-Saintine. (Paris: Hachette. 1860.)

besides of the rigorously exact measurements, and the patient and minute investigations of Dr. T. Tobler, the most conscientious of topographers.

Thanks to this plan, which will henceforth be an indisputable authority, the discussions of archæologists will, for the future, have a solid basis to proceed upon, whereas till now there were scarcely any data bearing upon the present topography of Jerusalem, which either were not, or might not be, questioned.

The ancient Jerusalem was built upon four hills ; on that of Sion was the ancient castle of David, with the part of the city called *the High Town ;* the Temple occupied Moriah ; a third hill, called by the Greeks *Acra*, on account of the fortress erected by the Syrians upon it during the time of their dominion, was also named *the Low Town*. Lastly, the fourth hill, called *Bezetha* (the new town) was built to the north of the Temple ; it was at first no more than a suburb, but Herod Agrippa (some ten years after the death of Christ) included it within the circuit of the city, by surrounding it with a wall.

There is happily no room for doubt with regard to the two most interesting parts of ancient Jerusalem— Sion and Moriah. Their sites are sufficiently described in the Bible and Josephus, and it is impossible to mistake them. As to Bezetha, Josephus describes to us its position exactly, saying that it lies to the north of the Temple and the Tower of Antonia ; it is therefore easy to point it out. Part of this hill is included within the present boundaries of the city, to the north-east of the Mussulman quarter ; the rest is outside the walls. A trench, which was required for the fortification of the present city, made two hills of what was originally but one.

The great difficulty is to determine the situation of
Acra. More even than the Tyropœon, this Acra has
been the battle-ground of archæologists ; some place it
to the north of the Temple, others to the south, others
to the west. I have studied this question on the spot,
as well as I have been able, and am much inclined to
think that Acra was the little eminence situated at the
north-east corner of the Temple, and where the Via
Dolorosa begins. I am, however, far from having arrived
at certainty upon the point. I shall not be expected
to enter here into a discussion which might lead us far
afield ; it would require a volume, or, at the very least,
a whole chapter, to set forth, even summarily, the principal arguments adduced in favour of, or against, the
various sites which may be assigned to Acra.

I will, however, state the hypothesis of Robinson,
because it has found its way into most books and plans,
and many regard it as an ascertained truth. The learned
American traveller thought he discovered Acra in the
elevated ground to the north of Sion. This hypothesis
is the least admissible of all. What Robinson calls
Acra is not, properly speaking, a hill ; it is but the
prolongation of Mount Sion, or, if you will, the link by
which it is connected with the great backbone of rock
which forms the watershed of the mountains of Judah.
Further, Acra always was, according to Josephus, the
lower part of the town, and the same historian tells us
that this hill was reduced in height by Simon Macca-
beus, to such a degree, he adds, that it was made lower
even than that on which the Temple was built. But the
Acra of Robinson, on the contrary, is higher than Mount
Sion itself, and therefore than all the rest of the town.
Lastly, according to Josephus and the books of the
Maccabees, Acra was close by the Temple ; the fortress

of the Syrians was even principally intended to command
the entrance into it, and to observe what went on in
it ; the Acra of Robinson, on the contrary, stands quite
separate from Mount Moriah.   And finally, Robinson's
hypothesis is based upon his view of the situation of the
Tyropœon, which, as we have just seen, is indefensible.

Let us leave the uncertain ground of these archæo-
logical researches, and describe what Jerusalem now is.
Seen from without, girdled with its walls, embattled
and flanked with towers, above which are seen white
minarets and cupolas, standing out with clear outlines
against the changeless blue of the Syrian sky, it presents, from whichever side one approaches it, a most
picturesque appearance.   It looks small, it is true, to a
traveller arriving from the north or west; but when one
looks down upon it from the top of the Mount of Olives,
it is really imposing, and stands forth with so much
majesty upon the sides of its hills, that it might be taken
to be much larger than it really is.   It may, however,
be noticed that towns in the East always make much
more show than those of Europe.   This is not only
owing to the style of the buildings, the absence of red
or grey roofs, and the number of cupolas; the principal
cause is that there are no suburbs.   The approaches to
our towns are crowded with yards, stations, manufac-
tories, gas-works, tea-gardens, etc., which make it difficult
to see where the towns begin and where they end ; but
in Palestine, where no one ever ventures upon building
isolated houses, the towns stand out in the landscapes
with well-defined outlines, like those one sees marked
in the old maps.   So it is particularly with Jerusalem.

On the other hand, we all know that the interiors of
the towns in the East do not correspond with the idea
one might form of them when viewed from without.

Jerusalem is no exception to this rule ; it is, I think, the most miserable of all. And yet the houses are built of good materials ; they are not made of brick, like those in Egypt, but of large square stones. Moses, indeed, promised the Israelites "*a land whose stones are iron, and out of whose hills thou mayest dig brass.*"* One seldom sees in the *façades* of the houses those little windows adorned with wooden trellis-work which one notices at Cairo ; there are often in the houses here no openings but the door only. A European who should be suddenly transported into certain streets in Jerusalem might walk about in them for a long time without any idea that he was in a town.

The sweepings of the houses, heaped up in front of each door, make of the streets real *cloacas*. The dogs and jackals are the sole œdiles of Jerusalem ; to them one looks to clear the public streets of the remains of domestic animals which lie rotting in the open road-ways. Besides which, one finds oneself walking in the midst of the dust of ruins, and you stumble every moment over the *débris* of some fallen wall. One would think that the town had just been taken by assault. Modern Jerusalem has grown up upon the *detritus* of those which preceded it, as mosses and funguses grow upon the remains of an old oak. In building a house there, its foundations are generally laid upon a soil made up of ruins. When, in the year 1841, the English began building their Church upon Mount Sion, they wished to found it upon the rock, and before they could lay its foundations, they had to dig through rubbish to the depth of forty feet. I myself

---

* Deut. viii. 9. It appears to me that this passage must be understood in the figurative sense which I have given it, for we are nowhere told that mines are to be found in Palestine.

witnessed a similar sight during my stay in Jerusalem : at a corner of the Via Dolorosa they were digging foundations for a large and handsome house intended to serve as a lodging for the Austrian pilgrims ; it was not till they reached to a depth greater still than in the last case that they came upon the soil.

Jerusalem is divided into four great quarters : that of the Christians to the north-west, that of the Armenians to the south-west (or Mount Sion), that of the Jews to the south-east, and that of the Mahometans to the north-east. One must, besides, count as belonging to the latter the little quarter of the Mogrebins, to the east of the Jews' quarter, and the ancient circuit of the Temple, called in our day *el Haram.* The Haram, taken by itself alone, makes up the fifth part of the town, and extends over .more than half its western side.

It may, perhaps, surprise some to hear mention made of the *Armenian* as distinguished from the *Christian* quarter. The reason of this is that the Armenians are foreigners, and form a rich and important colony in Jerusalem, distinguished from the other inhabitants by their language and costume. The larger number of the other Christians (Greek or Latin) are, on the contrary, indigenous, and even constitute the most ancient part of the population; and, except the colour of their turban (when they wear one), there is nothing to distinguish them from their Mussulman compatriots. Their language, origin, character, and, up to a certain point, their manners and customs, are .the same. It is nearly as difficult to distinguish a Mussulman from a Christian in Jerusalem .as a Protestant from a Catholic among us.

It is well to recollect that in the east the different

religions are almost all designated by the names of the principal nations which represent them. Thus, when one speaks of a Turk, one understands by that a Mussulman in general, just as by the title of 'a Greek' one means a member of the Church called *orthodox*, and by that of a 'Latin' a Catholic ; but if this Catholic, possessing a European passport, finds himself under the protection of some consul, he is no longer a Latin only, but a *Frank*. But these Greeks, these Latins, these Turks, and sometimes even these Franks, are Arabs by language and nation. All this causes much confusion and many mistakes; and it takes some time to learn to orientate oneself in it all. There are besides at Jerusalem some schismatic Greeks,—some Catholic Greeks—(that is to say, some who, while still practising the Greek ritual, have joined the Roman Church), some schismatic Armenians,—some Catholic Armenians,—some Catholic Syrians, and some Maronites (both of them subject to the Pope, but saying mass in Syriac), some Syrians, properly so called (that is to say, Jacobites), some Abyssinians, etc. Each of these various sects has in Jerusalem its churches and its convents. For the last twenty years the Protestants have been here represented by a Bishop. I shall have to return to the subject of these different Churches ; I only wished to mention them here in passing, in order to put the reader in possession of the existing state of things. In order to complete these general statements, it remains for me to give an approximative estimate of the population of Jerusalem.

This has been diversely estimated ; some make it no more than 11,000 souls, others 20,000. M. Schultz, who has been Prussian consul at Jerusalem, has made some researches upon this subject which seem accurate, from which it follows that Jerusalem contains about 15,500 inhabitants—that is to say, 3,400 Christians, 5,000 Mussulmans, and 7,100 Jews. According to this, the Jews would still constitute almost half the population of their ancient capital ; but the area of the quarter of the town inhabited by them is one-twelfth less than the other quarters taken together.

III.

THE WALLS OF JERUSALEM.

It takes only an hour to walk round Jerusalem ; I have several times done it, either at the foot of the walls or upon them.   It is the best way of getting a general view and an exact idea of the situation and configuration of the town.   And besides, I do not think there can be found in the world a walk which in so short a space evokes such a swarm of varied memories.   To walk from the western gate by which one goes to Bethlehem to the eastern which commands Gethsemane takes five-and-twenty minutes; in that time one has traversed the ancient City of David and the top of Mount Zion, looked into the depths of the valley of Hinnom, admired the fresh vegetation watered by Siloam's spring, surveyed the sepulchres of the valley of Jehoshaphat, passed round the walls of the Temple of Solomon, and then finds oneself opposite the Mount of Olives, and within a few steps of the pool of Bethesda and the palace of Pontius Pilate.   Sometimes I took with me Hhannah, to tell me, as we passed, the present names of the places ; at other times I went out alone, to give myself up more freely to the thoughts which suggested themselves.   Nothing interfered to disturb my meditations; the solitude which reigns around is such, that I have sometimes completed the circuit of the town without meeting any living creature. At night only, a little before sunset, I saw a few people near the gate of Jaffa, for that is the *rendez-vous* of the Europeans who happen to be in Jerusalem. On Fridays and holy-days, I saw also in the orchards through which the Damascus road passes, a large number of Mussulman women, wrapped in their white mantles, smoking their chibouques on the grass, or hanging their swings to the branches of the old olive trees. I often remembered Nehemiah's sad and silent walk round these ruined walls—"*I went out by night by the gate of the valley, even before the dragon well, and to the dung port, and viewed the walls of Jerusalem, which were broken down, and the gates thereof were consumed with fire. Then I went on to the gate of the fountain, and to the king's pool; but there was no place for the beast that was under me to pass.*"* How many times since those days have not these walls, rebuilt by the faith of Nehemiah, fallen again into ruins! And how many other ruins have been added to these!

If it is difficult to study the interior of Jerusalem, nothing is easier than to picture to oneself its external form. The defensive wall which surrounds it forms something like a square—very irregular, it is true, and having the north side somewhat exceeding the others in length. The town has seven gates; but, of these seven, two are walled up, and another is almost always locked. The number of available gates, therefore, reduces itself to four, answering to the four quarters of the town.

The present walls of Jerusalem were built between the years 1536 and 1539, under the Sultan Soliman II., son of Selim; their thickness is from three to four

* Neh. ii. 13, 14.

(French) feet; their height is far from equal everywhere. Towards the east and west they probably nearly follow the line of the ancient walls ; at least, it would not be easy to conceive it could be otherwise.   The breadth of the town is defined by the valley of Jehoshaphat on the one side, and by the upper valley of Hinnom on the other, which two serve as natural trenches defending the town ; and the present wall follows the top of the slope accurately.   On the other hand, we know that, on the south side, the ancient town extended further than its present boundary.   In fact, to the south, the wall, as it is now, leaves outside of the town the top of Mount Sion and the whole hill which from thence descends gently to the valley of Hinnom, and the lower Tyropæon. The extremity of Mount Moriah is also now excluded from the town.

On the north side, the ancient city appears to have covered successively a less and a greater area than the modern one. The most ancient wall, which still existed in the time of Titus as the innermost line of defence, probably enclosed no more than Mounts Sion and Moriah, and to the north followed a line drawn from the Jaffa gate, at right angles to the western face of the Temple wall ; it is easy still to trace its course, which is indicated exactly enough by a little escarpment in a straight line,—that which Robinson took for a remaining fragment of the upper part of the Tyropæon, and against which abut two streets,* also very straight, built end to end, and forming the northern boundary

---

* These are the two streets which in the days of the kingdom of Jerusalem were called by the Europeans *the Street of David* and *the Street of the Temple*. Here and elsewhere I purposely omit the Arabic names, which are too difficult for most of my readers to remember and would only confuse their minds.

of the Armenian, the Jewish, and the Mogrebin quarters. I have spoken elsewhere of a roadway which cuts across the Tyropæon. It is probable that in the time of David, before the building of the Temple, the wall did not extend as far as Moriah ; when it reached the Tyropæon, it turned no doubt to the south and only enclosed Sion. We see by the Bible that Solomon, having built the Temple, wished to re-connect it with the town, and elongated the rampart to that extent ; it is to him, therefore, that we must attribute the formation of the still existing roadway, which cuts across the Tyropæon, and which forms precisely the extremity of the streets of which I have just spoken. " *Solomon built Millo,*" says the Book of Kings, " *and repaired the breaches of the City of David his father.*" * *Millo,* in Hebrew, properly signifies *filling up,* that is to say, an embankment or roadway. Everything inclines one to believe that the great king, having, by lengthening out this rampart, enclosed within his boundary-wall a part of the Tyropæon, built there a new quarter of the town, and that this quarter took the name (*Millo*) of the roadway at the foot of which it lay. It is by anticipation that the Second Book of Samuel calls by the name *Millo* that part of the Tyropæon which, before the time of Solomon, formed the boundary of the City of David.†

* 1 Kings xi. 27.

† 2 Sam. v. 9. I have just found in David Kimchi's Commentary (upon 1 Kings xi. 27) a remarkable passage which entirely supports the opinion I have expressed respecting the site of Millo. Kimchi does not seem to imagine for a moment that this quarter of the town owed its name to a roadway ; but, according to him, Millo was so called on account of the crowd of inhabitants who *filled it ;* for it was, he adds, *a place intended to be used for assemblies of the people.* This explanation of the word seems to me forced, but one

At a later time, as the town increased in size, it became necessary to build a second wall, and then a third, in order to comprehend the new quarters within the limits of the ancient city. It was not long after the third wall had been built, and Jerusalem had reached its greatest size, that Titus took the city, and reduced it to ruins. According to some, this third wall followed, on the north, nearly the same direction as the present wall; according to others, it enclosed besides a considerable extent of ground which now lies outside the town. Looking at the rubbish of which the soil of the tracts lying to the north of Jerusalem is in part composed, one feels compelled to accept this second opinion, and to conclude that in the time of Titus the town extended beyond its present limits, not only towards the south, but also towards the north.*

But what was the course of the second wall? In other words, what was the boundary of Jerusalem before the time of Herod Agrippa, who built the last wall? This question is interesting, for the Jerusalem of the days before Agrippa is the Jerusalem of the time of Jesus. It is the aspect of the Holy City at that time especially that one would like to picture to

should carefully note the fact upon which the learned Rabbi rests his case, a fact which he no doubt received from Jewish tradition. Millo would, according to this, have been the Forum of Jerusalem, and therefore the Xystus spoken of by Josephus. Now this Xystus of Josephus was precisely in that part of the Tyropæon which is now occupied by the Mogrebin quarter; that is, it was at the foot of the roadway.

* But not to the extent commonly believed. We know from Josephus that in his time the circumference measured thirty-three stadia, which amounts to six kilomètres if the stadium of Josephus is the great stadium, and only five if it is the average stadium. In our time the circumference of Jerusalem amounts to about four kilomètres.

oneself. And then, Jesus having been crucified and buried outside the walls, it is important, if we wished to construct any hypothesis respecting the place of His death and of His burial, to know what was the circumference of the town at that period. This question is the necessary preliminary to the discussions with regard to the authenticity of the Holy Sepulchre. We will pause awhile to consider it.

Judging of it *a priori*, it would seem likely that the new town was, like the ancient one, limited westwards by the valley of Hinnom; it was necessary, it would seem, to unite the second wall to the angle of the first —that is to say, to the *Gate of Jaffa (the Tower of Hippicus)*—and to continue it along the course of the natural trench formed by the ravine.

Such was, in fact, the course of the third wall; such is also that of the present one. But Josephus expressly tells us that it was not that of the second. No doubt, at the time at which it was built, the high ground that lies to the north of Sion was not yet inhabited, and they did not wish to give the wall a needless extension ; they did not therefore build it on the edge of the ravine, but further to the east. It did not begin at the Tower of Hippicus, but, as Josephus tells us, at a gateway called *Gennath*, or *the Gate of the Gardens*.

The researches undertaken with a view to the discovery of the remains of this wall have not hitherto led to any indisputable results. The defenders of the authenticity of the Holy Sepulchre have thought they might consider as belonging to this second line a fragment of wall having a considerable appearance of antiquity running north and south and situated in the midst of the ruins of the hospice of the Knights of St. John. If this is, in fact, a part of the second wall,

the question is settled; for, by prolonging northwards
this ruined wall, one obtains a line which passes exactly
over the traditional site of *the Gate of Judgment*, and
which leaves on the west, outside the boundaries of the
town, the present Church of the Holy Sepulchre.

But we should not like to rest any hypothesis upon
this vestige of a wall, of which it would be difficult to
prove with any certainty the age and destination.   Let
us admit, on the authority of M. Tobler, whose accuracy we may trust, that it is not possible to discover
unquestionable remains of the second wall; and let us
argue, from the mere look of the places, what is its
most probable course.

From the look, I say, *of the places ;* for I do not wish
to give up my character of traveller.   I leave to the
learned the domain of historical inductions, and confine
myself to bearing witness to what I have seen.

Let us, then, go through the part of the Jerusalem
of our day that lies to the north of Sion, and try to see
which way it would have been possible to make a wall
run formerly, and which way it might be made to run
now.

We can only see three lines that are *possible*.

The first would be that of the present wall, quite at
the top of the hill, along the upper valley of Hinnom.
But we have seen that that was the course followed by
the third wall, and Josephus expressly tells us that the
second did not begin at the Tower of Hippicus.

A second possible line would be at the base of the
hill, in the Tyropæon itself.   But then the new town
would have been but a few paces in breadth ; the
hypothesis refutes itself, and I do not know that any
one has ever ventured to suggest it.

The fact, then, must have been—and this is the only

alternative left us—that the wall followed a course intermediate between these two. Now, walking over this hill-side, one easily arrives at the conviction that this wall must have been situated on the only level step it offers. It cannot have been built upon the slope itself of the hill, and yet not have left some evidence of its existence in the shape of a levelled spot, a depression, or some kind of break in the outline of the hill, marking where it had passed. Now nothing of the kind is to be found on the slope which commands the step of which I have spoken. On the other hand, the foot of this slope, upon the step, runs almost in a straight line, and it is impossible not to conclude, on first seeing it, that it was there the wall must have passed. A long, straight street—the longest and straightest in Jerusalem— seems still to mark its course. It is the street called that of Damascus.

If the facts are so, as I am very much disposed to believe they are, the line of the second wall would have been in perfect harmony with that of the first with which it would have been almost at right angles. The *Gennath Gate*, the point of junction of the two walls, would have been situated in the middle of the ancient one—that is, just at the opening of the street which separates the Armenian from the Jewish quarter, and which is now called *Hâret-el-Djavâin.* It is, perhaps, interesting to notice also that a straight line drawn from the Jaffa to the Haram gate is only broken at that point ; the upper part of the street (*the Street of David*) descends straight from west to east as far as the bazaars; but beyond the bazaars, the street which is the continuation of this one (*Temple Street*) inclines,—almost insensibly, it is true,—towards the north-east.

Another fact that deserves notice is, that when once

the above hypothesis is accepted, the great divisions
of the modern wall correspond exactly with those of the
ancient Jerusalem.   It would be the line followed by
the first wall which would then serve to mark the
boundary between the Armenian and Jewish quarters
to the south, and the Christian and Mahometan to
the north.   The line followed by the second wall would
be the boundary between the Christian quarter on the
west, and the Mahometan on the east.   So the two
great arteries of the present town (the street of Damascus and those of David and of the Temple) would have
occupied exactly the place of the two walls of the
time of Jesus.

With regard to the street which used to lead up to
the Gennath gate, and which consequently must have
been the most central outlet of the ancient town, we
may see that it too would have retained its importance ;
it would, in fact, be the *Hâret-el-Djavâin ;* that is to
say, the street which still, as I have said, forms the
boundary between the Armenian and Jewish quarters.*

I beg the reader to notice that I do not adduce
these facts in order to support the hypothesis which I
have stated, which is independent of them.   I see in
them only corollaries, which undoubtedly have their
interest as soon as the hypothesis is admitted.   Many
people, I know, attribute no importance to them ; they
perhaps think that, after all the vicissitudes through
which Jerusalem has passed, it is scarcely probable
that the plan of the ancient should be found to be

---

* The principal objection which might be made to the above
hypothesis of the line of direction followed by the second wall
would be founded upon the position of the supposed *Pool of
Hezekiah.*   I refer the reader to a note upon the subject at the
end of this book.

reproduced in any way in that of the modern town. And supposing it should turn out to be so, it will be said that one can only consider that to be the result of a mere chance coincidence.

But it is impossible to share this opinion, when one has noticed the singular persistency with which the cities of the east preserve, and continually reproduce, the essential features of their original plan. I will only cite one example of this which has particularly struck me; it is that of Constantinople. No doubt the metropolitan city of the Greek emperors has never had to undergo a disaster so extreme as Jerusalem suffered in its capture by Titus; but nevertheless, it too has passed through some considerable crises; its conquest by the Europeans, and that by Mahomet II., have left their marks upon it. And how often since then has fire reduced to ashes its wooden streets and palaces! how often has it been rebuilt! Besides which, it passed suddenly from under the government of a nation, Christian and highly civilised, to that of one barbarous, and differing from itself in religion, race, manners, and traditions. And yet, notwithstanding these facts, we still find in Constantinople, even in the quarter inhabited by the Mahometans, streets wide and straight, and squares, of which the Turks do not know what use to make, and not in the least suited to their needs. The Atméidan of Stamboul is the still existing hippodrome of Constantinople; you see at once that it was built by a people, sociable, active, accustomed to games, to public life and public assemblies. The houses which surrounded these squares and these streets have been many times destroyed and rebuilt; but their form, their *idea*, so to say, has been preserved through all; the essential features have transmitted and perpetuated themselves,—just as a type which distinguishes a species modifies itself without losing its nature, from generation to generation.

It is easy, without visiting Jerusalem, to satisfy one-self of the truth of the topographic facts upon which I rest my opinion with regard to the plan of the ancient walls. It is enough to glance at the plan of the city published by M. Van de Velde. I make my appeal the more willingly to this plan, because no one can suspect it of partiality. M. Van de Velde and M. Tobler, to whom we owe this fine work, both of them hold opinions with regard to the boundaries of Jeru-salem very much opposed to mine. They place the second wall much higher up, above the Church of the Holy Sepulchre.

IV.

THE GATES OF JERUSALEM.

I have said that Jerusalem has seven gates, of which only four are open for use. They seem to answer exactly to those which existed in the time of the Frank kings, before the present wall was built. But if we go back to the times of ancient Jerusalem, we see that it had a larger number of gates ; which is easily intelligible, since the town was in those days much more thickly inhabited than it has been since. The Book of Nehemiah has preserved the names of six of these gates. It would be vain to try now to discover the exact situations, at least, of those towards the south and north, where the boundaries are no longer the same as they were ; to the east and west, however, it is possible that those which now exist, correspond, more or less, to gates which existed in the times of the kings of Judah.

Rather than describe here *ex professo* the present gates of Jerusalem, I prefer to take my readers with me in one of the walks which I took round the walls soon after my arrival. All the gates will come under our notice; and we shall have the advantage of dropping for a time the didactic style.

Wednesday, March 31st.—After luncheon (for the *Melita Hotel* conforms as far as possible to English habits), Hhannah, who awaits me on the terrace, proposes to accompany me in a walk round the town. We go out by the northern gate, that by which I first entered the town; it is undoubtedly the most beautiful. The Arabs call it Bâb-el-Amoûd ("*the Gate of the Columns*"), but travellers ordinarily give it the name of the *Gate of Damascus*. And it is by it that one passes to go to Damascus, as well as to Samaria and Galilee. Here, the ground instead of sinking as it does from the other gates of the town, ascends. Before us, slightly rising, is a fine plain, covered with olive trees. We take the road to the right, that is, towards the east, and pass on our left a little hillock, in which is a cave, where if we are to believe the legend Jeremiah uttered his Lamentations. On this hillock are a great number of Mussulman tombs. Everywhere tombs! The approaches to Jerusalem are literally paved with them. Here, and on the slopes of the valley of Jehoshaphat, by the walls of the Temple there are Mussulman tombs. On the other side of Kedron, near the road to Bethlehem, Jewish tombs! In the valley itself—on the mountain—at Aceldama—ancient tombs, hollowed out in the rock! Lastly, on Mount Sinai, Christian tombs! Jerusalem is but a necropolis, of which the living seem the appointed guardians and conservators, more or less negligent.

Opposite the north-east corner of Jeremiah's hill is a
gate now walled up ; it is *the Gate of Flowers (Bâb-es-
Saheri)*, called by the Franks the gate of Herod, of
Ephraim, or of Benjamin. Soon, on turning at a sharp
angle the north-east corner of the walls, we find ourselves upon the heights which command the valley of
Kedron.   On this eastern side of the city, parallel with
the Mount of Olives, we find the only gate which leads
into the valley of Jehoshaphat.   Two lions are sculptured upon it.   In the middle ages it was called the
Gate of Jehoshaphat ; in our day the Franks call it the
Gate of St. Stephen, because it is said that it was at
a few paces from this that the first martyr was stoned.
The people of the country prefer to give it the name of
Bâb-Sitti-Mariam (literally *the Gate of the Lady Mary*).
It is in fact by this gate that one passes to go to the
pretended tomb of the Virgin, an object of veneration
alike to Mussulmans and Christians.   Between this gate
and the Haram are to be seen, within the walls,
the ruins of a deep fish-pond, which is pretty generally
considered to be that of Bethesda.*   It is now dried
up ; the walls which surrounded it have fallen into ruins,
and have partly filled it up.

This fish-pond is certainly ancient ; but have we
sufficient grounds for identifying it with that mentioned
by St. John ?   To answer that question one should be
able to say with some certainty with which of the ancient
gates of Jerusalem the modern gate of St. Stephen
corresponds ; since we see by the Gospel that this pool
of Bethesda adjoined the Sheep Gate.†

* St. John v. 2.
† The Greek says ἐπὶ τῇ προβατικῃ. Whether we understand that
to mean the Sheep-*gate* or the Sheep-*market*, the conclusion will
be the same ; for a market of that kind cannot well be situated

Nehemiah, who also speaks of this gate,* does not tell us on which side of the town it was situated. But, comparing carefully the three passages of his book which refer to the boundaries of Jerusalem,† one is led to look for it on the eastern side of the town. It is there that Raumer, for example, places it, in the catalogue he gives of the gates of Jerusalem according to the Old Testament. This conclusion is supported by the fact that the small cattle that were brought into Jerusalem certainly entered it from the east, for on that side lie the immense pastures of the desert of Judæa ; and still, in our time it is by the gate of St. Stephen that a great number of the sheep wanted for the town are brought in.

Besides, the requirements of the Temple services and of the sacrifices would have made it scarcely possible for the sheep-market to be held at any great distance from the Temple. There seems even good reason to think that it was close at hand, since we see by the Gospel‡ that there was danger of its encroaching upon the sacred precincts. May it not have been the sight of these great flocks ·of sheep, crowded together at the gates of the Temple, which suggested to Jesus the images He uses in the tenth chapter of St. John ? Or even may there not have been a direct local allusion in the words, " Verily, verily, I say unto you, I am the door of the sheep"?§

anywhere but at the entrance into a town, and besides, in Palestine, that was the case with all the markets. At Samaria, as also in our day at Jerusalem, the corn-market adjoined one of the gates of the town. (2 Kings vii. 1.)

* Neh. iii. 1—3, xii. 39.
† Neh. ii. 13—15, iii., xii. 31—40.
‡ St. John ii. 14.
§ St. John x. 7.

At less than a hundred paces from the gate of St. Stephen, we come upon the outworks of the Temple, of which the eastern face runs in an unbroken straight line as far as the south-east angle of the walls. The outline of the mountain contracts, and the slope of the ravine becomes more abrupt ; the footpath passes in the midst of tombs at a few paces' distance from the wall, and almost on the edge of the precipice.

In this front of the Temple is a gate, long since walled up. Its style is antique ; the capitals of the columns are adorned with palms, arranged in the manner of the Corinthian acanthus leaves. One is tempted to take it for a fragment of Herod's temple ; in any case one cannot suppose it to be of later date than Hadrian. This gate, called by the Arabs the Gate of Mercy (*Bâb-er-Rahmeh*), or the Eternal Gate, has always been called by strangers the Golden Gate. It was, it is said, through it that Jesus entered the Temple on Palm Sunday, coming from Bethany, preceded by the shouts of joy and the hosannas of the multitude. This legend, of which for want of date one can neither affirm nor deny the truth, rests upon the fact that the Golden Gate is the only ancient one that still exists, and upon its situation ; indeed, a path, cutting obliquely across the side of the ravine, descends from there to one of the bridges over Kedron, and rejoins, a little further on, the principal road to Bethany.

Beyond this gate, but nearer to the south-east corner of the town, the base of the wall is composed, in places, of enormous stones, which evidently are contemporaneous with the Temple ; they justify the exclamation of the apostle, " *Master, see what manner of stones!*"* Those which remain seem left only to

* St. Mark xiii. 1.

increase our wonder that the others should have been
overturned, and to make us recognise in their destruction the sovereign intervention of God. I measured
one of these stones, chosen almost at random; it was
sixteen (French) feet in length, by four and a half in
height, but there are some much larger. Schulz mentions one twenty-nine feet long.

One must go back far into antiquity to reach the age
when men built with materials like these. And we
may accordingly safely refer these foundations to the
time of Solomon : they are the remains of walls which
he built to strengthen the sides of Mount Moriah. The
upper layers, and, in places, the whole of the walls,
have been several times overturned by the conquerors
of Jerusalem ; but a few of these lower layers have
remained unshaken like the mountain itself, of which
they seem to form a part. Men have built, many
times over, upon these same foundations solid as the
rock itself. It is remarkable that all the remains of
the ancient walls of Jerusalem are found within the
area of the Temple; some here, others a little higher
up, between the Golden Gate and˙ the gate of St.
Stephen, at the north-east corner of the Haram; others
in front of the Haram, facing westwards, and therefore
inside the town ; among these last is the fine and
imposing wall, at the foot of which the Jews meet to
weep the ruin and profanation of their Temple.

All these great ancient stones have this peculiarity
distinguishing them, that only their edges have been
cut ; the middle of them is left more or less rough, but
all round is a border from two to four inches in breadth,
carefully chiselled, in such a way that placed one upon
the other the stones fit each other exactly.

Arriving at the south-east corner of the Haram and

the town, let us diverge a little from our course, and follow a new path which will lead us, like that which we have just been considering, to Kedron, and the tombs of Absalom and of Jehoshaphat. Though I intend to devote one day to the inspection of the ravines which surround the town, I find myself so near these monuments, that I will not resist the impulse to pay them now a first visit. It is here that the valley is narrowest ; one crosses the bottom of it in three steps over a little single-arched stone bridge. Immediately facing the bridge, and actually on the foot of the Mount of Olives, you see rising before you four bizarre monuments, to which tradition attaches the names of Jehoshaphat, Absalom, St. James, and Zechariah. Behind them, a little higher up, stretches a long line of tombstones, quite plain, and more modern than the others ; they are Jewish sepulchres. But other ancient sepulchres, hollowed out in the rock, are to be seen in infinite numbers in the sides of the mountain.

One understands how it happened that even from the most ancient times the Jews should have preferred this place to all others for the site of their sepulchres, under the shade of the rocks of Moriah and of the walls of the Temple. The day will come, said the prophets,[*] when the Eternal, from the top of this holy mountain, will judge the nations assembled in the valley of Jehoshaphat. There the dead will rise out of their graves, and appear before His judgment-seat, to receive the reward of their deeds. It is, no doubt, to the thought of this that we must attribute the eagerness of the Jews to be buried in this valley, and especially in the part of it nearest to the throne of the Eternal. But, alas! the time came when this place no

* Joel iii.

longer sufficed for the resting places of the dead ; it became necessary to bury them " *at Tophet, and in the valley of the son of Hinnom, because there was no room for them elsewhere.*"*

The four monuments which I have mentioned are sepulchres hewn in the rock, according to the ancient custom of the Jews; but that which distinguishes them is that they have been isolated from the mass of the rock by large trenches dug round each of them. Besides which, there are sculptures here, columns, pilasters, pediments ; so that looking at them from a distance, one pronounces them unhesitatingly to be buildings constructed of stones brought from a distance; but on coming near, one perceives that these singular structures are monoliths hewn out of the rock itself.

The tomb of Absalom is in a very curious style ; on its fore-part are figured columns ; the top is crowned with a capital, of a conical or cylindrical shape, which has, I believe, no parallel elsewhere. We read, in the Second Book of Samuel, "*Absalom had taken and reared up for himself a pillar, which is in the king's dale ; for he said, I have no · son to keep my name in remembrance ; and he called the pillar after his own name ; and it is called unto this day, Absalom's hand.*"† It is with this passage of Scripture that the name of the tomb before us is connected ; nothing forbids our admitting its authenticity ; and some critical and mistrustful travellers—M. Van de Velde, for instance—have not hesitated to accept it. It is certain that Absalom,

* Jer. vii. 32, and xix. 11.
† 2 Sam. xviii. 18. I translate literally (as do also the LXX. and the Vulgate) the two last words, יד אבשלם. But we must remember that the word *hand* in Hebrew is used of everything which serves as an index, a notice, or commemorative sign.

wishing to immortalise himself, could not have erected
a more durable monument ; the originality of its architecture appears also to be a proof of its high antiquity;
even this singular capital, with which it is crowned,
seems to me to be hinted at in the Biblical records,—
it is like a *finger* pointing to heaven, and it is easy
to understand how the people were led to give this
monument the name of *Yad Abshâlom* (the hand of
Absalom), rather than that of *Matztzébeth,** given it by
the historian.

Further, whatever may be the age of this monument, and of those around it, they are generally
considered rare and precious remains of Hebrew architecture.   Perhaps they do not, all four, belong to the
same epoch ; that of Absalom is the one which presents the fewest points of likeness to the architectural
works of other nations, whereas in that of St. James
one could hardly overlook indications of the influence
of Greek art.   It dates, no doubt, from the time of the
Asmoneans or Herods.

It seems to me very probable that many of these
caves may have served as sepulchres for a considerable
time before they were cut into the form of little temples, and that afterwards, no doubt, it was thought an
honour to those who were buried in them to decorate
their sepulchres in this way.   Perhaps Jesus alluded to
the building or decoration of these monuments, when
He said to the Jews, " *Ye build the tombs of the
prophets, and garnish the sepulchres of the righteous,*"†
and when He adds, " *That upon you may come all the
righteous blood shed upon the earth, from the blood of
righteous Abel unto the blood of Zacharias.*"‡

These words incline me to believe that, even in the

* מצבת.   † St. Matt. xxiii. 29   ‡ Ibid. 35.

time of Jesus, tradition gave the name of "the tomb of Zacharias" to one of the sepulchres in the valley of Jehoshaphat, and that Christ, who uttered these words *in one of the courts of the Temple,** had at the time before His eyes one of these monuments. This hypothesis would also account for a fact which has always perplexed interpreters in expounding this passage. The question is asked why Jesus here mentions Zacharias rather than any other prophet. But if we suppose that His first words (ver. 29) referred directly to this tomb, the mention He afterwards makes of Zacharias would be sufficiently accounted for.

This tomb of Zacharias is rather like that of Absalom, with the exception that it is crowned, not with a cone, but with a pyramid. The adjoining cave has been called that of St. James, because, according to the legend, that apostle hid himself in it after the apprehension of Jesus, in order to escape from his Master's enemies. It also is a sepulchre, but open in front, and adorned with a colonnade.

The tomb of Jehoshaphat is close to that of Absalom it is now almost entirely buried in the ground ; the upper corner of the façade alone remains visible.

Let us hasten to re-ascend. We have now to follow the southern face of the walls ; it will not occupy us so long as did the eastern ; for, with the exception of the east angle (which still belongs to the area of the Temple), and probably the part in which is the Mogrebin Gate, the situation of this wall is modern, and leaves outside of it a large part of the City of David.

The ancient wall, according to all appearances, instead of cutting across the heights of Moriah and Sion, as the modern wall does, nearly surrounded the southern

* Cf. St. Matt. xxiv. 1.

extremities of these two hills, and marked their outlines; it therefore left outside of it the lower Tyropæon,
and curved inwards there in a very marked way ; and
at the bottom of this curve probably was the gate
called in our day the Mogrebin Gate. We see from
Jeremiah and II. Kings,* that when Nebuchadnezzar
took Jerusalem, the soldiers who had defended the
town fled by night by the way of the king's gardens,
by the gate which is between the two walls, and took
the direction of the Araba.   As there can be no doubt
respecting the situation of the king's gardens, any more
than on that of the way to the Araba, it is probable
enough that the gate of which Jeremiah here speaks
was at the bottom of the curve which I have mentioned, and corresponded accordingly with the Mogrebin
Gate.†   It would also, no doubt, be the same as that
which is called by Nehemiah ‡ שַׁעַר הָאַשְׁפֹּת—that is to
say, the Dung Gate, or the Gate of the Sewers.   The
existence of a cloaca near the Mogrebin Gate, and
the situation of this gate at the mouth of the Ouâd,
at the lowest point of the town, makes this conclusion
very probable; accordingly, the Europeans have long
since given to the Mogrebin Gate the name *Porta
Stercoris.*

The present gate is, like the Bâb-es-Saheri, generally
locked; it is opened in summer, when the town cisterns

---

* Jer. xxxix. 4, lii. 7, and 2 Kings xxv. 4.

† I should now be inclined to believe that the *gate between the
two walls* was in the valley of Hinnom, to the south-west of
the town, between the first wall and the outer one built by
Manasseh (see, at the end of the volume, the note on *the Pool of
Hezekiah*).   A gate so placed, a little below *the Pool of the Sultan*,
would also have corresponded perfectly with the road to the Araba.

‡ Neh. ii. 13, etc.

run dry, in order to make a direct road in that direction to the spring of Siloam.

The latter, with the pleasant gardens that surround it (the king's gardens), is beneath us, at the end of the Tyropæon. The village of Siloam extends over against us, on the steep side of the Mount of Offence. It is said to be wretched enough; from here it is a very picturesque object. Two flocks of goats and sheep— each of about a thousand head—are at this moment descending, by different roads, from the top of the mountain; the shepherds urge them on with loud shouts, and bring them back for the night into the caverns of Siloam.

The sun sinks, and we have to redouble our pace; we arrive at the Gate of David, also called the Gate of Sion, situated nearly at the top of the mountain. The view from there is exceedingly fine. Still following the wall, one finds oneself, after two hundred paces, on the edge of the upper valley of Hinnom. Here the wall turns at a sharp angle, and runs north and south.

Here then we have reached the west face of the walls, and come near to the last gate we have to visit. This gate, to which travellers are pleased to give different names, is only known at Jerusalem under the title of the Gate of Jaffa, given to it by the Europeans, and of Bâb-el-Khalil (the Gate of Hebron), given to it by the Arabs. *El Khalil,* which properly means *the well-beloved,* is the epithet by which the Mussulmans commonly designate Abraham; the name has been transferred to the town which contains the tomb of the patriarch.

Each name fits this gate; for two roads lead up to it, the one from Jaffa, and the other from Hebron and Bethlehem.

By the side of the gate, within the walls, is a massive

building, on which every Friday the Ottoman flag is to
be seen waving. It is the Castle of Jerusalem, in Arabic
Kalâah. This castle, rebuilt for the last time by the
Saracens, after the final expulsion of the Franks,
dates from a high antiquity, as may be seen by the
great stones of which its lowest parts are composed.
Archæologists are agreed—as much, at least, as archæologists can agree—in recognising in this castle the Tower
of Hippicus, mentioned by Josephus, and which formed
the north-west angle of the first wall, and the starting-
point of the third. Most of the authorities make this
building date from before the time of Herod, and the
Europeans commonly give it the name of the Tower
of David. In that case, was it the residence of the
kings of Judah, or, perhaps, even the ancient citadel
of the Jebusites? or was it only a fortress built for
the defence of this angle of the original town ?

We hasten back into the town, for the gates are
shut at sunset, and they are not re-opened till the
morning. This rule, wisely ordered no doubt, much
shortens the traveller's journeys. Neither can one
employ the evening in walking about the town. It is
needless to say that it is not lighted ; the bazaars are
closed as soon as night sets in ; no ray of light falls
from windows, for there are no windows except towards
the courts. You stumble among the rubbish, you slip
in the mud ; accordingly, you meet no living creature
in the streets but the dogs, who are then in sovereign
possession, and whose barkings are the only break in
the silence of the night. If, notwithstanding all this,
one is determined to go out, one is obliged to arm
oneself with a *fanoûs,*—a long paper lantern, which can
be shut up, like a pair of bellows, when one wishes to
pocket it. The same rules are in force in the greater

number of the cities of the East. Any one who should disobey them by walking in the evening without a *fanoûs*, would be liable to be apprehended by the police. It is true that there exist no police.

V.

THE TEMPLE AND THE HOLY SEPULCHRE.

These two names sum up for us the greatest and holiest memories which belong to Jerusalem. The Temple, which God Himself had chosen to make His glory to dwell there, and to serve Him for a tabernacle in the midst of the habitations of men,—the Sepulchre into which Jesus descended for our offences, and from which He came forth victorious for our justification,— these are the most august monuments which the eye of man can contemplate, or his imagination conceive. Accordingly, the first questions a pilgrim to the Holy Land is asked on his return home are sure to be these,—" Have you seen the Holy Sepulchre ? and do you believe it to be the real one ? What remains of the Temple of Jerusalem ? "

These questions have this in common with all the greatest questions, that men are not agreed what are the true answers to them. I will try to make the truest and most compact answer I can. Let us begin with the Temple.

Before describing what it is in our day, it will be well, perhaps, in the interests of those to whose minds Hebrew antiquities are not as familiar as is desirable, to recollect what it was in former times. Holy Scripture,—when it speaks of the Temple, as when it speaks of the Tabernacle which had preceded it,— uses this word, sometimes in a limited, and some-

times in a more general, sense. So it is that to
this day, when mention is made of the Constantinople
seraglio, that expression is sometimes taken to mean
the palace itself, which was formerly the dwelling-
place of the Sultans and their wives, and sometimes
that vast area in which is included this palace and
its numerous appendages. Just so, in the narrowest
sense of the word, the Temple meant only the building
erected by Solomon to the glory of the Eternal, and
which, later on, was destroyed by Nebuchadnezzar,
and rebuilt by Zerubbabel. It was an edifice walled
in and roofed, like all houses, and distinguished by
its magnificence rather than its size. Its walls were
wainscoted inside with cedar wood, elaborately carved,
and even overlaid with gold in the part of the edifice
called the Holy of Holies. The dimensions of this
structure were anything but colossal ; sixty cubits in
length, twenty in breadth, thirty in height; add to
that a porch of the same breadth as the building
itself, and ten cubits in height, and we shall get as
the total length seventy cubits; that is to say, about
thirty-five metres, by ten metres in breadth, and fifteen
in height. One sees that these are proportions of
very moderate extent, somewhat like those of a village
church, and not comparable with Cologne Cathedral
or the Basilica of St. Peter.

It would have been useless to make it larger ; for,
far from being intended, like our churches, to contain
the multitude of the faithful, it was a sanctuary,
entrance into which was forbidden. The priests
alone entered it in the order of their course once a
year to pour upon the mercy-seat the blood of their
victims.

But if it was of little consequence that the House

of the Eternal should be of great size, since its destination was not at all practical, but only symbolical,
it was, on the other hand, necessary that the courts
which surrounded it should be capable of containing
an immense multitude, for the Temple of Jerusalem
was not the Temple of a town only, but of a whole
nation ; it was to it that the Israelites flocked from
all parts of the world to worship the Lord at the
solemn feasts.

They arranged, therefore, round the Temple, un-
roofed courts; first, one for the priests, a second for
the people, and a third for women. There were;
besides, chambers and other buildings, some of them
belonging to the Temple, others surrounding the
courts ; it was in them that they kept the furniture,
the sacred vessels, the treasure ; in them also lodged
the priests and the Levites employed in the service
of the sanctuary. Large porticoes offered places of
shelter for the lectures and discussions of the doctors,
the meditations of the learned, the prayers of the
devout. And, besides, we know from Jeremiah, that
there was even a prison in the House of the Eternal.*
So that it was a little world in itself, open at all
hours for the devotions of the Israelites. This enclosure was sacred, and accordingly it was often
called, in a more general sense, the Temple, or House
of the Eternal. It was there, in these courts, that
Jesus, still a child, stayed for three days, occupied
" *about His Father's business,*" hearing and asking
questions of the doctors, and astonishing them by
the wisdom of His answers. Later on, it was there
that, during the feasts of the Jews, He used to spend
His days,† surrounded by His disciples, *walking in*

* Jer. xx. 2. † St. Matt. xxvi. 55 ; St. Luke xxi. 37.

Solomon's porch,"* teaching the multitude, and disputing with the Pharisees and scribes, like Socrates with the sophists in the porticoes of the Agora. It was there that the first Christians, assembled "*with one accord*" in the same porch in which their Master used to teach, continued His work by bearing witness to His resurrection.†

I have taken care to record the two different senses in which the word Temple is used in Scripture, for it is above all necessary to make oneself clearly understood; and if the question is now asked, "How much is still left of the Temple?" we shall be able to answer confidently, that of the Temple, in the narrower sense of that expression, that is to say, of the *House* of the Eternal, there is left absolutely nothing; nor yet of the other buildings that surrounded it. The sentence pronounced against it by Jesus has been literally fulfilled; "*there has not been left of it one stone upon another.*" ‡ But if by "the Temple" is meant the enclosure, the terrace, which crowned Mount Moriah, and upon which were erected these various buildings, one may, on the other hand, answer that that exists still, and even that it is in the same state now as it was in the time of Jesus.

On three sides, in fact, the modern walls, built partly upon the foundations of the ancient ones, leave no room for any doubts; the boundaries of the present *Haram* are evidently, on these three sides, the same as those of the Temple. To the north, the modern buildings which are built against the wall do not allow us to demonstrate this identity in a manner as indisputable, but it may nevertheless be considered extremely probable.

* St. John x. 23.   ‡ St. Mark xiii. 2.
† Acts v. 12. See also iii. 11.

This enclosed space, which forms the south-east angle of Jerusalem, and which in area constitutes of itself the fifth part of the town, is called by the Arabs *Haram-ech-Chérif,* the Noble Sanctuary, or simply the Sanctuary *el Haram.* This last title it bears in common with the two other sanctuaries of Islamism, that of Medina, which contains the tomb of the Prophet, and that of Mecca, which contains the Kaaba. Entrance into it is strictly forbidden to all but Mussulmans.' I cannot therefore speak as an eye-witness of the wonders it contains, and do not choose to amuse myself with making a compilation of what one is told about it. All I know is, that it is useless to try to enter, and dangerous even to go too near it.

One day—it was not twenty-four hours after my arrival in Jerusalem—I had been for a long time wandering about the town, and was going down the Street of the Temple, looking right and left, and not enquiring whither I was going. Passing through these streets, though they were so Oriental in character, and so different from ours, I did not feel myself a stranger in them, as I did at Cairo or Jaffa; for I had been too long accustomed to live in them in imagination, and it seemed to me that the city of David and of Jeremiah was my own home too. I was, however, very roughly awakened out of my dream. I heard myself sharply questioned by some Turks. As I did not understand what they said, I continued my walk, but the shouts became louder, and took a tone of fury. I was on the point of entering the sacred precincts of the *Haram.*

I afterwards, however, regretted that I had not used the opportunity for casting at least a glance from without upon the Holy Place, and I returned one day to the neighbourhood of this gate, accompanied by Hhannah.

We were still at a very respectful distance from it, when we were pelted with a shower of stones thrown by some boys, provoked at seeing us walk in that direction. Stoning is still in our day, as it was in that of the Jews of old, the penalty to which a sacrilegious person is exposed; the rash infidel who should be caught in the *Haram* would not be brought before the Cadi or the Pacha : popular indignation would make an example of him.

As I am upon the subject of stoning, I will notice, in passing, that this punishment, prescribed by the law, and so often mentioned in Scripture, was more easily practised in Judæa than anywhere else, unless in the desert of Sinai, where we see it inflicted for the first time. The soil is everywhere strewed with stones. This is even one of the features which give to Judæa its characteristic look, and which stamp this whole country with its aspect of sterility and desolation.

Seeing the stones falling round us, I wished to draw back; but Hhannah, "young and proud," was delighted with this fine opportunity of shewing, by not giving way, that he understood the new rights which had a year ago been conferred upon him by the *hatti-houmaïoum.*

" So long as we do not enter the gate of the Haram," he repeated, "no one has a right to say anything to us."

I might have quoted to him Scapin's saying, " *Talk of justice to a Turk!*"* but an inhabitant of Jerusalem is not bound to know Molière. I agreed therefore to hold our ground. But the shower of stones continued : one larger than the rest striking me in a very perceptible way, proved to me that we had made a false step, and I gave up the contest. But Hhannah was furious, and would have insisted upon my complaining to the consul.

* Molière, *Les fourberies de Scapin.*

Some travellers, however,—few in number, it is true, and their names have been recorded,—have succeeded in effecting their entrance into the Haram by help of a disguise ; others, happier still, have entered without difficulty, under the protection of the Pacha but always without the knowledge of the people. The last person, as far as I know, who obtained this signal favour, was the Duke of Brabant, son of the king of the Belgians. The Pacha himself took him, surrounded by a troop of Turkish soldiers to protect him from the sight and from the fury of the devout. Many Europeans accompanied him ; amongst the number were the several European consuls, as well as the Anglican Bishop, M. Gobat. At this moment, I am told, it would be impossible even for a prince to obtain this favour ; the present Pacha would never grant it, and besides, the Mahometan populace is on its guard.* The *hatti-houmaïoum* granted by the Sultan in 1857, with a view to guarantee more extended privileges to the Christians of his empire, has led to an intensification of Mussulman fanaticism. I could see indications of it sometimes during my stay in Palestine, and soon after my return to Europe the Syrian massacres gave frightful proofs of it.

Notwithstanding all this, it is not difficult for the traveller to form a general idea of the Haram. Mount Moriah, on which it is situated, is not so high as the other Jerusalem hills, and one need only climb to the top of the neighbouring houses to get a good view into it. And it is also the first object which

---

* Things have changed since then, and now by the help of a small baksheesh one is allowed to visit the Haram. On the other hand, what I have said of the exasperation of Mussulman fanaticism has been unhappily confirmed, and has far surpassed all that might have been feared.

catches the eye on looking down at Jerusalem from the top of the Mount of Olives.

At about the central point of the area there is a great octagonal mosque, surmounted with a most imposing cupola ; travellers often call it the Mosque of Omar, as it is to the caliph of that name that its foundation is attributed, but the Arabs call it only the Cupola Rock, *Kubbet-es-Sakhrah.* At the further extremity of the Haram, to the left, (looking, that is, from the top of the Mount of Olives,) one sees the Mosque of Aksa, and other smaller ones belonging to it. Here and there are scattered oratories and schools. Elsewhere there are some fine trees, particularly cypresses, whose dark tints stand out clear against the light colours of the rocks and buildings. The soil is not cultivated, but grows naturally a thin carpeting of turf. I have called the Haram a terrace; and it is certain that, in fact, the walls which surround the mountain were not intended only to enclose, but also to support it ; but we are not to imagine that its soil has been regularly levelled. One cannot exactly tell what transformation it has undergone since the ancient times ; there is now a very perceptible incline, rising from the east westwards, and a depression on the north side.

We should form a mistaken idea of this Haram, or Mahometan sanctuary, if we imagined its use to be as restricted as is that of a church in Europe. A religious Mahometan does not go there only at certain hours to say his prayers, he often spends whole days in it, absorbed in meditation, sitting under the beneficent shadow of the great cypresses, contemplating the mountains and valleys which unroll before his eyes their splendid panorama, and, above all, enjoying the happiness of feeling himself actually on holy ground, without any risk of having his eyes defiled by the sight of an unbeliever. When I met Mussulmans bending their steps towards this ancient sanctuary of the Israelites, or caught sight of them from a distance walking upon the grass-plots of the Haram, the religious life of the ages of antiquity, as the Bible represents it to us, pictured itself vividly to my mind. I recollected ˙ the fine image under which one of the Psalmists figures the righteous, comparing them to those trees, ever verdant, which, *"planted in the house of the Lord, flourish in the courts of the house of our God;"* *—the sighs of the sons of Korah, *" My soul hath a desire, and longing to enter into the courts of the Lord. . . . One day in Thy courts is better than a thousand."*† *" When I think thereupon, I pour out my heart by myself; for I went with the multitude, and brought them forth into the house of God; in the voice of praise and thanksgiving, among such as keep holy-day."*‡

Alas! these blessed memories that made the hearts of the sons of Korah beat,—these regrets, these fervent aspirations which consumed them, are to this day the portion of the Israelites. In the Holy City itself, it is not granted them to tread the floor of that Temple which was their pride and their joy, and it has been only by paying for it that they have obtained the right toenter it; itis a known fact that for a long time they had to make an annual payment, to the Romans first,§ then to the Turks, for permission to come every week

* Psalm xcii. 12.
† Psalm lxxxiv. 2, 10.
‡ Psalm xlii. 4, 5.
Miles mercees postulat, ut illis flere plus liceat, says St. Jerome, who had himself witnessed it.

and weep under one of the walls.   This wall, the
finest of the remains of the ancient supports of Mount
Moriah, forms part of the western wall of the Haram,
and is separated from the Jewish quarter by that of
the Mogrebins.   Some years ago, a rich Israelite,
Sir Moses Montefiore of London, purchased for them
once for all the right of coming, as often as they
please, to pray and weep here.

   This same Sir M. Montefiore has done all that was
in his power to better the sad condition to which his
unhappy fellow-countrymen are reduced in Jerusalem.
He gained possession, outside the Jaffa gate, of a
large piece of ground, which he enclosed within a wall,
and in which he proposes to build dwelling houses
to serve as a supplement to the Jewish quarter, may
certainly too small.   The place is already indebted
to him for the foundation of one school or more, and
he contributed largely to the building of a spacious and
handsome synagogue.   MM. de Rothschild on their
part have founded a hospital.   Nevertheless the Jews
are still, to this day, the most miserable part of the
population of the Holy City.   Most of them live only
upon charity.   They are heaped together in some
streets unequalled for repulsiveness even in Jerusalem.
One wonders why the plague is not endemic there,
and certainly nothing could have prevented its being
so, but the singular healthiness of this climate,—of
this mountain air, always fresh and always stirring.
Misery decimates these poor people ; religion recruits
them.   They arrive in Jerusalem, not only from all
the provinces of the Ottoman Empire, but also from
the various countries of Europe and Africa,—not,
like the Christian pilgrims, to live there for a few
weeks, but to spend the remainder of their lives.

The larger number, however, of the Jews in Jerusalem are indigenous, and are Turkish subjects. Though the national Israelitish type of humanity is, as to its general characteristics, ever the same, the Oriental Jew has nevertheless a character and a physiognomy which are peculiar to him, and which distinguish him from the European Jew. This is how he is described by a traveller :—

"His glance," says A. C. Didier, in his *Promenade au Maroc*, "is askance, and restless; he masks the terror with which his heart is possessed under a honeyed smile, painful to contemplate when one studies it. He does not speak out, he whispers, like a prisoner afraid of awakening his sleeping executioners. He does not walk, he creeps stealthily along the walls, his eye and ear suspiciously on the watch, and he turns sharply at every corner, like a thief pursued. Often he carries his shoes in his hand, to make less noise; for there is nothing he so much dreads as to draw attention to himself. He would like to be wrapped in a cloud to make himself invisible. *If one looks at him, he doubles his pace; if one stops, he takes to his heels.*"

A Frenchman, M. du Couret, who has embraced Islamism, and who now calls himself *Hadji-Abd-el-Hamid-bey*, quotes, in his *Voyage à la Mecque*, the passage I have just copied, and adds: "But it is particularly at Jerusalem that the Jew exhibits in all he does that spirit restless as the remorse which the lapse of so many years has not been able to wear out. In presence of the places which witness against him,—branded, so to say, with a stigma of reprobation,—the Jerusalem Jew only half lives,—scarcely daring to breathe."

I detect here a hardness of tone, which displeases me ; I should like to see this great and heroic Israelitish people spoken of more respectfully,—a people sacred on account of its memories and its hopes, more sacred still from its sufferings. I have however quoted these passages, because the portrait they present to us of the Oriental Jew is drawn from the life, unhappily too truly. It is curious to compare it with the threatenings of the Law, "*I will scatter you among the heathen. . . . And upon them that are left alive of you, I will send a faintness into their hearts in the lands of their enemies ; and the sound of a shaken leaf shall chase them ; and they shall flee as fleeing from a sword ; and they shall fall when none pursueth.*" *

And yet, though Israel is fallen, though he is a stranger and a fugitive in his own land, the promises made to Jerusalem have not ceased to realise themselves. "*The hill of Sion*" is still "*the city of the great King, the joy of the whole earth.*"† "*It has come to pass, that there have come people, and the inhabitants of many cities, . . . yea, many people and strong nations have come to seek the Lord in Jerusalem.*" ‡ But it is no longer the Temple which attracts them, neither is it the glory of Solomon, nor the learning of Gamaliel ; it is the sepulchre of a Man who had no splendour, and no literary fame, "*in whom neither the Pharisees nor the rulers believed,*" but "*who,*" as the event has proved, was "*greater than the Temple.*" §

The Church called that of the Holy Sepulchre is situated in the Christian quarter, that is, in the north-

---

* Lev. xxvi. 36.   ‡ Zech. viii. 20—22.
† Ps. xlviii. 2.   § St. John viii. 48; St. Matt. xii. 6.

western part of the town; it is made up of three churches quite distinct from each other, but so connected as to form a single edifice. The whole is so closely flanked with convents, that only one gate is left free; it is reached by going through a small court, and it is from this side only that one can get a sight of one of the *façades* of the church.

To the west of this, the one entrance, is the principal part of the building,—the Church of the Holy Sepulchre, properly so called. It is a large and lofty *rotunda*, in the style of the Pantheon. It is lighted from the cupola. Round the whole are columns; in the centre is a chapel built of black marble, containing the sepulchre of Jesus.

To the east of the gate, in other words, to the right, is *the Church of Calvary;* one climbs up to it by stairs, consisting of eighteen steps, steep and narrow. I will not describe all the altars,—all the memorable places pointed out for the devotion of the pilgrims. These details, were they trustworthy, would add nothing to the grandeur of the place as a memorial; in such a spot history itself pales, no less than legend; and when on the hill of Calvary they shewed me the tombs, undeniably authentic, of Godefroi de Bouillon and of Baùdouin, I felt, I confess, no more interested than when I was shewn the hole in the ground in which it is said that the skull of Adam was found.

The third church, on the other hand, is built much lower down than the first; the descent to it is by twenty-one steps; it is the subterranean Church of St. Helena, or of the *Invention of the Cross.* Here, according to the legend, the Empress discovered *the true Cross*, which was thrown by the Jews, together with those of the two thieves, into a cistern.

I shall spend no more time describing the places ; the most important question is not what they are in themselves, but, principally, whether they are authentic. That is the point which I am about to investigate. I wish it to be clearly understood that I am not intending here to enter into a discussion with regard to the authenticity of each of the sacred places comprehended within this Church, and made sacred by legend. All I here enquire into is this general question,—Is this triple church called that of the Resurrection, or the Church of the Holy Sepulchre, really built upon the places in which Jesus Christ died and was buried ?

It is, in fact, clear that the authenticity of the supposed Calvary and Holy Sepulchre does not involve the truth of all the legends which have gathered round it, and is not bound up with them. It is admitted that the Louvre in which Charles IX. lived is really the palace which in our day bears that name ; but that does not oblige us to believe in the identity of the famous window from which he is said to have fired upon the Huguenots.

The defenders of the authenticity of the Holy Sepulchre allege in its favour the *tradition*, which they declare to be constant and uninterrupted ; their adversaries oppose to this tradition a certain number of *facts*, which, they say, cannot be harmonised with it, but demonstrate its falsehood. Let us first examine these facts; and then weigh the worth of the tradition.

One of the few things which we know from Scripture with regard to the place in which the death of Jesus took place is that it was situated, not in the city, but " *nigh to the city*,"* and " *without the gate.*"† But the Calvary and the Sepulchre which are now

* St. John xix. 20.   † Heb. xiii. 12.

shewn, lie within the walls. Here is a glaring contradiction. But we must remember that the boundaries of the city were not in the time of Jesus either those of our day, or those of a date a little later, when the third wall had been built. The city was as yet only enclosed by what is called the second wall ; now this second wall (as we know from Josephus, and his statement has not been disputed) did not begin, as the present wall does, at the *Tower of Hippicus* (by the Jaffa Gate), but lower down, at the *Gate of the Gardens*.

Where was that gate ? Where was this wall ? I have elsewhere examined this question, and I have endeavoured to shew how improbable it is that a wall should ever have passed over the slope now occupied by the Christian quarter, and how probable, on the other hand, it is that the track of the second wall nearly coincided with that of the Street of Damascus, and the Gate of the Gardens with the bazaars. If that was the case, the traditional site of Calvary and the Holy Sepulchre would fall outside the line of the walls as they existed in the time of Jesus. It would be *close to them*, it is true ; but that is precisely what we must conclude from the narrative of St. John was the case.

Neither must we object, as we might be tempted to do, that the Calvary and the Sepulchre indicated by tradition are too near to each other ; for St. John expressly tells us that the garden belonging to Joseph of Arimathæa was " in the place" where Jesus was crucified ; and it was on account of this proximity of the Sepulchre, that the Body was laid there, because it was "*the Jews' preparation day*."* But the present form of the Holy Sepulchre suggests a more plausible objection. One expects to find a cave hollowed out in

* St. John xix. 41, 42.

the rock ; for such were the tombs of the ancient Jews, and such was that of Jesus, according to the express statement of the Gospels,* and one is shewn a sort of marble mausoleum, in the form of a chapel, isolated in the middle of a perfectly flat piece of ground, on which is erected the round-domed Church. Here is a fact, it might seem, which settles the question ; the present Sepulchre is modern, or at least Roman ; it is not a true Jewish sepulchre ! But yet, on examining this mausoleum more closely, one can convince oneself that the black marble slabs of which it appears to be composed are no more than a coating with which the bare rock is covered, and that the sepulchre itself, which is concealed from view by this marble, is an integral part of the rock upon which the Church is built. We have then here a monument of the same sort as the tombs in the valley of Jehoshaphat, which were, no doubt, originally only caves cut out in the rock ; afterwards they must have been detached from it and isolated in order to do them honour, and to draw more attention to them. One may then imagine that the rock upon which is built the Church of Calvary extended originally as far as the place where is shewn the Holy Sepulchre ; Constantine may have had the western part of it cut away and carried off, leaving nothing of it but the sepulchre itself, which, later still perhaps, was overlaid with marble and arranged in the form of a chapel, as it is seen now.

This, then, is another instance of an improbability which turns out to be only apparent ; and,—I may be mistaken,—but it seems to me that these cases of im·

---

* St. Matt. xxvii. 60 ; St. Mark xv. 46.

probability, as soon as they are shewn to be groundless, turn into presumptions in favour of the authenticity of the fact disputed. No one would willingly allow appearances to be enlisted against him, unless he had the actual truth on his side. If there had not been, in the time of Constantine, a positive tradition respecting the site of the Holy Sepulchre, if that prince had only wished—as has so often been done with regard to other facts of the sacred history—to associate with some place or other the memory of the Death and Resurrection of the Saviour, — it is scarcely possible to doubt that, in default of truth, he would have endeavoured to have at least appearances on his side. He would easily have found, *outside the walls,* a sepulchre answering to all the conditions required, and it would not have occurred to him to choose one within the area of the town,—that is to say, in a situation the least likely to be the true one that could be conceived. Moreover, far from effacing the features that existed at first, of the original form of this tomb, one would have expected that he would rather have made an effort to preserve in it the distinctive look of those ancient Jewish sepulchres of which he saw before him so many specimens.

This is but a presumption, I know ; but let us now look into the tradition. Is this tradition no more than a legend which makes its appearance for the first time in the journal of a mediæval pilgrim, or—like so many other legends respecting Jerusalem—adopted by the members of one Church, and rejected by the rest? No, we can, in the first place, trace it up without interruption to Constantine ; and accordingly no one questions that the present Church of the Holy Sepulchre is situated on the spot on which Constantine had built his;* it is even granted that the existing Church still contains considerable fragments of the edifice erected by that emperor. That is not the question in debate. What is disputed is that Constantine knew what was the real site of Calvary and the Holy Sepulchre.

In fact, it is said, the whole of the history given us of the building of this Church bears the stamp of legend upon it : St. Helena causes searches to be made; she discovers the three crosses in perfect preservation, though they had been buried in the earth for three hundred years, and she discovers which is the Saviour's Cross by the miracles it works ! That is enough to deprive the historian of all credit, and the tradition of all trustworthiness !

This conclusion does not appear to me legitimate; on the contrary, on carefully reading this story, so full of the supernatural, we are struck with one fact,—namely, that the chronicler who so easily accepts miracles, and who accumulates so many of them, in order to explain the discovery of the true cross, does not bring in any when the object is to ascertain the site of Calvary and the Holy Sepulchre. He does not affirm that for that any revelation, or even any search, was needed. He speaks of this site as of a place well known, and he has no suspicion that there has been the least difficulty in determining it.

It is indeed certain that this site must have been easy

---

* A Scotch antiquarian, Mr. Fergusson, has nevertheless called this in question. According to him, the domed *Church of the Rock*, in the centre of the Haram, is no other than *the Church of the Resurrection*, erected by Constantine. His opinion, which for a long time was considered an untenable paradox, has, of late, found new defenders. See, for instance, a dissertation by M. S. Smith (*The Temple and the Sepulchre*), which was published in London in 1865.

to distinguish, since we must suppose—and besides, St.
Jerome confirms it—that, up to the time of his conversion, Constantine had allowed the idols which Hadrian
had, as I have said, set up in it, either with a view to
desecrating or doing honour to it in his own way, to
remain there. It is then to the time of Hadrian that
the tradition ascends, or even indeed a little higher still;
for to have made that emperor judge it necessary to
pervert the sacred memories which attached to Calvary
and the Sepulchre, those places must have been before
his time—and, no doubt, some time before that—an
object of veneration to the Christians.

Here then we find ourselves brought to the first
century of the Church's history without having discovered any break in the continuity of the tradition
respecting the Holy Sepulchre, and without having
perceived that it gave occasion for any hesitation, any
doubt, any dispute,—such as we find arising even in
the first centuries, when a decision has, for example,
to be arrived at with regard to the ecclesiastical
tradition respecting Easter.

I am well aware that we have here reached the limit
of our knowledge, and that we cannot ascend any
higher ; and I confess that, so long as there shall
exist an interval (if only of a few years) between the
death of Jesus and the first appearance of this tradition, it will be possible for those who choose to do so,
to question its truth. It is for that reason that
the authenticity of the Holy Sepulchre, though highly
probable, will never take rank among indisputable
truths. But I should be glad to clear out of the
way at least one objection which I have often heard
raised. It is not probable, some have said, that the
memory of the site of Calvary, and of the Sepulchre

of Jesus, should have been preserved during the first century of Christianity; we are not to think that the first believers would have thought of perpetuating their memory; the importance attributed to the sacred places is an effect of spiritual degeneracy, and we could not attribute that feeling to the Church of the apostolic age. The disciples of Jesus cared little, it is said, to know where was the tomb of their Master ; they looked for Him only in the Heaven whither He was gone before them.

It is true, I answer, that such was the view of St. Paul, and no doubt of the other apostles.   But it would be a great mistake to attribute an equal degree of spirituality to the masses who, from the Day of Pentecost, composed the Christian Church.   We see on the contrary by the Epistles of St. Paul that, from the beginning, attachment to external and visible things, the need of forms—in a word, the Jewish tendencies—existed in all the churches, and led always to the same abuses.   That was the spirit which St. Paul had ceaselessly to contend against ; he reminds some that we are no longer to know any one after the flesh, and that even " *though we have known Christ after the flesh, yet now know we Him so no more ;* "* he warns others not to attach themselves to the observance of " *holy days, or new moons, or sabbath days.*"† We know that it was principally in the churches which had come forth from Judaism, and particularly in the Palestinian ones, that these tendencies prevailed; at Jerusalem everything must have combined to favour them ; and if the Colossians attributed to particular days an idea of sacredness alien to the spirituality of the Gospel, we must suppose with very much more reason that the

* 2 Cor. v. 16.   † Col. ii. 16.

Jewish Christians in Jerusalem already regarded with special interest, and perhaps attributed an exaggerated importance to' the Holy Places which existed in their city.

If I insist so strongly upon the reasons which may be urged in favour of the authenticity of the Holy Sepulchre, it is because I have seen some persons entertaining prejudices upon the subject, and making it, so to,say, an article of faith to reject that belief. For my part, I cannot see that Christian doctrine is at all concerned in these questions ; but it will be intelligible that, as a Protestant, I have a still greater dread of Protestant than of Catholic prejudices.

Among the many reasons pleaded against the authenticity of the Holy Sepulchre, I have often heard a moral one urged :—God, it is said, would not have permitted the sepulchre of Jesus to become an object of idolatrous veneration, and to be profaned, as it is to this day, by the superstitions and the quarrels of Christians. Alas ! where are we to find sacrileges which God has not permitted ! or idolatries which man has not invented ! or outrages to which the name of Jesus has not been subjected! crimes in defence of which it has not been pleaded ! Really I should think it much more wonderful if the sepulchre of the Saviour were an exception to the general rule.

The following then is, as I believe, a true picture, such as one may represent it to one's imagination, of the state of the Holy Places in the time of Jesus :—

The space contained within the angle formed by the wall of the ancient and that of the modern city, constituted no doubt a sort of suburb ; the central position which it occupied must have led to its being selected, by preference over others, for gardens, that is to

say, plantations of fruit trees, such as may still be
seen at the gates of Jaffa, of Nablous, and generally of
all Oriental towns that are in a state of less profound
decadence than Jerusalem is in our day.   It was to
these plantations that the Gate of *Gennath* (that is, " of
the gardens"), which formed the door of entrance from
this quarter of the city into the ancient City of David,
owed its name.   And, no doubt, in the time of Jesus,
these gardens were already beginning to disappear, to
make room for houses; since a few years later this
suburb was so important, that it was thought right to
enclose it within the bounds of the city by building the
third wall.   But, nevertheless, some gardens would still
have been left there, belonging, no doubt, generally,—
like that in which Jesus was buried,—to persons of
wealth and distinction.

In this corner then, there was a little hillock or
crêt—as we say in .our mountain country—very like
those which one finds in considerable numbers to
the north of the Jerusalem of our day.   It had in
front of it, to the south, the top of Mount Sion,
—to the east, the Temple and Tower of Antonio,
with the palace of the Roman Governor.   It was
called *the place of a skull*, in Hebrew, Golgotha.   It
was, no doubt, a bare rock, such as *crêts* of this sort
commonly are ; but the proprietors of the gardens
which surrounded it had utilised its sides by cutting
out tombs in them.   Perhaps it was to these sepulchral
caves that it owed its name ; or, perhaps, and more
probably, this name was given it only on account of
its rounded outline.

This hillock is situated at the intersection of the streets
of the ancient and the modern city; nearer, however, to
the modern than to the ancient, and at only a few

paces' distance from the gate called, at a later date, the Gate of Judgment. It was the first object on which our eyes fell on issuing from the city, and perhaps this was the reason why it was selected on other occasions as the place on which to erect the crosses of criminals ; for it was thought desirable that these formidable examples of Roman justice should draw the attention of the people; and for that purpose they were often placed by roadsides, and in frequented pathways. Perhaps also it may have been by the Jews that this spot had been pointed out to Pilate's soldiers, that so to the ignominy of the execution they might add' that of a public exposure. We know that the enemies of Jesus had soon to repent of this refinement of cruelty. If the execution of their victim was made as public as possible, Pilate's inscription upon the Cross was equally so; and so many more of the people * had the opportunity of reading the famous words, *Rex Judæorum*, by which the Roman governor revenged himself upon the fanaticism of the Jews.

This spot would be found in our day to be com-prehended within the area of the church ; the eastern part of the rock would constitute the floor of the Church of Calvary,—at a much higher level, as I have said, than the rest of the edifice ; the greater part of the west of it would have been removed by the axes of Constantine's architects, and they would have left nothing untouched, but the cave which contained the Sepulchre.

It is, in fact, certain that the ground upon which the Church of Calvary is build is not an artificial ter-race ; it is easy to convince oneself that it is erected

* πολλοί, St. John xix. 20.

13

upon the rock itself. One can also see that this rock contains, besides the Holy Sepulchre, many other excavations absolutely similar to those which form all the ancient Jewish tombs, and which, it is singular to remark, have only recently been noticed.

I only regret, in quitting this subject, that I have not been able to treat it more thoroughly. I should have liked to have cited some of the researches, as learned as they are ingenious, to which the controversy respecting the authenticity of the Holy Sepulchre has given birth ;* but I have made it my object, on the contrary, to forget what has been already said by others ; as I wished to keep to my character of traveller, and to limit myself as much as possible to communicating my own impressions, my own observations, and the results to which I was myself led.

VI.

SOME DAYS IN JERUSALEM.

I do not intend to give a complete account of Jerusalem ; and accordingly I shall omit a great number of notes which I collected on the spot, which would be far from having the same value for others as they have for me. I must be satisfied with extracting here what I wrote of a few of the most interesting days I spent in Jerusalem—at Easter-tide.

Good Friday.—I went out alone this morning, intending to go and sit upon the Mount of Olives and do

---

* The reader may consult upon this subject almost all the accounts given by travellers of Jerusalem; for there are few of them which do not treat of this question. I may mention, besides, the excellent monograph by M. Albert Schaffter, published at Berne in 1849.

absorb myself in the memories of this day. After having followed through its whole length the *Via Dolorosa*—the road I naturally take whenever I wish to go out of the city eastwards, for the *Melita Hotel* adjoins the Gate of Judgment—I descend by the Gate of St. Stephen, to the bottom of the valley of Kedron.

The brook Kedron is completely dried up; in ascending the valley, one can no longer find any trace of it; but here its bed is still indicated by a number of pebbles, and it is crossed by a little bridge. Once or twice a year, at most, when rain has been abundant, it serves to carry off the water which runs into it from the slopes of the neighbouring hills; and then the inhabitants of Jerusalem collect in crowds on its banks, to see the unusual spectacle of the running water. Indeed it is known that even in ancient times, when the country was less arid than it now is, the Kedron never was more than a torrent; and it is always so spoken of in Scripture.

Immediately after crossing the bridge, I leave on my left the subterranean Church of the Virgin, and on my right, at the foot of the mountain, I come upon the traditional site of the *Garden of Olives, Geth-semane.* In it are some old and venerable olive trees, the finest probably in all the Holy Land. It would be difficult to find proofs of the truth of the tradition which assigns the name of Gethsemane to this spot; but there is nothing against it. We know that Gethsemane was near Jerusalem, and on the other side Kedron; there is no temptation to look for it higher up on the sides of the mountain, for its name signifies *oil-press,* and no one would choose for the site of an oil-press any part of the mountain but the lowest and the most accessible from a vine or olive yard.

Gethsemane belongs to the monks of the Latin convent; and as these monks are all Europeans, they have thought themselves bound, lately, to turn it into a garden like those of the Western world; they have adorned it with brickwork and trim borders, and surrounded the whole with a rectangular wall, neatly whitewashed. So we have to knock at the door to gain admittance; but we knock in vain; the man in charge is not often at his post. How fortunate it is that the greater number of the Holy Places are still under the protection of Oriental barbarism! Thanks to it, the Mount of Olives is not yet, under pretext of restoration, become a complete English park, to be seen by strangers only on presentation of their passports, and under an express prohibition to touch the trees, or walk on the grass.

While I am there, a Mahometan procession passes, with cymbals and tambourines. It is returning from the so-called tomb of Moses, which is in the direction of Jericho. The time of this pilgrimage, I am told, always coincides with the Holy Week of the Christians. I stopped, to see this assembly pass, in front of a tent pitched by the roadside, and used as a café. Still, to this day, tents play a great part in the lives of the inhabitants of Palestine: they serve often as cafés and shops. During the hottest time of year, the inhabitants of Jerusalem put up their tents on the roofs of their houses, or, if their circumstances allow of it, in the open country. M. Gobat told me that he spent in his tent four months of the year, at a few miles' distance from Jerusalem. And it is in tents, also, that the pilgrims are lodged, who cannot find room in the houses. This week the courts of the convents and of the churches are full of them.

It is easy, then, to picture to oneself the Feast of Tabernacles. I understand also how the Israelitish pilgrims who in ancient days came up to Jerusalem in such great numbers for their solemn feasts found means to house themselves. With our climate and our European habits, such a gathering in a town of moderate size would be an impossibility. But here, the streets and squares were no doubt filled with tents, as well as the country close round the town. We know from the Gospels, that when Jesus sojourned in Jerusalem during the feasts, He lodged upon the Mount of Olives. Thither He retired every evening to spend the night; in the morning He used to go to the Temple, and stay there all day, instructing the people.*

I climb rapidly, almost in a straight line, the steep sides of the mountain. The olive trees, which have given it its name, are still the only trees to be seen upon it, at least on this side. It was the road which David took when flying from his rebellious son. "*He went up,*" says the Second Book of Samuel,† "*by the ascent of Mount Olivet, and wept as he went up, and had his head covered, and he went barefoot; and all the people that was with him covered every man his head, and they went up, weeping as they went up.*" That is a picture which recalls the ancient *bas reliefs*. It is impossible for a Jew to travel by this road without having this short record, drawn from the *epopée* of the most glorious of his kings, recalled to his memory. He will also think of that magnificent

* St. Luke xxi. 37, xxii. 39 ; St. John viii. 1, 2.
† 2 Sam. xv. 30.

passage in which Zacharias represents the Eternal
"*standing upon the Mount of Olives,*" and contending
against the enemies of His people, and then coming
with His saints to reign over the whole earth.*   One
can see that this mountain had, even in the Old Testament, a sort of prophetic sacredness, which is confirmed
and realized to us by the sojourning of Jesus upon it.
An exceedingly remarkable Jewish tradition, recorded
in the Mishna, referring to a passage in Ezekiel, says
that when the *Shekinah* (that is, the Glory of the
Eternal, which dwelt in the Temple) withdrew from
the Holy of Holies and from Mount Moriah, it did
not immediately re-ascend to Heaven ; a season of
grace was granted, during which, before it departed
finally from Jerusalem, it sojourned before the Temple,
upon the Mount of Olives, *for three years and a
half !*

I leave on my right the mosque of the Ascension,
and take my way along the narrow plateau at the top
of the mountain.   At its extremity—just where one
loses sight of the city—is a little village, which I should
be much tempted to take for Bethphage ; a few paces
further on is a well and a plantation of fig-trees.   As
we know, the name Bethphage signifies *House of figs*,
as that of Bethany, close by, means the *House of dates*.
It seems that fig-trees thrive particularly well here ;
I saw none on the western slope of the mountain,
nor yet lower down on the eastern slope.   As if to
remind me more pointedly of the village mentioned
in the Gospel, an ass and her foal were grazing in
the orchard.†

I would not dogmatise upon the site of Bethphage ;
the data furnished by the evangelists with regard to

* Zech. xiv.   † St. Matt. xxi. 1, 2.

this village, are insufficient. We ought, however, I think, notwithstanding the fact that St. Luke mentions it before Bethany,* to look for it between Bethany and Jerusalem; this seems to follow from the narrative of St. John; † and the Talmud tells us that Bethphage was considered a part of Jerusalem.

At any rate, it is interesting to find still in our day a plantation of fig-trees on the road to Bethany; for it was upon that road that Jesus cursed the barren fig-tree. ‡

Descending the eastern slope from thence, without leaving the beaten track, we soon see in front of us, a little to the right, another round-headed mountain not visible from Jerusalem. I climb to its top in a few minutes. One cannot hesitate, it seems to me, to call this the scene of the Ascension of the Saviour; for the Ascension, St. Luke tells us in his Gospel, took place *at Bethany*, and the same historian reports to us, in the Acts, that after the Ascension the apostles came down *from the Mount of Olives*. The mountain-top on which I find myself is the only one which reconciles the two narratives, and it does so perfectly. This idea occurred to me on the spot, and I discovered afterwards that it was now generally accepted.

If, as is the common opinion, the Ascension had taken place on the summit upon which the mosque called after it is built, St. Luke could not have said it happened at Bethany or in its neighbourhood ; for *the Hill of the Ascension*, so called, is nearer Jerusalem than Bethany. That hamlet is situated, on the contrary, right at the foot of the hill of which I am

---

* St. Luke xix. 29.

† St. John xii., compared with St. Matt. xxi. 1, 2.

‡ St. Matt. xxi. 17, 19.

speaking, and which is still, to this day, called the hill of Bethany—*Djebel-el-Asarieh.*

Returning into the road, I sit down under the shade of a carob tree, at a few paces' distance from that sacred village where, in the ancient times, lived Martha and Mary and Lazarus. It was there that the Son of Man wept over the tomb of His friend; there He spent, in the midst of those whom He loved, the last Sabbath He celebrated on earth, before He returned to "*the glory which He had with the Father before the world was.*"*

I stop there for an hour or two, turning over the leaves of the Gospels, and reading, one after another, the histories of the sufferings of Jesus, of the raising of Lazarus, of the triumphal entry into Jerusalem, of the sayings of the Saviour with regard to Mary, "*She hath chosen that good part, which shall not be taken from her;*"† and "*wheresoever this Gospel shall be preached in the whole world, there shall also this that this woman hath done be told for a memorial of her.*" ‡ Sometimes my eyes rest upon the hamlet of Bethany, nestled in a recess of the hill, and as if sleeping at its foot ; sometimes they wander over the mountainous wilderness undulating before me. Far away on the horizon I can discern the Dead Sea, the Jordan, and the mountains of Moab, wrapped in a transparent mist, which veils and softens their outlines. Those are the regions "*on the other side Jordan,*" where Jesus was, during the illness of Lazarus. How many times must the anxious looks of Martha and Mary have turned in that direction, longing for the arrival of the Friend, the Physician, the Saviour, who should restore to them their brother !

* St. John. xvii. 5.   † St. Luke x. 42.   ‡ St. Matt. xxvi. 13.

The moments I passed under that carob tree—reading, praying, meditating—are among those blessed ones of which nothing can ever efface the impression. The memories of that day on which Jesus died for us, the sight of the places amongst which He so often wandered, concurred to make the Evangelic records live again in my mind. It seemed to me as if nothing here was changed; it was as if I saw, as in the Jewish legend, the glory of the Eternal arraying the Mount of Olives once more in its splendours.

The radiancy and serenity of the sky was unbroken, and the vast horizon which spread out before me had, in its grandeur and solemnity, something imposing,— I might call it august. Silence reigned around me, one felt one was near to the desert; no sound of voices or footsteps, no murmur of running water, no whispering of the wind amongst the leaves, or through the corn. Everything seemed to combine to do religious honour to the memories of that sacred day on which the covenant between God and man was sealed with the blood of the Saviour.

The perfect quiet was only broken at long intervals by the salutation of some little maiden returning into the village with her pitcher on her shoulder, crying *Marhaba !* When I rose to return, another came up to me, and offered me water, crying *Hadjï, Mâyi,* (Pilgrim ! some water !) How pleasant does this word *Mâyi* sound to me ! it is almost the same as the Hebrew. I often fancied I observed that the Arab dialect of Palestine is more like Hebrew than that spoken in Egypt. There are many words, particularly those used to describe the commonest things, which are still said here as in the days of David or of Josiah.

I return by the straightest path.   A woman, picking
up pistachio nuts in the field, brings me a fine branch
of them laden with fruit.   She has no basket, and I
notice the way in which she carries off her gleanings
between her frock and her bosom.   The country women
are dressed only in a simple frock, or rather shift, parti-
coloured for festive days, and of plain blue cloth for
work in the fields.   This cloth smock is also the
ordinary dress of the men in the country.   It is quite
open in front : if they have to carry grass or fruit, they
put it in their bosom ; the sash supports the load.
This explains that expression in the Gospels, taken,
like all the images used by Jesus in the Sermon on the
Mount, from the scenes of rural life,—" *Give, and it
shall be given to you, good measure, pressed down and
running over, shall men give into your bosom.*"*

I measure the distance, watch in hand, and find that
from Bethany, the village on the top of the mountain
(Bethphage ?) it is a twenty minutes' ascent.   From
the summit to the Gate of St. Stephen is a good quarter
of an hour.

At three o'clock I go to the wall of the Lamentations ; it is the day on which the Jews visit it in
great numbers to weep there.   In the long street, called
that of the Temple, I see a sad spectacle.   A sick woman
lay on a little bed in the middle of the street, and
held out her hand to ask alms of the passers by.   I
had never before, except in the Gospel story, come
across these portable beds laid out in the public streets.

The place to which the Jews have for so many
centuries resorted to weep over the ruins of their
Temple, is a street a few paces in breadth, having on
one side of it the wretched hovels of the Mogrebin

* St. Luke vi. 38.

quarter ; on the other, one of the walls of the Haram, a wall of great height, and built of enormous stones, like those of which I have already taken the measure, at the south-east corner of the city. A great number of Jews, men, women, and children—some in festive garb (as it is, for them, the Passover week), others in rags—are there, praying and weeping. Some are sitting on the ground, chanting in plaintive tones the Lamentations of Jeremiah, accompanying their song with that *rhythmical* swinging of the head from side to side usual with Jews when they read ; others stand up, pressing their cheeks against the wall of the Temple, and kissing the stones, and wetting them with their tears. I was drawn hither by mere curiosity; but the grief of these mourners is contagious, and I could not help weeping in sympathy with this fallen race, who, from the days of Abraham to those of Jesus, had been the high priests of humanity. One prays with them,—" *O God ! have mercy upon Sion ! For it is time that Thou have mercy upon her, yea, the time is come. And why ? Thy servants think upon her stones : and it pitieth them to see her in the dust.* "*

Yes,—and it is an impressive sight from another point of view also; especially in days like these. The blood of Jesus has been visited upon the heads of the children of those who demanded His death. It is the answer to their own imprecation upon themselves ! †
Strange fact ! In our day we see the Christians re⁻ joicing around the sepulchre of their crucified Master, and the Jews, who procured the death of Him whom they regarded as the enemy of their Temple, weeping over the ruins of that very Temple !

* Psalm cii. 15.   † St. Matt. xxvii. 25.

A little boy runs up to me, to ask for a baksheesh; he lays hold of the corner of my coat, and strokes my beard with his hand,—which we should not consider good manners, but in the East expresses the profoundest respect. I give him half a piastre ; instantly I find myself surrounded by a cloud of Mogrebin women, who, encouraged by this example, hope to share my liberality ; I gave away all the piastres and parahs I had in my pocket, in the hope of getting rid of them the sooner. But this expectation was too simple-minded ; their numbers kept continually increasing ; many Jews, leaving their prayers, joined the group gathered round me. In vain did I cry, *Ma fiche, ma fiche*, and shew by turning out my pockets, that I had nothing more to give ; their importunity did not flag. One of them made a sign that he would like my neckcloth ; another wanted my hat, a third my watch ; I was compelled to run—I might say to swim—away; no other word expresses the ceaseless struggle with hands and elbows, by which I succeeded in making my escape out of this hubbub.

I have already described what is meant by a baksheesh, and in what relation it stands to what we call alms ; to-day I was asked for one by a little girl, who wore, as a necklace, coins to the value of nearly two hundreds franks, all made up of Spanish talaris, shillings, and medjidiehs. To receive a baksheesh, far from being considered a humiliation, is rather an honour ; the recipient looks upon it as a compliment ; pride and cupidity, which among us often play each other such tricks, have come to a very good mutual understanding in this low region of life. Travellers often tell us with a certain complacency, that they have been entertained by this or that Arab émir.

That is an honour which it is not very difficult to obtain, for it is always a present which serves as a letter of introduction. This recommendation is not more absurd than many another. The larger or smaller amount of your baksheesh is taken as an indication at once of your position in the social scale, and of the degree of respect you feel to the person to whom you present yourself.

I pass behind the Mogrebin quarter. It is here that the Tyropœon is most clearly indicated ; for, between this quarter and the southern wall of the city, there are no houses, but only a forest of thorny fig-trees growing out of heaps of rubbish. Here also one observes in the wall of the Haram some antique layers composed of enormous stones ; I measured two, placed alongside of each other; one is seven métres twenty-five centimétres long, the other six métres, thirty-five centimétres. It may even be doubted whether these two stones did not originally form one ; in fact they seem only separated by a fissure ; and just there may be noticed in the wall the spring of an arch which, to all appearance, formed part of the bridge built over the Xystus to connect the Temple with Mount Sion, which is here very steep. The Xystus was a square open to the public in the Tyropœon, within the circuit of the first wall. It was, according to Josephus, used as a place for public assemblies, the forum or pnyx of Jerusalem.

I climb up again through these cactus plantations, from the Mogrebin gate to the Sion gate, and at a little distance from the latter I find some miserable hovels : it is in these, at some distance from the other houses, but still within the circuit of the walls, that lepers are lodged. The little huts of these unhappy beings are built against the walls, and make a sort of court. The lepers are not forbidden to walk about the town, and they like to go and sit near the gates to ask alms of the passers by.

I return into the middle of the town, passing through the Jewish streets ; the middle of the street is a deep morass in which one cannot set one's foot,—besides other filth, rags and sweepings of all kinds are thrown into it ; and on my way I come across a donkey and two horses far advanced in decomposition, exhaling a pestilential smell.

Passing near the Church of the Holy Sepulchre, I have the curiosity to enter it once more. I have already mentioned that, on the only side that is accessible, it has in front of its façade, a court. The two streets which lead up to this court end in very low gateways, through which one can only pass by stooping, which makes them the easier to guard.* Just now, on account of the great number of pilgrims, they are guarded by Turkish sentries; they search my clothes to see whether I do not carry arms ; for as quarrels often arise in the Church, it is in the interest of the public that they should not be too murderous.

* It is probable that these low, narrow gates were common in Palestine even from the earliest times. There is probably an allusion to them in the words of Jesus, "*Strive to enter in at the strait gate; for many, I say unto you, will seek to enter in, and shall not be able*" (St. Luke xiii. 24), and in the passage in the twenty-fourth Psalm, "*Lift up your heads, O ye gates, and be ye lift up, ye everlasting doors.*" It is not only the gates of houses and courts that are made so low, but often those of towns also. In entering Tiberias from the south, I could only pass through the town-gate by leaning down on the horse's neck. If the gates of Gaza were like those of Tiberias, the feat of Samson in carrying them off on his shoulders (Judges xvi. 3), though it would still, no doubt, have been remarkable, would not be at all inconceivable.

The court is filled with merchants sitting cross-legged on the pavement ; they sell candles, rosaries, bread, fruit, bracelets. These bracelets are made of terra cotta, and sell for ten parahs (five centimes), for the use of women who cannot afford to load their arms with coins ; as they are brittle, the demand for them is immense, and the dealers have them piled up before them in truly mountainous heaps.

On entering the Church, the first object one sees is the stone called that *of unction.* Many pilgrims are on their knees, devoutly kissing it ; near it, squatted on a stone seat, some Turkish officers are smoking their chibouques, and amusing themselves watching the stir which goes on around them ; the floor is covered with worshippers, squatting, lying on the ground, heaped one on another. They have arranged to spend the night in the Church. They talk, they walk about, they bestir themselves; some Turkish soldiers in great-coats, their guns rested on their feet, are drawn up in line, or walk about the Church, cane in hand, trying to keep some order in the crowd ; they strike at the pilgrims, and seize them by the collar to make them obey more quickly.

They march in single file before the chapel of the Holy Sepulchre. Its door is so low and narrow that we can only enter one by one, and stooping. Twice I am on the point of getting in, twice I find myself pushed back, either by men coming out or by others who wish to enter with me. I return after dinner; there are four sentinels at the door, and they take care not to allow more than a few at a time to come up to the door. I expect therefore to get in; but a great clamour arises round me. I see plainly enough that it refers to me, but I cannot make out its object. At last I catch the words, *"Le scarpe! Le scarpe!"* (his shoes!)

I observe that I am the only person who has not taken off his shoes, and I hasten to do so.

I enter a chapel called that of the *Angel;* then crawl, on all fours, into the sepulchral cave, in which there is only room for three or four persons. Its walls are lined with white marble. The actual tomb in which the body of Jesus was laid is a sort of long basin, about two feet in height; it is covered with a marble slab. Silver lamps are always burning in the cave. There is a picture, of the Spanish school, representing the resurrection of the Saviour, over the sarcophagus. In such a place, a picture, far from aiding the imagination, offends and irritates it, limiting its flights.

The different parts of the Church are to-night· splendidly illumined with many-coloured lamps. I ascend Calvary; there also is a great crowd, lying or sitting on the ground. They all in turn kiss the hole in which the Saviour's cross stood, after having three times prostrated themselves, touching the ground with their foreheads, and making the sign of the cross an infinite number of times.

On going out of the church, I see a great number of people, every one carrying in his hand a little wax taper. A Greek procession is coming out of the convent. The people rush to kiss a copy of the Gospel brought by a priest.

There is something in all this, resist the feeling as one may, that offends one much; these Turkish soldiers set to keep order in the Church, like police at a public dance,—the enmities, the quarrels, the displays of superstition, the idolatries seen by Mahometans in Christians, all this is sad! And yet, it is not to be denied, if there is a lack of enlightenment in these festivities, true life is not altogether wanting in them. It will be said, perhaps, that the only object these people have in making this pilgrimage is to do a meritorious act, and that they do it therefore from a dry sense of duty, and on calculation. No! I do not think an act of duty, felt to be merely legal and compulsory, can be done with so much *empressement* and vivacity. Self-interest—even if misguided—is not so passionate; there is here an element of life and of love. And, besides, it is not fair to compare these festivities with the small and infrequent gatherings of the enlightened Christians of the West. What we see here before us is not a Council, nor a meeting of the Evangelical Alliance,—it is a popular festivity. All these pilgrims are "men of the people." They are mostly Syrian Christians : they bring hither their rags and their ignorance ; they come once a year to make a profession of the Christianity which they have retained, faithfully, if not in its purity, in the midst of the Mahometan populations and during twelve centuries of servitude. One can see by their expression and their whole bearing, that to them it is a great feast :—a tumultuous feast, I allow ; but what popular feast is not so ? Is there ever one in France in which the presence of soldiers, and the aid of the police are not as much needed ? But here, unenlightened and rude as these people are, and noisy as this popular festivity is, there is in it something much nobler than in most of ours ; it does not consist of eating and drinking, dancing and playing. Listening to canticles, looking on at the illuminations of a church, kneeling in the places in which Christ died and was buried,— these are the acts which inspire all this multitude of

14

human beings with such joyous feeling and so genuine an enthusiasm. Perhaps they entertain very false ideas respecting Christ ; at any rate they worship in Him something higher than Earth. Quite recently, people were admiring the *empressement* shewn by the Parisian populace at the funeral of a poet;* they believed they saw in this homage evidence of a noble aspiration rising superior to the coarse instincts of mere bodily life. . . . We should learn to admire, and respect also, as they deserve, these poor Christians of the East, who so joyfully assemble around the tomb of Jesus Christ.

Imagine for an instant what it would be if the light broke in, and the Spirit of Truth irradiated these races, —nothing then would be a fairer sight than these pilgrimages. Christendom will hold its feast in Jerusalem, as the Israelites used to hold theirs ; all the churches will come, no longer to quarrel with each other, but to shake hands and give each other the kiss of brotherly love in the places in which Christ taught us by His Death what Love is.

Holy Saturday.

This day, during which Jesus rested in the tomb, the Church of the Holy Sepulchre is the scene of a most curious spectacle. Every one has heard of the *sacred fire;* every year, on Easter Eve, the fire of Heaven descends upon the Holy Sepulchre, in answer to the prayer of a Greek Bishop, who for that reason is called the *Fire Bishop.* He enters the Chapel of the Holy Sepulchre with some extinguished tapers, and a moment after he presents them to the people all lighted, through two round holes that have been made on purpose in the wall of the Chapel. These are the facts : there is no need

* That of Béranger, in July, 1857.

even of conjuring to effect this miracle ; the credulity of the people is enough.

The Armenians and the Greeks both believe it, and contend for the honour of lighting their tapers at this sacred fire. Accordingly an opening has been made on each side of the chapel ; the fire issues on the left for the *Monophysites*, on the right for the *orthodox*. Many of the priests blush at this custom, and regret its existence ; " But," say they, "it is now a necessity ; if we were to put a stop to it, the people would think we had been hitherto imposing upon them !" Others quiet their consciences by saying to themselves that they do not pretend it is a miracle ; if the people take it for one, so much the worse for them. Nevertheless a Greek priest was mentioned and pointed out to me, who refused the office of Bishop of Jerusalem to avoid taking part in this odious farce.

But the laity of the orthodox Church do not at all doubt the miracle. M. de Lukieff, my old Cairo travelling companion, even used it as an argument in favour of his religion.

" It is, at any rate," he used to say to me, "a fact that deserves consideration, that the sacred fire descends at the bidding of a Greek, and not of a Latin priest !"

The Latins are not of that opinion. They do not dispute the miracle on principle ; for during some time they worked it themselves ; but they say now that it is no more than the counterfeit of a miracle, and a sacrilegious imposture.

" It is infamous !" said l'Abbé R. to me.

I wished to witness this ceremony ; but it is not easy to do so ;—the crowd and press is unequalled. One has to stand in line for whole hours, and to use one's fist vigorously. I had no fancy for such an undertaking, and I preferred at all hazards to wait till noon. I purposed attaching myself to the Latin pilgrims who lodged with the Franciscans; but they had started long before for the Church. I went therefore alone with Hhannah.

As I enter the Chapel I am asked to what religion I belong,—*Turco?*—*Greco?*—*Armenico?*—for all visitors are classified according to their different religions, to prevent quarrels.

" *Frandji,*" my guide answers for me.

They direct us to the right, towards a flight of steps leading up to a platform appropriated to spectators. For this ceremony the Franks and all the Latins take their place among mere spectators, as do also the English and the Turks. We make our way, not without difficulty, through a dense crowd, and reach the bottom of the steps. But the door is shut. Hhannah knocks with great blows of his fist, crying—

" *Fra Giacomo! Fra Giacomo!*"

At last the door opens slightly, and a Franciscan shews the tip of his moustache through the opening.

" *Ecco un signore,*" says John.

" *Un milore?* " asks the monk.

" *Frandji,*" again answers my guide.

And the officer lets me pass.

The Church of the Holy Sepulchre is a little world in itself; besides the multitude of chapels of which it is made up, it contains numerous apartments for the Coptic, Latin, Greek, and Armenian monks employed in guarding and taking care of it; the Francisans, who here represent Catholicism, consist only of a dozen men; and they are changed every three months, for it is a damp and unhealthy place to live in.

After climbing many flights of steps, I arrive at a

little ante-chamber, in which many monks are taking
their modest repast. Here is another closed door ; we
are told we cannot be allowed to pass further. It is
discouraging. Happily I catch sight, in the crowd of
monks, of the excellent Abbé Pascal : he is the French
Missionary who was my companion on board the *Céphise*.
He is making a three days' *retreat* among the guardians
of the Holy Sepulchre ; he has the key of the platform,
and agrees to take me with him.

We find our way into a vast gallery, half-way up
to the roof, in which, between large columns, are
balconies commanding a view of the interior. The
difficulty is to reach these balconies ; they are already
occupied, and it is only by standing on tiptoe that I
succeed in seeing anything. The Church, as I have
already said, is in the style of the Pantheon, but of
different proportions ; it seems to me higher relatively
to its breadth. The gallery in which I find myself is
reserved for spectators—*Frandji*, or *Milori;* below are
two stories of galleries occupied by Greek and Armenian
women ; a very wise precaution ; for they would be
crushed to death in the crowd, if they stayed on the
ground floor.

The women in their galleries, the men in the body
of the Church, are all provided with a bundle of small
tapers, wherewith to carry off the sacred fire. Everywhere the crowd is dense. Round the Holy Sepulchre
one might call it a stormy sea, of which the waves
come and beat upon the walls of the Chapel. All arms
are stretched out with frenzied eagerness to the openings
through which the sacred fire is to come forth ; they
shove, they knock each other down, to get as near
as possible to the Heaven-blest spot, and light their
tapers with the sacred fire the first moment it appears,

and at first hand. The soldiers with smart blows of their sticks manage to control, to a certain degree, this tumultuous herd of wild creatures. Murmurs, shouts, resound through the place ; a fetid smell pervades it. Listening to these vociferations, looking down from above upon all these red caps, upon all these ragged creatures, and their outstretched arms, one fancies one-self taking part in an insurrection, or in one of the days of blood of 1789 or 1792. One would think the Holy Sepulchre was about to be taken by storm, like the Bastille.

. Above us there are more people,—in the windows, into which one climbs by the terraces of the convents, or, higher still, in the balconies of the cupola. This cupola is half ruined,—knocked into holes for want of looking after,—and leaves the Church exposed to the attacks of the weather. The Greeks and Latins have together collected between them more money than would be wanted to put it in repair, but they quarrel with each other for the right to do the work. The Church suffers in consequence, and it would fall into ruins if the Sultan who does not choose to allow so valuable a source of income to be further injured had not decided to have it put into repair at his own expense, and in his name.*

Upon the platform on which I am standing are two French pilgrims, a Spanish priest, two *Milori*, an Aus-

* It seems, however, that nothing has yet been done in this work. A correspondence in the *Augsburg Gazette*, of June, 1860, makes mention of a considerable number of new buildings erected in Jerusalem of late, and adds : "While so much building in different ways is going on in Jerusalem, nothing has yet been done to the cupola of the Holy Sepulchre damaged ten years ago. The Christians cannot be brought to an understanding about it. I believe it is very nearly falling to the ground."

trian count, with whom I made acquaintance on board the *Imperatore*, and a young German prince. These gentlemen have been here since break of day, and begin to feel faint. A Franciscan takes pity on them, and goes to fetch them bread and fish, and vinegar and water in large brass pots. This vinegar is the wine most used by the Franciscans of the Holy Land. It is the custom, in this country, to let the wine turn sour. I do not think this is from mere carelessness; no doubt it is found to be more refreshing in that state. Accordingly, if the drink that was offered to Jesus before He was crucified is called by St. Mark *wine*,* and by St. Matthew *vinegar*,† there is no inconsistency.‡

Meantime we see janissaries coming up to us, who call upon us to withdraw, as the place we occupy is reserved for the pacha. We obey, but with regret So, then, I shall have to push about with the crowd in the outer edges of this gallery, with no chance of getting near the balcony, and see nothing but the backs of the spectators. But what is to be done? I only move off to a few steps' distance, and as soon as the pacha's attendants have spread carpets and cushions enough upon the platform to make a comfortable place for him, I return, provisionally, to the place I had just vacated. Soon the pacha enters. A chant is heard. The pacha comes up to the divan prepared for him. I hastily jump off the platform; but with a very gracious gesture he motions me to take the place by his side. One of

* St. Mark xv. 23.
† St. Matt. xxvii. 34.
‡ It was in contrast with this *sour* and refreshing wine, that all wines not turned sour, and therefore intoxicating, were called *sweet wines* (Acts ii. 13). These were the wines for feasts : "*Eat the fat, and drink the sweet, for this day is holy to the Lord*," said Nehemiah (Neh. viii. 10).

his attendants holds out his hand to me to help me up again, and I find myself once more seated on the official divan, by the side of the representative of the Porte.

The pacha is a fine-looking young man, dressed in European fashion, or rather in the style now adopted at Constantinople ; he wears a black overcoat and coloured neckcloth ; his beard, cut very short, his fault-less waistcoat, and kid gloves, give him the look of a "lion" of the western world. His dress and his manner altogether are the perfection of grace and refinement.

No sooner is he comfortably settled, than the miracle at once takes place. A man, standing near the Chapel, in front of the mysterious aperture, inserts his taper into it, and draws it out lighted ! The cries which then break forth, the frantic eagerness of all the attendants to distribute the sacred fire, are wonderful. Some of them, more ambitious than the rest, are set upon light-ing their tapers also directly from that which burns in the interior of the sepulchre, but the rush of the crowd makes it impossible for them to stop for an instant.

The fire is distributed rapidly; every one, except the Turks and Europeans who occupy our platform, holds in his hand his bundle of tapers. In a few moments the Church is illuminated up to the roof; the Chapel of the Holy Sepulchre sparkles with the light of the tapers with which it is filled. Loud shouts of joy resound, from all the chapels, fragrant incense surrounds and veils with a sort of mist all the details of the scene. It is really a fine sight.

After taking a glance at the scene, the pacha, who has only been present for ten minutes, retires with his suite, smiling with much benevolence and dignity. I stay where I am for a long time. A Greek procession forms: some standard-bearers, some priests, with gilded mitres and cloaks richly embroidered, march round the Holy Sepulchre, chanting full-throated chants.

It is difficult to conceive a more frightful act of sacrilege than that committed by this Greek Bishop, who pretends to call down fire from Heaven into the Holy Sepulchre. The sacredness of the places he asso‑ ciates with this act makes the sacrilege still more horrible. He realizes what is said of the Beast in the Apocalypse.* Whilst he was in the Chapel, going through this frightful farce, I trembled at the thought that the real fire of Heaven might fall upon him in vindication of the glory which belongs to God only.

Leaving out of sight the crime committed by the priests in making that into a pretended miracle which originally, no doubt, was meant only as a symbolical act, this ceremonial seems to me very full of beauty. If it is tumultuous, that is partly because these people are almost on the level of savages, and still more from the vast mass of human beings crowded into one place. But if the noise and tumult are inevitable, I do not feel them scandalous. What are these vast buildings for, if not to hold these multitudes, and to provide a covered space the walls of which will not be burst asunder by their loud shouts of joy ? How beautiful a symbol is this fire to represent life issuing as in a moment from the Sepulchre of Jesus Christ, and this instantaneous illumination, in the production of which all take part, to celebrate the Resurrection of the Saviour !

Here again, as in so many analogous cases, there is nothing to find fault with in the form the thing has taken. Did but the spirit of truth take possession of it, that would become admirable, which now repels

* Rev. xiii. 13.

and justly pains us as a proof of the credulity of some, and the imposture practised by others.

EASTER.

To-night the various Christian communions have together celebrated the Resurrection in the Church of the Holy Sepulchre. I repeat, it is a striking testimony this, of all these Churches rivals or enemies to each other agreeing in recognizing in this great event the eternal foundation on which their faith rests, and thus, in spite of themselves and of their mutually exclusive principles, doing homage to the unity and universality of the Church.

I have to-day attended the various religious services of the Protestant Church, and spent the day with the Anglican Bishop, M. Gobat. M. Gobat and his family upon whom I called as soon as I arrived here received me with the greatest cordiality, as a friend and fellow-countryman.

The establishment of a Protestant Church at Jerusalem is a very recent event. This Church owes its origin essentially to the missionary spirit of our age, and especially to the interest felt in the Jews. There was a wish to make them some return for the blessings which had been received from them, to preach the Gospel to them in the very place from which, by their means, it disseminated itself over the whole earth. From 1820 to 1840, bodies of English and American missionaries were periodically seen arriving to settle in Jerusalem, to labour at the work of converting the Israelites who come there in such large numbers from all parts of the world. These attempts had had but small success; for the resistance offered by Judaism to influences from without is stronger in Jerusalem, than anywhere else, as if it had gathered new strength at the touch of its native soil. This is, however, a fact which it is easy to account for : the Israelites who come to Jerusalem are the devoutest, those most attached to the traditions of their fathers ; they are the Zealots of our times.

The Protestant missionaries in Jerusalem were few in number, isolated and with no influential friends to support them ; at first they placed themselves under the protection of the Greeks, who for some time shewed them great benevolence, but ended in distrusting and endeavouring to counterwork them.

The year 1840, a great epoch in the history of Palestine in general, is also a great turning-point in that of the Protestant Church in Jerusalem. Austria and England had just done the Turks a signal service in replacing Syria under their power. Never had the European powers been on better terms with the Ottoman Porte. The new king of Prussia, Frederick William the Fourth, thought this state of things ought to be made use of to secure for the Protestants of the Turkish Empire protection and guarantees which they had not as yet obtained. To this he drew the attention of the British Government and the Anglican Episcopate. It was determined to found at Jerusalem an Anglo-Prussian Bishopric, which served as a central point for all the Oriental Protestants, and which carried on amongst the Jews of Palestine the missionary work which had been begun.

The Protestant Bishop of Jerusalem is nominated alternately by England and Prussia; but the Archbishop of Canterbury has the right of a veto.

The first Bishop was nominated by England in 1841; he was a converted Jew of Prussian origin,—Doctor

Alexander.   He died in four years' time, and Prussia
proposed as his successor a Swiss of the Bernese
Jura, M. Samuel Gobat, well known for his mission in
Abyssinia.   M. Gobat has been in Jerusalem since the
year 1846.   No one could have been better fitted than
he for this important post.   He has passed the greater
part of his life in the East, he thoroughly understands
the character and the customs of the Arabs ; and their
language is as familiar to him as his native tongue.
And accordingly he does not inspire Orientals with that
feeling of distrust which one feels instinctively towards
a man belonging to a different race and a different
civilization.   The Abyssinians have placed under his
direction the convent which they maintain at Jerusalem,
and the school of Theology which is attached to it.
M. Gobat has already been able to render great services
to these institutions, which up to that time had been an
object of attack to other Churches, richer, with more
members, and better supported, than their own.

The long absence of M. Gobat from Europe also
tends, together with his living faith and his great
breadth of mind, to raise him above the petty disputes
which divide the Protestants from each other.   In
relation to the different elements of which the Evangelical Church in Jerusalem is composed, he possesses
all the characteristics which could be desired as guarantees for his neutrality.   Born a Swiss, and of the
Reformed Church, he cannot be suspected of partiality
towards either the Episcopalians, the Lutherans, the
Germans, or the English.   The character of M. Gobat,
and his well-known merits, procure him a degree of
respect and of influence far higher than could belong
to him merely as a Bishop.   If he is officially head
only of the Anglo-Prussian Church, he is in reality, and

by the common consent of all, the patron of all the Protestant communities in Jerusalem.

There are indeed here some religious bodies, which are not officially connected with the Bishopric, as for instance, the German Hospital, distinct from the English Hospital, and attended by the Kaiserswerth deaconesses, and an Arab Church, founded by the English Episcopal Church, and which employs itself exclusively with the evangelisation of the Arabs, whilst the Anglo-Prussian Mission has limited its field of work to the Israelites.

I this morning attended their service. It takes place in a large room in the School-House. M. Klein, of Strasburg, preaches there in Arabic ; there were present some five-and-twenty men, in the costume of the country, and three or four women in full dress with wide cherry-coloured pantaloons and blue vests embroidered with gold.

After the sermon and prayers were finished, the whole assembly repaired to Christ Church, to receive the Holy Communion with the English congregation. It is with this united service that they celebrate Easter.

Christ Church—so they call the Protestant Church—is built upon Mount Sion, in the Armenian quarter. The foundations were first laid in 1841, but the inauguration did not take place till the beginning of 1849.

This church is not large, but it is handsome,—I mean well built ; for I cannot help feeling that this architecture, which may be called a sort of commonplace Gothic, these great ogees, these ceilings of polished walnut wood, are strangely out of harmony with Jerusalem and the East. This walnut wood was brought from England at a great cost, as well as the slates with which the roof is covered. We have often been, not unjustly, criticised for our misuse in our northern climates of classic Architecture ; but this intrusion of our northern styles under the blue skies of Palestine offends good taste still more cruelly.   It is a refinement of Vandalism, of which civilised men alone could be guilty.

The work of the Protestant Churches in Jerusalem is a work of *faith* in the strictest sense of the word. The mission to the Jews has already, it is true, borne some fruit, but very much less than one could wish. One has to learn to "cast one's bread upon the waters," to sow seed for others · to reap, and to wait without murmuring or impatience for the time when the Spirit of God will breathe upon these dry bones.

EASTER MONDAY.

The weather is cloudy.   There is a cold wind from the west.   One looks out from day to day for "the latter rains," * which generally come in at the end of March or beginning of April.   These rains are not heavy, but they are necessary, for they come at the time when the wheat begins to sprout.   M. Gobat has not hitherto known them fail.   The early rains come in November; they are indispensable for the sowing ; if they fail, as M. Gobat tells me he has sometimes seen happen, it becomes impossible to sow, and there is a year of scarcity.   These rains seem to come now at the same seasons as they did in the Bible times, but they are no doubt less heavy than then, on account of the smaller number of trees now.   The winter rains (in January and February) are of no importance for the vegetation.

I had thought of going, the first opportunity, to Hebron, but I was told last night I must not think of it.

* Deut. xi. 14 ; Jer. iii. 3 ; St. James v. 7, *et passim.*

The Bedouins are making war there. At this moment, new troubles are reported in many directions. Two *moukres* have been killed this morning on the Jaffa road. These disturbances are not unexpected events ; they take place regularly in spring. It is like what one reads of France, in the time of Bertrand de Born ; * when the meadows are in flower, the knights take the field.

"Much do I love sweet Easter-tide, bringing with it its green leaves, and its flowers. I love to see the tents and banners enlivening the plains. And I am greatly delighted when I see armed knights and horses decorating the landscape with their ordered ranks."

So it was in the days of David : "*It came to pass at the return of the year,* (margin) *at the time when kings go forth to battle.*"†

I go out with Hhannah, to make once more the circuit of the city. Passing near the Church of the Holy Sepulchre, I wish to ascend to the terrace of the Church of the Abyssinians, which is close by. This terrace is on the same level with the Calvary, and above the cave of the *Invention of the Cross,* the cupola of which it surrounds. It is crowned with shabby little houses constituting the Abyssinian convent, which is very poor, and is supported by the Armenian convent. A few negro pilgrims are still there.

The Abyssinians call their convent that of *the Angel;* it is here, they say, that the angel appeared to Abraham, to prevent his sacrificing his son. The Greeks, on the other hand, affirm that this apparition took place on the other side of the Church of the Holy Sepulchre, where their convent stands ; "and," says Hhannah, "it is not known which is right."

Descending from there, we enter by the street of the

* A famous troubadour of the twelfth century. † 2 Sam. xi. 1.

Patriarch, into the ruins of the Hospice of the Knights of St. John. Their *débris* have been made into a heap, and the site now forms a grassy terrace, with a palm-tree standing in the middle of it. The panorama seen from this point is magnificent; this is the point from which to take a view of Jerusalem. It seems to me nearly certain that these *débris* did but enlarge and heighten a natural hillock which stood in a line with Golgotha. Or perhaps, even, these two hills may have originally formed but one, and only came to be separated from each other by the building of the Church of the Holy Sepulchre.

We go out of the town by the Gate of Damascus. The wind drives clouds before it which are rapidly crossing the sky at a little distance over our heads : this again is one of those little indications which remind us that we are in a mountain district.

We turn to the right to see the excavations which exist under Jerusalem, and out of which, to all appearance, have been drawn the stones used in the construction of the town, and especially of the Temple. These catacombs are seldom visited, and most travellers do not mention them. The entrance into them, which is at the foot of the wall of the town, is very low, and is blocked up with putrid remains of offal left from some butchering done here ; for it is here that they now slaughter the sheep and the goats; the oxen are never slaughtered ; only those that die natural deaths are eaten. This place of slaughter used formerly to be within the town itself; at the suggestion of the consuls, it was transferred to its present site for sanitary reasons. We light our tapers. After descending a few steps, the catacomb becomes wide and lofty: it is supposed to extend under half the town. Near the bottom one finds here and there some enormous blocks of stone ready hewn, like those to be seen in the ancient foundations of the wall at the south-east angle of the town. They lie there ready for use ; one might fancy that the chisels of Hiram's workmen had just finished them, and they were about to be carried to the places assigned them. But there, for three thousand years, they have lain sleeping in their gloomy resting-place. And how many times during that long period has the town overhead fallen into ruins! how many times has it risen again, and no echo of its glories and disasters reached the place of their repose !

The sight of these blocks ready hewn in the depths of these catacombs interprets to me a curious passage in the First Book of Kings ; for it is there said that *" the house, when it was in building, was built of stone made ready before it was brought thither : so that there was neither hammer nor axe nor any tool of iron heard in the house, while it was in building."**

Further to the east, in the side of a little hill facing the walls of the town, is a fine cavern, with a wide entrance, which bears the name of Jeremiah. I mentioned it before, when speaking of another excursion. To-day I inspected it. In front it is shut in with a wall. We knock at a back door ; a young man comes and half opens it, but will not let us pass till he has agreed with Hhannah on the baksheesh we are to give him. We see coming up to us the Dervish who lives here ; in one hand he holds his long stick, in the other his long pipe. In one corner of the cave is his whole family, seated on mats ; in another his horse, ready saddled (as is the custom), his donkey, his fowls and pigeons. It is a fine and spacious dwelling. This

* 1 Kings vi. 7.

15

troglodyte-like interior has its charm; it is a realization of the peaceable family life which La Fontaine
attributes with so much *bonhommie* of spirit to his rustic
divinities:—

"Dans un antre solitaire,
Un satyre *et ses enfants !*"*

The Dervish shews me the great cistern in which
Jeremiah was shut up; but we cannot now go down
into it,—it has water in it.   The legend of this cave
and cistern being the scene of Jeremiah's imprisonment †
was, no doubt, suggested by their proximity to the
Gate of Benjamin ; for we know it was in the neighbourhood of a gate called Benjamin's, through which
one passed on the way to that tribe's territory, that
the prophet was arrested by the captain Irijah.‡   Had
I not had what appeared to me good reasons for
accepting the tradition with regard to the site of
Golgotha, and had I been willing to plunge into con-
jectures, I should have been inclined to have placed
it on this spot, which seems to fit all the required
conditions so well.   The hill called that of Jeremiah
was, in the time of Jesus, as it is to this day, near the
city, and outside it ; it contains sepulchral caves, and
is surrounded with gardens ; and lastly, supposing that
Golgotha was so called on account of its configuration,
the name would perfectly fit the rock of which I am
speaking, which has very much the appearance of a
skull.

On closely examining this rock, it is clear that it was
originally only the northern extremity of a hill (pro-

* "In a solitary cavern, a satyr *and his children.*"
† Jer. xxxviii. 6.
‡ Jer. xxxvii. 13, 14.

bably *Bezetha*), of which the southern part is now comprehended within the limits of the city, and in which a large trench has been dug for the wall and the ditch.

Coming down from thence to Gethsemane, we ascend the southern summit of the Mount of Olives, in order to inspect the sepulchral cave known by the name of *the tomb of the prophets.* It is an underground cavern divided into many compartments ; in its sides have been worked niches, in which bodies used to be deposited. Here the niches are perpendicular to the wall, and look like ovens ; this arrangement has the effect of economising space, and allows of a considerable number of bodies being buried in the same cave. In many other ancient burying places the niches are parallel with the walls ; so it is, for instance, with the Holy Sepulchre.

I find here no trace of sculpture or of masonry inside or outside; whatever may be the origin of the name given in our day to this sepulchre, it is not to it that the words of Jesus apply, "*Ye build the tombs of the prophets, and garnish the sepulchres of the righteous.*" * I have said elsewhere that these words were probably spoken with reference to the tomb of Zechariah, and to the other similar monuments which lie beneath us in the valley.

It is towards these monuments that we are now descending. That of Absalom is the largest and the most curious. It is surrounded with a heap of small stones which conceal its base from view; for still, to this day, every Jew and every Mahometan who passes by, throws a pebble at this monument, repeating the Biblical malediction, "*Cursed is he that setteth light by his father or his mother!*" †

* St. Matt. xxiii. 29.   † Deut. xxvii. 16.

So has Absalom, who so much feared lest his memory should perish with him, succeeded in keeping it alive,—a malediction ceaselessly repeated has preserved his name for this cenotaph ; and this imperishable monument secures for its builder an immortality of anathema.

By the help of breaches which have been made in its walls one manages, though with difficulty, to effect an entrance into the interior of the mausoleum ; there also the ground is covered with stones thrown into it by passers by. I have spoken before of the cone which crowns it ; it is possible to climb into its interior, like a sweep into a chimney. While I am trying to do so, I hear a noise above me. I raise my eyes, and find myself face to face with a jackal. He looks at me with some terror, and wishes to get away. I have time to examine him leisurely; his head and his yellow coat make him very like the dogs of this part of the world, but he has a thicker neck : his tail is very fine, and like that of a fox. This is the animal so often mentioned in Scripture * as the denizen of desolate places. But I should not have suspected that he would have chosen the very gates of Jerusalem for his dwelling.

We are at about the level of Siloam ; I put a few questions to Hhannah respecting this village ; he tells me, in answer, that it is a place inhabited by Mahometans, and that he has never been there. This gives us an idea of what life is in the East,—of the lack of

---

* The word jackal does not, it is true, occur in our versions ; but it is generally agreed that this is the animal known in the Bible by the name of א (Isa. xiii. 22, xxxiv. 14 ; Jer. l. 39), and perhaps also under those of ןי (Job xxx. 29 ; Micah i. 8), and of לעוש (Judges xv. 4 ; Psalm lxiii. 11).

curiosity in Arabs, and the insurmountable barriers which religious differences establish between them. To have been born in the little town of Jerusalem, to have spent five-and-twenty years there, and yet never to have felt moved to enter the only village in the suburbs, at a gunshot's distance from the walls—strange!

I, then, shall have to do the honours of Siloam to Hhannah. At the top of the village are tombs now half buried in the ground, but of which the edges may still be seen, decorated with sculptures; one may notice, too, remains of terraces and of steps cut in the rock. It was here, perhaps, that the tower stood which fell in the lifetime of Jesus;* at any rate, this would have been a well-chosen site for a fortress intended to defend the town, and especially the Temple, for it is just over against the south-east corner of the Haram.

Siloam has retained to this day, almost unaltered, the name which it bears in the New Testament, (*Silouân* in Arabic,—in the Gospels *Siloam*).† It is very beautiful, seen from without, but on a near view, one of the poorest villages one can imagine. The houses are built against the rock, or rather they are nothing more than natural caverns or ancient sepulchres, cut in the sides of the mountain, and into which the entrance was imperfectly closed by a few scraps of wall. Some tombs serve as ovens, others as sheepcotes.

Thus there are, as far as I was able to judge, three rows of houses built one above the other, like the steps of an amphitheatre; the roofs of the lower rows forming

---

* St. Luke xiii. 4.

† It would seem that the termination of this name underwent slight changes between the days of Nehemiah and of Jesus. St. John and St. Luke both of them write it *Siloam*, whilst in the Old Testament one reads *Shélakh*, *Shiloackh*.

a street for the houses of the higher. Villages of this sort are not uncommon, I am told, in Judæa, where it is desired to utilise the caverns which exist there in such numbers. When you have seen one of these, you can understand more easily these words of our Lord : *" Let them which be in Judæa flee into the mountains, and let him which is on the housetop not come down to take anything out of his house."* * For here it is the fact that in order to flee into the mountains it is not necessary to come down from the housetop.

The foot of Mount Moriah, opposite Siloam, is covered with kitchen gardens, arranged in terraces, on which are planted pomegranates, artichokes, and other vegetables. These are the ancient *gardens of the king;* they have the freshest verdure of any I have yet seen in Palestine. They owe this to the waters of the reservoir of Siloam which is above them, and by means of which they are irrigated. The spring, properly so called, is a little higher up the valley, still nearer to the village, and is now called *the Fountain of the Virgin.* It communicates by a subterranean conduit with the fountain of Siloam.

The latter *"flows softly"* † in a cave at one end of the Tyropœon, into which one descends by steps ; in front of the cave is the reservoir to which Jesus sent the man born blind.‡ We find there a woman drawing water. I have tasted this water, which did not strike me as very cold, nor did I perceive in it the slightly salt taste which many travellers attribute to it.

This double fountain of Siloam, springing out of the

---

* St. Matt. xxiv. 16, 17, comp. v. 3.   Jesus was upon the Mount of Olives, and had at His feet the village of Siloam, when He spoke these words (see v. 3).

† Isa. viii. 6.   ‡ St. John ix. 7.

very rock on which the House of God was built, was to the Israelites a symbol of the spiritual life, and it is often alluded to in Scripture. Ezekiel, in his magnificent visions of the kingdom of God, sees these waters become a great river, spreading fertility on its banks, and restoring life to the accursed waters of the Dead Sea. "*Everything that liveth, whithersoever the rivers shall come, shall live. . . . And by the river, upon the bank thereof, on this side and on that side, shall grow all trees for meat, whose leaf shall not fade, neither shall the fruit thereof be consumed, . . . because their waters, they issued out of the sanctuary.*" *

The valley of Hinnom, or of Gehenna, into which we come, is narrow, like that of Kedron, and has rather the configuration of a *combe;* it does not seem ever to have formed the bed of a torrent, and from being planted with olive trees, it has not the repulsive aspect which one might have expected. It was in consequence only of its historic associations that among the Jews of the times of Jesus the name Gehenna had come to signify hell. In that delirium of idolatry which had seized the Jews in the age of Isaiah and Jeremiah, they had erected altars there to Baal and Moloch ; they made their sons and daughters pass through the fire to the honour of this latter deity, and we know from the books of Chronicles that the kings Ahaz and Manasseh themselves set the example of practising these abominations. The pious Josiah made an attempt to put a stop to these crimes by desecrating the valley of Hinnom ; that is to say, by making it a charnel house, or at least a burying place. No doubt the Jews kicked against the decrees of Josiah, and attempted to preserve for this place its sacred character; but the

* Ezek. xlvii. 9, 12 ; comp. Zech. xiv. 8.

days came when, willingly or unwillingly, they had
to bury their dead in the valley of Hinnom, because
there was "*no place*" elsewhere ; for the dead bodies
of this rebellious people covered the ground,—food
for the beasts of the field and the fowls of the air.*
One can understand how it happened that all these
memories of death and idolatry, of crime and punishment, made of this place a symbol of the torments of hell.
Christian tradition or legend—it is difficult to say
which—assigns to the sides of this valley another spot
of sinister memory,—*Aceldama*, or the *Field of Blood*,
which, bought from a potter with the money paid to
Judas for his treachery, thenceforth was made the place
to bury strangers in.†

This *Field of Blood*, still called by the Arabs *Hakel*,
(the field), or *Hakel Forar* (the potter's field), is on the
top of a rock which overhangs the lower part of the
valley.   This commands a fine view of the town and of
the Mount of Olives, and the field itself is planted with
trees which make it a very pretty spot.   Hhannah
tells me that it is usual for the Catholics in Jerusalem
to come and spend the Day of Pentecost here with their
families ; they bring their provisions with them, sit
under the shade of the olive-trees, and do their cooking
in some of the numerous sepulchres which have been
cut out of the rock all round the field.

One of these sepulchres, much larger than the rest,
and vaulted with masonry, has, it is said, for a long
time served the purpose of what we call the *fosse
commune*, where the bodies of the pilgrims who died at
Jerusalem, leaving no money to pay the expenses of
their burial, were thrown.   It is this receptacle particularly which is now called *Aceldama*.

* Jer. vii. 30—33.   † St. Matt. xxvii. 8 ; Acts i. 19.

Has the custom of burying strangers here existed since the time of the Apostles ? or was this *fosse commune* made in this place in order to justify the name *Aceldama*, which, it was thought, there was reason for giving to this field ? Men will, no doubt, answer this question according to the prejudices, favourable or unfavourable, which they may entertain with regard to the tradition.

There is, at any rate, nothing incredible in the belief that this place is the original Aceldama. It contains clay for making pots, and we know that, in the time of Jeremiah, the gate by which one went out of Jerusalem towards the valley of Hinnom, bore the name of " *the pottery gate.*" *

Leaving on one side the upper part of the valley, in which are still to be seen two fine fish-ponds, we climb the sides of Mount Sion, which are here very steep. On this side of Jerusalem is its only suburb, if one may so call three solitary buildings, not comprehended within the circuit of the walls, which have endeavoured to make up for this disadvantage by fortifying themselves as strongly as possible.

Of these three buildings, one, at only a few steps' distance from the gate of Sion, is an Armenian convent, built upon the legendary site of the house of Caiaphas. The second, close by, is the celebrated Mosque of David, which contains, it is said, the tomb of the prophet king. Entrance into this tomb is as strictly forbidden to unbelievers as into the *Haram*, but they are allowed

* *Porta fictilis* (Jer. xix. 2). Such is the sense of the expression, according to the Rabbis and the Vulgate. The French (and English) versions render it erroneously, "*the east gate.*" According to the Targum of Jonathan, this *pottery gate* would be the same as the *dung gate.*

to visit the so-called *supper chamber* over it.   The choice of this spot by the monks, as that to which to attach the memory of the supper-room, is an instance of the method of induction most commonly used by them in similar cases.   As St. Peter said to the Jews, " *The sepulchre of the patriarch David is in the midst of us (apud nos) to this day*,"* they thought they might conclude, by pressing the literal sense of these words, that the upper room inhabited by the Apostles † was situated in the same building as the tomb of David.

A little lower down, a building just finished is attached to a school belonging to the Anglican Bishop's palace, in which little Jewish and Arab children are educated.   I have several times visited it.   It is a sort of fortified house, which you enter, as you do most of the houses in Jerusalem, by a small low back door ; in doing which you have to bend double.   Around is a great cemetery, enclosed with a white wall, European fashion. I was walking there yesterday, between two rows of tombs, with the wife of the guardian of the cemetery, while her children,—fresh-looking, blooming and rosy creatures,—were looking for Easter eggs, which had been hidden from them under the tufts of grass, and enlivening with their laughter and loud shouts of joy the silence of Gehenna.

As we drew near the Gate of Sion, some lepers squatting on the ground, after their manner, stretched out their hands to me, asking alms.   Of all the human infirmities which display themselves in the sight of the sun, none is more piteous to see than this hideous disease.   Leprosy does not affect only the skin, as the uninstructed in medicine commonly suppose, it disfigures the limbs and the features, and so swells them as to

* Acts ii. 29.   † Acts i. 13.

make them unrecognisable. The heart bleeds at the sight of these miseries that cannot be cured.

As it is a holiday to-day, Hhannah proposes that I should pay him a visit at his house, and make acquaintance with his family. I eagerly assent, delighted with the opportunity of penetrating into the interior of the family of a real Jerusalem bourgeois. We enter the house through a passage very low and pitch dark; I expect to emerge into some wretched sort of home. But, in these countries especially, one must not trust to first impressions. After reaching the top of the stairs, we find ourselves on a pretty little terrace, and we enter a room, lofty and very well lighted. It is vaulted, and built entirely of hewn stone, and has no wainscoting or plastering. This style of construction gives to all rooms here a sort of monumental character; they have an austere simplicity, a striking bareness, which fits Jerusalem well. There is no furniture, or only a carpet to cover the stone floor; all round are cushions. In one of the corners of the room (the corners are always places of honour) sits, cross-legged, the father, Ahouâd, with his blue turban and grey moustache. He is smoking a narguileh. Some neighbours are squatted on the ground near him, and, like him, are smoking in silence. They have left their slippers at the door; I do the same, and, at the invitation of Hhannah, I sit down in the other corner of the room *vis-à-vis* his father. Madame Ahouâd,—a benevolent-looking person, in a muslin gown, cloth vest, and wearing a green cap on her head,—goes to fetch me a long pipe, ready lighted; which she transfers from her mouth to mine. Then she hands me a glass of *raki*, which she pours out from a crystal vase, with handles, and open at the top, like those represented

on Asmonean coins.   Then follows a glass of lemonade,
a cup of coffee, and some sweetmeats made by her for
this entertainment.   They consist of cakes of fine flour,
very coarsely ground and very slightly baked, stuffed
with some preparation of nuts or dates.   I find it very
good.

They bring me besides a red egg.   Here, as among
us, the Latin and Greek Christians give out at Easter
to their children, eggs, coloured red, which they amuse
themselves, like us, with *pricking*.   The Mahometans
have the same custom, only with them it is not at
Easter, but at their great festival, which takes place in
summer, (they have not told me its name,) and they
colour their eggs yellow.

Conversation is not at first very animated, but is
none the less cordial.   After saying *marhaba* ("good
morning"), *catakhérek* ("thank you"), I find myself
almost at the end of my Arabic.   But I manage two
more words, which I make use of to convey to Madame
Ahouâd the most agreeable sentiment, without doubt,
that one can express to a mother,—praise of her son.

Hhannah taib!—*John is good!*   An affirmation,
this, of the most elementary sort, but which won for
me, from Madame Ahouâd, the sweetest of smiles.

By the intervention, however, of Hhannah, we succeed
in carrying on a little conversation.   Madame Ahouâd
begins by enquiring whether I am married, and then
whether my mother is still living.   On my answering
in the negative, she expresses the wish, which Arabs
never omit whenever any allusion is made to death :
" May God grant you for yourself a long life ! "   Then
she wishes to know if eggs are dear in France, and tells
me she should be interested in visiting that country, to
see how marriages are managed there.

The father, Ahouâd, talks less, but tells me many times over how gratified he is at my visit. He also communicates to me his views on politics,—which I will not repeat for fear of compromising him with the Ottoman government.

John's brothers and sister, surrounded by his children, are present during our conversation, but they take no part in it, and keep at a distance, with the reserve to which young people are trained in a patriarchal family. When I take my leave, there is a repetition of the mutual compliments and thanks.

I return home to occupy myself in writing. The sky is overcast, and a storm comes on; it thunders; several smart showers succeed each other, but each lasts only a few minutes. This evening, at eight p.m., the thermometer stands at 10° centigrade.

The climate of Jerusalem is generally very agreeable, from a light breeze which blows every day, specially in the afternoons. It only fails in the months of May and October; accordingly these two months, particularly May, are the most severe. From about the 10th of June to the end of September, the heat is more moderate. The cold of winter never lasts long; this year it has been severer than usual; there has been ice, and for two days running two feet deep of snow; but on the third day it melted.

I spoke just now of the custom that prevails in the East of taking off one's shoes before coming into a room. In private houses this is simply for cleanliness; as the carpet is at once couch and table, it is important not to dirty it. In entering sacred places (mosques, or churches), shoes are taken off from a different motive; one shrinks from mingling the dust of profane earth with a soil accounted holy; it was for that reason

that Moses at the Burning Bush was commanded to
"*take off his shoes from off his feet.*" *   It was for that
reason also that the Israelites, when they left a foreign
country to re-enter their own, used to shake off the
dust from their shoes before crossing the frontier.
Jesus alludes to this custom when He says to His
disciples : " *Whosoever will not receive you, when ye go
out of that city, shake off the very dust from your feet,
for a testimony against them.*"†   This saying is equivalent to this other,—which is, so to say, its translation :
" *If any man will not hear the Church, let him be unto
thee as an heathen man.*"‡   With the preaching of the
Gospel another covenant was inaugurated; those who
rejected the disciples of Jesus, rejected Him who had
sent them ; § they shut themselves out from the kingdom of God; they no longer formed part of the holy
people, nor their cities of the Holy Land.

VII.

From Jerusalem to Jericho.

I should like to be able now to give an account of
my several excursions into the environs of Jerusalem,—
to the tombs of the Kings, to that of the Judges, and
specially to Emmaus and Nebi-Samuel. But I must
not forget that the first duty of a traveller is to
abstain from exhausting his subjects, and, as I am
compelled to make selections out of my recollections
and notes, I will limit myself to two of these excursions,—one to Jericho and the Dead Sea, the other to
Bethlehem.

I had been but twenty-four hours in Jerusalem,
when an opportunity presented itself of visiting the

* Exod. iii. 5.   ‡ St. Matt. xviii. 17.
† St. Luke ix. 5.   § St. Matt. x. 40.

plain of Jericho and the shores of the Dead Sea. I
say an opportunity, for it cannot be done just when
one pleases. That district is dangerous for travellers ;
even more so than any other part, of the Holy Land.
This need not surprise us : we know by the Parable of
the Good Samaritan that, in the time of Jesus, under
settled Roman government, a man might be stripped
by robbers on the high road from Jerusalem to Jericho.
Imagine then what must be the state of things under
the Ottoman government! It is therefore necessary to
take an escort—not certainly of Turkish soldiers, which
would but attract the foe—but of Bedouins of the
desert. These Bedouins consider themselves legitimate
sovereigns of the plain of the Jordan, and, on principle,
I do not very well know what objection could be made
to their rights. It is with them that one must come
to an understanding ; a ransom is paid in advance to
some head of a tribe, who declares himself satisfied
with it, and binds himself in the names of Allah and
of Mahomet not to rob you of the rest, and accompanies you during the journey, ready " *to give you help
and protection in case of need*," and to defend you against
both his friends and enemies.

This ransom, this tribute,—or, as we should say in
Europe, this *visa*,—sometimes costs travellers a large
enough sum. It is, however, best to submit to it. I
made the acquaintance in Palestine of an English
painter, who made this excursion shortly after me,
and who, from having neglected this form, reached the
shores of the Dead Sea as naked as the mountains he
had just crossed.

It is usual therefore to organise one's party as a
caravan, and then to pay so much a head to make up
the sum demanded by the Bedouin Scheikh. These

Bedouins are generally brilliant soldiers, well mounted and well armed, a sort of knights errant,—with this drawback, that they inflict more injuries than they redress. One must not conclude from this that all the scheikhs are alike. The Arab tribe, like the *commune* with us in the primitive times, is but an enlargement of the family; and the scheikh accordingly answers, very nearly, to our *maire de village.** There are some of every sort. It is not, however, indispensable for the scheikh, as it is for the *maire*, to be able to sign his name at the end of a document. Here, people are satisfied with dipping into ink the ring they always wear on their finger, and stamping with it the document to which they wish to attach their signature.

On the day after my arrival in Jerusalem, the four Americans I had met at Ramleh proposed to me to join them in making the expedition to the Dead Sea. They had provided themselves with an escort, and they had an excellent dragoman. These dragomans—whom one generally engages in Egypt—are not only interpreters, as their name indicates; but they are often *travelling agents*, with whom the tourist makes a bargain beforehand, and who accompany him at so much per day, undertaking to supply him with provisions, tents, horses, and servants. It is a very convenient arrangement, and is only open to the objection that it reminds one too much of our *excursion trains*.

But enough of preliminaries. I return to my journal, and copy from it the account of this excursion.

Monday, March 29th.—We start at ten a.m., with our dragoman and two Bedouins who serve us as an

---

* With wider jurisdiction, it is true, for he has the right of life and death in his tribe.

escort. One of the two wears the coarse woollen dress, with broad white and brown stripes, which is the ordinary costume of the Bedouins ; the other is a scheikh ; he is dressed in a red silk robe, and on his head wears a large yellow silk handkerchief, fitting closely, of which the long fringes frame his face in a most picturesque manner; he is mounted on a splendid white horse, and holds in his hand a long spear ; one might fancy oneself looking at one of the Saracen heroes of Ariosto. His gentle and calm expression, his regular features, his short and fine beard, through which one can see the lips and the outline of the mouth, make up a striking likeness to the traditional face of Christ.

We leave the town by the Gate of St. Stephen, and descend into the valley. Arrived in front of Gethsemane, we leave it on our left hand, and go up by the road which cuts diagonally across the side of the Mount of Olives. Then we follow the ridge which connects that mountain with the Hill of Offence.

Large companies of Mahometan pilgrims accompany us up the hill, chanting as they go. They are on their way to the tomb of Moses. Most of them are women and girls in holiday attire. I am never weary of admiring the gracefulness of their dress ; it consists of a simple tunic, striped in all manner of colours; these colours are brilliant, but harmonized with extreme good taste. They carry on their heads their little packs, which they hold on with both hands; from their naked arms, each loaded with a double silver bracelet, hang wide sleeves, open, Chinese-fashion, and reaching down below the knee. Their figures are slender and graceful, and their faces most pleasing, notwithstanding their extreme thinness.

16

They are country women, and accordingly wear
no veils. I like to think that this style of dress, so
different from that worn by the women of the towns,
is the ancient Israelitish costume, retained unchanged
in country places through all the revolutions that have
passed over the land and the mingling of races. At
least, we know from the Bible that among the ancient
Hebrews the holiday dresses of the children and girls
were many-coloured. Such was the coat in which the
tender love of his father clothed Joseph;* such, also,
the dresses worn by the daughters of David.†

The chant of these pilgrims is joyous, very different
from that which I have hitherto heard among the
Arabs : it sounds like a *souvenir* of past times, an echo
of those joyous songs that used to be sung in chorus by
the Hebrew pilgrims returning from the Passover.

Others are on horseback. Here is a man with a
great beard,—his children mounted behind him ; there
an equipage of a quite peculiar character,—two women
seated in great wooden cages, balancing each other
on either side of a horse. A red dais extends over the
whole.

After turning the flank of the Mount of Olives, we
come, on the slope which faces Jerusalem, upon the
village of Bethany. It has a look of misery, but its
situation between two mountains and the few trees
which stand about it give it a charm which harmonizes
well with the sweet and touching memories belonging
to it. Our dragoman takes us to a ruined hovel, in
which we are shewn the tomb of Lazarus. We descend

---

* Gen. xxxvii. 3.

† 2 Sam. xiii. 18. The Hebrew word פסים כתנת is the same as in
the passage of Genesis quoted above. The Vulgate unjustifiably
renders it by two different words.

into it ; it is a deep cave. There is no proof that this tomb is the real one, but I could not pronounce against it absolutely, as some travellers do.

From this place we descend by a steep and stony path, like the one we saw on the way from Ramleh to Jerusalem, and like many others which we shall see to-day. We continue our journey along valleys, and over hill-tops, rounded like backs of sheep,—that is the image which first presents itself to one's fancy. The strange comparison of the psalmist seems less so in Judæa than it would be elsewhere : " *What aileth thee, O thou sea, that thou fleddest? and thou, Jordan, that thou wast driven back? Ye mountains, that ye skipped like rams, and ye little hills like young sheep?*"* These mountains, all sheep-backed, in which no sooner do you reach the top of one, than you see another, rising beyond it,—these "mountains of division," as the Song of Solomon calls them,† give to several passages of Scripture a singular appropriateness ; for this character of the country suggested to the Hebrew poets many images which would not have occurred to others. "*How beautiful upon the mountains,*" cries Isaiah, "*are the feet of him that bringeth good tidings!*"‡ And the Shulamite, "*The voice of my beloved! Behold, he cometh, leaping upon the mountains, skipping upon the hills.*" §

* Psalm cxlv. 5, 6. It is to this class of images that belongs the name of *bull* (*Taurus*), given by the ancients to so great a number of mountains. The Mount of Olives is in our day called by the Arabs *Djebel-et-Tûr*, Mount Bull. The same name is given to Gerizim, to Tabor, and to the Sinai group. It was natural to pastoral nations so to call a hill-top which towered above those around it, like a bull lifting his head above the rest of the herd.

† Song of Solomon ii. 17. See margin.

‡ Isaiah lii. 7.

§ Song of Solomon ii. 8.

We come upon no traces of human habitations; here and there, however, are a few cultivated fields; the country is deserted, but its look is not at all melancholy, and from the hill-tops the view is extensive.

Ere long, all traces of cultivation cease, and we are in the desert,—not the sandy desert, such as we saw in Egypt, but the steppe, the pasture land,—called by the Hebrews *midbar.* Not a tree, not a shrub, nothing but a thin carpeting of turf, which colours in patches ground covered with large stones. Was it into this very desert, so close to the Jordan, or was it into another, of the same kind, that Jesus was "led up of the Spirit," after His baptism, and spent the forty days? However that may be, one cannot pass through it without being reminded of the story of the Temptation. "*Command that these stones be made bread;*" *—I do not clearly see in what other way this place could have furnished, so to say, the *material* for the miracle which Satan demanded of Jesus. The high mountain from which he shewed Him the kingdoms of the world, and the glory of them, is also not difficult to identify. There is no lack, upon the mountain-tops which stand around us, of the widest panoramas ; legend has associated one of these heights with the memory of this history, and has called it *Quarantania,* in memory of Jesus' forty days' fast.

Large flocks of goats and sheep graze upon the slopes of the mountains. There are no spotted goats here, such as I have seen in Egypt, or fawn-coloured, or white, like many in our countries ; they are almost all as black as ebony, and the sheep are perfectly white.† One can the better understand from this, how these two, almost always seen together, and which never-

---

* St. Matt. iv. 1—11.   † Compare Song of Solomon iv. 1, 2.

theless offer so marked a contrast to each other, should have furnished Jèsus with a very natural image to picture the complete distinction which exists between the good and the bad among men. Goats and sheep graze in distinct flocks, under the care of one shepherd, —the sheep gathered together in a compact flock round the shepherd, according to their well-known habit, the goats more scattered, and led by their vagabond instincts. Often a goat intrudes his black coat amidst the white fleeces, introducing confusion among the quiet ranks of the sheep. Accordingly, it is at times necessary for the shepherd to restore order, and disentangle the two flocks. We remember the picture of the Last Judgment. All the nations will be "*gathered like a flock before the Son of man*" (*congregabuntur ante eum*), "*and He shall separate them one from another as a shepherd divideth the sheep from the goats.*" * Jesus speaks of this as an every-day sight. Perhaps He had it before His eyes while He was speaking; for He was then sitting upon the Mount of Olives, which commanded a view over these same plains in which I am now walking.†

Whilst looking at this little scene of pastoral life, I see another parable of the Saviour ‡—the most beautiful of the parables, if one may allow oneself to have preferences—also enacted before my eyes. Drawn off by I know not what caprice, one sheep has escaped and run off towards the top of the mountain. I see the shepherd *leave the ninety and nine*, and run after the one wanderer. Haslin, our dragoman, whose horse is better than mine, or who understands managing him better than I do, takes pity on the poor man, and helps him in the pursuit of the fugitive. He soon compels it to

* St. Matt. xxv: 32.   † St. Matt. xxiv. 3.   ‡ St. Luke xv. 4—7.

retrace its steps; the shepherd gets hold of it, lays
it on his shoulders, and *brings it back rejoicing.*

We come upon a khân in ruins; it is the only building, even in ruins, that I have seen since Bethany in
the whole length of road from Jerusalem to Jericho.
Orientals use the term *khân* of what our writers call
a *caravanserai:* it is the inn of the East, an inn without bed or kitchen, where the traveller finds nothing
more than a shelter from the rays of the sun or the
cold of night. I shall have an opportunity of speaking
elsewhere of what the khâns are in the towns; in the
country they are mere sheds. One comes upon them
often enough in the different countries of the East; and
even in Greece, with rare exceptions, they are still the
only inns. They formerly were to be found in Palestine; but in this respect, as in others, that country is
now degenerate. In our day the ruins only of these
primitive hostelries exist. It was for one of these
hovels (*diversorium viatorum*) that Jeremiah longed,
when he had to witness the turbulence and the
crimes of his fellow-citizens: "*O that I had in the
wilderness a lodging place of wayfaring men; that I
might leave my people, and go from them! for they be
all adulterers, an assembly of treacherous men."* * And
below, in the same chapter, he weeps over the destruction of this one remaining place of shelter, and the
immense devastation, which has not spared even these
poor hovels: "*For the mountains will I take up a weeping and wailing, and for the habitations of the wilderness
a lamentation, because they are burned up, so that none
can pass through them."* †

The khân in which we are now settled is upon the
high ground, in a picturesque situation commanding

* Jer. ix. 2.   † Jer. ix. 10.

a pretty extensive view. Near it is an ancient cistern not yet entirely crumbled into ruins. This khân is situated just half-way between Jerusalem and Jericho, that is, at three hours' walk from each of these towns ; one may suppose it was the halting-place, and probably the only one, between these two great towns. Who can tell that it is not the "inn" to which the merciful Samaritan conveyed the traveller? At any rate, it was on this road that Jesus spoke this admirable parable ; for we see that, on leaving the spot, the first place He came to was a certain village, in which Martha received Him into her house;* and we know from St. John that Martha lived in Bethany, the first village, in fact, one comes to on the way to Jerusalem from Jericho. Here, as was so often the case, the circumstances of the moment, and the scenery in which He happened to be, suggested to the Saviour the images He used.

I will here remark that the synoptic Gospels, and St. Luke in particular, keep much more strictly to the chronological order in their narratives than is commonly supposed. The study of the New Testament, carried on on the spot, suggests many proofs of this. What I have just said is an instance of it. St. Luke, who did not belong to that country, seems not to have known that the village in which Martha lived was Bethany; but the course of his narrative agrees perfectly with the order in which the places he mentions occur.†

I return to my sheep and shepherds,—for the *Khân-*

* St. Luke x. 38.
† St. Luke even appears not to know that all this took place in Judæa, but St. John makes particular mention of this journey of Jesus to Jerusalem.

Kadrûr furnishes me with a new opportunity of observing these shepherds of the desert. We have dismounted, and arranged ourselves for breakfast, not near the khân—for, at this hour of the day, the remaining fragments of its walls give insufficient shade—but under the shelter of a large cave worked in the side of the mountain ; the natural inn has outlasted that erected by the hand of man ; this fine cavern had existed before it, and no doubt suggested the spot as a halting-place for travellers. Haslin spread a carpet on the ground, and set out our provisions before us. A shepherd boy who has caught sight of us runs down from the top of the mountain ; he is twelve or fourteen years old—the true goatherd of the classic poets, with naked legs and feet, a grey smock-frock with loose sash and, thrown over his shoulder like a scarf, the woollen coverlet in which he wraps himself at night.* But you must not complete the picture with "*de collo fistula pendet.*" No, the rustic pipe of Polyphemus would not be in place among the shepherds of Judæa ; what you see hanging from his neck is a long pistol, and in his sash shines an enormous powder-flask, at this moment unfortunately empty, and he presents it to us with supplicating gestures, begging us to fill it. Unluckily I cannot do so.

According to our notions, the life of a shepherd is the very ideal of peacefulness. But in Palestine I do not think I ever saw a shepherd, old or young, not well armed. They must be so, especially in these wildernesses ; one must be prepared to defend oneself against brigands and wild beasts ; it was just at the age of my little shepherd, and in these same mountains,

* "*He shall array himself with the land of Egypt, as a shepherd putteth on his garment*" (Jer. xliii. 12).

that David, keeping his father's sheep, had to deliver them out of the paw of the lion, and out of the paw of the bear.*

This fact, if I am not mistaken, gives meaning to many Biblical comparisons, of which we often miss the force by reading into them the ideas of our western pastoral poetry. One must try to forget Némorin.† The expression, " *Shepherds of the nations,*"—applied to kings in the Bible, and in Homer,—is very far from being meant to suggest none but images of peace, as we might have thought beforehand.‡ The good shepherd is he who not only "*feeds his sheep in green pastures,*" and " *leads them forth beside the waters of comfort,*" but also " *whose rod and staff comfort them;*"§ who lets no one pluck them out of his hand, and is ready to fight in their defence, and to " *lay down his life for them.*" ‖

I am sorry to make so many digressions, and really do not know when I shall reach Jericho. At every step in a journey through the Holy Land, one comes upon sights associated with some memory, which arrests one. A journey in this country is a perpetual commentary upon Holy Scripture. This is a remark which has been made a hundred times, but I make it once more, because I find it a hundred times more true than I had expected. There is no need of much learning, or of any uncommon powers of observation or of thought, to profit by such a journey. One has not to seek for objects of interest ; they come to one

---

* i. Sam. xvii. 34—37.

† Némorin is the hero of one of Florian's pastoral romances entitled *Estelle* (1788), which was for many years popular, but is now out of fashion.

‡ Psalm xxiii.

§ See, for instance Jer. vi. 3.

‖ St. John x. 1—16.

of themselves.   The only regret one experiences is
in finding how much one has missed ; it is indeed the
embarras de richesses.

This is a great pleasure during the journey, but there
is a difficulty in writing an account of it.   That which
is real does not always look so ;* and one is afraid
of being thought influenced by prejudice.   Indeed, a
traveller who has observed too little is more likely to
be forgiven than one who is suspected of having seen
too much.   I will not, however, for that reason abstain
from recording what is a fact,—that, as if to make my
experiences during my three hours' journey on this
historic road complete, I did not fail to come upon an
illustration of what the Gospels tell us as to its being
infested by robbers.   I met one of those brigands
bound with cords, driven by another man.   But in our
day on seeing such a sight one feels a doubt as to
which of the two is the robber.   That, however, does
not affect the case on the point that interests us ;—
either way, we saw a robber.

At last we catch sight of the Dead Sea, of a beautiful blue colour, rather lighter than usual at this moment,
like our Swiss lakes ; and   soon   after, on   our left,
the valley of the Jordan.   This view, seen from above,
is very grand in effect, particularly on coming out of
the desert which we have been crossing.   The solitude
and sterility of the shores of the Dead Sea does not
affect us with sadness or wonder ; we have already
become accustomed to such scenery ; and the eye now
only tries to take in the beauty of this great expanse
of water.

For those of my fellow-countrymen who delight in

---

* "*Le vrai peut quelquefois n'être pas le vraisemblable,*"—a line
Boileau's *l'Art Poétique.*

comparing one country with another, I will here remark
that this view reminds me rather strikingly of the end
of the lake of Neuchâtel and the plain of Yverdon, as
seen from the old Lausanne road. The mountains
of Moab and Ammon fairly represent those of the
Jura. The site of Jericho would stand for that of
Valentin. But all this is here of course on a very
large scale, and it is better lighted up,—a painting
instead of an engraving,—for such is always the image
which occurs to one on comparing the scenery of eastern
with that of northern lands.

We have but one more descent to make, but it is
long and steep ; my tired horse stumbles at every
step ; soon, as we cross a pretty little brook, he dips
his smoking nostrils into it and refreshes himself with
long draughts of the water.

Here we are in the valley. We follow for a few
moments the base of the mountain diverging from the
lake. Vegetation here begins once more to shew itself,
—nothing, however, but little shrubs prickly with thorns.
The prettiest bears lilac flowers with yellow stamina
like those of the potato, and a round fruit, of the
size of a biffin apple or of a large lemon, full of little
grains. We visit the stream which is called *Elisha's
fountain*, in memory of the story narrated in 2 Kings
ii. 19—22. It is probable this is really the spring
to which the Biblical story refers; for to a considerable
distance round this spot in the neighbourhood of
Jericho no other is to be found.

Jericho, to which the name of "the City of Palm-
trees" is given in the Bible, was formerly surrounded
with a forest of those fine trees. Some were still to
be seen here at the beginning of this century ; there is
not one left now ; neither is a sycamore to be seen,

like that climbed by Zaccheus. A square tower, built by Franks, and three parts ruined, a poor little hamlet, protected by a thorny hedge,—that is all that remains now of Jericho.

In the times of Elijah and Elisha, Jericho had a school of the prophets. But it was not that which made its fame. The names which are its glory are neither those of prophets, of kings, nor of priests ; they are the names of persons outside the chosen people, but inscribed in the *Golden Book* of Divine grace ; as, for instance, that of the woman which was a sinner, who, as the firstfruits of the Gentile world and precursor of the sinful woman of the Gospel History, was saved by her faith, amidst the ruin of a whole city;* or that of the publican Zaccheus, to whom was addressed that saying, expressive of a new covenant of grace, " *The Son of man is come to seek and to save that which was lost ;* " † or again, that of the blind beggar, sitting by the gates of the city, who cried to Jesus :

" *O Son of David, have mercy on me !* "

" *What wilt thou that I should do unto thee ?* "

" *Lord, that I might receive my sight.*"

" *Go thy way; thy faith hath made thee whole.*" ‡

Near the ancient tower which I have just mentioned, in the bed of a dried-up river, we see a great number of tents ; it is the encampment of the Coptic and Greek pilgrims, who arrived before us from Jerusalem, and who, to-morrow morning, will go and bathe in the Jordan. Whole families are there, going and coming ; some are preparing their repasts, others are seated on the grass. One hears nothing but singing and shouts

---

* Josh. ii.; Heb. xi. 31.   † St. Luke xix. 10.

‡ St. Mark x. 46—52.

of joy. It is a joyous and animated scene, a fine Oriental festivity of a kind of which we have no idea. We pitch our tents on the opposite side of the ravine, and soon retire to rest, as we have to start early in the morning. Much later into the night I overhear near my tent the songs and the noise of the games of the Copts. Their principal amusement seems to be singing a sort of catch : one man sings, and all the rest accompany him with a rhythmical beating of hands, and they repeat many times, enthusiastically, the burthen of the song. It sounds primitive—almost savage ; and yet it is self-restrained and decent. The influence of Christianity has passed over it, and though past and gone, its perfume still hangs about it,—*Servabit odorem testa diu.*

I meditate, as I fall asleep, on this ruined Jericho, on this Dead Sea so near me, and I say to myself that if the Eternal, our God, had not had mercy on us, "*we should have been as Sodom, we should have been like unto Gomorrah.*" *

VIII.

THE JORDAN AND THE DEAD SEA.

To M. L. B—— A——

Jerusalem, April, 1858.

I have already made many excursions in the neighbourhood,—to Emmaus—to St. John of the Wilderness—to Bethlehem—and elsewhere. My expedition to the Dead Sea is one of those which have most interested me ; there, as in all that I have seen of Judæa, the country is infinitely more picturesque than

* Isa. i. 9 ; Rom. ix. 20.

I had imagined it; it has a character of *roominess*, which I had not expected to find; it is, as the phrase is, in the *grand style*. But if geographically very fine, it is in a state of desolation truly frightful; it is the ruin of a ruin. It might seem as if all trace of human activity having long since left it the land itself had at last become decrepit and meagre with age. The underlying rock crops out everywhere, the soil is crumbling; on all sides are the beds of dried-up rivers. But I must except the Jordan, in which I narrowly escaped drowning.

We had slept at Jericho, or rather on the site where Jericho once stood. At two o'clock in the morning —eight by Arab time—we set off to visit the Jordan. The full moon of the month *Nisan,*—for it was the very night of the Jewish Passover,—was lighting up around us the most beautiful and novel scene on which my eyes ever rested. Some hundreds of Coptic pilgrims, —men, women, children,—in turbans, in tarbouches, walking, riding on horses or donkeys, were arranging themselves for a start, in the white moonlight, in the middle of a plain full of bushes. Their priests were at their head. In the stillness of this desert, one heard conversations carried on in many languages,— shouts, all the confusion of a departure. I was picturing to myself the Israelites going out from Egypt in such a night. But ere long order is re-established, and no sound is heard but the neighing of the horses and the cracking of the thorns which they trample under their feet.

We ride on, ahead of the rest, and after an hour and a half's trotting reach the Jordan. A pleasant sound of running water announces its neighbourhood. It runs in graceful curves between tufted trees, which bend over its waters, drinking in their freshness. This range of the Jordan runs like a ribbon of fresh green across the sands of the desert, a living pathway decked with flowers, traversing a burnt-up land that seemed under a curse. That fine image of the Psalmist,—" *a tree planted by the waterside, whose leaf shall not wither*," * has, in these burning regions of the earth, much more of literal and striking truth than elsewhere.

While reflecting upon this, I was admiring the beauty of the scene that surrounded me, further enhanced at the time by the indefinable effects produced by the subdued light of the moon,—the broad plain overhung on one side by the round-topped hills of Judæa, and on the other by the hills of Gad and Reuben forming an upright wall, of which the long horizontal summit carries the eye far into the distance. Meantime the Copts had arrived. With loud shouts of joy they had dismounted; in a moment they had taken off their clothes, and were bathing, or rather washing themselves on the banks of the river.

The Jordan is no broader than the Thiéle. I also plunged into the water, a little higher up the stream than the Copts (for good reasons), and like an old *habitué* of the *Môle de la Guillotine*,† wished to swim across the river to the other side, to gather some of the *Idumæan palms* which grow there. But the stream is so strong that it carried me away with great rapidity ; I struggled my utmost against it, and at last, exhausted, began to cry out for help. But the Copts are no swimmers, and do not understand French; they stayed

* Psalm i. 3 ; Jer. xvii. 8.
† The name of one of the piers which formed the harbour of Neuchâtel, and near which the boys used to bathe during the author's childhood.

quietly on the bank, and were content to wade into the water up to their knees. And I was being floated away further and further from the bank, and now found myself at a long distance from my companions. But by the blessing of God, after five minutes' agony, I succeeded in getting near enough to the river's bank to lay hold of a branch, landed, ran through the crowd, and got at my clothes, though not without difficulty.

The danger had been a real one, and I have since heard many stories of travellers drowned in the Jordan. One must not, however, suppose that it is as full, or its stream as rapid, at all times of the year. It is in the spring, during the melting of the snows on Mount Hermon, that it swells to this extraordinary degree. Joshua, who passed it near this spot, and at the same season of the year—only four days earlier *—expressly says that "*at this season of the year the Jordan overflows all its banks.*" † God does not always make use of an evident miracle, as in the case of Joshua, to make us clearly see that He watches over us.

After having bathed themselves, the Copts plunge into the river the little children they have with them, three times in succession, and wash their clothes in the sacred waters. Then they climb the trees that grow on the banks, cut down or break off a number of sticks, great and small, dip them also three times in the Jordan, and carry them off as *souvenirs.* After this, the whole multitude resume their march, starting, as always, with their characteristic shouts of joy unknown to us of the western world, and which one must have heard to understand what is meant by the songs of triumph, of which the Bible so often speaks. ‡

* Joshua iv. 19.   † Joshua iii. 15.
‡ In Hebrew רנה.   Psalm xxx. 6, xlii. 5, and elsewhere.

Meantime, day has dawned. We start at the same time as the Copts ; but we turn towards the shore of the Dead Sea, across the plain which is still covered with thorn-bushes. The two Bedouins who escorted us have just been relieved by a third, armed with a lance of fabulous length. He gallops in magnificent style over the plain.

The water of the Dead Sea is clear and limpid, and to look at, is not different from the purest water ; accordingly, our horses eagerly dip their noses into it, and draw them out again instantly, with disgust. I taste it, and find it even much more salt than I expected. If you take a single mouthful of it, spitting it out immediately, you retain, for a long time after, an intolerable nitrous taste. If you dip your hands into it, you find it impossible to wipe it quite off, and the skin still feels a very disagreeable, astringent sensation. The pebbles on the shore are always wet and shining. In short, it is sea water of an intenser sort ; a sea whose salt is nitre, not kitchen salt.

Of course, as a loyal subscriber to the Challandes collection, I picked up, for the Neuchâtel Museum, some pebbles and shells,—not sea-shells, there is no animal life in the Dead Sea,—but fresh-water shells, mixed with fragments of reeds, from the *detritus* of the Jordan. One of my travelling companions drew my attention to this distinction. How often had I cause to regret my want of knowledge of zoology, of botany, and geology ! Some amount of knowledge of this sort would often have enabled me to perceive, with more of accuracy, the distinguishing characteristics of a country. Open your eyes as wide as you may, you cannot feel you understand anything really unless you know its name ; it is the story of Adam and the animals. In a journey

17

such as this, one finds how great is the use of all one
knows, even on the smallest matters. Accordingly, in
my ignorance of Arabic, of which I felt regret, almost
remorse, that I had not continued the study, Hebrew
was often very useful to me. I was also very fortunate
in knowing a little English, and in having the impudence necessary for coining Italian, as the need for it
arose. These two languages (Italian and English) are,
of all those of Europe, the most serviceable in the East ;
French is of secondary importance ; the times of St. Louis
and of the "*beau Dunois,*" are fled,—the days when
all Europe was *Frangistan*, and all Europeans *Franks*,
are of the past. In these days they are rather called
Inglesi. The Frenchman, the Austrian, the *Milore*
(that is, the Englishman, properly so called, under which
head is included the American), are considered by the
Arabs only varieties of the genus *Inglese.* Not, I think,
that English travellers are much more numerous than
the others, but they count for twice as much, here,
as in Switzerland, and for the same reason. But, once
more, why did we not pursue our studies in Arabic ?

Travelling in the East has its difficulties. In the
first place, there are in Palestine roads,—or, rather,
places through which one passes,—which are truly
frightful, and two or three days of slow trotting over
hills covered with rolling pebbles cannot but be tiring
enough to a "*Sunday horseman,*" as they used to call
me at Berlin in my first week of lessons in the art of
riding. That renowned horse which is said to have
walked without hesitation down the great stairs at La
Rochette,* might nevertheless have thought twice before
undertaking the descent to Jericho.

I will not go any further into my adventures ; you

* At Neuchâtel.

will find all my acts and doings recorded in my diaries. I will not repeat what I have said of the religious impressions left upon one's mind by a visit to Jerusalem. They are very real, and I now understand what is meant by a pilgrimage. A visit to Judæa would not, it is true, convert an unbeliever; but such faith as one has, however feeble it may be, is reawakened and strengthened in these regions. Like the material creation, like the sacred history, the Holy Land is itself a page in the records of Revelation.

IX.

THE RETURN FROM THE DEAD SEA BY MAR-SABA.

Whilst the climate of the greater part of Palestine is temperate, that of the valley of the Jordan, and, above all, of the plain of Jericho and the basin of the Dead Sea, is tropical. This is partly owing to the situation of these districts, which lie very much below the level of the Mediterranean, and partly to the great walls of bare rock which stand around them. In summer the heat here is intolerable; the inhabitants of Jerusalem will scarcely venture to come hither. Winter is Jericho's only spring. One can imagine what a charm there was for the Jews of old in the vicinity of these two cities, which were at about the same distance from each other as Paris and Versailles. By spending the summer amid the fresh air of the hill-tops of Jerusalem and Bethlehem, and the winter under the palm-trees of Jericho, and beneath the shadow of these great rocks heated by the sun, one could, without difficulty, live continually in a climate always mild and beneficent, and as in an eternal spring.

When we left the shores of the Dead Sea,—at eight

or nine o'clock in the morning,—the rays of the sun
were beginning already to be overpowering. We returned to Jerusalem by a different road from that by
which we came, taking a more southerly direction, and
passing under the convent of Mar-Saba. We climb by
steep and narrow paths cut into the face of mountains,
even higher and more bare than those of yesterday.
Here, for a long distance, we see no vegetation,—only
sand,—for ever, sand. Far away in the distance, on
one of these mountain-tops, they point out to me a
pyramid believed by the Mahometans to be the tomb
of Moses. At last, here and there, appear a few blades
of grass,—not tufts, nothing but solitary blades. On a
large plateau we find a hundred or so of camels, grazing,
under the care of a single shepherd. Further off are
flocks of sheep and of goats. We come upon an encampment of wandering shepherds; their tents, arranged
in a circle, are made of black wool. It is to these tents
of Arab shepherds that the Shulamite compares her
complexion, tanned by the sun : "*I am black, like the
tents of Kedar.*" * It was here, or rather a little further
to the south, that the shepherds of Abraham and of Lot
pastured their enormous flocks. It must have been
from here, too,—from the top of the mountain which
we have just crossed,—that Lot must have seen this
valley of the Jordan, at that time so well watered.†
One understands how fascinating to him must have been
these smiling landscapes, seen from the tops of these
barren rocks. No contrast could be greater ; here the
desert,—below, the luxuriant vegetation of the tropics.

* *Song of Solomon* i. 5. Kedar was the son of Ishmael (Gen. xxv.
13). His descendants were shepherds (Isa. lx. 7), and they lived in
tents,—that is, they were nomads (Isa. xlii. 11).

† Gen. xiii. 10.

I call it luxuriant vegetation, and yet what I have said of the plain of Jericho cannot have conveyed such an idea. Its vegetation is luxuriant only on the actual banks of the Jordan. But it is easy to see that all that is needed is more of moisture, and one can imagine what must have been the fertility of this country at the time when Jericho still had its great forest of palm-trees, and consequently more rain than it can have at present. And the southern extremity of the Dead Sea is in our day still remarkable for its exuberant vegetation. Some time after my return from Jericho, I met, at the house of M. Gobat, a Swiss naturalist, Dr. Joos, of Schaffhausen, who has often explored Palestine and the neighbouring regions. He had just arrived from the country of Moab, and the Araba, and was still possessed with a feeling of great wonder at the force of the vegetation to be seen in this fine oasis to the south of the Dead Sea ; the *asclepias*, for instance, he told me, which at Jericho is but a shrub, is there a magnificent tree.

The shepherds receive us hospitably in their tents ; they offer us camel's milk, and ask for tobacco in exchange. After a short halt, and some hours' march, during which we see no trace of life, we arrive at a road worked in the rock, and fenced in with a wall, built of unhewn stones. Soon we see at our feet a deep and narrow ravine, at the bottom of which a row of white pebbles marks out, between the rocks of yellow limestone, the dried-up bed of the Kedron. This scene is very different from that of yesterday. Instead of dome-shaped sandhills, we have now before us pointed rocks of a height which it makes one giddy to look at, and frightful precipices,—in a word, what is called romantic scenery. Our road follows the ridge of one of the mountains that close in our ravine, and soon we catch sight, on the nearly perpendicular side of the rock, of the Greek monastery of Saint Saba.

This ancient convent looks like a fortress, and, indeed, it is one. Compelled to defend itself against robbers and against unbelievers, it is fortified, on the side facing the top of the mountain, with a battlemented wall, flanked by two large towers ; on the opposite side, the precipice is protection enough.

On the steep flanks of the ravine, on both sides, are openings into a great number of caverns, apparently inaccessible. It is said that there are thousands of them, and that they are to be found over numbers of square miles in the valley of Kedron. Some of them are the work of man, others of nature, only enlarged by human art. These caverns are a characteristic feature of the geography, as well as of the history, of this country. They are constantly mentioned in the Bible, as, for instance,—without speaking of the other sepulchral vaults,—the cave of Machpelah, in which Abraham was buried ; * that in which Lot took refuge after the disaster at Sodom ; † that of Makkedah, in which the king of Jerusalem and his allies hid themselves after the battle of Gibeon ; ‡ and, lastly, those which served as fortresses for David and his men, during their life of adventures.§ We see by these and other instances, how, even from early times, these caverns were made use of as resting-places, not only of the dead, but often of the living also. It would even seem, from a passage in the Book of Judges, that, during one period of their history, the Israelites found themselves driven, from fear of the Midianites, still further to multiply these caves,

* Gen. xxiii. 9, etc.; xxv. 9.　　‡ Josh. x. 16.
† Gen. xix. 30.　　§ 1 Sam. xxii. 1, xxiv. 4.

and to turn troglodytes.* When Gideon had freed them from the tyranny of Midian, they came out, one by one, from their caves ; but the memory of this kind of life did not altogether die out, and in times of panic the people were very ready to betake themselves once more to these subterranean hiding places.† Accordingly, this image recurs continually in the threatenings of the prophets, in which it represents the extremity of fear and distress.‡

At a very different period of history, under the reign of the Asmonæans and the Herods, these cells were again occupied by pious Israelites, who came to seek shelter from the evils of civilized life in the same places in which their fathers found refuge in times of barbarism. The mountains to the west of the Dead Sea were in the time of Pliny§ the principal resort of the Essene cenobites. At a later date, in the first ages of Christianity, they became the asylums of the Christian hermits. It is asserted that there were as many as eleven thousand of them !

It is a strange, romantic history, which sets one dreaming for a long time,—that of this race of solitaries, suspended like ghosts, between earth and heaven, without laws and without the restraints of society, with no king but God, no utterance but prayer;—a mysterious history, all the more attractive that it never was, and never will be, written, and which had no spectators but the silent rocks of the valley of Kedron. In our day one sees, sailing on outstretched wing from out of these caverns, flights of the fair blue pigeons, piping their sweet plaintive notes, || who "*take up their dwelling*

---

* Judges vi. 2.   ‡ Isa. ii. 19; Rev. vi. 15.
† I Sam. xiii. 6.   § Plinii Hist. Nat., lib. v. 15.
       || Isa. xxxviii. 14.

among the clefts of the rock in the secret places of the cliffs." *

At the end of the fifth century, St. Saba congregated into the cœnobite life the hermits of this Thebaid desert. St. John Damascene, and others besides, brought glory to this convent, which is still to this day existing, a venerable relic of the ancient ages of the Church. Many a time, and even in our own day, it has been seized by the Mussulmans ; many a time it has had to undergo pillage, and the monks who inhabited it have been massacred, or tortured to death.

We pitch our tents a little higher up, and after a few minutes' rest present ourselves at the gate of the monastery. No woman is ever allowed to enter it ; if a woman begs for hospitality, she is lodged in one of the towers which defend the wall. Men can only be admitted on presenting a letter of introduction ; we have two, one from the American consul at Jerusalem, the other from the Greek Patriarch. We are received by two old monks, of benevolent countenances, with long white beards (one of the two is the head of the convent), and by a young ecclesiastic, who has a gentle and modest expression. They belong to the order of St. Basil ; their dress consists of a robe of blue cloth, with a black cafetan over it ; they wear black caps, round and flat, and their hair and beards long.

The monks do the honours of their retreat very graciously. The church is fine, its collection of images very large, and the pictures with which it is hung are all presents from the Emperor of Russia. In the court is the tomb of St. Saba.

We are shewn the cells of the monks; upon the door of each is invariably written, in Greek letters, the in-

* Song of Solomon ii. 14.

scription, " *Christ be with us !* " Then they bring us to
a little garden, in which grows a date-tree, considered
to be the great marvel of St. Saba ; its fruits, which
have no kernel, give children to women that have
none.

Another curiosity of this convent are the bells, said
to be the only ones in the whole Ottoman empire.
This may at one time have been the case ; but in our
day the intolerance of the Turkish government has
been to a remarkable degree relaxed, and I have seen
many other bells in Palestine. What interests me more
is the ancient church of this monastery, which is a cave,
a *laura*, such as were the dwellings of the monks themselves in old times. I noticed a very deep baptistery
that is used—or, at least, that formerly was used—for
baptizing by immersion, according to the Greek use,
adult infidels converted to Christianity.

The monastery of St. Saba has, I am told, among its
vassals some families of Bedouins, who undertake to
defend it by mounting guard round its walls. And it
is they, also, who bring to it, from the Patriarch at
Jerusalem, the provisions it requires for its use. This
feudal relationship with Jerusalem, of which I was not
told the origin, is kept up by a custom binding the
monks to place, every day, in a certain tower, some
provisions of which the Bedouins have the use. It is
even possible that that is the whole secret of this pretended vassalship.

Many rooms, very cleanly kept, their floors covered
with carpets or mats, and with cushions round the walls,
are provided as lodgings for the pilgrims. We are
taken into a little divan ; the two old men take their
seats by our sides, and the young monk goes to fetch a
flagon of *raki.* It is a sort of aniseed, much used in

the Levant. He pours out a little glass of it, and presents it to each one of us in turn. As soon as a guest has drunk a few drops of it, the cup-bearer refills the glass to the brim, and passes it on to the next. The glass passes round in this way several times, and the little refection ends with figs and dried raisins, and then a cup of coffee.

Scarcely are we back in our tents when we see the venerable Superior coming up. His step is heavy with age. He brings with him a servant, carrying a bottle of the wine of the country. The Superior drinks it with us. It is a wine which might be very good, but, like all the wines of Palestine, it is badly made, thick and sour,—in short, detestable.

When evening came, I went out alone, to climb the nearest hill-top. How easily one understands, in this country, what is so often said of Jesus,—"*Departing to a mountain apart to pray.*"* The air is clear and fresh, after a day of burning heat. The towers and the dome of the convent, the rocks of Kedron, the round tops of the mountains, the range of the Moabitish mountains far away in the distance, the whole scene fades, and is lost amid the gathering shades of night. The sound of our horses' bells dies away. All around is night and silence,—that complete and absolute silence which is to be found only in the desert, and does not exist, even for an instant, in our atmosphere impregnated with the ceaseless stir of human activity. I could imagine that the day just ended, and my whole journey, was a dream; I find it rather hard to realize that it is all real, and that I actually am upon those mountains of Judah on which lived the hermits of the first ages, and which were trodden by the patriarchs.

* St. Matt. xiv. 23, and elsewhere.

I rise early, as one does on the mountains. The *moukres* set to work foraging, while Haslin and his men busy themselves preparing breakfast. A moment after, the four Americans come out of their tents, and shake me warmly by the hand, saying, *"Fine morning,"* and *"Rather warm,"*—the safest of remarks under these Palestine skies, of implacable radiancy! After breakfast I climb the mountain-tops once more. When I come down again, all is ready for a start. The Americans are in the saddle, the tents have been struck, and are ready rolled up on the backs of the mules. I look in vain for the spot on which they were pitched. Five minutes sufficed to clear away every trace of what was our encampment. *"Its place knows it no more."* One must have lived in a tent to understand the charm of a nomad life, and the pleasure, unlike anything else, of being able to carry off one's home, tacked on, if not to the soles of one's shoes,* yet to the back of one's horse.

It is but a three days' march from Mar-Saba to Jerusalem. We follow, all the time, the direction of the Kedron ravine, also called *the Valley of Fire* (Ouâdi-en-Nar), but keeping to the high ground. The scenery continues desert and desolate. Here and there, however, at a little distance from Mar-Saba, are to be seen some cultivated plots of ground. The same pleasure that it gives one, in Europe, to come from time to time upon bits of nature that are still wild and unsubdued by man, and that have hitherto escaped the measuring rod of the surveyor, the pipe of the drainer, the axe of the woodcutter,—the same, or greater, does

---

* An allusion to a famous expression of Danton, " Does one carry away one's fatherland on the soles of one's shoes?" (Thiers' " Histoire de la Révolution," cap. xviii.)

one feel here on suddenly seeing in the midst of the desert, some trace of the action of the intelligence or of the will of man.

On this road Jerusalem is seen from a great distance,—at least an hour before one reaches it. The city stands forth in her full height, on the summit of her mountain. In the upper part of the *Wady*, on the left of the road, there are some plantations of olives and fig-trees. When the fig-tree begins to put forth its first leaves, it is a sign *that summer is nigh at hand.** Most of the trees in Palestine, not losing their leaves in winter, do not serve to mark the changes of the seasons. The olive tree, the cypress, the terebinth tree, do not change their appearance in any perceptible way ; and the almond tree, which changes its leaves every year, renews them some time before the end of winter ; it gives, therefore, only, as its Hebrew name indicates,† a sign that summer will come, but not that it is already near. On the other side of the road there are only thorns and thistles. *"Do men gather grapes of thorns, or figs of thistles ?"*‡ This illustration is quite natural, and offers itself spontaneously in Palestine. Wherever there is no cultivation, thorns and thistles abound. The

---

* St. Matt. xxiv. 32 ; St. Mark xiii. 28. In the parallel passage, St. Luke (xxi. 29), being less well acquainted with Palestine, and writing for all countries, uses the expression,—*"the fig-tree,* and ALL THE TREES ;" but St. Matthew and St. Mark mention the fig-tree only, *"Learn a parable of the fig-tree."*

† שָׁקֵד, the almond tree, means properly, *he that is awake* (during the sleep of the rest of nature). See Jer. i. 11, 12 (in the Hebrew text and in the Vulgate).

‡ St. Matt. vii. 16 ; St. Luke vi. 44. If I were not afraid of being accused of over-minute criticism, I should draw attention to the fact that from this passage again one can perceive that Palestine was the native country of St. Matthew, whilst St. Luke betrays his

thorn spoken of in the Gospel is certainly the little woody and almost creeping thorn, which covers the ground in the neighbourhood of Jerusalem. It is very much used for lighting fires; walls are also crowned with it, to make them a better fence against trespassers. I have no doubt it was of this kind of thorn that the Saviour's crown was made; for it naturally suggests itself for making garlands; its prickles are fine, and its branches curl naturally; its flowers are very small, but of a fine purple tint; and the whole has a look of refinement and grace about it. These thorns are hard, and very sharp.*

At the extremity of the Valley of Fire, at about the point at which it meets those of Hinnom and Jehoshaphat, of which it is but an elongation, is to be seen a well of antique construction still in pretty good repair, to which the country ·people give the name of *Job's Well.* Travellers call it also *the Well of Fire, Joab's Well, Jacob's, Jeremiah's, Nehemiah's, Nahum's.* None of these names are very instructive; I only mention them to shew the wealth of the supply of synonyms in the topography of the Holy Land. We are here upon a soil which belongs to the whole of human-kind;

foreign origin. What the latter really says, is: "*One does not gather figs of thorns, nor grapes of a bramble bush.*" An inhabitant of Palestine might, in strictness, contradict the first half of this assertion, or at least it would not have awakened in his mind the idea of something essentially impossible, like the expression used by St. Matthew; for it is upon thorny bushes that the cactus figs, so common in Jerusalem, are gathered. Further, the name *bramble bush*, mentioned afterwards, is a very general one, whilst the *thistles* of St. Matthew are drawn from nature.

* This is the *poterium spinosum.* This little thorn, of the family of the rosaceæ, is very widely diffused in the countries round the eastern part of the Mediterranean, from Sicily eastward.

European and Arabian conquerors, Jewish, Christian, and Mussulman pilgrims, have trodden it in all directions, leaving nothing on their track but new names and new ruins. One may conclude, from the situation of this well, that it is the ancient *En-Rogel* (the fountain of the fuller or of the spy), mentioned in Scripture as one of the points which were to mark the boundary between the territories of Judah and Benjamin.* It was there that, during Absalom's usurpation, the sons of Abiathar, Jonathan and Ahimaaz, hid themselves, not daring to enter the town, and carrying on enquiries on what was happening in it, to report it to David.† It was near there that, at a later time, Adonijah, when just about to proclaim himself king, learnt from this same Jonathan that David had discovered his plot.‡

X.

BETHLEHEM AND ITS NEIGHBOURHOOD.

The Convent of St. Saviour, at Bethlehem, has under its direction the other Latin convents of the Holy Land. Accordingly, though they all of them generally shew a disposition to be very hospitable, even to those who present themselves at their doors without any other recommendation to their kindness than the fact that they are travellers, it is well to demand from the Franciscans of Jerusalem a letter of introduction for their brethren of Bethlehem, of St. John of the Desert, and of Nazareth. Hhannah undertook to procure me one ; it authorises the fathers of the various convents to receive " *colla consueta ospitalità il signor Felic Bovet,*

---

* Josh. xv. 7, 8 ; xviii. 16, 17.　　　† 2 Sam. xvii. 17.
‡ 1 Kings i. 9, 42, 43.

svizzero protestante, e graziosamente soccorerlo nella sua divota pellegrinazione."

Of all places in the Holy Land, there is, no doubt, not one of which the name is more popular with Christians than that of the little town of Bethlehem. Associated in our memories with the thought of that *"babe, who was the Saviour, Christ, the Lord,"* it imprinted itself more deeply than any other upon our childish imagination. It calls up in our hearts the memory of the sweet Christmases of the past, and of the most sacred impressions of our earliest years.

Bethlehem is only two leagues' distance from Jerusalem, and the communications between these two towns are frequent. During the season for pilgrimages, one can easily go as far as Bethlehem from Jerusalem without incurring the least danger. On April 7th, I set off with Hhannah ; we go out by the Damascus Gate, to avoid the obstructions of that of Jaffa. By our side walks an Arab hunter (a Christian, it is needless to say—Mussulmans do not hunt), who is going to shoot partridges and gazelles at Beit-Djala and at St. John's in the Desert. Our moukre sings his melancholy song, which John interprets to me :—

"Rest, rest,
Let the fair one rest."

Our road takes us over a broken tableland, but on the whole it ascends ; for Bethlehem stands at a level three hundred feet higher than Jerusalem ; the soil is a stone-besprinkled pasture, enamelled with those fine "lilies of the field," whose glories threw into the shade those of Solomon's royal robes,—and covered almost every-

* *i.e.,* " To receive with the accustomed hospitality Mr. Felix Bovet, a Swiss Protestant, and courteously to assist him in his devout pilgrimage."

where with those dwarf thorns, which at one time furnished a crown for the Son of David. The comparison in the Song of Solomon, "*a lily among the thorns,*"* is suggested by nature itself. I have already spoken of the little thorn of Judæa. As to the lily, I have no doubt it is the large red anemone (*anemone coronaria*), so common in the neighbourhood of Jerusalem. In Judæa the spring flowers are almost all scarlet coloured. The hills are covered with anemones, tulips, and poppies.†

In front of us march some Coptic pilgrims, with tall, white or yellow, round felt hats. One of them plays on a pipe ; pacing by his side is a tall donkey, on which are mounted a woman and child. It is the kind of picture I have so often seen in Egypt, but which is not so often to be seen now in the Holy Land, as it used to be formerly. In our day Egypt is the land of donkeys, Palestine of horses. In the Bible times it was the reverse ; the first rule prescribed by Moses for kings was, "*He shall not multiply horses to himself, nor cause the people to return to Egypt, to the end that he should multiply horses.*"‡ Solomon, it is well known, on this point, as on others, set himself above the law ;§

---

* Song of Solomon ii. 2. The Hebrew word is שׁוֹשַׁנָּה ; the Vulgate says "*lilium,*" and our old French versions, "*muguet*" (lily of the valley).

† The poppy and the *anemone caronaria* are very like each other at first sight, and often found together. They may very well have been, both of them, described by the generic name *lily of the fields.* The poppy is one of the species common to our flora and to that of Palestine. That of Palestine, however, constitutes a distinct variety ; its stalk is more hairy, and the spots on the petals of a darker colour.

‡ Deut. xvii. 16.

§ 2 Chron. ix. 28.

he aimed more at competing in magnificence with the
other kings of the East, than at being a truly Israelitish king. But the spirit of the Mosaic legislation was
always living in the prophets ;* and when in times of
humiliation Zechariah wishes to picture the re-establish-
ment of a national kingship, he represents the King of
Jerusalem mounted, like the ancient judges of Israel,†
not on a horse or a mule, but on a thorough-bred ass,
" *a colt the foal of an ass.*" ‡

Rich as is this route in great historical associations,
men have not been content with them. Everywhere
legendary lore has inscribed its romantic traditions
upon this soil, already consecrated by history ; it may
be compared to one of those ancient palimpsests on
which the fictions of our forefathers are written across
the history of Thucydides or the Decades of Livy.
Here we are shewn the tower in which the aged
Simeon lived,—there the site of a terebinth under
which the Virgin used to sit,—the well of the Magi,—
Habakkuk's chapel, — Elijah's convent,—or Rachel's
tomb.

This last deserves notice ; the antiquity of the tradition, and its coincidence with the text of Holy Scripture, give probability to its authenticity, and it is held
in equal veneration by Mahometans, Christians, and
Jews. We know from Genesis, that Rachel died on
her way from Bethel to Bethlehem, and close to the
latter town ; that Jacob buried her by the wayside, and
that he erected over her sepulchre a monument which
was still standing in the days of the historian.§

The tomb of Rachel is a little builing crowned with
a cupola, just like the tombs of Mahometan saints. I

---

* Judges v. 10, x. 4. ‡ Zech. ix. 9 ; cf. St. Matt. xxi. 5.
† Isa. ii. 7.   § Gen. xxxv. 16—20.

18

hear with satisfaction that for some years past, thanks to Sir Moses Montefiore, the Turks have given up this monument to the Jews.   It might seem as if the great lamentation of Rachel were beginning to be heard, and that she must soon be comforted with the sight of her children, now oppressed and scattered, returning to her.*

One catches sight of Bethlehem some time before arriving there.   It is the very model of "*a city built on a hill, that cannot be hid.*"   This city has given to the world a great light, and all nations have rejoiced in it.†   Its situation is in many respects analogous to that of Jerusalem ; like it, it crowns the top of a mountain ;   it is encompassed by deep valleys, and forms a kind of promontory or peninsula which is connected with the principal chain only towards the north.

We all know that we cannot feel strongly attached to places that have no likeness to those familiar to us from our infancy.   But the great likeness to each other of these two cities explains how David was able to transfer to Jerusalem the love which he felt for his native city.   Indeed, Jerusalem is but a Bethlehem on a larger scale, better fortified, and capable of more extension and of being made into a capital.

Though Bethlehem stands higher than Jerusalem above the valleys that surround it, and presents still more the appearance of a mountain city, its aspect is less imposing and more attractive ; for the neighbouring hills are not so precipitous, and there are traces of cultivation upon it, which one looks for in vain upon the hills surrounding Jerusalem.   *Bethlehem*

* Jer. xxxi. 15; St. Matt. ii. 18.
† St. Matt. v. 14, 15.

Ephratah is still *the House of Bread* and *the Fertile*, as is indicated by these two Hebrew words. Wheat is cultivated either in the town itself, in little enclosures attached to the houses, or in the olive-yards, or between the fig trees and the vines. Terraces propped up with walls are the supports of these plantations. On all sides are to be seen round towers, to a great degree in' ruins, in which are oil presses, and which serve for shelter and for *vedette* for the guardians.

Another peculiarity of the situation of Bethlehem is that, in contrast with Jerusalem, the former is surrounded with hills of less elevation than that upon which itself stands ; and it therefore commands a very extensive outlook. From hence Ruth the Moabitess could see plainly her native mountains, and could return thither from hence in a day's journey. This situation of Bethlehem also justifies an expression in the Bible which may seem perplexing ; we read that Ruth *went down* to the threshing-floor of Boaz ; * it might seem more natural to say that she went *up* to it, for we know that in all Judæa they choose by preference high situations for their threshing-floors. But, from the very circumstances of the case, Bethlehem is an exception, since here the town towers above all that surrounds it ; and whether we suppose that the threshing-floor of Boaz was situated on one of the slopes of the hill of Bethlehem, or that it occupied the summit of one of the adjoining hills, in either case it was at a lower level than the town, and the expression used is the only one that would fit the facts.

These little details have their interest, however insignificant they may seem, or rather on that very account. They indicate that the historian was a native

* Ruth iii. 6.

of that country, familiarly acquainted with Bethlehem, and rendering faithfully the characteristics of the place, not from having made a special study of that region, but because he had so long lived there.

At the eastern end of the town is the triple convent of the Nativity, including the Latin, Greek, and Armenian convents, brothers but enemies to each other, like Esau and Jacob in the womb of their mother. Like the convent of St. Saba, it has the look of a fortress, with its high walls, low posterns, and iron doors. The convents in Palestine are, in fact, the only fortresses still maintained there by the Christian powers ; and it is necessary that they should be safe against *coups de main.*

Around these convents, and under their protection, the remains of the Christian population of the Holy Land have grouped themselves. Just so among us, in the Middle Ages, villages were seen forming and developing themselves under the shadow of the castles of the barons. Accordingly, thanks to the Bethlehem convent, the great majority of the population of the little town is Christian ; it is made up of Latin, Greek, or Armenian Arabs, who, in contrast with their spiritual guides, live on fairly good terms, and even intermarry with each other—" which," John tells me, " is not the case in Jerusalem."

One must have seen Oriental countries to form an adequate idea of the civilising power of Christianity. In Europe it sometimes seems to us as if Oriental Christianity in its degenerate state, atrophied by ignorance, disfigured by formalism and superstition, must be little better than Mahometanism. But it is not so. There is in the Gospel an immortal power of light and life, which the world's darkness may in some degree

overshadow, but can never completely destroy. One
is struck with this on visiting Bethlehem : the influence of Christianity makes itself felt ; the passengers
salute you with a certain affability ; they have in their
conduct, manners, and expression, more of vivacity and
of openness than the other Arabs. They are more
energetic, more industrious, more cheerful. Here the
people work, and in front of the houses the children,
instead of looking askance at us, continue their games
in our presence.

Notwithstanding the variety and play of fancy which
prevails in Arab costume, the following may, I think,
be said to be the ordinary dress of a Bethlehem man :
a white turban, a scarlet robe, and over it, picturesquely
draped, a dark-blue cloak. Some of the women wear
the parti-coloured gowns of their sisters in the country;
but the greater number a light-blue gown, and over
it a short, brick-dust coloured mantilla, with sleeves
covering only the shoulders. This costume must be
traditional in Bethlehem, for we see it used in the
most ancient pictures of the Blessed Virgin. All these
women also wear a head-dress which I have not ob
served elsewhere : instead of the little round cap, they
wear a taller one, and over it a white veil, which passes
in a straight line across their foreheads, and makes a
square frame for the face.

As I am upon the subject of dress, I will add that
the women of Palestine do not disfigure themselves, -
like those of Egypt, by a bizarre and complicated
system of tattooing ; they only print a stamp upon the
palms of their hands, another between the eyes, a point
upon the chin, and sometimes a row of small points on
the mouth, along the lower lip. Kept within these
limits, tattooing has a not unpleasing effect ; it gives

piquancy to the face, and brings out the brilliancy of the complexion, like the *patches* still in use in Europe, so much in fashion during last century.

The noble and regular features of the women of Bethlehem, their clear complexions, their fine noses slightly arched, the point bent a little downwards towards the mouth, the oval shape of the face, its outline more rounded and less sharp than in the Arab type, properly so called, distinguish them from the other inhabitants of these countries. I like to believe that here we see the characteristic type of countenance of the ancient Jewish race still preserved ; and this is a very probable supposition. The Christians of Palestine are certainly the primitive part of the population, dating from before the time of the Arab invasion, and not amalgamated with the conquering race. What I have said of the costume of the Bethlehemites is equally true of their faces ; one recognises in them at once the traditional type of face of the Virgin.

They pique themselves—though without alleging any proof of their assertion—upon being descended from the Crusaders. It is strange that people should pride themselves upon being the scarcely legitimate descendants of our adventurers of the twelfth century, when they might, on better grounds, call themselves cousins of Jesus and of Mary. But it is well known that the nobility of the sword is the most esteemed.

Bethlehem, which, in the days of Micah, was "*little among the thousands of Judah,*" * is now one of the largest towns of this tribe,—which, however, is not saying much. I am assured that its population amounts to 4,000 or 4,500 ; but this seems to me an exaggeration ; I doubt its exceeding 2,000 souls. Its Hebrew

* Micah v. 2.

name has survived unaltered, and the Arabs pronounce
it in strict conformity with Masoretic orthography.*

We dismount at the Latin convent, and are very
well received. The rooms are clean and spacious ;
the fare is extremely simple, but *Brother Cook* is clever
at his trade. The monks are affable, and have an
expression of honesty, gaiety, and cordiality, which
expands one's heart. After breakfast, I walk through
the town to get a more exact idea of it. In the days
of Ruth it was already walled, for we read of Boaz
and the elders "*sitting in the gate;*" † later on Rehoboam made it a fortress.‡ There is nothing now left
of its walls or gates.

Compared with Jerusalem, Bethlehem may pass for
a clean and handsome town ; it has indeed its heaps of
rubbish, but the houses are generally well built, and
some new ones even are now in building. Here, as
at Siloam, I have noticed that the roofs of many of the
houses serve for a street to those higher up.

A Catholic Bethlehemite,—whom I have sometimes
seen in Jerusalem, and from whom I have often bought
articles of his making,—George, the son of Issa,—meets
me, and presses me to come into his house. On a
level with the street is a large room,—vaulted, as they
all are here, and, as usual, without furniture. Three
women are squatted on the floor ; one sewing, by
the side of a cradle, another winnowing wheat ; the
third fetches me a chibouque and a glass of *aqua vitæ*,
while George displays before me the wares he makes
for sale ; they are rosaries, crucifixes, little boxes

---

* BETH-LÈKHEM. The first E very compressed, the second
very open, the last moderate. The accent is on the syllable LÈ.
† Ruth iv. ‡ 2 Chron. xi. 5, 6.

made of olive-wood, of mother-of-pearl, of red stone *of
the Holy Cross*, of black stone of the Dead Sea. The
manufacture of these little articles, which are sold in
great numbers to the pilgrims, is the trade of Bethlehem.   In the course of conversation he mentions that
a *Broushiân* lives in the adjoining house ; I express a
wish to see him, and they send for him.   He comes
from Lindau, on the borders of the Lake of Constance,
but the erudite Arabs give the name of Prussian to
every German who is not a Catholic.

I will not attempt here to describe by what con-
currence of circumstances this excellent man was led
to settle in Bethlehem, with his wife, a German like
himself, to cultivate the vine and make wine *à l'Européenne.*   This is an uncommon case, but less so than
one might suppose ; at a league from Bethlehem,
another *Brushiân* has brought the gardens of Solomon
into cultivation as a market garden.

As I re-enter the convent, a number of children come
in with me, to attend a class; for the Latin monks
are the only teachers and the only pastors of the
Catholic population of Bethlehem.   Though they are
all Italians or Spaniards, they quickly set themselves
to learn Arabic, and are in a short time ready to fulfil
their various functions.   No sight certainly could be
pleasanter, in the birthplace of the Saviour, than this
multitude of little heads, these children filling with
their merry shouts the great bare, solemn-looking courts.
One's thoughts ran back to the little ones who here
perished by the fury of Herod,—infant martyrs for an
infant God.

I visit the church and the caves.   The church,
called that of *St. Helena*, belonged formerly to the
Latins; now it is the property of the Greeks and

Armenians; but the Latins have retained or recovered a place in the caves under it. Fourteen steps lead down from this church into the Cave of the Nativity. I do not know whether it is authentic; but in this case, as in that of Calvary and the Holy Sepulchre, I feel that to be a question of secondary importance. One cannot enter these places otherwise than with head bowed before the mighty mystery of the Incarnation, the central point of history and of eternity. I cannot express what I felt, when I read upon a marble slab let into the ground, these simple words: "*Here Jesus Christ was born*"—HIC DE VIRGINE MARIA JESUS CHRISTUS NATUS EST.

I pass, without stopping, before the altar of the Three Kings, the stone crèche, the tomb of the Holy Innocents, and the place where St. Joseph used to put down his stick. Such sights here are like the Apocryphal Gospels by the side of that of St. Luke. I only just note, in passing, the tomb of St. Eusebius of Cremona; I look, however, with interest at the cave in which St. Jerome translated the Bible. I like to recall the memory of the great man who, having given up everything on earth besides, ended by giving up even the glory of being, as he expressed it, a *ciceronian*, to make himself nothing more than a humble Christian, a child in faith, fasting and praying in the places in which the Son of God was pleased to be a child. The body of the saint rests in an adjoining cave.

Whether the Cave of the Nativity is authentic, it would be difficult to prove or disprove. In Judæa, to this day, caves are very commonly used as stables. The fourteen steps leading down into this do not constitute a valid objection, for they are quite at the bottom of the Church of St. Helena, and it is possible that the soil has here been raised in order to make a level site on which to build the church.   However that may be, of all the traditions upon the Holy Places, this is the most ancient ; and even so early as the second century, Justin Martyr, who was an inhabitant of this country, says that Jesus was born in a cave.

The birthplace of Jesus Christ at Bethlehem, and His sepulchre at Jerusalem, are possessions of inestimable value for the Christian powers ;—they offer a difficulty always available, an ever-present subject for diplomatic notes, a *casus belli* ready to their hands.   Whatever may be the object in view, the *Question of the Holy Places* is an excellent point to start from.   As is well known, it was from the cave at Bethlehem that the last Oriental war took its rise ; the Franciscans accused the Greeks of having carried off the stone with the Latin inscription, which I mentioned just now, and of having substituted another, with an inscription in Greek ;—it was another case of a " *chant du Lutrin,*" and the quarrel might have been settled in Barbin's shop, had there happened to be a Barbin at Bethlehem ; * but the Greek monks had Russia on their side, the Latins France, and diplomacy intervened—*et voilà la guerre allumée!* †   I do but mention all this, without going into an examination of the facts.   As to the first question, which is not yet completely solved, Solomon would perhaps have cut the knot by proposing that there should be a Latin inscription, with a Greek one over against it.

Talking of Solomon,—there are some remarkable monuments of his power to be seen close at hand here.   The famous pools which bear his name are at scarcely a league's distance from the city of David.   We

---

* An allusion to *Le Lutrin,* a comic-heroic poem by Boileau.
  A quotation from La Fontaine.

descend from Bethlehem by the southern slope ; on this side particularly the town looks well, and forms a perfect crown to the mountain. The fertile territory of Ephratah does not extend far round ; within a few minutes we leave it behind, and see before us nothing but rocky mountains ; to the left rises the *Mount of the Franks*, a hill-top cut off sharply from everything round it ; in form a truncated cone ; one might think it an extinct volcano, or a work of human art. Its close neighbourhood to Tekoa gives much probability to the supposition that it is the *Beth-hakkérem* of which Jeremiah speaks : "*Blow the trumpet in Tekoa, and set up a sign of fire in Beth-haccerem.*"* It would not be easy to find in this part of Judæa a mountain more noticeable, or visible from a greater distance.

According to a tradition,—for the truth of which, however, there is no other evidence,—a party of French knights defended themselves upon this hill-top for thirty or forty years after Jerusalem had fallen a second time into the hands of the Saracens ; and this was the reason it was called *the Mount of the Franks*. The Arabs call it *Djebel-el-Feredîs* (*Paradise*, or *Park*, *Mount*) ; that is almost a translation of the Hebrew expression *Beth-hakkérem* (the house of the vine or vineyard). It has been supposed that it owes this name, either to the plantations which used to cover it, and of which the existence there in former times is still attested by some remains of terraces,—or to the gardens of Solomon, close by, to which we are just coming.

Accordingly, very soon, between two rocky mountains we discover a narrow valley clothed in the freshest verdure. On coming near it, we hear the unaccus-

* Jer. vi. 1.

tomed sound of a little stream running over the grass.
We are in the *Wady Wurtâs,* the garden of Solomon,
also called *hortus conclusus,* on account of its situation
at the bottom of the valley, and in allusion to the
poetical metaphor of the Song of Solomon.* It must
have been easy to water it abundantly by means of
this stream and of the large reservoirs which Solomon
had had excavated on the adjoining mountain. To
this day it is still, thanks to the little stream which
runs down the wady, a charming oasis, an Alpine or
Lebanon valley amongst the arid hills of Judæa.

The whole of this valley of Wurtâs is carefully cultivated ; it is, as I have said, a German who has made
these fine kitchen gardens. We pass in front of his
house, which is surrounded with rose trees, limes, and,
above all, peaches ; it all has an indescribable look of
order and of *plan,* in which one recognises at once the
presence of a European.

From thence, following the lines of the mountain, we
climb up to the pools ; they are at a considerable
height, in a *combe* near the summit. They consist of
three basins cut out of the rock, and lined within with a
wall of masonry; they are arranged one above the other,
and communicate with each other. Robinson measured
all three. The lowest basin is 50 feet deep and 582
feet long ; its breadth is 207 feet at one end, and 148
feet at the other. The dimensions of the second are a
little smaller ; the third, which is the smallest, is 380
feet long, by from 229 to 236 broad. They are still
full, up to a certain height, of clear limpid water ; but
as the bottom is a good deal worn, it allows a large
quantity of the water to escape, so that in summer
they are nearly empty.

* Song of Solomon iv. 12.

These reservoirs are filled partly from the rain-water brought down from the neighbouring slopes, and partly from a fine spring, issuing from the mountain-side, two or three hundred feet higher up. This spring is enclosed and roofed over with a vault ; the Arabs call it *Ain-Sâleh,* and the Franks *the sealed fountain* (*fons signatus*).

"*A garden inclosed is my sister, my spouse ; a spring shut up, a fountain sealed. Thy plants are an orchard of pomegranates, with pleasant fruits ; camphire with spikenard. Spikenard and saffron ; calamus and cinnamon, with all trees of frankincense ; myrrh and aloes, with all the chief spices ; a fountain of gardens, a well of living waters, and streams from Lebanon. Awake, O north wind : and come, thou south ; blow upon my garden, that the spices thereof may flow out. Let my beloved come into his garden, and eat his pleasant fruits."* *

Was it near this limpid spring, under these pomegranates in bloom, of the Wurtâs valley, that the writer of this incomparable idyll, fresh as the spring, fiery as love, was inspired? At any rate, it is difficult to doubt that, at least as he wrote the following passage in Ecclesiastes, Solomon was thinking of the great works of which I now see the remains. We have been listening to the words of a youth, let us turn now to those of an old man : "*I made me great works : I builded me houses ; I planted me vineyards,*† *I made me*

---

* Song of Solomon iv. 12—16.

† Our versions say *vines.* But in Palestine there are no vineyards like ours ; the vine, the olive, the fig-tree, and the other fruit trees are all cultivated together. A plantation of this kind called in Hebrew כרם, answers pretty nearly to what we call an *orchard.*

gardens and orchards,* and I planted trees in them of all kinds of fruits: I made me pools of water, to water therewith the wood that bringeth forth trees. I got me servants and maidens, ... men singers and women singers; .... and whatsoever mine eyes desired, I kept not from them; I withheld not my heart from any joy. .... Then I looked, ... and, behold, all was vanity and vexation of spirit. †

The tradition which gives the name of Solomon to the pools and gardens of Wurtâs is not very ancient, or rather it is not a tradition, but evidently a simple induction which suggested itself spontaneously to the minds of travellers. The places I have just described do, in fact, correspond perfectly both with the allusions in Ecclesiastes, and with what Josephus tells us of the gardens of Solomon. If the pools of Wurtâs are not the works of that king, I cannot see to whom we could attribute their construction. I look in vain in the history of Judæa for any other age or for any other king that would have been capable of executing, or even of conceiving the idea of these great works. One is reminded involuntarily of the fountains at Versailles. Solomons and Louis the Fourteenths do not, for obvious reasons, repeat themselves in the history of a nation.

At a few steps off is a square castle flanked with four towers, and with no entrance but a gate now closed. Its architecture is Saracenic, and perhaps it was built only as a protection to the pools; for, during

---

* Literally *paradises.*. It is again the same word which is used in the Song of Solomon in the passage cited above. A *park* is really the equivalent, in our modern way of speaking, for what the Persians, and after them, the Hebrews and the Greeks, called a *paradise.*

† Eccl. ii. 4—11.

eighteen centuries, these pools have supplied the fountains of the Jerusalem Haram with water. After they
had raised Judæa to the rank of their other provinces,
the Romans, who were men of practical minds, did not
choose to leave unemployed these great stores of water,
at that time used only for the maintenance of a pleasure
garden for which there was no use in a country without a king or a capital. Pontius Pilate determined to
bring this water to Jerusalem by an aqueduct. He
executed this purpose, and the aqueduct still exists.
But, to construct it, money was wanted, and Pilate diverted to this object the sacred treasure of the Temple
—the *Korban.* We owe these details to Josephus and
the Talmud. This act of spoliation was one of the
causes which most alienated the minds of men from
him ; they considered it sacrilege. Pilate perceived,
but a little too late, that he had not allowed sufficiently
for the strength of the religious prejudices of the Jews :
he did not wish to fall again into the same mistake,
and to come a second time into collision with a fanaticism which he had now learnt to appreciate ; accordingly, when the Jews demanded with loud cries that he
should pass sentence upon Jesus as a breaker of the
law, he was afraid to oppose them, and notwithstanding his contempt for the canting hypocrites of Jerusalem,
he gave up into their hands one whose innocence he
acknowledged.

The top of the mountain, near the pools, is bare and
treeless ; but there are to be found in abundance, in the
midst of the thorns that are so common in Bethlehem,
the beautiful blue irises, which I noticed at Sharon,
and the large red anemones, which are the flowers
most characteristic of Judæa. The glory of Solomon
has long since vanished, but the lilies of the field are

still, as in the time of Jesus, clothed in their robes of splendour.   Donkeys and camels are grazing on the heights.   Three bachi-bazouks are stationed on guard on the road ; they are from the castle garrison.   I have already mentioned that fighting was then actually going on, on the road from Bethlehem to Hebron.

We return to Bethlehem, not by way of the valley, but following the line of Pilate's aqueduct, along the crests of the hills.   Hhannah tries to draw me into conversation, and to make me notice the places through which we are passing ; but these words recurred to my memory, and I could not turn my attention from them: "HE SUFFERED UNDER PONTIUS PILATE." There is indeed in these words a something which eclipses, and makes one quite forget, all the glory of Solomon.

On coming back to Bethlehem, my eyes have the unexpected pleasure of falling upon a familiar figure ; —my old companion on ship-board, M. Basson, of St. Stephen, one of the French pilgrims of the *Céphise.*   He has been for some weeks at Jerusalem, and before leaving, he wishes to revisit Bethlehem, which interests him more than all else.   He has just returned from the *Shepherd's Field,* but wishes to go there once more with me.   There, according to tradition, the angels appeared to the shepherds.   We go there toge-ther.   The sun is setting, herds of oxen are returning into the village, the air is cold, the night-wind is blowing upon these bare hill-sides; we might fancy ourselves on one of the plateaux of the Jura.

Except an ancient subterranean church, the *Shep-herd's Field* has nothing remarkable belonging to it but the tradition which attaches to it, in support of which no further authority can be pleaded.   These fields in the valley seem fertile, and never can have served for pastures. I should prefer to take them as illustrations of the stories of Ruth and her gleanings, and of Boaz's reapers, and to me it would seem more natural to refer the scene reported by St. Luke to one of the numerous hills which surround the town towards the south. There are, in fact, in Bethlehem three regions perfectly distinct from each other. The tops of the hills are bare of trees, that is the region of the pastures ; their sides are covered with vines ; and lower down in the valleys are those fine fields of corn which have given to Bethlehem its name. I cannot doubt that David had present to his imagination the district round his native city, when in one of his psalms he wrote, " *The little hills shall rejoice* * *on every side. The folds shall be full of sheep; the valleys shall stand thick with corn.*" †

This evening I have withdrawn peacefully into my Franciscan cell, to write an account of my journey. I have before me a copper lamp, which, but for the fact that it has only three branches, represents very faithfully the lamp in the Tabernacle, as the Bible describes it. Above the reservoir which contains the oil is a disc, from which is suspended by four little chains an extinguisher, a pin to draw out the wick,‡ pincers to snuff it, and a little dish to catch the snuff that falls from the lamps.§ I am quite aware that this lamp is not an Arab one, but imported from Italy, where this kind of lamp is very common. Nevertheless,

---

* The sign of this *joy* is the vines. Allusion is intended to the Hebrew proverb : " *Wine which maketh glad the heart of man.*" See Judges ix. 13 ; Psalm civ. 15 ; Eccles. x. 19.

† Psalm lxv. 13, 14.

‡ " *Et producit acu stupas humore carentes.*"—VIRGIL, *Moretum.* Exod. xxv. 38.

19

I am inclined to believe that, at least, in these general characteristics, it is of an antique pattern, like many other implements still in use in Italy.

XI.

St. John of the Desert.

Thursday, April 8th.—In that adventurous *épopée* in the life of David, which has been preserved for us in the books of Samuel, there is no episode breathing more of the spirit of chivalry than the history of the well of Bethlehem.   It occurred at the time when David had entrenched himself in the cave of Adullam. Thirty captains had joined him there.   The Philistines had garrisoned Bethlehem.   It was harvest time. Overcome, perhaps, by fatigue, and consumed with that home-sickness which sometimes takes possession of the heart of an exile, David let fall this expression of a longing desire : " *Oh that one would give me drink of the water of the well of Bethlehem, which is by the gate !   And the three mighty men brake through the host of the Philistines, and drew water out of the well of Bethlehem, that was by the gate, and took it, and brought it unto David ; nevertheless, he would not drink thereof, but poured it out unto the Lord, and he said, Be it far from me, O Lord, that I should do this ; is not this the blood of the men that went in jeopardy of their lives ?   Therefore he would not drink it.*" *

The interest which I had always felt in this story made me eager to see this well in which centred for the son of Jesse the sweet memories of his native place.   In the little cities of the East, the well, with the gate which is generally near it, constitute the forum, the focus of their social life; and there, night and morning,

* 2 Sam. xxiii. 13—17 ; 1 Chron. xi. 15—29.

meet the shepherds who during the day have been scattered among the pastures, and who now come to water their flocks, the maidens coming to fill the tall pitchers which they carry on their shoulders, and the travellers stopping to have their meals,* or to pitch their tents.

I set off with John, at six in the morning. A sort of suburb extends a little distance outside the town ; it consists of neat and pretty houses ; as a whole, Bethlehem has the look of a new town, and the stone of which it is built is of a clear, fresh colour, which gladdens the eye. The well is at the entrance into the town, as the Bible expressly says, and as, besides, all wells are in Palestine ; it is a few paces off from the road to Jerusalem, by which I arrived yesterday ; one may even make a probable guess that when the town was walled, this was the only entrance into it ; it is the only one allowed by nature, since, as I have said, the town of Bethlehem is a sort of peninsula, with steep sides to it, surrounded by valleys on every side but this.

The situation of this well, north of the town, and consequently on the opposite side to the cave of Adullam, where David had entrenched himself, makes it easy to understand what dangers the three heroes had necessarily to face ; this well could not be reached by any other road than that which they took, that is to say, boldly traversing the enemy's camp.

We dismount, and I proceed to take my measures. The well has five openings arranged in a triangle of considerable extent,—for the longest side is about twenty metres in length. It is partly filled with stones ; its depth must at one time have been much greater than it is now ; in our day it has great inequalities. Measured at one of its openings, the well is found to

* St. John iv. 6—8.

be eight metres in depth ; at this spot it still holds a certain quantity of water (about fifty or sixty centimetres). Sounding the depth at a second opening, I find it six metres deep, with scarcely any water in it. Finally repeating this process in the other openings, I find about the same depth, but the bottom quite dry.

This water seemed to me fresh and good ; I feel certain that there must be a spring here, but that most of it is lost, owing to the wearing away of the bottom of the well. Bethlehem has no other well of running water, but only cisterns.* The convent has seven of its own.

Instead of returning to the high road, we follow for a moment Pilate's aqueduct. It is a canal constructed of masonry, almost level with the ground round it, and covered with great unhewn stones ; one would not know it from the low walls so common in this country, were it not that at intervals there are openings through which one can see the water running.

Arrived over against the tomb of Rachel and the Christian village of Beit-Djala, where the Latin patriarch, Monsignor Valerga, is now erecting a large and handsome seminary, we turn aside from the way towards Jerusalem, and quitting the beaten tracks, canter freely across the pastures. Soon a wide smiling valley opens before us. In front, on the high ground, are the two villages of Sérâfat and Safâfa. We pass near one of those magnificent terebinths, of which the lonely majesty used in former times to impress the people of the country with a feeling of religious veneration, and which, even in our own day, are often considered sacred by the Arabs of Palestine. It is not

* Wells באֵר (beér), and cisterns באוּר (beôr), בוּר, are always carefully distinguished in the Bible.

uncommon to see some of these terebinths with their branches all hung with little woollen rags, a sort of token of homage, or *ex voto* offerings, with which the Mahometans also deck the tombs of their saints. In enclosures around are fine growths of fig, almond, vine, and rose trees ; cyclamens, coquettishly bending down their lilac or violet petals on their stalks, grow in tufts by the roadside ; the birds are singing, and my moukre too chants a song in ascending gamut, reminding me of some of the Paris street cries. I make Hhannah interpret it to me. It is a song common to all coun-tries :—"*Never will my heart love any other than her ; my heart melts at the sight of her, like wax at the fire.*"

Soon we enter another valley, narrower and longer than the last, at the end of which stands the convent of St. John of the Desert. It opens again into another, filled with olive trees, said to be the valley of the Terebinth, in which David killed the Philistine giant. So that we had nearly followed the footsteps of the young son of Jesse, when he went from Bethlehem to take to his brothers the loaves and the parched corn, and to their captain the cheeses. It was a three or four hours' journey, and, by starting early, the boy could easily go and return before night, and not lose sight for more than a day of his sheep, which he had "*left with a keeper.*"* A tower which here comes in sight, on the hill which stands between us and this valley, is called by tradition *Goliath's tower.*

By the side of the convent of St. John is the village of *Aïn Kârim* ; it is said to be inhabited by from two to three hundred Christians, and nearly a thousand ·Mahometans. The whole of this corner of the country ·is well cultivated ; the hills are covered with terraces,

* 1 Sam. xvii. 17—20.

growing vines, wheat, and fig-trees. No part of this
land belongs, as I was at first led to think it did, to
the convent.

We leave on one side the convent, which we shall
not enter till later ; for we wish first to visit St. John
the Baptist's spring, and the desert in which, according
to tradition, the Forerunner of Jesus Christ passed his
childhood, before "*the day of his shewing unto Israel.*" †
Not that this tradition, of comparatively very modern
origin, inspires me with much confidence ; but I am
pleased with anything which leads to my exploring the
country. We make our way along the sides of the
mountains. In this country, in which the roads very
generally run along the heights, the view from them is
always wide and open ; and besides, it is not blocked
by houses, trees, or walls ; for the walls of the vineyards are never more than two or three feet in height.
Here we are in the wilderness of St. John, a cheerful-
looking, flower-bedecked wilderness, which less deserves
to be so called than many other parts of Judæa not so
designated. It is a mountain-top covered with white
cistuses, yellow papilionaceæ, and a quantity of different kinds of flowers, and of woody plants scarcely
raising themselves above the ground. After crossing
this summit, we reach St. John's spring ; it issues
from a hole in the rock; and, at two paces' distance,
on the same steep slope, is the cave in which the Forerunner lived ; according to others, it is that in which
his mother Elizabeth hid herself with him, to escape
the massacre of the children by Herod. One sees how
legend allows itself free play here. I forgot to mention
that we had just now passed in front of the Cave of the
Visitation, and of the ruins of a country house of St.

* St. Luke i. 80.

Elizabeth ; her principal home was, no doubt, at Aïn Kârim, since it was there that her son was born.

I am prevented from seeing the interior of St. John's cave. The Superior of the Franciscans has bought it, given it a door, and put the key in his pocket. There is no porter to open it. This mania for protecting monuments which sufficiently protect themselves, must, it seems, penetrate even into Palestine. If ever the taste for restoring them, and for marking them off distinctly, grows up by the side of the other, there will be an end of the Holy Land.

Opposite, on the side of a high mountain, stands the little village of Sâtâf. It is but seldom that the villages in Judæa are, like that in La Bruyère, "*painted on the slopes of the hills.*" As they are of the same colour as the rock, the eye can only with difficulty distinguish them, unless they happen to be on the top, and so stand out against the sky. Accordingly, though this one is near enough for me to be able to see the inhabitants sitting in front of their houses, I should never have noticed its existence, had not the noise of the human voices and the cries of the domestic animals, reaching my ear across the silence of nature, revealed their presence. This is easily understood when one remembers the grey colour of certain southern villages—about Avignon, for instance—which do not stand out any better than these against the background of the bare hills which border the Rhone. One always fancies them ruins.

On our return to the convent of St. John, Hhannah, who has an attack of fever, goes to lie down for a while. I enter the divan, in which the house-servant, a Catholic Arab, who knows a little Italian, comes to keep me company till his masters come out of the church. He questions me as to what country I belong to, asks if Switzerland is subject to England, France, Italy, etc. The Arabs often call Austria Italy, because the Austrian navy speaks Italian and is essentially Venetian. In compensation, I have sometimes heard the language of Petrarch and of Monsignor Valerga called *Austriaco*.

In a short quarter of an hour, half a dozen Francis-cans with great white beards make their appearance ; they take their seats on the divan, and make me the warmest offers of hospitality, assuring me that I may stay with them as many days as I please. Then they give me my dinner in one of the cells. The St. John's wine is very superior to that of Bethlehem ; it is con-sidered the best in the country.

The convent is large, and has a fine walled garden, growing cypresses and other evergreen trees. There are here, as at Bethlehem, only ten monks ; they are all Spaniards or Italians. By the side of the Church is the Cave of the Nativity of St. John the Baptist. But why should they think he was born in a cave ? It is evident that the cave at Bethlehem, the most ancient of the Holy Places—whether it is authentic or not— has had followers in Palestine.

On St. John the Baptist's day it is the habit of the Latins of Jerusalem to visit St. John's of the Desert. The feast is of long duration, like all Oriental feasts ; it does not last less than twelve days. The visitors lodge with the *bourgeois* of Aïn Kârim, and they spend their time joyously, Hhannah tells me, singing, dancing, and, above all, indulging in discharges of musketry.

We choose for our return journey a road which is to take us direct to Jerusalem. On reaching the mountain-top which overhangs the convent of St. John, we catch sight of the Holy City. There still intervene between it and us four successive ranges of hills ; but as they are much less high than that upon which we are standing, they are not distinguishable to our sight ; one fancies one is looking down on a plain. I am never weary of dwelling upon all there is of grandeur in most of the views in this country, for I find that this characteristic has not been sufficiently noticed.

These mountains are not absolutely sterile. Their summits, it is true, are but rocky pastures ; but on their sides there are a few wheat-fields. Pastures of this kind make the Parable of the Sower * perfectly intelligible ; one could not cast a handful of seed on them, without some of it falling on stony ground, and some among thorns.

In the last valley we have to cross, we see, at two hundred yards to the right of our road, a handsome building with lofty walls ;—the convent of the Holy Cross. It is inhabited by Greek monks, famed for their hospitality and tolerant spirit ; one might also praise their courage, for they are much exposed to the attacks of marauding Bedouins and fanatic Mahometans. It is not many years back that the Arabs invaded them in the night, and murdered the Archimandrite.

Every convent in the Holy Land wishes to connect with its name some consecrating memory. This one claims to possess in its chapel, not the cross itself of Jesus, but at least *the hole in which was planted the tree of which it was made.*

But we have had enough for one day of legends and of convents. *Guardi e passa.*†

* St. Matt. xiii. 3—9.
† Vid. Dante, *Inferno*, cant. xiii.

IV.

SAMARIA AND GALILEE.

Devenere locos lætos, et amœna vireta.

I.

FROM JERUSALEM TO NAZARETH.

THE moment had arrived for leaving Jerusalem. I should have liked to have put it off indefinitely. I could not make up my mind to bid a final farewell to these walls, which I had so long desired to see ; to relegate to the past, to the world of memory, that of which during so many years I had been in the habit of keeping the image before me as a hope and a vision of glory. But I was urged to start at once; for the spring was advancing, and it was already some days since Coptic and Catholic pilgrims, English and American tourists,—all who knew the seasons,—like the crane and the swallow, had taken flight in the direction of Carmel or of Jaffa, to be in time to avoid the warm month of May, when the hot sun burns the ground to dust, and the Bedouin goes forth to war. I therefore made up my mind to set out as soon as possible to visit Samaria and Galilee.

I mentioned that in travelling in Palestine, one generally makes a bargain with a dragoman, who pro-

* An allusion to the well-known fairy tale, *Blue Beard.*

vides one, at so much a day, with tent, horses, and provisions. For the sake of economy and, still more, of safety, one travels in caravans. This way of travelling is convenient in one sense, as you have not to trouble yourself about the little material necessities of existence ; you find under your tent each night the bed in which you slept the night before, and having once become accustomed to the cookery of the dragoman, you are not obliged every day to make dangerous experiments.

I had appreciated in former excursions the comforts that belong to this manner of life ; but none the less did I remain convinced that the thing in the world which is most comfortable is freedom. The thought of being handed over by contract to a dragoman, who fixes the occupations of your days, the hour of getting up and going to bed, and who may come in at any moment to interrupt your siesta or your meal, like Don Juan's Commander, or like the "conductors" of diligences in the old times ; this thought, I say, was only moderately agreeable to me. It seemed to me, also, that to carry one's tent with one, like a snail, to sleep in every night, was to rob travelling of its principal charms, the liability to surprise, and the local colouring of the journey. One might as well go through those long flights by railway, in which, from Paris to Bayonne, you are exposed to no greater shock than finding at each station the identical buffet and waiting-room.

I told my faithful Hhannah, therefore, of my wish to travel alone, without tent or cook ; I asked him if this idea could be acted upon, and I proposed to him to accompany me. Hhannah (I must confess that generally I called him simply John, to spare my lungs) answered that he was willing to accompany me whither

I pleased, and that the plan I proposed could perfectly well be executed, if I was not afraid of sometimes sleeping in a stable, and could be satisfied on occasion to live on oranges and café, not *au lait;* and we should find, into the bargain, an inn at Tiberias, and a convent at Carmel.

Accordingly, he brought me some *moukres*, and I prepared to start.

I hired three horses, one for John, another for my luggage, a third for myself. The two *moukres* were, according to custom, to travel on foot. For safety I carried in my girdle two pistols which I bought at Marseilles on the eve of my departure. In the East, to be respected you must go armed. It is true I had no bullets, and I had tried in vain to buy a little gun-powder at Jerusalem. In my heart of hearts I was glad of it ; it would have gone against me to stain the Holy Land with bloodshed. Of these two pistols I was robbed of one in the convent at Nazareth, and the other slipped out of my girdle at Argos, as I was coming down from the castle of the Atridæ. May they have fallen into hands as pacific as my own, or at least never have been used but in defence of order and of property ! . . . . It is more than I dare hope.

To finish what I have to say of Jerusalem, I give here some fragments of the last letter I wrote before quitting it ; it contains some details for which I have not found a place in my journal :—

A. M. L. B., A——
Monday Evening.

My intention is to continue my pilgrimage to-mor-row, going to Nablous, Nazareth, and Tiberias, and from there to Beyrout, either by Damascus or by the coast of Tyre and Sidon. It is not without regret, nor without some effort of self-control, that I leave this Jerusalem, in which I have spent such delightful days, and which will leave ineffaceable impressions upon my memory. But all the caravans are already gone, except a small party of Englishmen who start to-morrow, and whom I shall follow at a greater or less distance. M. Gobat urges me not to set off at a time when I should be quite alone, for the country is not in a safe state ; there is fighting going on in several places. The other day, I was spending the evening with Consul R——, a very amiable man, whom I am very sorry not to have seen oftener. Suddenly a janissary comes in, and informs him that two guests who lately left him have just been robbed on the Jaffa road, at a few steps' distance from the gates of Jerusalem. They were stripped of everything but their shirts. The consul hurried off to the pacha, who promised to have enquiry made ; and to-day I hear that the robbers have been caught. But one is not always so fortunate; and the pacha himself did not expect it. Like his predecessor, Pilate, he does not believe in the attainableness of truth. He was expounding to the consul the other day his scepticism as to the course of justice in the world, and cited in support of his argument a criminal case, in which his father, a pacha like himself, had put seventy persons to death by torture, without succeeding in discovering the real criminal. You see, people do, at any rate, what good they can. Anyhow, my pacha is a *perfect gentleman*,* as I had the honour of realising in my own experience at the ceremonial of the sacred fire.

To-day I have made my preparations for starting— some indispensable purchases. There is no great variety

* So written, in English, by the author —*Tr.*

of resource at Jerusalem. In Switzerland, where civilization reaches an altitude of eight thousand feet, where
one finds a telegraph on the top of the Righi and
pianos on the Faulhorn, one finds it hard to believe
that there can anywhere be towns with a population of
twenty thousand souls into which it has not yet pene-
trated. The sole representatives of European industry
and commerce here are three or four Greeks, who inscribe
on their sign-boards " *Tailor and Merchant,*" or else
"*British Magazine,*"* and who display together on their
counters Swiss absinthe, coloured shirts, cheese from
Cyprus, artificial flowers, and china. I had the greatest
trouble in finding a knife of any kind. The Arab
merchants are Arabs. Their good point is that they
never fail to offer a purchaser a narguileh ready lighted,
and a cup of coffee boiling hot. But for myself my
needs are few. I bring away with me only a tin cup,
which I was obliged to have specially made for me, of
course. You see, my *ménage* is even more simple than
that of Diogenes; I carry no tub; Hhannah tells me
it is not indispensable; he will get the Arabs to lodge
me. Where there are no Arabs, one may take refuge,
like David, in caves. This manner of travelling was
pleasant to me; one finds oneself more in contact with
the natives, and one sees their home ways. I shall be
very glad to make close acquaintance with the hospitality of the sons of Ishmael; I have already had
occasion to see in what respects it differs from that of
the Scotch mountaineers,† and to remark how well they

* So written, in English, by M. Bovet.—*Tr.*

† An allusion to a couplet in the opera *La Dame Blanche*, by
Boieldieu—

" Chez les montagnards écossais
L'hospitalité *se donne*
Elle ne se *vend* jamais."

know its value in *piastres* and *mejidiehs.* Good-night.
I hope you have got home again happily, and that this
letter will find you amongst the trees and flowers of your
orchards. As for me, notwithstanding all the pleasure
I have in travelling, I long, I assure you, to have done
with the bournous and the turban, to lay down at your
gate my pilgrim's *courbache,* and to come and " *mingle the
dust of Africa and of Asia with the ashes of your fire.*" *

P.S.—I write on the best paper to be had in
Jerusalem.

First Day's Journey.

FROM JERUSALEM TO BIREH.

My first day's journey is recorded in a letter which I
wrote that same evening. This letter is absolutely
unpublished, for it was not even sent. I had forgotten,
when I wrote it, that there was no means of forward-
ing it.

EL-BIREH, *Tuesday Evening.*

How I wish, dear friend, you could see me seated
here at the heart of the most primitive civilization,
squatted in the middle of an Arab family, who look
with curiosity at me as I write, the father holding
my candle over my paper, the women and children
communicating their remarks to him. How much
would I give to understand them ! Really, I call this
one of the most charming evenings of my life. At any
rate, it is one of the least commonplace.

It was yesterday that I suddenly made up my mind
that I would leave Jerusalem to-day. Many bad omens
seemed to gather round my departure. My poor John
this morning lost his brother, a youth of eighteen, who

* A sentence of V. Hugo in the *Feuilles d'Automne.*

died after six days' pleurisy. They buried him some hours after. I put off starting, that I might not take John away from his family at such a moment. I wished to delay longer still ; but he insisted that I should not change any of my plans.

At three o'clock in the afternoon we leave Jerusalem. The olive trees of the orchards soon hide the town from me ; but on reaching the Scopus, it stands before us once more in all its beauty, facing the Mount of Olives, and I salute it for the last time. The road to Damascus is continued over a plateau of broken ground ; on the left the lofty summit of *Nebî-Samuel* is visible for a long time ; but at last it disappears, and no more mountains are to be seen, for the hills which rise at intervals on each side of the road are not to be so called. Such little hills, crowned with a poor village, or with the ruins of an ancient town, are common in the territory of Benjamin. Here particularly the towns are commonly built upon the summits of the mountains ; the names of the most famous belonging to this tribe indicate clearly enough where to look for their remains—*Rama* (height), *Tsélah* (rock), *Mizpah* (sentinel), *Gibeah*, *Geba*, *Gabaon* (hill). It is, no doubt, due to the geographical sense of these words that they have been preserved to our times.

The road which I follow is the great road of the caravans, by which St. Paul travelled on his way to Damascus. The ancient Roman road may still be clearly traced ; it is paved with enormous stones, which, being now much worn and often displaced, make the most frightfully rocky road to be found even in this country. Accordingly, one prefers travelling by the side of it.

Many sad feelings come over me. I cannot get

over my sorrow at leaving Jerusalem ; I should like
to turn back there, never to leave it. I am uneasy at
the journey upon which I am entering ; I seem to
myself to have been utterly wanting in judgment and
foresight. After cutting short my stay at Jerusalem,
that I might have the protection of the little English
caravan which left us this morning, I have allowed it
to start long before me, and now it is late ; we shall
only reach Bireh at night, and that is almost as much
as to say that we shall certainly be robbed. So, at
least, my *moukres* insist; and their hang-dog counte·
nances appear to hint that they will themselves, if
necessary, see to the fulfilment of their prophecies. As
for Hhannah, his habitual silence and reserve would
suffice, of themselves, to incline one to the spleen, and
to-day one is not surprised that, after the loss which he
has just suffered, the poor youth should be even more
morose than usual.

Like little clouds rising out of the horizon on a summer
day, which soon grow larger, swell out, and at last cover
the whole heaven, my sadness gradually darkens my
view of my whole existence. Oh, what memories rise
within me ! Oh, what regrets ! Oh, what despond-
ency ! . . . .

*   *   *   *   *   *

*   *   *   *   *   *

I am lifted out of this state by some familiar musical
notes that ring in my memory. They are the air of
the forty-second Psalm : "*Like as the hart desireth the
water-brooks.*" . . . . I echo them with the most ardent
sighs of my soul ; I am now in the place in which this
Psalm was sung for the first time, where this same
experience of the Divine help has so often and so

20

strikingly been realised : "*My God, my soul is vexed within me ; therefore will I remember Thee concerning the land of Jordan. . . . . Why art thou so vexed, O my soul ? and why art thou so disquieted within me ?*" Then I make the mountains of Benjamin echo to these other ancient and simple words : "*Gracious and righteous is the Lord ; therefore will He teach sinners in the way.*" *

The sun sets, night draws on, our way is desert. We enter a shallow *wady;* then, after a short ascent, appears, on the high ground to the east, the village of Bireh. At the foot of the hill, a fine spring, with abundant water, announces its proximity. Round the spring are women come to fill their pitchers from its waters.

In our time, as in the days of Rebecca, of Rachel, and of the daughters of Jethro, when after a silent day's journey the traveller, coming within sight of a village, wishes to lodge there, it is to the neighbourhood of the well or spring that he must betake himself. Accordingly, thither John leads me ; for we too arrive "*at the time of the evening, even the time that women go out to draw water.*" † My guide addresses one of them ; she calls her husband ; an Arab comes up, with a black beard and ragged turban ; his only dress is his white shirt, open over the chest, and his heavy striped cloak ; a great sword hangs from his girdle. This costume in its simplicity gives a look of dignity even to the poorest villager. The Arab offers us hospitality, which I eagerly accept.

He takes us to his house. It is a stone building, vaulted in the interior, like a cave, and admitting the

* Psalm xxv. 7. † Gen. xxiv. 11.

light only by the door.* It consists of only one room, of which I cannot better describe the distribution than by comparing it to the part of a theatre which contains the orchestra and the stage. The front of it (the orchestra) is on a level with the ground outside, the back (the stage) is six or eight feet higher— a sort of terrace resting on two small vaults. Under these vaults, and in the *orchestra*, are the domestic animals, calves and sheep. The *stage* serves as a barn, and as a dwelling for the owner and his family. One climbs up to it, with the help of hands and feet, by a staircase of which only the lowest and highest steps are left. Its only articles of furniture are a hand-mill, and large earthenware jars in which grain is kept.

Here we are to sup, and spend the night with our hosts. The only light is a little lamp, consisting simply of a saucer full of oil. There being no table, it rests on an inverted bushel. Jesus was, no doubt, thinking of this rustic custom when He said, "*Men do not light a candle, and put it under a bushel.*" † I have already drawn attention to the fact that, in our Saviour's discourses, the images He employs are always suited to the customs of His hearers. In the *Sermon on the Mount* He addresses Himself to the multitude,—common people and country folk. Hence His allusion to the bushel ; it is the only implement of the household of a peasant, such as that now before me. It serves alternately as a table and a dish, for it is in this same bushel—like those in use among ourselves—that they will presently bring the curds which

* This is the reason why the poor woman in St. Luke xv. 8, who had lost a piece of money, had to light a candle to look for it.
† " Under *the* bushel," not " *a* bushel," as it is in our versions.

are the supper of the family. And when He added that the lamp "*gives light to all that are in the house,*" He was not thinking of the town houses, with many rooms, but of rural dwellings, such as that in which I now find myself.*

This little lamp gives some sort of light, but really only makes the darkness visible. If you want more light, or to look for anything, you light a handful of thorns.

The ground is covered with mats, upon which I am glad to sit down. My hosts bring me the usual curds and cakes. John takes out of my bag some travelling provisions,—oranges, hard eggs, and even a bottle of Cypress wine, bought of Antonio. My hosts are too good Mussulmans to drink wine, and I willingly give them my curds ; but the rest we divide, and make a delicious pic-nic. Then the master of the house offers us his *jôsé* (a sort of narguileh) ; I hand it over to John, light my chibouque, and pass it on to my host, He gives it me back in a moment or two ; I pass it back to him a little later, and so we smoke turn-about, as is their manner.

It would not be easy for me to write, had I no other light but that of the lamp ; happily I have taken the

---

* In St. Matthew (v. 15), Jesus says simply, "*Men do not light a candle, and put it under the bushel.*" This image suggested itself quite naturally to the Jews for whom St. Matthew was writing. But it might seem strange to foreigners. And accordingly St. Mark who wrote for the Romans, and St. Luke addressing Greeks, take care to add a word or two which explain, as well as generalise. The former says (in iv. 21) "*under the bushel, or under the bed,*" the latter (in xi. 33) "*in a secret place, or under a bushel,*" and again (in viii. 16), "No man, when he hath lighted a candle, *covereth it with a vessel, or putteth it under a bed*" And Mark and Luke do not say that it gives light to *all that are in the house.*

pains to provide myself with a taper ; I stick it into
the neck of my bottle, but my host insists upon holding
it for me himself. His children are boys of from eight
to ten years old ; one of them plays a musical instru-
ment, which is simply a reed pierced with small holes,
(the *leves calami*, or *gracilis avena*, of Virgil), and the
whole family look on at me as I write with a curiosity
scarcely as great as my own. Here I am, living quite
the life of antiquity !

Meanwhile the hours pass away,—it is bedtime.
Every one goes to rest where he is. The night toilet
does not take long. A man takes off his girdle, and
simply lets himself slip on to the ground, wrapped in
his cloak. The women and children, who have nothing
on but their shifts, spread a large coverlet over them
all. That is all. I take my bag for a pillow, wrap
myself in my cloak, pull my tarbouche over my ears,
and prepare for the sweetest sleep, for I had but a
few minutes' rest last night. Long, however, after that,
I indulge in listening to the snoring of the calves
beneath us, the tinklings of the bells of the horses in
the courtyard, and the regular breathing of the peaceful
family party round me.

But sleep will not come. The fleas—*horribile dictu !*
—settle on me in legions, and do not allow me a
moment's rest. It is difficult to imagine the number
of fleas one of these primitive habitations can hold ! At
last, towards two o'clock, the cock begins to crow, the
cat mews in answer, and the whole family awakes.
Without at all seeing the good of such early rising, I
hasten to follow their example. I go out to look at
the sky, which is clear and starlit. The *moukres* are
asleep by the side of their horses. The courtyard is
very small, enclosed in high walls built of large unhewn

stones, like the cyclopean buildings, and crowned with
stunted brambles.   These walls are not less than eight
feet thick! In this country, where security is unknown,
the smallest cottage is a fortress.   In the middle, a
large vine shadows with its strong branches almost the
whole court.   These branches are propped, not on posts,
but on enormous stone pillars.   Here, where stone is
to be found everywhere, and wood almost nowhere, it is
easier to procure a stone column than a wooden one.

My hosts begin breakfast,—curds and cakes, as
usual.   If they did not interrupt their slumbers now, to
eat, they would have to pass the whole day fasting, for
to-day is the first day of *Ramadan.*   This is a month's
fast, recurring once a year.   While it lasts, they are
forbidden to eat, drink, or smoke, from sunrise till sunset.   One can see what a disturbance this makes in
the whole way of living of the Mussulmans, as they
generally keep this fast with extreme scrupulosity.

As soon as the meal is over, every one lies down
again at full length upon the ground, and resumes his
interrupted sleep.   One of the women alone keeps
awake; she sits down by the hand-mill, and begins
grinding.   This mill consists simply of a great stone
mortar, in which the stone is turned by a handle
like those of our coffee mills.   This work is always
reserved for women : thus Jesus says, "*Two women shall
be grinding at the mill; the one shall be taken, the other
left.*"*   Where there are maid-servants, this work is
handed over to them, and it takes up much time, and
is very laborious.   In the Bible, the condition of the
slave who turns the millstone is spoken of as the lowest
in the social scale.   For instance, in Exodus we read :
"*All the first-born in the land of Egypt shall die, from*

* St. Luke xvii. 35 ; St. Matt. xxiv. 41.

the first-born of Pharaoh that sitteth upon his throne, even unto the first-born of the maid-servant that is behind the mill."* And the prophet Isaiah announces the fall of Babylon by this fine *prosopopeia* : " *Come down, and sit in the dust, O virgin daughter of Babylon ; sit on the ground; there is no throne, O daughter of the Chaldæans. . . . Take the millstones, and grind meal. . . . Sit thou silent, and get thee into darkness; for thou shalt no more be called, The lady of kingdoms.*" †

This hand-mill, with the two vessels which hold the grain, make up, as I have said, the whole furniture of the house. This mill is an indispensable implement, and Hebrew legislation which forbids the creditor to keep the raiment he has taken to pledge after sunset, does not permit him either to seize the hand-mill,—"*or even the upper millstone*," says the Deuteronomist, "*for that would be to take a man's life to pledge.*" ‡ One is not surprised to find Scripture often mentioning an implement so universally used—or Jeremiah, for instance, when picturing the devastation of Judæa, adding, as a finishing touch, "*I will take from them the sound of the millstones, and the light of the candle.*" §

Second Day.

FROM BIREH TO NABLOUS.

I assure you, my dear friend, it requires often an effort of will to bring oneself to write the journal of each day, regularly every evening. At this moment, for instance, after the sleepless night which I described to you, after twelve hours spent since then on horse-back, on a Turkish saddle, I should much prefer to

---

* Exod. xi. 5.
† Isa. xlvii. 1, etc.
‡ Deut. xxiv. 6.
§ Jer. xxv. 10.

smoke my chibouque on the terrace, or to drink in
the sweet odours of the orange trees of Nablous, or,
better still, to go to sleep upon the cushions which are
ready for me.

Is *Bireh* the *Béeroth* of the Gibeonites, as its name
and situation would suggest, and as Robinson would
have us believe? or else is it, as has long been supposed, the *Michmash* of Scripture? I incline rather to
the first opinion. According to the legend, it is there
—in a house of which they still point out a fragment
—that Mary and Joseph observed the absence of Jesus,
on their way back from their pilgrimage to Jerusalem.*
In our time, Bireh is ordinarily the first station for
travellers going to Nablous and Nazareth. The ancient
road, which we follow, is that by which Jesus often
travelled on His way to Jerusalem ; it used to be, and
still is, taken by the Galilean pilgrims.

Though we started at daybreak, the heat of the sun
soon became extreme ; this intolerable heat, my bad
night, and my bad horse, brought back my yesterday's ill
humour. Again a fit of the blue devils seized and
saddened me, and I only succeeded in getting rid of it
by the same means. But as I almost fell asleep as
I rode, I let slip without engraving them on my
memory the names of the places through which we
passed, and even the features of the scenery.

Do you remember a very pretty picture by our friend
Léon Berthoud ? It represents Don Quixote and his
squire riding on an August day, side by side, up the
steep ascents of some *sierra*. What truth to nature
is in that picture! what clouds of dust! what a dryness in the atmosphere! How, looking at it, one feels
the oppression of that merciless sun of the dog-days,

* St. Luke ii. 44.

which pulverises the limestone rocks, melts Sancho
under his woollen cloak, and irresistibly forces its way
through Mambrin's helmet, into the unhappy knight's
brain !

I was often reminded, I assure you, of that picture,
while wandering with Hhannah amongst the environs
of Jerusalem, and climbing with him in silence, seated
on my stumbling Rosinante, up the dried-up torrent
beds or the long mountain paths. I thought of it particularly this morning amongst the passes of Benjamin.
I did not, it is true, detect in myself any great likeness
to Don Quixote ; but John called up irresistibly the
thought of Sancho. He would go on insisting in every
variety of tone that the road to Nablous was the haunt
of cut-throats, and that our fate was sealed if we did
not succeed in overtaking the English who had gone
on before us. Then I was taken with the suspicion
that his reason for encouraging me in the idea of
travelling by myself was that he was afraid that if I
attached myself to some caravan, I might no longer
require his services. But now we had started, and he
had taken upon himself the responsibility of the enter-
prise, it began to weigh upon him.

As far as near Bethel, we travel over a tolerably level
plateau. Bethel, on our right, stands on its edge, and
commands a view over a small valley. It has been
remarked by others before me what disappointment one
feels on seeing *the unimpressive situation** of the ancient
and venerable sanctuary of Jacob. The scenery has
nothing picturesque or characteristic about it—it is
hardly to be called scenery ; there is nothing to draw
the attention of passers by. The pagan sanctuaries are
marked by a character of grandeur and mystery, which

* *Sic*, in English, in the original.—*Tr.*

is very impressive, and accounts for the veneration they
inspire. But here,—as also at Shiloh, where we shall
arrive presently,—there is nothing for the imagination
to lay hold of ; it is evidently not the character of the
place, but its history only, that made it a *Beth-el,*—that
is to say, a *House of God,* to the Israelites.

Soon after, we find ourselves once more among
those passes of Benjamin, which serve as a gateway
into Judah ; but soon nature changes ; the country
assumes an appearance which I had not before observed
in Palestine ; the cultivation becomes richer and more
general. We are in the fine country of Ephraim, very
different from Judah. It would not be so true to
say that we were here among *mountains separated by
valleys,* as among *valleys separated by mountains.* This
distinction, I allow, is not scientifically geographic, but
I do not pique myself on my scientific geography; my
only wish is to render accurately the impression made
upon me by the places I see. One does not any longer
feel oneself, as in the whole of Judæa, "*in the mountain
country ;*" it is a delight to find oneself once more in
*the rich country ;** one feels much as one does in Switzerland, on passing from the stern uplands of the Jura
into the fair and pleasant valleys of *l'Argovie.*

It is particularly on arriving at the great valley
in which is Jacob's Well, that this change becomes
apparent. This plain has, it is true, no trees, and the
mountains which enclose it are still bare and rocky ;
but the bottom of the valley is filled with cultivated
fields, and with meadows of the freshest and most
brilliant verdure. In a few days' time the fields will
be "*white to harvest.*" This corner of the country, so
smiling and so fertile, attracted, even in their remote

* "*Le bon pays.*"—*Tr.*

day, the notice of the patriarchs. It is still called *the valley of the encampment* (*Wady-el-Mokhna*). Here Abraham first pitched his tents, and built an altar to the Eternal.* Here at a later time Jacob came to settle on his return from Padan-Aram;† and he gave this tract of country—true gem, as it is, of the Holy Land—by preference, to his favourite son.‡

Scripture bears witness to the richness and beauty of these places, and of that land of Joseph in general, on which the benedictions of Jacob and of Moses were poured forth. "*Joseph is a fruitful bough by a well.*§ . . . *Blessed of the Lord be his land, for the precious things of heaven, . . . and for the precious things of the earth, and the fulness thereof.*"‖ . . .

This country, in fact, has not that austere nakedness, that sadness of look, if one may so express it, which gives to Judæa its peculiar aspect, and fits so well with the character of the people, and the religion of the Jews. In the rocky pastures of Judah, on the monotonous dome-shaped tops of its mountains, the scenery has no other beauty but its grandeur; it raises the thoughts of the poet, without interesting the eye of the painter; from the absence of details, and the uniformity of the colouring, there is no variety of beauty to attract the eye, which therefore naturally turns towards the vast celestial horizons here so wide open to view,—towards that curtain of light behind which the Lord hides the rays of His glory.¶

* Gen. xii. 6, 7.
† Gen. xxxiii. 18. *Before the city*, that is to say, to the east, as I shall presently explain.
‡ Gen. xlviii. 22. Compare St. John iv. 5.
§ Gen. xlix. 22.
‖ Deut. xxxiii. 13, etc.
¶ See Psalm civ. 2.

Here, again, it is easy to understand how the
religions of nature should have more easily gained
access to the heart of man than elsewhere. The territory of Joseph is one of those brilliant and richly
planted countries, in which the earth exerts an almost
irresistible attraction upon man. This influence made
itself felt from early times, in morals, and in religion
itself. The inhabitants of that district were much
inclined to debauchery; the prophet Hosea lifts up his
voice against their orgies;* in the time of Isaiah, who
reproaches them in the same way, *the drunkards of
Ephraim* seem to have had a reputation that had
become proverbial.† We see also that—even long
before the time of the Samaritans—the religion of
Jehovah itself became in the kingdom of Ephraim a
sort of paganism, through the symbolic worship of the
golden calves of Jeroboam. And from this country,
from Shechem, came to us the one attempt at profane poetry known to us among the Hebrews, I mean
the *apologue of the trees;* ‡—unless indeed we class
under that head *the Song of Songs*, which moreover
borrows from this part of Palestine the larger number
of its images, and, according to Ewald, must have
been also composed in the kingdom of Ephraim. And
in Jotham's apologue on *"the time when the trees spoke,"*
there is a faculty of personification, a sort of poetic
pantheism, of which no other example is to be found
among the remains of Hebrew literature.

But we come to ' *Jacob's well*,' where for the first
time the great principle of a new worship was laid down

---

* See, for instance, Hosea vii. 4, 5. And in another passage
(iii. 1), " *They look to other gods, and love flagons of wine.*"
† Isaiah xxviii. 1, 3.
‡ Judges ix. 8, etc.

by Jesus, in contrast with the semi-paganism of the
Samaritans and the formalistic theism of the Jews:
"*God is a Spirit, and they that worship Him must worship Him in spirit and in truth.*" This is undeniably
one of the most interesting spots in the Holy Land,
not only on account of the grandeur of the event of
which it was the scene, nor only of the importance of
the words there uttered by the Son of man, but also
because there is no site more exactly defined, or more
easily to be distinguished. The Gospel is chary of
pictures, and presents us with few so vivid as that of
the conversation of Jesus with the Samaritan woman.*
It was here, upon the margin of this well, that Jesus
sate at noon, wearied with His journey, and asked the
woman of Sychar to give Him to drink. This is the
spring of which He said, "*Whosoever drinketh of this
water shall thirst again; but whosoever drinketh of the
water that I shall give him, shall never thirst.*" These
stones, this plain, these hills, witnessed this conversation. These fine fields of wheat, which I see spread
out before me, are those which Jesus shewed to His
disciples, asking them, "*Say not ye, There are yet four
months, and then cometh harvest? Behold, I say unto
you, Lift up your eyes, and look on the fields; for they
are white already to harvest.*" There, above us, is that
mountain-top of Gerizim, to which the words refer,—
"*The hour cometh when ye shall neither in this mountain,
nor yet at Jerusalem, worship the Father. . . . . The
hour cometh, and now is, when the true worshippers shall
worship the Father in spirit and in truth.*"

Jacob's well is in an admirable situation, at the point
of junction of the narrow valley of Shechem with the
great valley of Mokhna. But it belongs rather to the

* St. John iv.

latter; which indeed constitutes the picture, for it is towards the east and north-east that one's eyes are attracted. Contemplating this magnificent possession which Jacob "*took out of the hand of the Amorite with his sword and with his bow, and which he gave to his son Joseph,*" * I have behind me Gerizim, on whose top are still to be seen the ruins of the temple of the Samaritans, on my left, Ebal, and at its foot, at a short distance, the sepulchre of Joseph.†

It was here, at the entrance of the valley of Shechem, that the Israelites, in their conquering march across the land of Canaan, stopped, to renew their covenant with the Eternal. The ark, surrounded · by priests, was in the valley, the whole of the people covered the sides of the two adjoining mountains, six tribes, encamped on Mount Gerizim, recited with loud voices the blessings pronounced in the Law upon those who fear the Eternal, the six other tribes, grouped upon the sides of Ebal, opposite the others, uttered the curses. And all the people answered, Amen!

* Gen. xlviii. 22.

† The maps differ very widely as to the true site of Jacob's well. I have before me those which Raumer (*Palæstina*), and Stanley (*Sinai and Palestine*) have appended to their excellent works. According to that of Raumer, the well would be actually in the valley of Shechem, and about equidistant from Ebal and Gerizim. According to Stanley's map, it would be almost at the foot of Mount Ebal. Robinson and Van de Velde place it, with good reason, at the foot of Gerizim, but Van de Velde a little further south than Robinson. One sees by this what uncertainty and caprice have prevailed, up to these latter days, on the geography of Palestine, even with regard to sites so famous, and so often visited.

‡ Josh. viii. 33—35. Compare Deut. xxvii. 12—26. It is not easy to picture this scene to oneself, clearly, in all its details; but, as to its general features, it cannot have been very different from

These two mountains resemble each other closely, and nothing at first sight indicates what motive led to the choice of one of them for the curses, and the other for the blessings. Each of them is, on this side, steep, bare, and rocky; perhaps even it may be said that the rocks which form the base of Gerizim have a more rugged aspect than the corresponding ones of Ebal. Further on, towards the bottom of the valley, both are equally green and smiling. It is true that Gerizim is the most thickly wooded. Nevertheless, if the highest function has been assigned to it, it is, I believe, simply and only, because it lies to the right, that is, to the south.

It is clear that the mass of men do not *Orientate* themselves, as geographers do, by first settling where the north lies. The easiest way to do this is, in the first place, to determine the east—the *Orient*. So did the Hebrews. To find what we call "the points of the compass," they set themselves opposite to the rising sun. And they called this the *front*, or *fore-part*, of the world (קדם); *behind* them was the west;* what we call the north was *the left*,† and the south had no other name but *the right*.‡

Now among the Hebrews, as well as Greeks, the right was the place of honour and advantage. This is clear from many examples in Scripture—among others, from the name of *Benjamin* ("the son of the right hand"),

my description. I place it at the entrance into the valley,—a little further on, however, than Jacob's well,—because it is at this point that the two mountains approach each other most closely.

   * For instance, see Isaiah ix. 12. Look at this passage in the Hebrew text : "*Syria before, and the Philistines behind.*"

   † Gen. xiv. 15.

   ‡ For instance, 1 Sam. xxiii. 19 (see margin).

which in Genesis xxxv. 18 is contrasted with *Benoni*
(" the son of my sorrow ").

The neighbourhood of Nablous announces itself by
large and ancient olive yards, of singular beauty.
Nearer the town, behind and above it, on the south
side, are other orchards containing a number of trees
of all kinds : orange, citron, rose trees, etc. ; these are,
in this place, no longer mere shrubs, but great trees
of the finest growth.   In any country this would be
charming ; in so bare a country as Palestine it is a
delicious surprise, a real feast to the eyes.   One can
understand perfectly how Jotham came to take the
dramatis personæ of his ingenious apologue from the
trees.   Only here could this fable have been imagined
or spoken ; it would never have occurred to the mind
of a dweller in Jerusalem, or have been felt to be very
appropriate in that part of the country ; olive trees,
vines, thorns are to be found there, it is true ; but,
except some wretched fig trees, and here and there an
almond tree, I do not well see what electors could call
them to the throne, or what rivals could have arisen to
contest it with them.   Here, on the contrary, it is no
slight honour to reign over this innumerable host of
citrons, myrtles, peach, apricot trees, pomegranates, of
fruit trees of all sorts, with brilliant foliage, sweet-smelling flowers, and exquisite fruit.

The situation of the modern Nablous, and that of
the ancient Shechem, do not seem to be absolutely
identical.   If the Shechem, or Sychar, of the Gospels
had been on the site of the present town, the inhabitants would not have come from such a distance
to draw water from Jacob's well ; for they have in the
town itself springs in abundance nearer at hand.   The
ancient town, which still existed in the time of Jesus,

must then have been at the entrance into the valley,
close to Jacob's well; signs of its former existence
are still to be seen in the plantations of olive trees
through which one passes before reaching the present town. This latter (*the New Town, Nea Polis,
Naplouse*) is built a little further on in the valley.
St. Jerome alternately distinguishes and identifies them
—a manifest contradiction, which he himself explains
when he tells us elsewhere that Shechem has become
a suburb of Nablous. I had first doubted whether
the Sychar of St. John might not be some locality in
the neighbourhood, distinct from Shechem, and situated
in some other part of the valley of Mokhora, on the
sides of Gerizim, perhaps even at a few paces' distance
from the well, near the tomb of Joseph, to which,
according to this, it would have owed its name.* But
what prevented me from resting in this opinion was
that St. John calls Sychar a *town* (πόλις), and not a
suburb or a village (κώμη). Clearly it is impossible to
imagine that there could be a town of Sychar distinct
from Shechem, and at only some hundred yards' distance
from it. Let us, then, hold to the general belief which
identifies Sychar and Shechem. Without even supposing,
with St. Jerome, that the first of these two names is but
a mistake of a copyist, it is not difficult to understand
how the name Shechem may have been disfigured by
the malignity of the Jews into Sychar, or Sichar
(*drunkenness*), in allusion to *the drunkards of Ephraim*
(שכורי אפרים), of whom I spoke above.

Nablous, with its eight thousand souls, has the

---

* The word סור appears to have borne, in the Talmudists, the
sense of *sepulchre*, a translation open, it is true, to doubt, but which
has on its side the authority of l'Aruc and of Sebastian Münster,
and which harmonises well with the root of the word.

21

appearance of a large town.   It is beyond comparison
cleaner than Jerusalem.   The houses are in the same
style, built, too, of very fine stones ; but they show to
much greater advantage, because they are not, like those
at Jerusalem, lost amid ruins and rubbish.   Nablous.
reminds me, in miniature, of Cairo ; but here the streets
are straighter and handsomer.   One recognises, as
in Cairo, a town almost wholly Mahometan.   The
fanaticism of Islam has free play here.   At Jerusalem,
the disciples of the Prophet, forming only a minority,
and being under the eye of the European consuls, are
compelled to pay some regard to the Christians and the
Jews.   Here they are at home, and make use of their
advantages.   Everywhere, as I pass, the men cast sinister
glances at me, and make remarks aloud, which I do not
understand, but they do not seem to express good-will;
even the beggars will not condescend to ask alms of me,
and the little children, far from addressing me with the
honourable title of *hadji*, run after me, crying—

    " *Nazari ! Nazari !* " (Nazarene.)

In their mouths this word is an insult.   But I know
not what title I should prefer to this, or one which would
better please one's ear.   It is the name by which Jesus
and His first disciples* used to be designated.   This
name, of Palestinian origin, has continued until now
the only one in use among the Arabs, whilst that of
Christian, invented by the Greeks of Antioch,† has passed
into the language of the European nations.

    There is no hotel at Nablous.   In our day, as in
the time of Jesus, travellers halt by some spring, under
the shade of some olive tree, and send their servants into the city to buy provisions.‡   So do our
party of English, whom we have at last, to the great

---

 * Acts xxiv. 5.   † Acts xi. 26.   ‡ St. John iv. 8.

satisfaction of Hhannah, overtaken. They let us plunge into the populous streets of Nablous, while they themselves pitch their tents near one of the gates of the city.

As I have no tent, Hhannah takes me into a retired street, to the house of a Greek or Latin Christian, who offers us an upper chamber. This is more commonplace than our yesterday's resting-place, but we shall sleep better. Everything in it breathes peace and comparative cleanliness, which is refreshing and reposeful. The principal ornament of the room is a little map of Sweden turned upside-down. This curiosity, imported from foreign parts, a fragment from a Russian atlas, is hung against the wall as a pendant to an image of the Virgin.

While the beds are being spread on the floor and John goes to market to buy provisions, I avail myself of the last hour of daylight to visit the synagogue of the Samaritans, and to ascend Gerizim.

I need not remind you of the origin of the Samaritans and of their religion. We see in the Second Book of Kings * that, after the deportation of the ten tribes, the king of Assyria re-peopled Samaria with colonists taken from various provinces of his empire; and that this new population made itself a religion in its own way by adding the worship of Jehovah, whom they took to be the God of their new country, to that of its ancient gods. After their return from captivity in Babylon, the Samaritans tried to make friends with the Jews, and to make common cause with them in rebuilding the Temple; but their offers were rejected by the puritanism of the latter. Having failed in attaching themselves to the Jewish nationality, they gave themselves out as the

* 2 Kings xvii. 24—41.

heirs of the ten tribes;* and the same mutual hostility was seen springing up between them and the Jews which had formerly existed between Ephraim and Judah. A Jewish priest, named Manasseh, son of the high priest Jehoiada, and son-in-law of Sanballat, having been excommunicated by Nehemiah,† passed over to the Samaritans, and brought with him the rights of the race of Aaron and the traditions of the priesthood. Sanballat caused a rival temple to be erected on Mount Gerizim. The Samaritans gave up, it would seem, all that they still retained of the idolatry of their ancestors, and laid claim, like the Jews, to the exclusive title of "*the true worshippers*"‡ of Jehovah. It was from that moment that the mutual hostility of the Samaritans and the Jews became implacable. Without here mentioning the testimonies to this fact which are to be found in the Talmud, it is enough to recollect those we find in the Gospel. Observe, for instance, in the fourth chapter of St. John, this little word, " He *must needs* (ἔδει, oportebat) pass through Samaria." § We know that when it was not absolutely needful so to do, the Jews went a long way round to avoid passing through that country. Remember, too, how the woman of Samaria was astonished at hearing a Jew address her.‖ Further, we find from the same Gospel that to call any one a Samaritan was, among the Jews, the most deadly insult : " *Thou art a Samaritan, and hast a devil*," said the Jews to Jesus.¶

As to the doctrinal differences which separated the

* The woman of Samaria calls Jacob "*our father*" (St. John iv. 12) ; but the Jews call the Samaritans *strangers* (St. Luke xvii. 18).
† Nehemiah xiii. 25.   ‡ St. John iv. 23.   § St. John iv. 4.
‖ St. John iv. 9.   ¶ St. John viii. 34.

two races and distinguished their religions, the principal, and perhaps the only one, was, that the Samaritans received as sacred books only those of Moses, and rejected all the rest of the Jewish canon.

They have in their possession, even now, an ancient copy of the Pentateuch, of which they trace the origin as far back as the early days of the history of Israel. This Pentateuch is in Hebrew ; but instead of being written in Chaldaic, like the manuscripts of the Jews, it is in Samaritan characters, which are probably of greater antiquity, and have been retained by the Samaritans for writing Hebrew as well as their own language.

There are still existing in Nablous a hundred or so of Samaritans, the sole remaining representatives of their race, the sole adherents of their religion. This nation, reduced to a few families—this religion, professed by only a few persons, but still through all time retaining its identity, is one of the most interesting historic phenomena in existence. I asked to be shewn their synagogue. It is a small room, with nothing remarkable in it. But I was not allowed to enter it till I had taken off my shoes, and left them outside the door. The priest was sent for. He is a man of about forty years old, of a very noble and dignified countenance. He solemnly displayed to me the roll of parchment on which the Pentateuch is written, but strictly forbade my touching it. I had once gone through a course of lessons in the Samaritan language, at the University of Berlin, and Doctor Petermann (if he is still living, as I hope) would even assure you, were it needful, that I was one of his best pupils ;—it is true that he had only three. I confess that since that time I have forgotten much of what I learnt of the language, having never had occasion to make use of it. I remembered the alphabet, however, and that was all I now wanted, as the text was Hebrew.   I set to work to decipher a few lines under my breath.

"*Hayôdéa attâ leschôn hakkôdesh?*"   (Dost thou understand the sacred language?) the priest asked me, in Hebrew.

On my answering in the affirmative, he entered into conversation, and we had a few minutes' talk.   You see the Samaritans as well as the Jews call Hebrew the sacred language.   This member of the race spoke very good Hebrew ; his pronunciation was that of the *Sephardim* Jews, and in entire conformity with that in use in the Christian schools.   He told me that the number of Samaritans amounts at the present moment to a hundred and fifty ; but others of the inhabitants of Nablous have assured me that that is a great exaggeration.   As to the manuscript they shewed me, it is evidently modern. But nevertheless the priest warranted it to be the original.   Some travellers affirm that they have two, and that they do not shew the most precious.

A point often discussed *inter doctos* is that of the origin of the Samaritans.   Are we to consider this people as composed essentially of foreign colonists, and did the remains of the tribe of Ephraim, who had not been carried captive into Assyria, enter only as a small and almost inappreciable element into the formation of this new nation? Or are we to suppose, on the contrary, that the heart and substance of this race is Israelitish, and that the Assyrian colonists are only a secondary element ?   This latter hypothesis has in its favour the language of the Samaritans, which is but a dialect of Hebrew adulterated by the intrusion of a considerable number of foreign words.   Nevertheless the narrative of the books of Kings favours the former hypothesis.

I must also say that, looking at the Samaritan high priest, I was struck with his face, which did not in any way recall the Jewish or Arab type. His aquiline nose, his handsome face, with full, rosy cheeks, were of the pure Indo-Germanic type.

I take a guide to shew me the way to Gerizim. He is a Mussulman, but he uses also, and murders in the using, a few Hebrew words, among which he introduces continually, *Yes sir.** These two monosyllables are the only European words he knows. This man is a thorough Arab, not inferior in rudeness to any of his fellow-citizens in Nablous. Far from piquing himself on the obsequiousness usual with men who have an eye to a baksheesh, he treats my horse and its rider with a shameless brutality which draws from me, many times over—I confess it with regret—exclamations which ought never to have been heard on the Mount of Blessing. On issuing from the town, we climb straight up to Gerizim, through the sweet-smelling orchards. Nablous has been compared to Heidelberg; it is as seen from this side that it resembles it,—as much, at least, as an Oriental can resemble a northern town. The crest of the mountain forms a plateau sloping from east to west, in which are some fields of wheat, alternating with stone-sprinkled pastures. We ascend this plateau, up to its highest summit. It has an elevation of eight hundred feet above the valley of Shechem, and of two thousand four hundred above the sea. It is generally considered the highest summit of the mountains of Ephraim, but M. Van de Velde nevertheless assures us that the top of Ebal is some feet higher. This fact explains why it was on Ebal, and not Gerizim, that the Israelites erected an altar to the

* *Sic*, in English—in the original.—*Tr.*

Eternal.* Ebal was the highest mountain-top in the country.

On this height, which looks down upon Jacob's well, there is a wide space, enclosed in fragments of wall and great heaps of stones, many of which are sculptured in relief. These remains formed part, no doubt, of many buildings in succession ; it is probable that among the number are included fragments of the temple built by Sanballat and destroyed by John Hyrcanus. And here also is the Samaritan sanctuary; towards this spot they turn in their prayers. The only building still standing is a small cubical edifice, crowned with a cupola. It contains a single chamber, four yards square, which serves as a synagogue for the Samaritans. They still celebrate on Mount Gerizim the solemnities commanded in the Law of Moses, the Passover, the Feast of Pentecost, the Feast of Tabernacles, the Day of Atonement. A notable fact!—while the Jews have been for a long time deprived of their Temple and their sacrifices, the Paschal lamb is still sacrificed by Manasseh's heretical sectaries, and their worship still celebrated by a junior branch of the family of Aaron, a quasi-legitimate priesthood.

Third Day's Journey.

FROM NABLOUS TO DJENNIN.

This morning, on waking, I saw light clouds floating over the top of Ebal. It was a real Swiss morning. I found my host, in his white cotton robe with lilac spots, smoking his narguileh on the terrace. I settled accounts with him,—not a very easy thing to do. In

* Deut. xxvii. 4. In this passage, the Samaritan Pentateuch, as is well known, gives Gerizim instead of Ebal.

this country the inn-keepers have too much delicacy to hand you in their bill. You give them what you please, and you may be quite sure that they will never be satisfied, and that they will ask for more.

Leaving the town, we stop at the encampment of the English. We are to travel with them to-day, as it is particularly on the road from Nablous to Nazareth that there is danger, and that it is important not to be alone. I hear from them that, yesterday evening, as they were ascending Gerizim, half-an-hour in advance of me, they were attacked ; and, notwithstanding their numbers and their arms, they were compelled to capitulate, and pay a ransom to the Arabs. It was no doubt owing to them that I met no one on my expedition to Gerizim ; the robbers must have been content with this success, and, in a hurry to dine after a long Ramadan day, must have returned immediately to the town without waiting for the chance of perpetrating more robberies.

While our English are busy with their preparations, and my horse, wandering along the orchards, takes leave of the fine pastures of Nablous, some lepers come up, and hold out to me their swollen hands,—a sad spectacle amidst the glories of nature !

At a little distance from Nablous, we are shewn, by the roadside the tomb of Joshua. There we meet a caravan of fifty camels, and are obliged to stop to make room for them to pass, on account of the narrowness of the road.

Arrived in the neighbourhood of Samaria, we part from our baggage and our moukres ; they take the straight road to Djennin, while we visit the ruins of the town. Samaria stands on a long-topped hill standing by itself in a plain. This plain is surrounded

with higher mountains, not round-topped, like those of
Judæa, but, so to speak, throwing themselves backwards,
and rising by terraces. Upon the ascending steps of
this amphitheatre, in the prophecy of Amos, the kings
of the nations are summoned to assemble themselves to
contemplate the spectacle of the crimes of Samaria.*
This situation is very like that of Jerusalem ; but
Samaria, seated "*at the head of the fat valleys,*" as says
Isaiah,† is richer and more smiling ; also its position
is stronger, the mountain being here surrounded by
valleys on all sides. Samaria is an island, Jerusalem
is only a peninsula, and one knows that the isthmus
which, towards the north, connects her with the plateau,
has often proved fatal to her, and has many times furnished a bridge by which her enemies have gained
entrance.

Who can tell whether this similarity of situation did
not count for something in deciding Omri to choose
the mountain of Samaria as the site of his new capital ?
The likeness of Jerusalem to her rival, " *her sister,*" as
Ezekiel ‡ calls her, only served to bring into greater
relief the advantages of the latter. But neither was the
one nor the other able to escape from its appointed
chastisement. They both justified the malediction of
Amos, "*Woe to them that are secure§ in Zion, and trust
in the mountain of Samaria!*"‖ Samaria is only as "*an
heap of the field, and as plantings of a vineyard; its stones
have been poured down into the valley, and the foundations
thereof have been discovered.*"¶ In fact, these ruins
still standing on the mountain-top, are those, not of
the ancient Samaria, but of Sebaste, which succeeded

* Amos iii. 9, 10.   § See margin.
† Isaiah xxviii. 1.   ‖ Amos vi. 1.
‡ Ezek. xvi. 46.   ¶ Micah i. 6.

it. Even the name of the capital of the ten tribes has disappeared, and the hamlet which, in our day, stands in its place is called Sebustieh, after the Roman town. We come upon a pretty stream, running under the grass, amongst green shrubs. In front of us rises the hill of Samaria, upon which there stands, spectre-like, a fragment of wall, high and narrow, part of an ancient Christian church. Further to the left is a long line of broken columns. It is a most picturesque scene.

While I am surveying these ruins, to which attach no great memories, and counting these columns stretching along the whole top of the mountain, some men at work in the fields come and offer me small medals. I buy all they bring, hoping to find among them some Greek or Asmonæan coins. But they are all of the date of the Roman emperors.

The heat is very moderate ; the verdure which surrounds us all day long is rest at once to eyes and mind. It is true the vegetation is not everywhere as vigorous and varied as at Nablous ; but, at any rate, one is always within sight of trees, of shrubs, of water, and of cultivable land. The soil is not stony, as in the environs of Jerusalem ; the footpaths are even sometimes very good and level. From one end to the other, Samaria presents a striking contrast to Judæa. I quite understand why the Jews did not like passing through it. It must have been heart-breaking to them to see the fairest district of their country in the hands of the unbelievers.

More fertile than Judæa, Samaria is much more thickly inhabited ; travelling through it, we come upon a large number of villages. The reception we meet with is not hospitable ; wherever we go, the children pursue us with insults, and make a show of throwing

stones at us.   But we are not attacked, for we are a
large party.   From time to time Bedouins, armed to the
teeth, appear from behind the rocks ; they look at us, as
we pass, with a curiosity which is, no doubt, not dis-
interested, and seem calculating how many shots our
revolvers may hold.   I was told, in the evening, that
our moukres, less fortunate than we, had been attacked
on their way; but they fought bravely, and our goods
only suffered slightly.

Going on from mountain to mountain, we pass, in
succession, Burka, Fendekumieh, and Djeba, which
seems to be the " Gibeah of Mount Ephraim," where
Eleazar, the son of Aaron, was buried ; we then find
ourselves in a valley, by the side of a little lake, low-
lying, and without outflow for its waters,—an *agâm*, no
doubt, which is quite dried up in summer, but in winter
must be of greater extent than now, if one may judge
from the heaps of reeds which litter the fields.   Close
at hand is Sanoûr, encircled with a low wall, and
crowning, like Gibeon, the summit of a round, regular-
shaped hill, which stands like a tower at one extremity
of a range of low hills.   Some travellers have thought
they recognised in it Judith's Bethulia, but others identify the latter town with Djennin, where we shall sleep
to-night ; others again with Kubâtiyeh, where we are
just arriving.

But as, in any case, I am close to Judith's city, it
will be in place for me here to say a word about the
women of this country.   Their costume differs a little
from that of the women of Judæa.   Some of them, it
is true, wear the many-coloured gown ; but the greater
number a tunic of unbleached linen, (not blue, as in
Judæa,) girt round the waist with a many-coloured
sash, like those worn by the men.   Their head-dress

is original ; it consists, in the first place, of a cap of
graceful shape, of which the edge, forming a roll, is
covered with pieces of engraved silver. Often also they
wear, instead of this cap, or over it, a handkerchief,
—black, or of some other colour,—which covers the
head, hangs down over the cheeks, is tied under the nose
so as to cover the mouth, and then falls down square,
like an apron, over the middle of the chest ; a corner
of the same handkerchief falls behind, over the nape of
the neck. Their foreheads are bound round with a
coloured scarf, folded length-ways. You might call it a
diadem. Their faces, framed between the straight line
of this *bandeau* and the straight line of the veil which
covers the mouth, acquire thereby a singular severity,
or, perhaps one might say, dignity, of expression.

Arrived at Kubâtiyeh, we enter a narrow pass enclosed between very low hills, which is to take us into
the plain of Esdraelon.

It is still early in the day when we reach this plain.
At the extremity of the pass, at the foot, and on the
slope of the last hill, is the suburb Djennin, in which we
are to spend the night. Our party of English pitch
their tents at the entrance, near a clump of palm trees.
I enter the village with John ; a Coptic inhabitant
offers us hospitality in his house. It is an asylum
of a simple and primitive kind ; nevertheless our host
appears to be of a higher rank than our friend at Birch.
The house has, in this case, a second apartment, in which
we are lodged; it is, as usual, a great vaulted chamber,
opening upon the courtyard, and admitting the light
only by the door and by a little opening made in the wall
above it, for the pigeons to pass through; for we are to
share our room with them. As to a chimney, such a
thing is never thought of in the villages of Palestine.

To roast coffee, they make a fire of thorns in the court-yard; and bread is baked in great ovens detached from the houses, in the street.

I avail myself of the last gleams of sunlight to climb to the top of the hill.   The sunset is beautiful in its perfect serenity.   The view extends into the far distance; I am never weary of gazing at this picture, which is a refreshment to the eyes.   At my feet, beyond the great cactus orchards, is the village of Djennin, with its white terraces, overhung by a minaret, and a few tall palm-trees.   And then, to the left, is the wide plain of Jezreel or Megiddo, stretching, almost further than one can see, up to the range, shadowy in the distance, of the moun-tains of Galilee.   This plain is the battle-ground of Palestine; it was here that Josiah perished,* and the greatest battles of Israel were fought.   Accordingly, it is here that in the Apocalypse the *"spirits of devils gather together the kings of the whole world for the battle of the great day of God Almighty."*†   There also was Jezreel, the city of Jezebel and of Ahab, of which the remains have disappeared, and the name alone recalls terrible judgments

"of God found true to all His threatenings."‡

In front of me, at a little distance, I see another memorial of the judgments of the Eternal.   It is that Mount Gilboa on which King Saul perished, and which seems still to lie under the malediction pronounced upon it by David:—*"Ye mountains of Gilboa, let there be no dew, neither let there be rain upon you, nor fields of offerings; for there the shield of the mighty, of Saul, was vilely cast away."*§

Behind this mountain rises Little Hermon, with the

* 2 Kings xxiii. 29.   ‡ Racine, in *Athalie.*
† Rev. xvi. 14—16.   § 2 Sam. i. 21.

villages of Shunem and Nain, of blessed memory; * towering in the distance is seen the snowy top of Great Hermon.

The children of my host, who saw me start, come to meet me on my return, and accompany me down the hill. They are, as I have said, Copts, and one of them bears upon his countenance that peculiar stamp, so easy to recognise, which every one may have noticed in copies of Egyptian pictures and bas-reliefs. It is curious that this type of countenance, which has to a great degree effaced itself among most of the Coptic race, occasionally reappears among them in all its purity. I have often observed it in Egypt, and always in children. It would seem that as they grow up, education, and the context of circumstances in which they live, have a tendency to denaturalise them, and to assimilate them to the Arabs.

On re-entering the courtyard, I find supper prepared for us; John has brought out of the bag the eggs and oranges, which are our usual fare, and our host contributes some cups of exquisite coffee. Then, while I smoke my chibouque, stretched upon the ground, and making painful efforts to write, in this awkward position, the children gather round me again, try to draw me into conversation, and empty my bag, to examine, one by one, the things it contains. At each fresh discovery they make, they are full of wonder, and run to tell their father what they have found.

* 2 Kings iv. 8, etc. ; St. Luke vii. 11, etc.

Fourth Day's Journey.

FROM DJENNIN TO NAZARETH.

Last night I sate up till near midnight talking and playing with the children of my host. In a few more such evenings I should make great progress in Arabic. At last I fall asleep, notwithstanding the fluttering of the pigeons' wings and their insufferable cooings.

This morning I start early. The splendours of the sky are softened by a veil of thin clouds, through which the sun's rays penetrate, though with blunted intensity. Near Djennin, the plain of Esdraelon is well cultivated; on issuing from the village, we find fine gardens fenced with great cactus hedges. One can still recognise in its present name *Djennin* the Hebrew word *Gannim*, which signifies *gardens;* and may with great probability take this place to be the *Ain-Gannim* of the tribe of Issachar, twice mentioned in the book of Joshua.* A little further on I see two water-mills, with aqueducts of quite modern date, and in very good order; nothing strikes one more in Palestine than anything that looks at all new or in good order, or that indicates industry. Further off are prairies and fine fields of wheat. But as one advances further into the plain, the soil shews scarcely any trace of cultivation; its natural fertility expends itself in useless products; the adonis spreads out, more widely than usual, its superbly brilliant corolla; and the wild artichoke thrives. Herds of gazelles gallop by, flights of storks alight near us, and great eagles and great white vultures, with black wings, hover a few feet overhead.

Travellers have thought they have discovered in the

* Joshua xix. 21 and xxi. 29.

hamlet of Zerin the site, and even the name, of the town of Jezreel. It is built upon a little isolated hill, at the foot of Mount Gilboa, in the lowest part of the great landscape before us,—a magnificent site, almost worthy to be compared with that of Memphis ; a beautiful specimen of a city in a plain, as Samaria is of a city on a mountain, with which the Israelitish kings must have unfavourably contrasted the comparatively austere look of Jerusalem. One pictures to oneself the chariot of King Ahab disporting itself at large in this truly regal plain.

Between Gilboa and Little Hermon we come in sight of the blue mountains of Gilead bounding the horizon towards the east. After passing Hermon we find ourselves near Tabor, with its regular and graceful outline. At first it seems quite isolated, but is soon seen to be connected at its base with the chain of the mountains of Galilee.

This beautiful and fertile plain of Esdraelon, in which Issachar had "*couched like a strong ass between two burdens, for he saw that rest was good, and the land that it was pleasant,*" * constitutes, as it were, a broad trench, making a well-marked boundary between the two mountain districts of Palestine,—that of Samaria and Judæa to the south, that of Galilee to the north. Esdraelon itself, and the plain of Acre, which is its continuation, do not belong geographically either to the one or the other. They form a great natural highway, the only one which connects the shores of the Mediterranean with the banks of the Jordan ; accordingly, they have been in all ages trodden by caravans and foreign armies. Issachar, who inhabited it, "*bowed his shoulder to bear, and became a servant to tribute.*"†

* Gen. xlix. 14, 15.   † Gen. xlix. 14, 15.

22

The mountains of Galilee are before us, and descend with a steep slope into the plain. Seen from hence, they present the appearance of a terrace with imperfectly defined profile, and look like the outer edge of a plateau.

After a short hour's march through a narrow ravine, we reach the top of the ascent, near a large orchard enclosed in cactus hedges. On one side is a fountain, whence flows a pretty little streamlet, running down into the ravine. At a few hundred yards' distance on our left, we see Nazareth.

This little town, or, one might say, village—for Nazareth has no walls—is charmingly situated. Three mountain gorges meet here, and form at their junction a wider valley, or, if you will, a little plateau, surrounded with rocky hills, and covered with shrubs. Nazareth rests upon the broadest and highest of these hills, and spreads itself out against it like an amphitheatre. Its white houses, and the orchards which surround it, give it a look of cleanliness and of elegance. It is a *friendly* situation, as a German would say, and I have seldom seen a town which more inspired me with the wish to live in it. There is here neither the majesty of Jerusalem, nor the less severe grandeur of Shechem or of Jezreel ; its proportions are of a humbler sort, and yet without anything cramped about it,—it is just the city of the Son of Man !

Nazareth calls up a whole class of memories which belong to it alone. The Saviour presents Himself here to us in His most human aspect. On the shores of the sea of Tiberias we are reminded of His mission as a Teacher ; we see the Master surrounded by His disciples ; the Prophet, mighty in deeds and words, followed by a great multitude eager for instruction, for

consolation, for healing. At Jerusalem, everything recalls His sufferings, His death, His resurrection, His
ascension; there we behold Him as sacrificing Priest and
Victim, "declared to be the Son of God with power."
. . . . But at Nazareth we find Him once more a
man like us. Here He grew up in the bosom of His
family; in these meadows He played as a child ; here,
as a youth, He laboured day by day in the carpenter's
workshop. Not a path which He has not trodden, not
a hill which He did not climb, not a hill-top on which
He did not pray ! There is not, within this narrow
horizon, one feature of this landscape, there is no part
of the outline of these mountains, on which His eyes
did not habitually rest, which did not imprint itself
upon His fresh childish consciousness, which was not
associated with the memories of His first impressions,
of the first wakenings of His intelligence, of His first
aspirations towards His Father !

I am going to visit the church and the cave of the
Annunciation, merely to quiet my conscience as a sight-
seer; for I no longer believe in caves,—legend has made
too free with them. After giving my horse a moment's
rest, I have him saddled again immediately, in order
that I may ride freely and in all directions, unac-
companied by monk, or *moukre*, or *cicerone*, about this
little corner of the world in which Jesus spent the
larger part of His life. In doing so, I at last lose my
way ; not that I lose sight of the city, but I so completely bury myself among the rocks and brushwood,
that I cannot see how to get out again. While I
am letting my horse wander as he pleases, leaving
all responsibility for the result, and the business of
getting me out of the scrape, to him, a young man,
dressed *à l'Européenne*, gallops up to me as if flying

to my assistance. He had heard that some English travellers—perhaps those I had left at Djennin—had just been robbed and dispersed by the Bedouins, and seeing me wandering alone and without definite aim, he made no doubt that I was a "waif and stray" of the caravan. I hastened to reassure him, and we entered into conversation, first in English, then in German; for he told me his name was Huber, and that he was one of the German missionaries settled at Nazareth by the Protestant Bishop of Jerusalem.

Whilst we are riding back together from there, at a foot's pace, he enlightens me on the present state of Nazareth. This little town grows and prospers. The Christians form the majority of its population; Greeks and Latins are in about equal numbers. The Greeks have a church there, but no convent. The Latins have a convent of Franciscans, and a nunnery, in which the nuns employ themselves in the education of Arab children; they are called *the ladies of Nazareth.* And accordingly this place is the one of all Palestine in which the Protestant missions have had the greatest successes; there are some, also, at Nablous, St. John D'Acre, and elsewhere.

M. Huber is accompanied by the little Arab girls belonging to his school; they disperse over the prairie, and amuse themselves gathering bouquets of immortelles. There is to be seen here a red species of immortelle which I have never seen elsewhere, and a great number of flowers of all sorts. I have been struck, as all travellers are, with the richness of this valley in flowers. If the name Nazareth signifies *a flower*, as is sometimes, on the authority of St. Jerome, admitted, it is perhaps to this peculiarity of the place, and perhaps also to the shape of the valley, that it alludes. "Nazareth is a rose," says Quaresmius, who visited it at the beginning of the seventeenth century; "the shape of it is round, like the flower, and the mountains stand round it, like the leaves round a rose." This idea will suggest itself naturally, I think, to every one who looks at Nazareth, particularly if seen from the high ground on the road to Kefr-Kenna. But as the word נֵצֶר, seldom used in the Bible, occurs in it only in the sense of a *shoot*, I should be tempted to give up St. Jerome's interpretation, and to derive the name of the town from the shrubs which cover its hills, and which also are a principal feature of the landscape."

I took up my quarters in the Latin convent, in which I was very well received, and found on my arrival a good supper and good lodging. However great a lover one may be of *local colouring*, and even when one has arrived only at the fourth day of one's travels, it is always pleasant to find oneself again among civilised people. The representatives of civilisation here are Italian and Spanish monks. In Europe that would by no means be the case, but everything is relative to circumstances. I have, besides, the pleasure of meeting, to my great surprise, my old friends of the French caravan. I am entertained with them in the refectory. After the meal, grace is said, and then the evening prayer, consisting of a *Pater* and a *Credo*, in which I join with all my heart. With regard to the *Ave*, which follows, it would have seemed to me *de trop* anywhere else ; but *here*—how should one not make mention of that lowly Nazareth maiden, whom "*all generations shall call blessed*," of that "*handmaid of the Lord*" who "*found favour in His sight*," and whose faith co-operated in the realisation of that supreme mystery of our salvation,—" *The Word was made flesh !*" How could one refuse to repeat, with thanksgiving to the Lord, the words which were once heard in this place—" *Hail, Mary, thou that art highly favoured ; the Lord is with thee ; blessed art thou among women.*"*

II.

THE LAKE OF GENNESARET.

The inhabitants of Lyons, in their *legend*, report that a Parisian, arriving in their town, heard for the first time men speak of the bridges over the *Saône.*

" *Saône !* " echoed he, slightly contemptuously ; " in Paris we say *Seine.*"

There are always travellers of that stamp, continually possessed with home prejudices. I should be sorry to pass for such an one ; and yet I cannot refrain from drawing attention to the relationship, so to say, between Galilee,—at least in the lower steps of its mountain region, the only ones I have visited,—and some of the more central districts of the Jura.

I made an attempt, above, to describe the impression produced upon me by the difference in the character of the scenery in Judæa and Samaria, the somewhat monotonous grandeur and somewhat bare simplicity which marks the former—the richness, variety, and brilliancy which draws one's admiration in the latter. I likened the environs of Jerusalem to our elevated plateaux ; I will now compare those of Nazareth with that middle region which, with us, separates the zone of the vines from that of the pines. The mountains here are no longer bare and ragged-looking, like those in Judæa ; they are *combes*,—undulations of the soil, covered with bushes and holm-oaks, the grass rich, and of a dark green, all pied with daisies and marigolds.

* St. Luke i. 28.

I had before been struck with this comparison on coming to Nazareth. I was so still more when I went to Tabor ; at a certain point of the ascent, in the midst of the bushes and underwood, I could have thought I was climbing up to the *roche de l'Ermitage.* It was with real emotion, I might even say thankfulness, that I recognised these points of likeness. Of the different countries that I have hitherto seen in the East, that in which Jesus lived is that which seems least strange to the eyes of a traveller accustomed to the typical regions of Europe. There is indeed nothing strange or novel to us in the look of the country ; it requires no great effort of imagination on our part to transport ourselves to these Galilean roads along which wandered the Son of Man as He went about doing good.

Mount Tabor, of which the height* is no wise extra-ordinary in a mountainous country like Palestine, has nevertheless always been one of the most notable of its mountains. The Rabbis say it would have been fit to have been chosen as the site of the Temple, and it seems that, even in the time of Jeremiah, its grandeur was proverbial.† And indeed it does draw attention by its isolated · situation ; and its outlines have that architectural regularity which I have, since then, often admired in the mountains of Greece. But I will not stop to describe my excursion to Tabor. The principal source of the interest felt by travellers in this mountain is their belief that it was the scene of the Transfigu-ration, and I must confess that I think there is little probability in that notion. The Gospel history connects

---

* At most 1,900 feet; according to Robinson, only 1,000. At any rate, it is not 3,000, as Rabbi Joseph Schwarz would have it to be.

† "*As is Tabor among the mountains*" (Jer. xlvi. 18).

the story of the Transfiguration with that of the visit of Jesus *to the coasts of Cæsarea Philippi.** He was therefore at that time far enough from Tabor, but, on the other hand, He was at the foot of Great Hermon, the highest summit of all Lebanon (10,000 feet), to which would best apply the title of a *high mountain* given to it by St. Mark and St. Matthew. St. Luke says simply, " *He went up into the high mountain,*" which is still more characteristic.† If any historian or modern writer of romance, after having brought his hero to Chamouny, told us afterwards that he went to *the mountain,* or to *a high mountain,* I do not think any one would be likely to imagine that he was referring, not to Mont Blanc, but to Chasseral, or Jolimont.‡

The principal historic *souvenir* which attaches to Tabor carries us back to the time of the Judges of Israel. By the advice of Deborah, Barak had taken

---

* St. Matt. xvi. 13.

† St. Matt. xvii. 1 ; St. Mark ix. 2 ; St. Luke ix. 28. See the Greek text; our versions translate inaccurately, " *a* mountain."

‡ These are mountains near Neuchâtel. However ancient this tradition may be, the above is a fact which seems to me to throw doubt upon it. On the other hand, I cannot attribute any weight to Robinson's argument. "It is *impossible,*" says he, "that the Transfiguration should have taken place upon this mountain, for at that time there was a town there." We see, I admit, by two passages in the Old Testament, that in the time of Joshua, and in that of Hosea (1 Chron. vi. 62, in our versions 77; Josh. xix. 22; Hosea v. 1), there existed on Mount Tabor a Levitical city ; we even know from Polybius that it was still in existence in the days of Antiochus. But was it so at the time of Jesus ? One may suppose so, but one may also doubt it, for it was no longer in existence at the time of the war of the Jews with the Romans. Josephus tells us that the top of Tabor is a plateau of twenty-six stadia in extent, and that he had enclosed it with walls. One could not conceive that if there had been a town there, he would not have mentioned it, but have spoken only of a plateau.

his position upon that mountain, with ten thousand
men of Naphtali and of Zebulun ; from thence they
threw themselves upon the army of Sisera, and upon
his nine hundred chariots.* That is the first time the
name of Tabor appears in history. The last military
distinction of this mountain is the battle fought upon
the plain of Jezreel by Bonaparte and Kleber in 1799.
Three thousand Frenchmen defeated there twenty-five
thousand Turks. The conquerors gave that feat of arms
the name of *the Battle of Tabor.*

We know from Flavius Josephus that Galilee was in
his time "a rich country, everywhere abounding in
pastures, and furnished with all kinds of trees. Its
soil," he says, "is of such excellent quality that it would
of itself tempt any one to cultivate it. And accordingly
it is all under cultivation by the inhabitants ; no
part is left vacant. The towns in that region are very
numerous, and on account of the goodness of the soil
the villages are all thickly inhabited ; the smallest has
a population of full fifteen thousand." In our day,
alas ! the largest of the cities of Galilee is far from
reaching that number, and one can hardly find any
traces of cultivation. Here and there, however, as one
contemplates the vale of Nazareth, for instance, or as
one passes under the blossoming pomegranates of Kefr-
Kenna, one can form some idea of what this country
was in former days, as Josephus describes it. The scattered villages are whitewashed, and have not that faded
and almost sinister look which marks those of the south
of Palestine. And besides, the country is green and
smiling, and one may still see remains of those "trees
of all sorts " with which it used to be embellished.
Galilee is a deserted country ; it is not, like Judæa, a

* Judges iv.

country desolated and ruined. If ever it came to have a government, such as to inspire its inhabitants with a feeling of security,—or, rather, I should say, if ever it came to have a government of any sort,—and began to be cultivated, it would again become extremely rich ; whilst, in the larger part of Judæa, many years of labour would be required to restore to the soil any fertility, for there is no longer any water, nor any cultivable soil.

The inhabitants of Galilee suffered from too favourable circumstances, from their daily intercourse with foreign nations, and from their too great distance from Jerusalem,— a distance practically increased by the settlement of the Samaritans in the territory of Ephraim. Local and material soon outweighed in their minds religious and national interests. Like the nations on the other side Jordan, they participated very indirectly in the religious and political life of the Hebrew people. Scarcely can they be said to have a place in its history;— it may be said to be only in the battles of Barak and of Gideon that they are recorded to have taken any part. Hardly any of their towns are mentioned in the Old Testament, and even the Lake of Gennesaret itself, under the name of the Sea of Chinnereth, only figures in it two or three times, with reference to a question of frontiers. But Galilee was to have its turn ; those who had been last were to become first in the kingdom of God. The obscure shores of the Lake of Gennesaret had been reserved in the counsels of Providence to become, one day, the native land of the Gospel. So that the prophecy of Isaiah fulfils itself: "*As the earlier ages left the land of Zebulun and the land of Naphtali without honour, so will the later cover with glory the way that goes from the sea to beyond Jordan, Galilee of the nations. The people that walk in darkness see a great* *light; they that sit in the region of the shadow of death, upon them hath a light shined."* *

The part played by Galilee in history, compared with that of Judæa, is about the same as that of Macedonia relatively to Greece. The Greeks considered their northern neighbours semi-barbarians, murdering their fine language, strangers to the civilisation, the arts, and the philosophy of Athens ; and yet it is owing to these Macedonians that this language, these arts, and this philosophy spread themselves over the whole East. Thus it is that *Galilee of the Gentiles* also has made the conquest of the world. The Galileans, so despised by the Puritans and purists of Jerusalem, have proclaimed through the whole world "*the salvation which comes from the Jews,*"—the God who has revealed Himself to them, —the Messiah foretold by their prophets.

The most beautiful part of Galilee, though in our time the most desert, is, beyond a doubt, the Lake of Gennesaret, also called the Sea of Galilee, or of Tiberias. Under the shelter of high mountains, fertilised by the streams which descend from them, by the vapours of the lake, and by *the dews of Hermon*, this district enjoys perpetual summer ; for it lies more than six hundred feet *below* the level of the Mediterranean. It is, as says St. Matthew after Isaiah, " *by the way of the sea.*"† The great route of the caravans which go from Damascus and Palmyra to the shore of the Mediterranean, cuts through the basin of the Lake of Gennesaret at its northern extremity. One can imagine what must have been

---

* Isa. viii. 23, ix. 1, 2 (compare St. Matt. iv. 14—16). I translate this passage from the Hebrew. The Septuagint, the Vulgate, and most of our modern versions give a rendering which is unintelligible.

† St. Matt. iv. 15.

the prosperity of a country so favoured, and one need
not be overmuch surprised at the immense population
which seems to have accumulated there in the time of
the Roman dominion.

When Jesus, rejected by His fellow-citizens, quitted
Nazareth, and came to settle by the Lake of Tiberias,
it was not, one may well believe, the charm of nature
there, or the delights of the climate which attracted Him
to these coasts. " *The Son of Man came to seek and to
save that which was lost.*"* That which attracted Him
was, no doubt, these great populations, active and industrious, but absorbed in gross earthly interests; it was
these multitudes, " *miserable and scattered abroad as sheep
having no shepherd;*" these masses of human beings
for whom, the Gospel tells us, " *He was moved with
compassion.*"† It was to these multitudes that Jesus
addressed the larger part of His instructions, and from
amongst them that He chose His Apostles. A little
later, after the fall of Jerusalem, it was into these same
regions that the Jewish doctors transported their renowned academies. It was there, in the city of Tiberias,
that they composed those admirable works of criticism,
which have come down to us under the name of *Masora;*
it was there that they drew up the Mishna, and then
the Jerusalem Talmud, which was the first commentary
upon it,—real pandects of Israelitish jurisprudence,
monuments of science, of erudition, of wisdom and
subtilty, upon which the fabric of Judaism rests.‡   Thus,

* St. Luke xix. 10.
† St. Matt. ix. 36.
‡ The Mishna was drawn up about A.D. 190, by Rabbi Jehuda,
surnamed *Hakhadôsh,* that is to say, *the Saint,* but commonly referred
to by the Talmudists as simply *Rabbi,* as being *the Master, par ex-
cellence.* The Jerusalem Talmud appeared about the year 230,
either at Tiberias, or, more probably, at Sephoris, another Galilean

—remarkable fact,—it was on the shores of this little lake that the two religions that issued from the Bible, Christianity and modern Judaism,—the worship of the spirit, and the service of the letter,—took their origin. Both of them existed in germ in ancient Judaism, and St. Paul very well compares them to the two sons of Abraham, Ishmael the child of the bondwoman—in other words, of slavery—and Isaac, the child of the free woman. " *Jerusalem which now is,*" he exclaims, " *is in bondage with her children; but Jerusalem which is above is free, which is the mother of us all.*"*

There are two solemn and ineffaceable moments in a journey in Palestine; one is that in which one salutes, for the first time, Jerusalem and the Mount of Olives ; the other, that in which one catches sight of the Lake of Gennesaret.

When, on reaching the top of the mountain which commands the view of the Lake of Tiberias, I suddenly perceived it at my feet, so polished and so peaceful, as if asleep amidst the solemn silence of its shores, I scarcely dared to go forward and descend into the valley,— I felt that these places were holy ground. My eye took in, at one glance, these waters into which Peter and Andrew, James and John, so often cast their nets; this shore, so often trodden by the feet of the Saviour; these so favoured tracts of earth, upon which the Eternal Word "*pitched His tent,*"† which "*beheld His glory,*" and

city. It is called the *Jerusalem* Talmud, not from its having been written in that city itself, but because it was composed in Palestine, and to distinguish it from the Babylonish Talmud drawn up a century and a half later, and on a much larger scale. It is well known that John Buxtorf, the elder, gave the title of *Tiberias* to his fine commentary upon the Masora, printed at Basle in 1620, as a sequel to his *Rabbinic Bible.*

* Gal. iv. 25, 26.   † Εσκήνωσεν, St. John i. 14.

which have borne witness to these things to all countries and all ages.

Should my book happen to reach readers, not of my fellow-countrymen for whom it is specially intended, I beg them to excuse, once again, the comparisons I am about to draw, which cannot have any interest for them. The Lake of Gennesaret, seen from the top of these mountains, has quite the appearance of a Swiss lake. It bears, particularly from its extent, as well as from the principal features of the landscape, a striking likeness to the Lake of Neuchâtel, as seen from one of the summits of the Jura. It has not the deep blue of the Mediterranean, or of Lake Leman ; rather it is of a greyish blue, and I see in it the same *spots* which one sees so often on our lake, and which have not, I think, as yet been satisfactorily accounted for. The mountains in front of me make a line nearly horizontal, like the eastern shore of the Lake of Neuchâtel. But they are higher, and intersected with ravines ; and their slopes, though abrupt, have a regularity which one misses in those of the Jorat ; and their effect is therefore more picturesque.

Behind this range of mountains rises, as with us, a second ; not, it is true, along the whole length of the lake, but only on my left, towards the north-east extremity. This second range, higher and more broken than the first, answers to what with us is the range of the lower Alps. Finally, to complete the parallel, is seen rising to the north, also beyond these mountains, the lofty and broad crest of Hermon crowned with eternal snows. But it is at a less distance from Tiberias than the Alps are from Neuchâtel. The distance is about the same as that from Geneva to Mont Blanc.

At my feet lies the little town of Tiberias ; it is the only one which still exists on this shore; it lies between the lake and the steep sides of the mountain, in a small area left open by the latter. Its aspect is most picturesque. Its walls, flanked with towers three-fourths crumbled into ruin, describe an arc, of which the edge of the lake forms the chord. Round the walls are here and there a few isolated palm trees and some tufts of cactus.

The fate of Tiberias is curious. Founded, or perhaps only rebuilt, by Herod the tetrarch, who gave it the name of his suzerain, the Emperor Tiberius, it was, under him, the capital of Galilee. It was a town altogether Roman, with a population almost entirely pagan ; and the Jews had a great prejudice against it. Later on, when it had become a place of refuge for their doctors, and their most illustrious school, they flocked thither from all parts of the world, to profit by their lessons. In our day, when these sources of light have long since been extinguished, they still come there to visit the sepulchres of their wise men. Tiberias is the city of the Rabbis, as Jerusalem is the city of the prophets.

But it is not these memories of the past only that in our day bring together such crowds of Jews within the ruined walls of Tiberias. It is also a hope,—the expectation of the promised deliverance of their nation. They have in Palestine four sacred cities, Hebron, where rests Abraham ; Jerusalem, the City of David ; and then, in Galilee, Tiberias, and Saphet. These two last are the cities of the future Messiah. According to an extremely remarkable tradition, He is to come forth from the waters of the Lake of Gennesaret, land at Tiberias, and then establish His throne at Saphet.

Still, to this day, in Tiberias we see the interesting phenomenon of a Jewish city. When one enters it on a Sabbath day, as I did, one is struck with a degree of order and silence not to be matched elsewhere. As the Mussulmans, while they specially consecrate Friday to religious exercises, nevertheless do not make it a day of rest, I had not seen a holy-day since I left Europe.

We entered Tiberias through a breach in the wall. On the 1st of January, 1837, an earthquake almost entirely overthrew the city, and buried under its ruins more than two thousand of its inhabitants. The walls were only partially destroyed; but the new city, which arose out of the ruins, has suffered from the poverty of its inhabitants; it scarcely looks like a town; the houses have no cupolas, and consist generally of one story; they are out of sight at the bottom of little walled courtyards, over which one may see hanging a fig tree, a large vine, a palm tree, or a pomegranate. It has, everywhere, its ruins and its rags; and yet, compared with Jerusalem, one might think Tiberias a clean, well-ordered town.

I ride on for a while without meeting a living creature, and hearing no sound but that of my horse's footfalls re-echoed from the walls. But a little further on are some Jews seated in front of their houses, or walking slowly up and down in holiday attire. The men wear long cotton robes with girdles round the waist, and fur-bordered caps, from under which escape their long locks of curled and greased hair; the gowns of the women have the gaudiest of flowers embroidered on a white ground; gold ornaments decorate their caps and the bosoms of their dresses, and from the backs of their heads hang many-coloured veils.

There is at Tiberias a Galician Jew, who keeps a sort of *locanda*. To this I am taken. His house, which in front is but two windows broad, is one of the largest in the town ; it has one story above the ground floor. I dismount, to pass through the gate of the courtyard. Two young Jewesses, very handsome and well dressed, come to meet me, and shew me into a very clean and pleasant divan. Then the host makes his appearance, and apologises for not being able to offer me anything, not even a glass of water or a light for my chibouque, because to-day is the Sabbath. Afterwards, a youth presents himself, dressed in a *redingote à l'Européenne*, but wearing over it a great white *thaleth*. He comes straight up to me, squeezes my hand warmly, expresses his extreme happiness at the sight of me, and makes a thousand protestations of his devotedness to my service. He explains that he is acting as consul here. He is a Polish refugee, a Jew by race and religion. He has found protection and employment in Austria. The imperial and royal government has sent him into Galilee to protect its subjects there ; for the European Jews in Tiberias and Saphet belong often by origin to the Austrian States.

As the Sabbath does not end till sunset, our host then, but not before, taking off his holiday dress, begins his preparations for our repast. It is already ten o'clock when I am invited to supper. We, the consul and I, are served by ourselves in the courtyard, according to custom, under the shelter of the vault, which takes the place of a *peristyle*. The supper consists, in the main, of excellent fish from the lake. The consul orders red Saphet wine, the best I have yet drunk in Palestine. The attendants of the consul,

23

his secretary and his *cawass*, are also Jews; they come and go, taking the orders of their master.

Some poor *ashkenázim* who saw me pass just now, come into the courtyard and ask an alms in German. One of them, a tailor by trade, begs work of me. In vain do I try to evade his offers of service ; my trousers, torn in many places by the thorns in Judæa, furnish him with an irresistible argument in favour of his *rights of labour.*, He squats at my feet, and puts me in repair then and there.

The custom of supping under the porch of the house, in a courtyard open to all comers, explains many passages in the Gospels which would not at all fit in with our European notions. For instance, we find that Jesus, having been invited to a supper by Simon the Pharisee, a woman of evil life having heard that He was among the guests, came and sate at His feet, washing them with her tears and anointing them with perfumes.* To my mind this supper in the open air on a fine star-lit night, these fishes served up, this whole Jewish *entourage*, carry me back to the days when Jesus used to visit the dwellers on the shores of this very lake, and sit at their tables.

There are but two rooms in this story; one for the consul, the other for me. This last has three great windows, unglazed, I need not say, but closed, after a fashion, with shutters. I only half sleep, though I have a real bed ; for the bed consists only of a duvet one inch thick, resting on iron bars which bruise my back. At cock-crowing there is a violent storm ; the wind blows my shutters· open with a loud clatter ; notwithstanding repeated efforts, I cannot keep them shut. But though my bed was in front of the window, and I

* St. Luke vii. 36, etc.

had neither clothes nor coverlets, I felt no disagreeable effects from these violent puffs of wind which blew straight at me. This shews the mildness of the climate on the shores of the Lake of Tiberias. In the rest of the country, on the other hand, I always found the nights cold.

The day after my arrival at Tiberias was a Sunday. The Jews had shewn, the day before, how they kept their Sabbath ; I wished also to celebrate, in my own way, the day which commemorates the glorious resurrection of the Saviour. I determined that on that day I would leave the city of Jehuda-hakkâdôsh, and seek to tread in the footsteps of the Nazareth Rabbi, on the seashore at Bethsaida and Capernaüm.

There may be differences of opinion as to the exact site of Capernaüm,* but at any rate we know that it was situated on the western shore of the lake, on the border-land between the territories of Zebulun and Naphtali, and consequently to the north of Tiberias. My road is therefore marked out for me. I have not even to decide whether to travel by land or water ; for the only boat in Tiberias is at this moment disabled. The Rabbi Schwarz, who lived for sixteen years in Palestine, and wrote a book upon it which is deservedly highly valued, pictures the Lake of Gennesaret as full of life :—" It is," he says, " continually crossed by little vessels, bringing wood and other articles of merchandise from the dwellers on the other side Jordan." *Tantus amor patriæ !*—love for the native soil of his ancestors has here drawn the learned Rabbi into a manifest exaggeration. For my own part, I am bound

* I write *Capernaüm*, as the received text has it ; but the best manuscripts and the Vulgate make it *Caphernaüm*, the authority for which seems, in fact, the best.

to say that, during the three days I spent in Tiberias, I did not see a single sail crossing the lake ; and all travellers say the same.

I must then make this expedition on horseback. I am accompanied by John, and by a *bachi-bazook* whom he insists on my taking with me as an escort; for the country into which we are going is infested by Arab robbers. I object that an escort of only one man seems to me an insufficient defence against a troop of bandits, and that it would be better to go alone, and so be less visible. But John judiciously answers that the bachi-bazook is not intended to defend us, and does not in the least dream of doing so ; what makes him valuable to us is that he is afraid of the Bedouins; and we can be very sure that at however great a distance he may catch sight of any of them, he will forthwith turn tail and give us the signal of retreat.

There was no answering such good reasons. And I felt them to be the more original as we were then on the very classic ground of chivalry. I recollected that Tiberias had been the city of Tancred, and that, according to an ancient romance, Saladin himself had wished to be knighted by Huon de Tabarie (Hugo of Tiberias).*

Our host, on our setting out, gives us provisions for our expedition : loaves—I say *loaves*, not *a loaf*, as they make them here very small—eggs, hard-boiled, as always, together with fried fish wrapped in a leaf of the *Khôbath hallebâbôth.*† The fish is a delicacy which I have not met with elsewhere in Palestine, but which

---

* See *l'Ordène de Chevalerie*, in the collection of Barbazan and Méon.

† A treatise on Morals, written towards the end of the eleventh century, by Rabbi Bechai, of Barcelona.

is commonly to be had on the shores of the Lake of Gennesaret. Evidently the eatables in use are absolutely the same as in the days of Jesus. When the multitudes followed Him, the provisions taken with them by the most provident persons were loaves and fishes.* "*If a son,*" He says to His disciples, "*should ask bread of any of you that is a father, will he give him a stone? or if he ask a fish, will he for a fish give him a serpent? or if he shall ask an egg, will he offer him a scorpion?*"†

Tiberias, as I have said, is built on a little corner of land between the lake and the mountain. But further towards the north the mountain projects into the lake, and the road we follow takes a line a little higher up. For a distance of four or five kilomêtres this shore is broken only by one valley, at the bottom of which runs a little stream called *Ain-el-Bârideh*. But on reaching Medjdal, the mountains recede and leave space for a fine plain of the shape of a half-moon, more than a league in length. This Medjdal is but a poor hamlet; but its name is pure Hebrew —*Medjdal* being but the Arabic pronunciation of *Migdal* (a tower). Its situation makes it easy to understand why it had been intended to build a fort here ; it was indeed a military position of considerable importance ; on one side was the plain of Gennesaret, on the other the bad road which leads to Tiberias ; behind the village opens the little valley of Hattin. Many Israelitish towns bore the name of *Migdal*, as may be seen in the Old Testament and in the Talmud. Which of these does the modern hamlet represent ? Is it *Migdal-El* (the tower of God), a city of the tribe of Naphtali, mentioned by Joshua ? ‡ or, as

* St. Mark vi. 38, viii. 5.   † St. Luke xi. 11, 12.
‡ Josh. xix. 38.

Schwarz will have it, *Migdal-Nunia*, of which the name
occurs only in the Talmud? It matters little to us,
since none of these ancient *Migdals* has any great
historic interest. At any rate, the one now before us
is evidently the *Magdala* mentioned by St. Matthew[*]
as being on the shore of the Lake of Gennesaret—that
from which, to all appearance, Mary Magdalene took
her name.

The steep sides of the mountain at the foot of which
I find myself are regular in shape, and lie, so to say,
in folds; there are no trees upon them, but the slopes
are covered with green turf. If the mountains of the
opposite coast have a slight resemblance to the eastern
shore of the Lake of Neuchâtel, these have none to
those of the Jura; rather they have a sort of Alpine
character. There is to be found, for instance, among
the environs of Vevey, a spot which strikingly recalls
the territory of Magdala.

The plain into which we are entering bears in the
Old Testament the name of Chinnereth, and in the
New that of Gennesareth. The former has been given
to it on account of its shape, which is rather like a
harp (in Hebrew כנור). The word Gennesaret signifies
the gardens of the prince. Of what prince? I do not
know. Can there be, in this name, any allusion to
those *princes of Naphtali* who are twice mentioned in
the Bible?[†] However that may be, this plain was
formerly a real garden, a kind of earthly paradise. I

---

[*] St. Matt. xv. 39.

[†] 1 Chron. xii. 34; Psalm lxviii. 27. I should be tempted rather
to trace the word נגוסר (used in the Talmud) to the root סור, *recedere*,
and to make the expression mean *gardens of retreat.* Or it might
be meant for *gardens of Zer*, a town mentioned with Hammath in
Joshua xix. 35.

have quoted the description given by Josephus of Galilee in general; that which he gives of Gennesaret is still more brilliant; one might fancy oneself reading of a journey to the *Land of Cokayne.* " This country," he says, "is equally admirable for its beauty and its fertility. There is no species of plant which does not thrive in it. Nuts, which love cold, grow there in large quantities by the side of dates, which belong to warm climates, and of the figs and olives of temperate regions. One might say that Nature here piqued herself on combining contrasts, and that each of the seasons of the year fought for possession of the country. The soil produces the different kinds of fruit, not only once a year, but at the most opposite seasons; bearing during ten months without ceasing those kings among fruits, grapes and figs.

Near Medjdal are market-gardens in which we see two men at work, stripped to the waist. The rest of the country is uncultivated; but one can still see how great must be the natural fertility of the soil, and richness of the climate, justifying the eulogies of Josephus. At this moment everything is flowering; the flower most prevalent is that large yellow star so common with us, and of which I am really ashamed not to know the name; it gives to all this country a golden colouring.* It sprouts in tufts, and attains to the height of a man. It is the same with the daisies, which I can gather without stooping while sitting on horseback. The thistles, which are very common, grow to a height of from ten to twelve feet.

* This yellow flower, of which I had forgotten the name, is none other than the *marigold* ("*le souci*"). That in the plain of Gennesaret is not a marigold, M. Boissier has since told me, but a plant of the same family, the *chrysanthemum segetum* of Linnæus.

I find also a number of thorns, not the little woody
thorn of the environs of Jerusalem and of the mountains
of Galilee, but a plant at least four feet in height, of
which the leaves, of a pale green colour, are armed at
the axilla with five long star-like spikes. The green
shoots of the palm-tree are sprouting in great tufts.
One does not, however, see in this plain any of the
trees which used to beautify it in old times ; but, as
the grasses attain to the dimensions of real shrubs, the
shrubs grow to the size of great trees. Some magnificent oleanders, laden with their great flowers, decorate
the shores of the lake and the banks of the streams ;
for this plain is perfectly watered. I have crossed three
pretty streams, and have found the beds of many others
now dry, but which no doubt also have their season.

All this, it will be seen, is very different from the
rest of Palestine ; one might fancy oneself in another
zone of the earth ; and such, in fact, it is—for the
climate of the banks of the Lake of Gennesaret is
much less dry and much warmer than that of the
Mediterranean coast of Syria ; it reminds one of that
of the tropics. In July and August the heat is extreme ; the consul told me yesterday that though he
had been for a long time accustomed to hot climates,
he found it impossible to spend the summer in Tiberias ;
he had to leave it for Saphet.

Two of the parables of Jesus bear indirect testimony
to the fertility of this country,—those of the Sower,
and of the Mustard Seed. Even if the Gospels had not
told us that they were spoken on the shores of the
Lake of Gennesaret,* we could easily have guessed it.
The seed " bearing fruit an hundredfold " is not, it is
true, anything extraordinary ; but yet this particular

* St. Matt. xiii.

statement in the parable would, I think, have astonished the country people of the neighbourhood of
Jerusalem, accustomed to sowing in a dry, light soil,
more suited for the cultivation of the vine than of
wheat. And as to the other parable, this country with
its tropical climate is, no doubt, the only one in all
Syria where a mustard seed could grow into a great
tree. The Jerusalem Talmud, which also was written
at Tiberias, mentions some extraordinary instances.*

I have drawn attention to the fact that the parables
of Jesus were always adapted to the customs of those
to whom, and to the country in which, they were spoken.
It is not difficult to detect by internal evidence which
were spoken in Jerusalem, and which in Galilee. The
life of the shepherd, and that of the vine-dresser, are
the sources from which the former are oftenest taken.†
On the other hand, when Jesus speaks of fields of
wheat, of harvests, of barns, of nets which fishermen
draw to shore,‡ we conclude that He is on the shores
of the Lake of Gennesaret. If, after drawing such
conclusions, we look back to the circumstances under
which each parable was spoken, and to the actual facts
which preceded or followed it, we shall find that we

---

* The mustard plant of the Gospels is called in the Talmud,
חרדל ; its seed is often taken by the Jews as a symbol of the smallest
things. (See Buxtorf, *sub voce*, and St. Matt. xvii. 20.) It is the
salvadore de Perse, also called by the Arabs *khadel*, or *khardel*.

† See for example, the parable of the Two Sons, whom their
father sends into the vineyard (St. Matt. xxi.), of the Unfaithful
Vine-dresser (ibid.), of the Shepherd who separates the sheep
from the goats (St. Matt. xxv. 32, 33), and of the Good Shepherd (St. John x.).

‡ So also the parables of the Sower, of the Tares, of the Net,
(St. Matt. xiii.), of the Rich Man rebuilding his barns (St. Luke
xiii.).

have rarely been led astray—the narrative of the evangelists almost always confirms the truth of what we had been in this way led to guess.

I make slow progress, sometimes walking through the tall grasses of the meadows, sometimes following the shore of the lake; this shore is a narrow strip covered with very fine sand, sprinkled with little shells of various kinds.

At its northern as well as southern extremity, the plain of Gennesaret—or, as it is now called, the territory of Magdala (*Ardh-el-Medjdal*)*—is completely shut in by a rocky promontory forming a natural wall. Probably this side was formerly also protected by a tower, and perhaps by a little town; there are ruins here of a khân, called Khân-Minîeh.

Climbing over this promontory in a few minutes, by the help of a little path cut in the rock, one reaches another valley, or alluvial plain, of the same nature as that of Gennesaret, but much narrower. It is watered by a stream breaking into several branches. At the mouth of one of these streamlets is a mill, and close by it I see some fishermen spreading out their nets to dry. Perhaps it was in this very place that Peter, Andrew, and the sons of Zebedee were plying their trade, when Jesus walking upon the same shore saw them sitting in the boat and said to them, "*Come, follow me.*" † Many travellers think this is the Bethsaida (*"fishers' house"*), which was the city of Philip, Andrew, and Peter.‡ Others find it in the Khân-Minieh, by which I passed just now. It is difficult, perhaps impossible, to discover its exact site; but

---

* This would lead one to think that in the Gospels these two expressions are absolutely synonymous.

† St. Matt. iv. 18—22.   ‡ St. John i. 44.

there are only two or three places on this shore, very near to each other, between which we can doubt. I am at any rate on the very native soil of the Gospel; I am on the strip of ground upon which was once cast that seed, small compared to all the rest, but soon to become a great tree, which was to receive all the nations of the earth under the shadow of its branches.

Here I stop for a moment, and I wish to drink of the brook. But the fishermen tell me that the water is brackish, and is used only to turn the wheel of the mill. James, the writer of the Epistle, was perhaps also an inhabitant of Bethsaida, or at any rate had often visited this region ; perhaps he was thinking of the different branches of this stream, and of the streams in the plain of Gennesaret, when he wrote the words, "*Doth a fountain send forth at the same place sweet water and bitter ?*"*

The mountains which, as far as Medjdal, and above the plain of Gennesaret, descend in abrupt precipices, begin here to change their forms ; the summits are further from us, and the sides of the mountain descend towards the lake in gentle slopes. The hill-side which I cross, after passing the Bethsaidan mill, is beautifully situated ; it is near the extremity of the lake, and spreads out towards the north-east ; so that the view from it embraces the whole of this fine sheet of water, and its picturesque shores. This was formerly the site of a town of considerable size. The soil is still, over much of its extent, strewed with large stones for the most part hidden under the thorns with which it is covered. Here the road ends ; the thorns grow to such a height, that it would be quite impossible to pass on foot. They tear my clothes, and make

* St. James iii. 11.

more work for my friend the Tiberias tailor ; my legs are torn ; my horse stumbles at every step against the stones, and wounds himself with the thorns ; he kicks, and stops short.

Here in old times was the site of that "*Capernaum which was exalted unto heaven ;*"* for it was, for three years, the dwelling-place of "*God manifest in the flesh,*" and the witness of His wonderful works. Now it is "*cast down to hell.*" This land, cursed above all lands, in our time produces nothing but briars and thorns ; and all that marvellous fertility of soil, which once made it an Eden, now only serves to give these frightful thorns a greater vigour than elsewhere.

Two or three little hovels, entirely concealed from sight amid this forest of thorns, are the only shelter to be found against the burning rays of the sun. They were built by Bedouins, John tells me, and serve them occasionally as hiding-places for the fruits of their raids. We force our way, not without difficulty, into one of these huts. Its walls are built of great hewn stones, gathered from the ruins of the ancient town ; the roof consists of mats made of rushes resting on three posts of fig-wood, and on a fragment of an ancient column.

We are within a hundred paces of the lake. John goes out to draw water from it ; but notwithstanding his efforts, he cannot reach it. I set off to fetch some for myself, being quite determined to reach the lake, in which I have absolutely made up my mind to bathe. I therefore get into the saddle again, and begin another determined fight with the stones, the thorns, and my unhappy horse, who rears, has a fall, and obstinately refuses to go on. After half an hour's struggle and a

* St. Matt. xi. 23.

world of trouble, I at last reach the shore. I undress upon a heap of the stones which strew the ground, and refresh myself with a swim in the limpid waters. They are much agitated to-day, there being a high wind, but they are very mild in temperature.

We have our meal in the hut. The bachi-bazook refuses to share in it, because it is the month of Ramadan. In vain do we urge that before we get back to Tiberias we shall have accomplished a more than seven hours' journey, and that the law allows dispensation from fasting to those who have to undergo exceptional fatigues. He is not to be seduced by such lax interpretations ; no doubt he puts us down as doctors of only just sufficient authority to establish a *"probable opinion."* He refuses even a glass of water, and will not so much as come into the hut, for fear of running into temptation. The good man stays at a few yards' distance, like a sentinel; still mounted on his horse, and in the blazing sunshine.

While John collects the fragments of our loaves and fishes, and puts them back into the sack, " *that nothing be lost,*" I take a New Testament out of my pocket, and turn over its leaves to find the passages relating to Capernaum. At this time of day—on Sunday morning—how many Christians in all the world are reading this name, and are borne away in spirit to these places in which I now am, alone with a Turk and an Arab! Jesus once lived here ;* the Gospels even call Capernaum " *His own city.*"† They inform us that it was here He paid tribute.‡ Here He taught in the synagogue, healed the palsied man,§ the centurion's servant,‖ the man that had an unclean spirit,¶—all the

---

* St. Matt. iv. 13.   ‡ *Ibid.* xvii. 24.   ‖ *Ibid.* viii. 5—13.
† *Ibid.* ix. 1.   § *Ibid.* ix. 1—7.   ¶ St. Luke iv. 33—35.

infirmities of the body, and all the miseries of the soul. It was at Capernaum that He spoke these words, "*Him that cometh to me, I will in no wise cast out; . . . . for this is the Father's will which hath sent me, that of all which He hath given me, I should lose nothing.*"* I would wish to lift my heart to Him, or rather to pray Him to come to me,—this Saviour now glorified, this Physician, this Friend so easily found. I would wish to hold communion with Him, and to feel His invisible presence in these places, in which, Himself a man, He lived among the sons of men. . . . . But one might think that the anathema which rests upon Capernaum would not suffer those who stop there to enjoy a moment of meditation and peace. My bachi-bazook never ceases crying out that the Bedouins are coming. This does not trouble me at first, as I say to myself that if they have to cross a bed of thorns like the one we have just passed, it will take them some time to reach us. However, I go out of the hut, and far away in the distance I catch sight of a little troop of Bedouins. We should have had, I believe, nothing to fear; for they were but a handful of men. It is true that neither John nor I was armed; two days before I had been robbed of one of my pistols, and I had left the other at Tiberias; but the bare sight of our bachi-bazook, with his lance in arrest, his sword in his girdle, and his gun on his back, would, perhaps, have been enough to overawe the robbers. For the second time to-day I thought of Tancred and Saladin; but I did not, I confess, dare to trust myself to the courage of a soldier who had not breakfasted. We remounted, and took the road to Tiberias.

The ruins at which we had stopped are, in our day,

* St. John vi. 37—39.

called Tell-Ilûm. Their proximity to the end of the lake, the extent of ground they cover, and various other circumstances concur in making it probable that they represent the ancient Capernaum. Robinson, who loves to be in opposition, prefers to place Capernaum at Khân Minîeh. Wilson undertook to refute him, and has succeeded in doing so to my satisfaction. I shall not embark in this discussion, for the data are not sufficient to enable one to arrive at any certain conclusion. It is remarkable that tradition, which has pointed out, rightly or wrongly, the sites of so many sacred places in Palestine, says nothing positively on Capernaum in which Jesus lived, nor on Bethsaida, the home of St. Peter. Of Chorazin, Robinson does not claim to have discovered any traces. They assured me, however, at Tiberias, that there exists on the mountain, a league and a half from Tell-Ilûm, a ruin still called Bir-Kérésoun (the well of Kérésoun). That might well be the Chorazin of the Gospels.

Some time after my visit to Capernaum, I was passing through Tyre and Sidon. On the sites of these queens of the sea I found shabby little towns, fallen far below their ancient splendour, but retaining still, intact, their old Phœnician names, and containing within their walls a fairly active population, which seems to retain some of the commercial genius of its ancestors. My thoughts reverted to the shores of the Lake of Gennesaret, and I was struck with the literal fulfilment of the sentence of our Lord : " *Woe unto thee, Chorazin! Woe unto thee, Bethsaida! it shall be more tolerable for Tyre and Sidon than for you !*"*

* St. Matt. xi. 21, 22.

III.

The Environs of Tiberias.

The principal regret which I have brought away with me from my journey in the Holy Land is that I did not stay longer by the shores of the Lake of Tiberias. I wish I had stayed long enough to imprint the memory of it for ever on my mind; I wish I had fixed in my imagination in ineffaceable lines each outline of its coasts, and had learnt to know each aspect of these waves, these skies, these mountains.

Nevertheless, I had the happiness, during the three days I spent at Tiberias, of seeing the country in many different aspects. Those who have lived by the shores of a lake know what unceasing variations are produced in the scenery, not only by the motions of the waves and their changes of colour, but above all by the vapours rising out of it which modify in so many ways the transparency of the atmosphere. When I came back from Capernaum, the wind had ceased, and the mountains on the opposite shore, instead of presenting those brilliant colours, those clear and well-defined outlines, which bring distant objects near, and are characteristic of Oriental scenery, were veiled with so much vapour, were so *sunburnt* (according to the happy expression used amongst us), that they seemed much further off than they really are. During the night there arose one of those great storms which make navigation on the Lake of Gennesaret so dangerous, and of which instances are given us in the Gospels. In the morning there was a slight fall of rain and the same north-west wind. The sky was overcast, and remained so till noon; the temperature, nevertheless, was of the mildest, whilst on the mountain and the plateau it was very cold.

I had still to visit the immediate neighbourhood of Tiberias, and especially its famed hot springs. They are close to the shores of the lake, a full quarter of a league to the south of the present town. It has been supposed that formerly the city extended as far as that. Hammath, of which the name signifies *warm waters*, and which is mentioned by Joshua as one of the cities of Naphtali,* would have occupied the site upon which Herod the tetrarch rebuilt Tiberias. On comparing the many passages of the Talmud which speak of these two cities, I should rather conclude that they are not identical, but very close to each other, and that, when Tiberias was built, Hammath became one of its suburbs. It is the Hammaus of Josephus. We come out of the city by a gateway with a depressed arch ; it is made, it is true, to admit a man on horseback, but only if he bends down over the neck of his horse. This, too, is a measure of precaution.

I have already spoken of the Alpine character of the mountains which overhang Tiberias. Seen from here, the ancient building erected over the thermal springs reminds one by its situation of the castle of Chillon.

There are two pools of these thermal springs, at two hundred yards' distance from each other ; one of them was the work of Ibrahim Pacha, the other is attributed to Solomon. Solomon and Ibrahim Pacha ! these in Syria are the only names *which live in the memory of the people ;* they do not imagine that anything great can have taken place between these two. The names of the Herods and the Saladins have perished. With us, too, the people date every event from Cæsar or Napoleon.

Ibrahim's bath-house, the first we come to, already

* Joshua xix. 35.

24

looks like a ruin, and soon will be one. Though it is very much frequented, no one will take the trouble to keep it in˜repair. The large room containing the spring is surrounded by several porticoes, in which we find a crowd of people heaped together, laid on couches, or wrapped in blankets, with a lamentable look of misery and suffering. How well we can picture to ourselves, as we look at them, the sick brought from all parts to Jesus ; or, still more vividly, the blind, the lame, the palsied, laid in the five porches of the pool of Bethesda ! *

There is, it is true, a sort of valet acting as a bath attendant, but nothing like a committee of administration, or police. We enter the bath-house ; some women who are in possession beg us to wait a little. They soon give place to us. John is eager to take a bath ; curiosity would incline me to do the same, but I am afraid that the warm water may weaken me, and I am content with only inspecting.

The bath is of white marble, circular in shape, and roofed with a cupola resting on columns. Round the bath itself, in the interior, runs a step which serves as a seat ; the middle is very deep, but nevertheless one can cross it without danger, for the specific gravity of the water is so great, that to reach the bottom requires an effort, but to float on the top requires none.

I forgot to bring my thermometer with me ; but happily other travellers, more careful, have tested the temperature of these waters. According to Robinson, it is $49\frac{2}{3}°$ Réaumur. The water which runs into the basin is now and then stopped, in order to allow that which is in it to cool a little ; it remains, however,

---

* St. John v. 2, 3.

very much hotter than that of most warm baths. I
could hardly keep my hand in it.

I found this water had a disagreeable salt taste.
However, it is not used for drinking, but only for
bathing.

Though the dome is high and pierced with holes, the
water in the bath gives out so much steam that I cannot stay long in the peristyle. I prevail upon Hhannah
to tear himself away from the delight of the bath.
While he is remounting the steps, and having a bucket
of the lake water poured over his shoulders, to wash off
the salt deposit left upon him by the bath water, I pay
a visit to the old pool—that of Solomon. It is smaller
and much more dilapidated. Many people prefer it to
the other, because its water it still hotter.

I would not leave Tiberias without paying my
tribute of veneration to the tomb of Rabbi Moses ben
Maïmon, better known to the Jews by the name of
Rambam (which is a shortened form of it), and to the
Christians by that of *Moses Maïmonides*. In the midst
of the constellation of theologians, learned men and
poets, who were the glory of the Jewish people during
the eleventh and twelfth centuries, at the time when the
Christian nations were plunged in the profoundest darkness, no name shines more brightly than his. Moses
Maïmonides aspired to be the reformer of Judaism ; he
was at any rate its glory, and the Jews, comparing him
to their great lawgiver, still have a proverb, " *From
Moses to Moses there arose no man like Moses.*" *
Though he was born at Cordova, and died at Cairo,
they buried him at Tiberias, by the side of the doctors
of the Mishna. His tomb is on the heights, at five
minutes' distance from the walls. A Jew offers to take

* ממשה עד משה לא קם כמשה׃

me there.   He shews me, a few yards lower down,
the tombs of many other men of learning, amongst
whom he mentions to me *Rabbi Khanin ben Zaccai*,
the author, he tells me, of the *Shené loukhoth habberith*.
Your imagination, no doubt, pictures to you these
tombs left in solitude and silence ; but no ! before each
of them sit Jews, reading their prayers aloud. Women
are kissing the stones, bathing them with their tears,
and uttering groans.   The sight of me excites curiosity,
they ask me endless questions, they pour out explana-
tions, they tell me anecdotes, with the eagerness and
volubility characteristic of the Jews among the people
of the East.   Almost all of them speak Hebrew with
much fluency and correctness.   When they see the
interest I take in the memory of their sages, they talk
to me of them with still greater vivacity, and a kind of
passion, as one might in Europe of some hero of the
day.   To the mind of a Jew, time seems to have no
existence.   They are always young, for they forget
nothing, and live upon a great hope.   They are patient,
because they are eternal, and know that " *the gifts and
calling of God are without repentance.*"*

Were I asked what Judaism is, I could hardly illus-
trate it better than by the picture now before me.
These venerable tombs, around which gather the pathetic
memories of the living ; this city, of which the crumbled walls have never been rebuilt, and yet in which
not a stone is wanting to the vast heap of ruins—what
a striking image of that vivacious nationality sym-
bolised by the Wandering Jew who suffers on through
so many centuries, and without being allowed to
die !

These tombs are constructed of masonry, and white-

* Romans xi. 29.

washed. So are all Oriental tombs—Jewish, Christian, and Mahometan. We know that the ancient Hebrews often hewed their sepulchres out of the rock; but it may be supposed that that kind was reserved for the rich, and that the common people were buried in the way usual now. The expression, "*whited sepulchres*," used by the Saviour, probably referred to tombs such as those in use now. As they are generally built near the gates of towns, along the high roads, they suffer from the trampling of horses and cattle, for they are made of soft stone. I recollect seeing at Alexandria, within a few yards of Pompey's column, one of these tombs, still quite new and white, but nevertheless already broken. If the breach in it had been at all larger, the dead body it contained would have been visible, for the grave is not generally dug to a depth of more than half a foot, or at most a foot, and no earth is thrown upon the body. This explains the forcible comparison used by Jesus in stigmatising hypocrites: "*Ye are like unto whited sepulchres, which indeed appear beautiful outward, but within are full of dead men's bones, and of all uncleanness.*"*

After I had, according to custom, deposited a little stone upon the tomb of Rambam, as a memorial of my visit, and an act of homage to his memory, many Jews who were there proposed to take me to the tomb of another of their sages, Rabbi Akiba, one of the most famous doctors of the Mishna, and one of the martyrs to Jewish independence, under the Emperor Hadrian. This monument is much higher up on the side of the mountain. Rabbi Schwarz, in his critical notes on

* St. Matt. xxiii. 27. St. Luke, in citing this parable (xi. 44), purposely leaves out the epithet "whited," which would have called up no recollections in the minds of his Greek readers.

Raumer's Palestine, rebukes severely enough the traveller Burkhardt for talking of the fourteen thousand disciples of Akiba buried near their master. I must defend Burkhardt, who certainly did no more than repeat what he had heard at Tiberias from the lips of the Jews themselves; for those who accompanied me told me the same story, only that they made the number twenty-four thousand.

Let Rabbi Schwarz take comfort, however! The imagination of the Christians has often run as wild as that of the Jews : with our eleven thousand virgins at Cologne, we cannot throw stones at the twenty-four thousand disciples buried at Tiberias. I have elsewhere recounted some of the legends current among the Jerusalem monks. In Tiberias, too, attempts have been made to discover, and collect within a convenient distance from the town, and not too far from the road to Nazareth, a certain number of the places mentioned in the Gospel narrative. I even discovered in Hhannah's possession a little book *ad hoc,* written in Italian, from which he drew his erudition. He took me to the mountain of the second miracle of the loaves,* and to what he called *the field of the ears of wheat,*† and then to *the Mount of Beatitudes.*

The last-mentioned site does really deserve to be noticed. Though I attach no authority to the legend or tradition which marks it as the place on which Jesus delivered the *Sermon on the Mount,* I was exceedingly struck, on examining it, to find it so perfectly in harmony with the data of the Gospel history. I asked myself whether it was possible to find on the shores of this lake, or even in all Palestine, another mountain which would harmonize so completely with the details

---

* St. Matt. xv. 29—38.   † St. Matt. xii. 1.

bearing upon this subject to be gathered from St. Luke and St. Matthew. Behind the mountain which over-hangs Tiberias is a large *plateau*, ascending in a gentle incline towards a rock which forms its summit. This would have been the rock upon which Jesus spent the night in prayer, and when it was day called His dis-ciples, and chose His apostles.* Then He would have descended again to the multitude who were waiting for Him upon the plateau, and from thence He would have addressed the people. The apparent contradiction be-tween the narratives of St. Luke and St. Matthew would thus be cleared up. According to the former, Jesus *came down*, and it was *in the plain* that He delivered His discourse. According to St. Matthew, He *went up into a mountain* with the people.‡ This we can explain, since St. Matthew says nothing here of the prayer of Jesus, or of the selection of the apostles ; he only reports the fact generally,—the preaching to the multitudes upon a mountain. St. Luke, who tells us one other fact, speaks of the Lord first going up to the top of the mountain, then coming down again *into the plain*, that is to say, on to the plateau.§

Just here, at the foot of the rock, at the top of the plateau, there is, in fact, a platform, a sort of natural pulpit, from whence any one could easily be seen and heard by a great multitude. It is there that, according to the above supposition, the Lord would have sate down. From thence His eyes would have

* St. Luke vi. 12, 13.
† St. Luke vi. 17.
‡ St. Matt. v. 1.
§ So our versions translate the passage ; but the original (ἐπὶ τόπου πεδινοῦ, *upon a level place*) seems here, by the turn of the phrase, to indicate that it is not a plain, in the strict sense, that is meant.

surveyed the multitude of the unhappy who had come
to beg from Him the healing of their infirmities.*
Then we can imagine Him looking towards His disciples,† who had left all to hear from Him the words
of eternal life ; and then beginning His Sermon. ‡
" *Blessed are the poor in spirit ! Blessed are they that
mourn !* . . . . *Blessed are they that hunger and thirst
after righteousness !* "

Then, looking at Tabor, of which the summit is seen
towering above the undulations of the mountain country
of Galilee, He points out to His disciples the town
which crowns it, and says to them, " *Ye are the light of
the world. A city that is set on an hill cannot be hid.*"

These words, thus spoken, are more important than
they might seem at first sight for determining the
place where the Sermon on the Mount was delivered.
We have already remarked that it was not the habit of
Jesus to fetch the imagery He used in His teaching
from far, but generally from things familiar to His
hearers ; oftenest He availed Himself of such as the
country itself in which He happened at the time to be,
offered Him.   Now a city on a hill-top was not so
common in Galilee as in Judæa.   In Judæa, cities are
so placed as a general rule ; in Galilee only as a rare
exception ; in the latter they are ordinarily built, not
on hill-tops, like Jerusalem and Bethlehem, but on the
sides of hills, like Nazareth.   As Jesus made use of
this image, it is a very probable conclusion that He
had a case of the kind at that moment before Him.
And—notable fact !—in the place we are considering
He would have had before His eyes the two most

* St. Matt. iv. 23—25 ; St. Luke vi. 17—19.
† St. Luke vi. 20. '
‡ St. Matt. v., vi., vii.

prominent examples—perhaps the only ones—to be found in Galilee. On His right, at two leagues' distance, would be the city of Tabor,* lifted on its gigantic pedestal ; behind him, Saphet, on a mountain summit much higher still.

There was another point of detail which interested me much. On arriving in Jerusalem I had been struck with the great number of red anemones with which the grass is enamelled, and I had become convinced that this flower, at once the commonest and the most brilliant in Judæa, must have been the "*lily of the fields*" of the Gospels. Travelling in Galilee, I was disappointed to find that there it was less universally prevalent. On the shores of the lake particularly, I did not remember having seen it. I began, therefore, to doubt the identity of the anemone and the lily of the fields ; for, according to all analogy, the imagery made use of by the Saviour in the Sermon on the Mount must have been to be found in Galilee. What then was my surprise when, on coming down again from the mountain-top to the plateau, I saw at my feet a magnificent bed of these scarlet anemones! This was a new confirmation of my conjecture with regard to the relative positions of Jesus and the multitude. If we picture to ourselves the multitude, on the plateau, and Jesus seated on the lower step of the mountain staircase, this beautiful bed of anemones would have been exactly between them and Him ; and here again His own words carry conviction : " *Consider the lilies of the field, how they grow ; they toil not, neither do they spin ; and yet I say unto you, that even Solomon in all his glory was not arrayed like one of these.*"

* Perhaps only its ruins ; for, as I said above, it is not certain that that city existed in the time of Jesus.

I cannot express the impression made upon me as I read in this region of the earth the *Sermon on the Mount.* My voice resounded in my ear with a peculiar vibration, which thrilled me. It sounded to me as if it was not my own voice, but that of the Master Himself proclaiming the Gospel Law upon the Mount Sinai of the New Testament. Never had His Sermon seemed to come so near to me ; the nearness of place annihilated the distance of time.

The beautiful name, *the Mount of the Beatitudes,* preserved by the traditions of the early ages, or attached to it by the imagination of the pilgrims, is not that by which this summit is commonly known. It is commonly called *Hattin's Horn.* This name, of sinister memory, commemorates the most terrible battle which ever stained with its blood the soil of the Holy Land in the days of the Crusades. Here it was that in 1187 Saladin defeated the Franks. The battle was fought on the plateau. The last king of Jerusalem, Guy de Lusignon, withdrew to the Horn itself, and valiantly defended that position. In the end the Saracens took it. The king was taken prisoner. Most of its defenders were cast down the precipices which form the boundary of the hill towards the north. The *true cross,* which had been taken with them into the battle, as the Israelites used to take the Ark of the Covenant, fell into the hands of the infidels. This battle put an end to the kingdom of Jerusalem.

Here is yet a new example of that law of irony which seems to govern history ! The Cross of the Saviour serving as a war signal on the mountain upon which He preached the Gospel ! These terrible disasters to the Christians on the very scenes in which He had said to them, " *Resist not evil !* " " *Blessed are the peace-*

makers !" What an example! What a solemn confirmation of these words of the Saviour! The cries of pain of the dying at Hattin respond to the Beatitudes from the lips of Jesus, as did the curses uttered on Ebal against the transgressors of the Law, to the blessings on Gerizim.

The Christians who had conquered the Holy Land were not able to keep it ; to them it never was anything but a field of battle and a cemetery. The Saracens who took it from them saw it in turn taken from them by the Ottoman Turks. These latter, who are still nominally its owners, have made it into a desert, in which they hardly dare to set foot without fear. The Arabs themselves, who are its inhabitants, can only be considered as encamped in the country ; they have pitched their tents in its pastures, or contrived for themselves a place of shelter in the ruins of its towns; they have founded nothing in them ; strangers to the soil, they never became wedded to it ; the wind of the desert which brought them there may one day carry them away again, without their leaving behind them the slightest trace of their passage through it. God, who has given Palestine to so many nations, has not permitted any one to establish itself or to take root in it ; He is keeping it, no doubt, in reserve for His people Israel, for those *rebellious children,** who will one day have become the "*men of a meek and humble spirit*," of whom Jesus said that "*they shall inherit the earth.*" †

* Isa. xxx. 1.   † St. Matt. v. 5 ; Psalm xxxvii. 11.

V.

PHŒNICIA.

I.

TYRE AND SIDON.

THE convent on Carmel is the best resting-place one meets with in a pilgrimage in the Holy Land. Thanks to the neighbourhood of Kaifa, at which the packets of the Austrian Lloyd touch, one can there enjoy the pleasures of civilized life—a bed, a dinner, glazed windows decorated with white curtains, a sitting-room with books and albums, and even European conversation, for it is but seldom one does not find at Carmel some belated traveller, who, under pretext of indisposition, is resting himself there after the fatigues of Turkish saddles and the severities of the Arab *cuisine*. I had found there two amiable abbés, stragglers from the French caravan, and I had indulged my inclinations by spending three days with them. The Fathers were full of kindness to us; they accompanied us in our walks, and placed their servants at our disposal. Too much of grandees to wait upon us themselves, as the Franciscans do, they used to come and sit with us at dessert, and did not even take offence at the freedom of Abbé R., who, to avoid making mistakes between " Fra Marco," " Fra Domenico," and " Fra Bartolomeo," took the line of addressing them all indiscriminately by the better known name of *Fra Diavolo.*

In the convent of St. Elias I felt what I have never failed to feel, every time that in my Eastern travels I have found myself brought into contact with Europe and civilization—namely, at first a lively feeling of pleasure, a sensation of repose and well-being,—and soon afterwards a mortal *ennui,* an irresistible desire to get away from social bondage, and to breathe once more unadulterated the free atmosphere of barbarism. I therefore made haste to return to my travels. I wished to follow the coast of Phœnicia, paying my respects in passing to Tyre and Sidon.

Our party remains the same. Hhannah leads the way, " *his eye downcast and his head bowed,*"* as his manner is. The *moukres* bring up the rear. One of them, Yoûsef, is a Maronite, a lively, laughing creature, shouting, singing, and begging shamefully and cease- lessly, for cigars and *baksheesh.* The other, Abdallah, is a Druse, with a melancholy face, admirably repre- senting the resigned fatalism of the East ; I do not think I ever heard him utter a word.

The road from Carmel to St. Jean d'Acre is beau- tiful. After passing Kaifa, and crossing the brook Kishon close to its mouth, we gallop over a tract of open sands freshened with the breaking waves. The city of Acre which is in sight, the range of Carmel which we are leaving behind us, and the blue expanse of the Mediterranean, make up a picture both simple and grand, refreshing to one's imagination.

St. John d'Acre ! what a name of romance ! Else- where, in this country, so rich in memories, those of Biblical antiquity either leave no room for others, or

* " *L'œil morne et la tête baissée,*" a well-known verse in Racine.

throw them into the shade. Here it is otherwise. *Accho*, assigned to the tribe of Asher, but of which it could never take possession,—*Ptolemais*, where St. Paul touched, on his way from Tyre to Cæsarea, are but obscure names by the side of St. John d'Acre, the last refuge of the Frankish knights in Palestine.

The latest *souvenir* belonging to this city is its bombardment in 1840, by means of which the English once more replaced unhappy Syria under the dominion of the Turks. St. John d'Acre was then fortified anew, and it now has, externally, quite the appearance of a fortified European town ; but within it bears, most markedly, the stamp of the East. One comes across here and there, it is true, some European costumes ; Levantines come to buy wheat. But, with that exception, nothing here reminds one of civilised countries.

Travellers who arrive at Acre can lodge either in the Latin convent or in the khân. I choose the khân, as the more Oriental. It consists of a great stable, roofed with a terrace paved with asphalte, upon which open little chambers with no furniture of any kind, except mats made of palm leaf. A *khândji* shews us into one of these little cells, in which we deposit our things. Then we go out to buy what we want for supper. John takes care to lock the door ; for whereas in the villages in Palestine no device for securing the doors is known but bolts, in the towns they use a sort of wooden lock of very simple construction, but exceedingly ingenious. I got John to explain it to me ; but I am so poor a mechanist that I cannot make it out. All I remember is that the key is nothing but a thick stick, into which are driven a certain number of nails arranged in different ways, corresponding with the wards of the lock for which they are fitted.

I go then to the market, swinging the "key" in my left hand, much in the same way that the exquisites in Europe used to swing their *sticks*,* which they carried with so much grace four or five years back. That was not, however, the way in which I ought to have held it. It is usual in the East to lean one's key on one's shoulder, as a sapper carries his axe. One often meets in the streets, at the hour when the shops are being shut, shopkeepers going home from their day's business, preceded by a little boy gravely carrying on his shoulder one of these great wooden keys. This custom, which I used to notice as I passed, without attributing to it any importance, became very interesting to me when, some time after, I read again this prophecy of Isaiah,† "*The key of the house of David will I lay upon his shoulder ; so that he shall open, and none shall shut ; and he shall shut, and none shall open.*"

That is a way of speaking unintelligible, or at least strange, to any one who has not lived in Syria. Accordingly, the author of the Apocalypse, who borrows this passage from Isaiah,‡ is careful to omit the words "*on his shoulder.*" This expression would not have been understood by the inhabitants of Asia Minor, for whom he was writing.

I like my recollections of our purchases of bread and sweetmeats in the bazaar at Acre, and the narguileh that I smoked there, in front of a café, sitting under a palm tree fronting a mosque. These are some of those pictures, so thoroughly Oriental in character, which remain imprinted on one's imagination, and on the contemplation of which one dwells with so much pleasure, when one comes across them by chance in turning over

* *Sic*, in English in the original.　　† Isa. xxii. 22.
‡ Rev. iii. 7.

the leaves of the book of one's memory. I will say nothing of our supper, except that I found the bread excellent, and that I said so to Hhannah.—" I daresay you do !" answered he ; " the Acre bread is famous ; it is the best in Palestine."

Here is a case of a reputation which dates from three or four thousand years back ! for the patriarch Jacob said in his time, " *Out of Asher his bread shall be fat, and he shall yield royal dainties.*"

On getting back into my little cell, I tried in vain to sleep. It is needless to repeat here what was the cause of my frequent sleeplessness. How could I expect to find for myself upon these palm-leaf mats a repose which had no existence within themselves ? Happily, the moon shone bright, the sky was beautifully illumined with stars ; I went out upon the terrace, and spent the night in contemplation. From the top of a minaret, hung with little lamps,—for it was still Ramadan,—the prayer of the muezzin fell in clear-dropping chants, responded to by chants from other minarets in the distance. From time to time a cannon shot sounded.

At six o'clock in the morning, I set off for Tyre. The plain of Acre, in which I have been walking for three or four hours, seems to be very fertile ; though a part of the soil is given up to thorns, a large part also is under cultivation. As we leave the town, we rejoin three Damascus merchants who are on their way from Jerusalem to Beyrout, and with whom we walk for some hours ; we pass near the palaces and gardens created by Ibrahim Pacha. Ibrahim did a great deal of planting. That is always the first thing to be done by those who wish to restore Palestine. These fine gardens are very numerous in the plain of Acre. We halt for breakfast in a great plantation of fig, almond, pomegranate, and, above all, orange and citron trees, amongst which murmurs a little stream of clear water. They are real gardens of Armida. Their only guardian is a negro wrapped in a great white robe, whose appearance produces quite a magic effect in the midst of this rich verdure.

The plain of Acre is separated from that of Tyre by a rocky tract of shore, which begins at *Rás-en-Nakhoûra*, and ends at the White Cape. This tract of shore between the two capes forms a natural barrier between Palestine and Phœnicia ; the narrow roadway which has been made through it was formerly called *the Tyrians' ladder.* As soon as we pass the first of these promontories, we lose sight of the plain of Acre, and see stretching before us another bay, at the further extremity of which one faintly discerns the city of Tyre. It is a rock-strewn path, which would be dangerous to travel over, were there not a little parapet on the left hand. This parapet is, I need not say, the work of ancient times. Such good ideas seldom enter the heads of the Turks.

The plain is uncultivated, and overgrown with brambles. Near Tyre it is of great width ; the nearer the town, the more dreary-looking. For a long time we walk over sand. On the horizon before us is a yellow hill projecting into the sea ; there is the city of Tyre ; further to the right are three ruined arches, the remains of an ancient aqueduct, and the lower spurs of Lebanon ; and behind them stretches a lofty ridge still covered with snow.

We reach the gates of Tyre without having met any one, or seen any traces of the neighbourhood of a town, except a few tombs surrounded with great tufts of violet irises, like those of our gardens.

Tyre has not lost its ancient name, as the geography

books tell us. That of *Soûr*, given it in our day by
the Arabs, is that which used to be given to it by
the ancient Phœnicians and Hebrews. From this name
that of *Syria* itself is derived. *Tyre* is but the Aramaic
pronunciation of the same word, and it is in that form
that it passed to the Greeks. So it is with the name
Jafo, or Jaffa, as ancient as the town itself, and of which
the Greek name Joppa was only a corruption.

Tyre is still "in the midst of the seas,"* upon that
island on which, for long years, like Venice, it defied
foreign conquerors. But the island has become a peninsula. Alexander, despairing of subduing it in any
other way, had a causeway built to connect it with the
continent. By successive accretions of soil, this dyke
has been considerably widened ; but one can still distinguish the original causeway, which forms, in the
middle of the isthmus, a ridge of slightly greater elevation. The peninsula of Tyre has been compared to a
hammer, of which the ancient island is the head and
the isthmus is the handle.

The city has walls only on that side, and only
one gate. The streets do not appear ugly to any one
who comes there from Palestine. The Mahometan
quarter, lying towards the west, consists, it is true, of
low houses, hidden in the recesses of little courts ;
but in the Christian quarter, nearer the gate, there are
good-looking houses of a fair height. Out of a population of four or five thousand inhabitants, Tyre numbers twice as many Christians as Mahometans. One
perceives it at once by the cordial greeting with which
one is received ; it is evident that there is as much of
friendly feeling to strangers, as of hostility to them
in Mahometan towns. Many people greet me as I

* Ezek. xxvii. 4, xxviii. 2, 8.

pass with a hearty *Buona sera !* and those who cannot
talk *Frankish* at least turn towards me and lay their
right hands in turn upon their heart, their mouth, and
their forehead, a silent but expressive salute, which is
like a sign of the Cross, and which symbolises very
well the Oriental form of speech, " *To love with all the*
HEART, *with all the* SOUL,* *and with all the* MIND."
A young man, dressed in European fashion, comes
up to us, and asks me in French to come and lodge
with him.   I accept,—also in French,—and I leave to
Hhannah the business of fighting out with him, in
Arabic, the question of the price to be paid for this
hospitality.   We follow our host.   His house is in the
harbour, in a charming situation.   Out of the upper
terrace open two rooms with divans, one of which is
assigned to me.   Everything in them has a look of
brightness and comfort ; two or three engravings out
of the *Journal des Modes*, framed and hung up on the
walls, are even indications of a wish to shew that the
host is no stranger to European civilisation.   The windows have, in the absence of glass, moveable trellis-
work and shutters.   My room opens both upon the
interior terrace and upon a little external platform
which commands the harbour, on the other side of
which I see the white mountain-tops of Libanus.

* The word we translate *soul* in Hebrew and in Greek, as well
as in Latin, signifies properly the *breath*, of which the mouth is the
organ.   The expression I here quote would seem to have been
current in the time of Jesus ; for in a well-known passage in St.
Matthew (xxii. 37) He uses it in lieu of that of Moses (Deut. vi. 5),
" To love with all the heart, and all the soul, and all the strength."
What shews that this change in the words is not accidental, is
that St. Mark (xii. 30) and St. Luke (x. 27), who reproduce the expression in Deuteronomy, nevertheless complete it also by adding,
" *with all thy mind.*"

My host—Michel—is agent for a maritime insurance company ; he learnt French at Beyrout, and his great ambition is at some future time to see the West. Europe, with its industry, its arts, and its police, exerts in the East, over many a young man's imagination, the same prestige that the East exerts over us. An *Almanach de l'Illustration*, which came under the notice of Michel, gave him a glimpse into more marvels than were opened to us by the tales so well told by M. Galland* and *les Orientales* of Hugo. He dreams of railroads, india-rubber braces, *trottoirs*, gas-jets, Great Exhibitions, and policemen, just as we in our romantic youth used to dream of palm trees, azure domes, minarets, dervishes, and narguilehs. He introduces me, however, with genuine Oriental gravity, to *my servants his brothers* and *my handmaid his sister.* The latter, Mademoiselle Camille, is a fine girl of twenty years old, with her gown open, according to the fashion of the country; her long hair, amidst which sparkle pieces of silver, hangs down to her waist. It is she who prepares our dinner. Scander, the youngest of the family, is a youth of eighteen, who leaves to his elder brother the privilege of a felt hat and paletot of coarse linen, and keeps to the embroidered vest and the ample cloth pantaloons, in which he looks quite graceful.

My hosts are Catholic Greeks in religion, and talk Arabic ; by race they are true Syrians, that is to say, they descend, like all the Christians of this country, from the Græco-Aramaic population† anterior to the invasion of the Arabs and the conquest by the Turks.

---

* Galland, a learned Orientalist of the time of Louis XIV., translated into French the *Thousand and One Nights.*

† Or, as says St. Mark (vii. 26), "*Greek, Syro-Phœnician.*"

Their faces, like their characters, remind one at once of the Greek and Jewish types.

Scander keeps a confectioner's shop; but a Syrian confectioner is not a confectioner in the odious sense which artists in that line attach to the word—no slave to routine, he gives two turns of the key to the lock of his shop door, and comes out for a walk with me, to do the honours of his native city.

The present city of Tyre, though a more considerable place than it seems to have been in the last century—in the days of Volney, for instance—still only fills a part of the island ; it only touches the seaside on the north-east ; on all its other sides an open space is left between the city and the sea. Here are found a great number of hewn stones of large size, and enormous columns of porphyry, blackened by the waves. The Tyrians, who have always had a mercantile turn, make these remains an article of commerce ; they sell them to any one who wants materials for building ; people come even from Alexandria to buy them, Scander tells me ; a stone of average size is sold for half a piastre, and the largest for a piastre (twenty centimes). The pacha of Beyrout, who is building barracks, has given an order for as many stones as can be got out of the ancient buildings belonging to the government. This order will be fatal to the Cathedral; it was the finest ruin in Tyre ; they are now busy demolishing a part, and to all appearance there will soon be nothing left of it.

Scander, seeing that I admire the columns, presses me to buy one ; he undertakes to procure me one for forty pence ; though the price is tempting, I do not agree. I should not like, however, to leave the place without having made some purchase there in

memory of the ancient commerce of Tyre.   But I look
through the bazaar many times without finding anything to my fancy.   I am obliged here, as everywhere,
to come down to attar of roses, the *hhatl'coum*, and the
sashes of woven silk (*ceintures de soie filochées*).   This
last article is indigenous ; they plant here numbers of
mulberry trees.   A cigar and a bottle of wine are things
not to be found in Tyre.

The Tyrians, however, still   consider themselves a
commercial people.   Though they no longer go themselves to bring from the Baltic the yellow amber with
which they adorn the ends of their chibouques, and
though they are satisfied to receive at second hand
the handkerchiefs of Lyons which the Greeks retail to
them, and   which are the   only articles of European
manufacture to be found in   their bazaars, they take
actively enough to the exporting of the wheat, which
the Lebanon merchants bring them on camel-back, and
which the Greek ships come to fetch from their ports.

I do not know whether the port of Tyre is still really,
as Scander assures me, the best or even the only good
one in all the coast of Syria ; all I   know is that it is
charming.   Only a few little vessels are to be seen
there ; but two enormous masses of masonry of bizarre
shape, remains of the walls which formerly guarded it,
still stand above the   water, and give the place a most
picturesque appearance.

After supper, which Scander brings me on the terrace, I am introduced into the rooms belonging to the
family.   Michel *sits down* by my side on the divan ;
Scander and Camille squat on mats.   I will not report the long conversation I had with Michel ; I will
only say that " *my servant his sister* " had availed herself of my absence for exercising the right of search

upon my travelling bag ; she had found a telescope, which she strongly pressed me to give her. It was the first time, said her brother, that she had seen anything of the kind ; and she added, it would be useful to her every minute for seeing from the top of her terrace what was going on in the neighbouring houses. What could one say in answer to so strong an argument ? or how withstand a request from a fellow country-woman of Dido ? For love of Virgil I presented my glass with *empressement* to the charming Tyrian lady. She gave me in exchange an engraved stone, which I shall have mounted as a seal, if I ever find it again among the knick-knacks I have brought home from my travels.

The distance from Tyre to Sidon is only six or seven hours' walk. Tyre, seen from the north, is very different from Tyre seen from the direction of Palestine. I walk on a long way without losing sight of her. She is always visible,—isolated in the midst of the waters, " *situate at the entry of the sea*,"* of which she still seems queen. At some distance from Tyre, I pass the Leontes, the largest river in Syria ; one crosses it on a hog-backed bridge, single arched, and with no rails. This bridge, and another close to Sidon, are the only ones still in use on this road. 'I have seen several others, but they are in ruins : rather than rebuild them, the natives prefer to travel by their side.

As far as Sarepta, the road offers nothing of much interest ; but on arriving there a new bay opens before us, forming a curve of wide sweep ; at the further end of which rises Sidon. It is the bay of Acre and Tyre over again.

The name of Sarepta has survived in that of Surafend, so they call this little village, situate on a high ground,

* Ezekiel xxvii. 3.

at a little distance from the road.   Like the villages of
Judæa, it looks like a picture painted in black and
white on the rock, from which it is difficult to distinguish
it.   The ancient town must be looked for on a promontory, like all the Phœnician towns ; it was beyond a
doubt built upon the spot we are at this moment crossing ; Sarepta and Sidon therefore faced each other, and
marked the two extremities of the bay.

There is, near the sea, a great orchard of mulberry
trees, and above it a fine fountain shaded by two old
mastic trees.   This is the usual halting place of travellers going from Tyre to Sidon.   We stop there at
about two o'clock ; for the khâmsin, which is in force
to-day, makes us appreciate rest ; it burns and reddens
one's face, as a large fire might ; though the sky is
clouded over, it feels as if the sun's rays were reflected
on us from all sides.   Many travellers are already collected round the fountain.   They are all natives of the
country,—Christians or Mussulmans.   The Christians
eat their meal, squatted on the border of the pool, or
else, kneeling down and leaning with both hands upon
the ground, they lap the water like Gideon's soldiers.
As for the Mussulmans, though the Ramadan obliges
them to play the part of Tantalus, I cannot detect
on their countenances any expression of vexation or
greediness ; they watch the water run by them with
that superb indifference of which the East alone knows
the secret.

Here, as on all the coast of Syria, with the remi-
niscences of the sacred history are mingled those of
the ancient mythology.   At Jaffa, one is reminded of
Andromeda as well as of St. Peter.   Sarepta, which
recalls Elijah and the widow's cruse of oil, brings up
the thought also of the rape of Europa, twice sung by

Ovid'; for, according to the myth writers, it took place on this same coast upon which we are now resting.

The situation of Sidon, built on the sea-shore, upon an isolated hill-top, is very similar to that of Tyre, but much more beautiful. Whilst Tyre looks like a ship wrecked on the sand, Sidon, surrounded with its fair gardens, meets the traveller's eye with an *air de fête.* Another difference is that the plain in which it stands is not so broad nor so uniform. The last undulations of Lebanon come down almost as far as to the town,— fresh, bright little hills.

A long time before reaching the town, the road inclines slightly downwards, winding its way among great plantations of figs and mulberry trees. These gardens have a border of mastic trees with twisted trunks, and their great branches make a bower over my head. As I come near the walls, I cross a little plantation of Persian lilacs in full flower. These lilacs are here great trees. At the bottom of the hill are tombs, amongst which I see the figures of some phantom-like Mussulman women wandering, wrapped in their veils and shapeless mantles.

Sidon is now called Saida ; these two names are synonymous ; both signify *fishing* or *fishery* in Phœnician and in Hebrew. Internally, as well as externally, Sidon is very superior to Tyre. And yet it is almost entirely a Mussulman town; but its population is larger ; it is estimated at six, eight, or even fifteen thousand souls. Here, as at Nablous, one quite feels oneself in a town. The houses are well built, the bazaar is full of life. The streets are covered in, either with mats, as in most of the towns of the East, or with trellis-work of vines, or, as at Jerusalem, they are *vaulted,* which darkens them, and gives them a sort of weird and

mysterious appearance. Passing through these gloomy
streets, in the midst of these Arab Mussulmans, who
seem to belong to another species of human beings,
one might fancy oneself living again in the ancient
Phœnician town, one of the most ancient in the world.
It is nineteen centuries since Virgil, speaking of Carthage,
said, " *There was once an ancient town,—Urbs antiqua
fuit.* . . . And Carthage was the daughter of Tyre,
and Tyre herself was the daughter of Sidon! Some
modern men of learning have wished to prove that
Tyre was the metropolis, but Justin expressly says that
Sidon was founded first. It is spoken of as early as
in the books of Moses, whilst Tyre is not even mentioned in them. Sidon figures in the tenth chapter of
Genesis as the eldest son of Canaan.

I come to a great building, in the middle of which is
a square court, with an arcaded gallery round it. In
its centre is a fine fountain shaded with banana trees.
This building is called the French khân. It was built
at the time when Sidon was *chef lieu de pachalik*,
and retained a degree of importance which it has
now lost. The French consul still lives there; another
part of the building is attached to the Latin convent.
The occupants of the convent are three in number,
two priests and a serving brother. From them I beg
hospitality.

I have by this time made enough progress in
conversation in Arabic to have no further need of
Hhannah in my walks. So I leave him to rest in
our lodging, and go out alone to visit the town and
harbour. The harbour, choked with sand by the
émir Facardin (*Fakr-ed-Dinn*), to prevent a descent of
the Turks, is as much deserted as that of Tyre; there
are now to be seen in it only some insignificant small

vessels. It is defended by an old castle built on an islet, and connected with the town by a bridge of seven arches. This bridge is now no more than a ruin, but it is nevertheless still in use. There are in the castle a few soldiers and a few rusty old Vienna cannons on their worm-eaten carriages. From this side particularly Sidon looks well. It comes forth, so to say, out of the water, and rises into an amphitheatre. The neighbouring plain is commanded by the Lebanon range, at the foot of which I find myself for the first time ; even . at Tyre I could only see it in the far distance. On the slope are great extents of garden ground, innumerable lilac shrubs, and, here and there, the ogee arches of a small mosque.

Meanwhile, the superior of the Franciscans had sent for John. The Vicar Apostolic of Syria had just arrived at the convent, and the question had to be settled whether I should have the honour of dining with him. The worthy Father therefore asked John whether his master was a *great personage.* John confined himself to throwing back his head and raising his eyes to heaven, as if to express the impossibility of conveying in words the high idea he had formed of me ; and then, as the superior wished for some more definite information, he declared that I was a man who never fasted. They therefore served me in company with Monsignor and his secretary.

Monsignor is an Italian ; he wears a long beard in Oriental fashion, and speaks well and agreeably the beautiful language of his country. His secretary is a young Piedmontese abbé, who speaks French with ease. After supper, we stayed by ourselves in the divan, and talked with great familiarity all the evening. The Roman Church has in the East three

Vicars Apostolic : one for Mesopotamia, the second for Egypt, the third for Syria. This last, who lives at Beyrout, is the one in whose company I have the honour to find myself; he has in his hands—1. The government of the whole Latin Church in Syria and in Palestine,—with the exception of the Holy Places which fall to Monsignor Valerga, Patriarch of Jerusalem; 2. The control of the various non-Latin Catholic communions in all Syria and Palestine, without exception. It must be remembered that the majority of the Christians in Syria are Catholics,—that is to say, subject to the pope, though they have their own ritual.

"But," says the abbé to me, "do not mistake as to these people ; the Catholic Greeks differ less from the schismatic Greeks * than from us. They are *ungovernable*. Scarcely any of their priests understand Greek, which is, nevertheless, their sacred language, and consequently they say their services in Arabic. But *one has to shut one's eyes*. It is asserted that the Roman Church aims at subjecting to the Latin ritual the members of the other churches ; nothing," continues the abbé, "is more false ; far from urging them to become Latins, they do not even allow them to become such. When a schismatic wishes to become a Catholic, he may attach himself to the Maronite, Greek, or Armenian, but not to the Latin ritual. If he insists upon adopting the latter, he must present a petition to that effect ; which is always rejected, unless the peti-

---

* The orthodox or schismatic Greeks are known in the East under the name of Roûmi (Romans), which is that of the Greeks of Europe. This name may give rise to misunderstandings, as one might be led to think that this *Roman* Church was here, as in Europe, that which recognises the supremacy of the pope, whereas the precise opposite is the case.

tioner makes it a *sine quâ non* of his conversion to Catholicism, that he shall be admitted into the Latin Church."

II.

ARRIVAL AT BEYROUT.

The ancient Sidon, with its picturesque streets and its enchanting groves of lilacs, might claim more space in the accounts of travellers, and in my own, than is given to it. Unluckily it is too near Beyrout, and suffers in consequence. Beyrout is an enchantress, who eclipses all around her, and easily makes one forget everything that is not herself. I should, however, be sorry to let drop out of my memory those fine rivers which, between Tyre and Beyrout, refresh the Phœnician shore. I call them rivers, that I may not contradict the geographers, for they run into the sea ; but, to speak good French, we must call them streams or very small rivers. They are very numerous. Even Solomon in his time sang the praises of "*the living waters and streams which flowed from Lebanon*,"* and which were an object of wonder to the inhabitants of Judæa. I could have mentioned three which I had to cross on my way to Sidon. Going out of the town, at about half a league's distance, and before leaving the gardens, one comes upon another larger than the rest,—the Bostrenus. It has, I need not say, no bridge, and one has to find a ford. That might be a dangerous undertaking ; but two men, naked from their waist downwards, come and lay hold of your horse's bridle, and conduct him over a sandbank known to them, which offers the means of arriving safe and sound at the op-

* Canticles iv. 15.

posite bank. So is the Bostrenus crossed. When the water is high, matters are simplified—one does not cross at all.

Let us stop a little further on the banks of a river, wider, but less deep, running in a pebbly bed, and which is crossed without difficulty. On the other side of the river is a little hut made of reeds, before which travellers halt in the middle of the day. I find some there sitting on the turf; they are Bedouins, their burnouses in rags, their wives and children round them, and Métoualis with embroidered vests, all glittering with swords, guns, and long pistols inlaid with brass. They fetch me from the hut a rush mat, on which I lie down to smoke a narguileh. The khandji roasts and grinds for his guests a handful of coffee berries, with which he then makes his coffee at a little sparkling fire of thorns, lighted on the pebbles. Meantime our horses graze among the oleanders, which cover the banks of the river; great herds of oxen come up to the river, but hesitate to cross the water; some camels lie down groaning. Close to us the Mediterranean dashes its waves against the shore. It is a complete and harmonious picture, which one would like to look at for a long time; we are upon this classic and mythologic coast of Syria, whither Greece used to send its kings, and from which they borrowed their gods. In the East, there is no need to run after the picturesque, it exists everywhere and in everything. With us, poetry shines from time to time through the realities of life, just as during some fine summer days the sun shines through our misty skies. In this country it is a universal and penetrating light, colouring everything with its rays. That is the reason why the poets of the East,—

Homer, for instance,—are at once so realistic and so poetical.

This river is the *Nâhr-el-Dhamoûr*, the *Tamyras* of the ancients,—a beautiful name, which, without recalling to me anything definite, has a sound nevertheless to my ear as of something familiar; it brings with it, like a breeze from beyond the sea, the sweet accents of the language of the Hellenes.

Sidon being, according to Genesis,* the last town of Canaan towards the north, the Bostrenus or the Tamyras probably formed the extreme limit of the Land of Promise. I cast one glance back, and bid adieu to the Holy Land. . . . .

My halt on the banks of the Tamyras was not the only one on my journey; I rested once more in a khân situate a little further on. Approaching Beyrout, the number of the khâns increases; it seems as if one had but to cross the borders of Palestine to find once more some beginnings of civilisation and sociability. The khân in which I stop is a stable built of stones, with a vaulted porch offering shelter to travellers. The people in charge of it are amiable and hospitable; the gloomy and egoistic temper of the Arab race is less perceptible in Syria than in Palestine; it is true that in Syria the Arab element is less predominant, as is proved by the fact that the parts of the population which are Christian, and therefore date from a period anterior to the invasion, are there much more numerous. Whilst I am drinking my coffee, the khandji brings a little bird, and cuts its throat. They catch here, with birdlime, a number of these little sparrows, which they take to Beyrout for sale. I enquire their price. It has not varied since

* Genesis x. 19.

the days of Jesus.   It is a piastre for a dozen, which
makes exactly *five for two sous*, as we see in St. Luke.*

Two full hours before we reach Beyrout, the scenery
completely changes, and surprises one by its richness,
to which there is nothing to be compared in any place
I have hitherto seen in the East.   Instead of the low
bare hills which had all day long hidden the mountains
from me, Lebanon arises before one in all its glory.†
Our high mountains in Europe, the Alps and the
Pyrenees, are perhaps more picturesque; but the
majesty of Lebanon seems to me still more imposing.
The summits are covered with snow, and the slopes
with fresh verdure, amid which a number of villages
stand out like the daisies in our meadows, dazzling in
their whiteness.

As the shore turns off to the left to form the promontory which bounds the roadstead of Beyrout, the
sea-coast is here much wider.   I lose sight of the sea,
which disappears behind some rising ground, and I
see nothing around but a large and fertile valley, a
very sea of verdure.   The bottom of the valley, at the
foot of Lebanon, is covered with olive trees; nearer to
me are plantations of mulberries, pinewoods, and some
pomegranate and citron gardens.   The road I am travelling by has been cut through the middle of these
gardens.   The soil is of very friable red rock, crumbling
into orange-coloured sand.

* St. Luke xii. 6.   The Roman penny was worth, in the time of
Cicero, about six centimes of our money.   The piastre is worth
about twenty-five centimes.   Comparing St. Matthew and St. Luke,
we see that, taken singly, sparrows were a little dearer; you got
only two for a penny, which would make their price to have been
about five *parahs* each.

† Isaiah xxxv. 2.

Beyrout is not visible from a distance ; it is on the opposite side of this promontory which we are climbing by an imperceptible incline. As we come near it, we see houses at intervals by the roadside, people walking, and children playing. Everything breathes safety and peace. It is a different world from that of the Mussulman countries. One's heart expands and brightens. The first building I came upon,—a chapel, no doubt,— was surmounted by a cross. You cannot imagine what a feeling of delight comes over one in these countries, when one comes upon this symbol of Christianity. It is the standard of our fatherland—of the Eternal fatherland —in presence of which all sectarian divisions vanish.

There is a great commotion at the gate of the town ; to avoid the obstructions of these narrow streets, we take a road on the left, outside the walls, and keep on the high ground. On arriving at the *new barracks*, I have beneath me a complete view of Beyrout, and of its bay. None of the brilliant descriptions that have been written of Beyrout can give any idea of the magnificence of its site, the roadstead, the great mountains so near at hand, upon which the setting sun pours his violet rays, the immense forest of fine trees in which the city is buried. I should hardly know whether to call Beyrout a city or a garden ; the houses are overhung by palm trees, and the groves of orange trees by minarets ; it is all redolent of the scent of roses, and resounds unceasingly with the warblings of birds. It is impossible, on coming into it, not to feel oneself under the spell of a sort of fascination ; one remembers Mahomet's saying about Damascus, and understands it. When from the slopes of Lebanon he gazed at that city in its magnificence, and, like this, all crowned with flowers, he would not enter it.

26

"We can have," said he, "but one paradise, and mine is elsewhere."

And he turned back.

I turned back also, but it was to enter the town. My heart beat very fast, for I was about to see old friends again, and feasts to the eyes and imagination cannot cloy one for those of the heart. I did but stop an instant at the hotel and hurried off to the Ottoman bank, to my fellow-countryman, M. B., my old travelling companion on board the *Céphise.* I found him sitting in stately style in his divan, under a cedar-wood ceiling, and apprenticing himself to Eastern ways by smoking *djébéli* from a chibouque eight feet long. Madame B., with her usual good nature, had gathered round her the French pilgrims who had just arrived at Beyrout from Carmel and Damascus ; even those who had been most tired out and half killed by the fatigues of the journey had here picked up again their health, their force and cheerfulness. Like Antæus recovering his energies on touching mother earth, they have been restored to themselves on treading once again a drawing-room carpet.

I was expected, and the room selected for me had been decked with flowers in preparation for my arrival. I tried in vain to decline the invitations of M. and of Madame B., who insisted that I should be their guest. On my return to the hotel, I saw a janissary coming up, bearded and moustachioed, who took possession of my things, and carried them off to the Ottoman bank.

I spent there, amidst all the delights of family life, eight happy days, of which I shall not lose the recollection. And now, when the memory of Beyrout recurs to me, and it recurs to me often, that which presents itself first to my imagination is not the roadstead with its blue waters, not the minarets and the palm trees, not the scent of the roses, or the song of the night-ingale,—it is the friends whom I left there.

But I was not yet at the end of my travels. I had gone through the land of the prophets and of the Gospel, I had still to visit the land of Homer—the Holy Land of poetry.

APPENDIX.

Note I.

HEZEKIAH'S POOL.

(See page 156.)

THE principal objection that may be urged against my hypothesis respecting the course followed by the second wall, is that it makes *the Patriarch's Pool*, with which, it is generally agreed, we may identify *Hezekiah's Pool*, lie outside of it. If the pool constructed by Hezekiah lay, as one is compelled by the Scripture narrative to allow, inside the town, it must have been within the circuit of the second wall, which was in existence in the days of that king. Consequently one would be forced to suppose that wall to have lain further west than my view would make it do.

Though this argument is not so strong as it seems, it would nevertheless have some weight, if one could admit the assertion upon which it rests—that of the identity of *the Patriarch's Pool* and that of Hezekiah. But notwithstanding the plausibility of the reasonings upon which Robinson rests his case, this identity, far from being proved, is in flagrant contradiction with the text of Scripture.

The following are the passages that refer to this Pool :—We read in the Second Book of Kings, " *The rest of the acts of Hezekiah, and all his might, and how he made a pool and a conduit, and brought water into the city, are they not written in the book*

*of the Chronicles of the kings of Judah ?"** And in the Second
Book of Chronicles, " *This same Hezekiah stopped the upper
watercourse of Gihon, and brought it straight down to the west
side of the city of David.*"† If the city of David here means
the ancient town, Mount Sion, as is generally admitted, and as
Robinson himself admits, some few pages further on, when
speaking of the "tomb of the kings,"‡ it is impossible that the
Book of Chronicles should mean to speak of the Patriarch's
Pool; for that lies not to the west of the city of David, but
quite to the north.

Even if we supposed for a moment, with M. de Saulcy, and
against the opinion of Robinson himself, that the name of " *the
City of David*" did not always apply to Mount Sion only, but
sometimes also to the whole of Jerusalem, our argument would
hold nevertheless ; for if the Patriarch's Pool lies to the east
of modern Jerusalem, its situation in ancient Jerusalem must
have been much more to the north than the west, since the
town extended in those days much further south than it does
now. .

But, it will be said, if the Patriarch's Pool is not the same as
Hezekiah's Pool, where do you place the latter ? I might meet
this question with a demurrer; for we are not called upon to
be ready with an answer to every question that can be raised,
or to discover in the modern town everything which existed
in the ancient one. It is permissible to be ignorant, but it is
not permissible to fix a site in a way that is contrary to the
express and positive data of history. And, besides, the argument from *débris*, so often appealed to, would be more applicable in this case than in any other. If it be admitted that the
débris of the ancient city might, as Robinson affirms, have filled
up the Tyropæon valley, one may, with much greater reason,
suppose that they may have completely choked and made un-

---

* 2 Kings xx. 20.
† 2 Chron. xxxii. 30.
‡ " Researches," vol. i., p. 534, at the foot of the page.

recognisable a mere pool. And we know that just here, on Mount Sion, *in the City of David,* there is no lack of *débris.*

Let us, however, make an attempt to investigate the question little more closely, and see whether there are none of the pools that still exist to which it would be possible to apply what the Book of Chronicles tells us about Hezekiah's PooL

Casting a glance upon the plan of Jerusalem, we see, *precisely to the west of Mount Sion,* a pool, now dried up, but which is much larger than any of those still existing in Jerusalem. It is *the Sultan's Pool (Birket-es-Sultan).* It is situate in the ravine which the archæologists (Robinson among them) are generally agreed in considering to be the Gihon of Scripture ; that is to say, in the upper part of the valley called that of Hinnom. It is not, it is true, in communication with the *upper pool of Gihon (Birket Mamilla)* ; but the respective situations of these two pools shew that nothing was easier than to put them into communication.* It is even so natural to look at them as connected with each other, that travellers commonly call them simply *the upper* and *lower pool of Gihon.*

Must we not then find in the *Birket-es-Sultan* the pool constructed by Hezekiah on the west of the City of David, and into which he brought down (he "directed downwards ") the waters of *the upper pool of Gihon* ?

That might in fact be the most probable view ; but here one is met at once by a serious objection which we must examine. Hezekiah's Pool was in the town, and the Birket-es-Sultan is outside the walls, not only outside the present walls, but also outside those described by Josephus, and consequently, it would seem, outside those which existed in the time of Hezekiah. In fact, the eastern side of the ravine of Gihon seems to form in so necessary a way the western boundary of the city, that it is difficult to suppose it ever passed it.

It is possible, however, to answer this objection, and it is once

---

* Robinson himself admits that the Sultan's Pool must have formerly een fed, at least partially, by the waters of the Birket Mamilla.

more the Book of Chronicles which will give us on this point precious information. No doubt the eastern boundary of the valley was even from the earliest times defended by a wall (Josephus's first wall), but we know that there was also a second one on the other side of this natural trench, that is, to the west of Gihon ; it was that which was called the *external wall.* It was no longer in existence in the time of Josephus, and one must not confound it with any of those of which he speaks ; but we read in the Second Book of Chronicles, " *Manasseh built a wall without the city of David, on the west side of Gihon, in the valley. . . .*"* Thus the Birket-es-Sultan would have lain between the ancient wall and this external wall. Now it is precisely so that Isaiah describes the situation of Hezekiah's Pool : "*Ye made also a ditch between the two walls for the water of the old pool.*"†

On comparing this passage of Isaiah with that in 2 Chronicles, which we have just cited, and with that which tells us that Hezekiah's Pool was on the west of the City of David, one cannot help considering the identity of the Birket-es-Sultan and of Hezekiah's Pool to be extremely probable. But we have not yet come to the end of all difficulties. It will be objected to me, no doubt, and with some appearance of reason, that the external wall of which I have just spoken was built by Manasseh, and consequently it did not exist in the time of his father, Hezekiah.

It is easy to remove this difficulty. We know by Isaiah that at that period " *the breaches of the city of David were many,*"‡ and nothing would have prevented Manasseh from being considered to have built the external wall, when in fact he had done no more than finish, repair, rebuild it, or make it stronger than it was before. The expression, *to build,* is often used in that sense in Scripture ; is it not, for instance, said in this same Book of Chronicles§ that *Rehoboam built Bethlehem,*

---

* 2 Chron. xxxiii. 14.   ‡ Isa. xxii. 9.
† Isa. xxii. 11.   § 2 Chron. xi 5, 6.

meaning that he fortified it? We need but to turn over the pages of the Old Testament, or to open Gesenius' Dictionary, to find many a passage in which " *to build* " means " to rebuild."*
What seems to me here to justify an explanation of this kind is a passage in 2 Chron. xxxii. After having narrated how, during the invasion of Sennacherib, Hezekiah stopped all the fountains which were outside the city, the author adds, in verse 5, " *He built another wall without.*" Is it not exceedingly probable that the wall here spoken of is the same as the *external wall* of Manasseh, and that when it is said of this king that he built it, the meaning was that he repaired it, or more simply still, that he finished building it?

This external wall, to the west of Gihon, was, no doubt, destroyed with the rest, by Nebuchadnezzar. We do not see in Nehemiah that it was rebuilt; at any rate, it was no longer in existence in the time of Josephus. Hezekiah's Pool from that time lost its importance, and the waters of Birket Mamilla were at least partially diverted, to feed a pool nearer to the gates, that of the Patriarch. Supposing that the conduit which forms the communication between these two pools is of ancient construction, it still would not date so far back as the time of Hezekiah.

However, even supposing that my hypothesis respecting the identity of the Birket-es-Sultan and Hezekiah's Pool is not accepted, and even supposing that the situation of the Patriarch's Pool was successfully reconciled with what Scripture tells us of that of Hezekiah, it would not necessarily follow that this Pool, because it was included within the walls in the time of the kings of Judah, must have been so in the time of Jesus and of Josephus. It may be supposed, with very much probability, that the direction of the second wall of Josephus was about the same as that of the wall which enclosed the town under the last kings of Judah, and which was rebuilt by

---

* For instance, 1 Kings xvi. 34; 2 Kings xiv. 22; Psalm cxlvii. 2; Amos ix. 14, etc.

Nehemiah. But that, after all, is but an hypothesis. We know, and Rabbi Schwarz proves it very well,* that after Nehemiah, and before Titus, the walls of the Holy City were again twice overturned and twice rebuilt.

NOTE II.

THE DEAD SEA.

(See page 257.)

I HAVE scarcely spoken at all of the Dead Sea, for I stopped but a short time upon its banks, and should have nothing new to say of it. Perhaps, however, my readers might be pleased to find here some further details upon this subject. I will therefore give a brief summary of the present state of our geographical knowledge with reference to the Dead Sea.

The Dead Sea, so called by modern geographers, and even in ancient times by Pausanias and Justin, was more generally known among the Greeks and Romans under the name of the *Asphalte Lake* (*Lacus Asphaltites*). The Arabs call it *Bahr-Loût* (Lot's Sea). The Bible calls it the Salt Sea (Gen. xiv. 3), the Sea of Araba, or of the plain (Deut. iv. 49), also the East Sea (Ezek. xlvii. 18, Joel ii. 20), in contrast with the Western Sea (the Mediterranean). Though already famous in antiquity, it was but very imperfectly known till our own days. Costigan, in 1835, was the first who undertook to descend the Jordan, and to go round the Dead Sea by water. He fell ill on reaching Jericho, and came back to Jerusalem to die there. Molyneux, in 1847, was not more fortunate. He succeeded, it is true, in making the circuit of the Dead Sea, but he fell ill in consequence of the extraordinary fatigues of the journey, and died at Beyrout before having been able to complete his diary. In the interval, Moore and Beek, in 1837, and Symonds in 1841, had made, with better success, some attempts of the same kind, and had brought back from the Dead Sea, and from the valley of the Jordan, some valuable

* *Das heilige Land*, p. 205.

barometric observations. Lastly, Lynch's expedition (made in 1848, by order of the United States Government), and the still more recent one of M. de Saulcy, have very much enriched our geographic knowledge, and put an end to many uncertainties.

The most remarkable fact gained for science by these various explorations is the greatness of the depression of the Dead Sea, of the Lake of Gennesaret, and of the valley of the Jordan, below the level of the Mediterranean. Schubert, who travelled through the Holy Land in 1837, first drew attention to this extraordinary fact. The measurements since taken by Symonds, Lynch, and others, have completely confirmed his observations; though, it is true, they are far from agreed as to the figures. According to Lynch, the level of the Dead Sea is 1,235 English feet (or 1,159 French feet) below that of the Mediterranean. According to others, it is very much lower still.

The length of the Dead Sea is forty English miles; its breadth varies from seven to nine miles. Its shores are unhealthy, from the excessive heat which prevails there; but all that has been said of its pestilential exhalations must be set down to the region of fable.

The specific gravity of the water of the Dead Sea, compared with that of distilled water, is, according to Gay-Lussac, as 1,228 to 1000. It is literally saturated with salt; no more can be dissolved in it. Maréchal Marmont, the Duke of Raguse, tells how, when he threw some sea-fish into this water, he saw them die after two or three minutes.

Lynch ascertained that the basin of the Dead Sea is divided into two very distinct parts; the one to the north, the other to the south. They are separated by a peninsula projecting from the eastern shore, and terminating in two points, to which Lynch gave the names of his two unfortunate predecessors—Costigan and Molyneux. The strait between this peninsula and the western shore of the lake received from Ritter the name of *Lynch's Canal.*

The southern basin of the Dead Sea is very different from the other. It is smaller and very much shallower. Its greatest depth is at most sixteen feet, but in many places it contains scarcely a foot deep of water. The bottom is covered with a salt mud, heated by thermal springs. The great basin, on the other hand, has almost throughout a depth of about 1000 feet, and in the northern part it reaches to as much as 1,227 feet.

The difference which exists between these two basins proves that they are not of the same formation, and that their origin must be attributed to different causes. This seems to confirm the account given in Genesis xix., according to which the catastrophe which overtook Sodom overthrew the whole valley of Siddim (Gen. xiv. 3, xiii. 10). "For us," says Lynch, "the result is decisive. We had come there with very divergent opinions. One doubted the narrative of Moses, another rejected it altogether. After twenty-two days, and a conscientious investigation of the question, we were, if I am not mistaken, all agreed in acknowledging the truth of the fact recorded in Genesis."

So then the northern basin must, no doubt, have existed before the time of Abraham, and the phenomenon to which it owes the saltness of its waters must be independent of that which previously had caused the depression of the Araba and of the valley of the Jordan. The catastrophe reported by Moses would, according to this, have had for its stage the ground which, in our day, forms the southern basin. It would be that "*vale of Siddim which is the salt sea*" (Gen. xiv. 3).

N.B.—The passages of Holy Scripture cited in this book are drawn sometimes from the various French versions, sometimes from the Vulgate, oftenest from the original texts. As, in some books of the Old Testament, the versions do not agree together in their division of chapters and verses, I have followed that which is adopted in the Hebrew Bibles.

FINIS.

PASSAGES OF HOLY SCRIPTURE
REFERRED TO IN THIS BOOK.